My Pregnanc

white
LADDER

Important note

The information in this book is not intended as a substitute for medical advice. Neither the authors nor White Ladder can accept any responsibility for any injuries, damages or losses suffered as a result of following the information herein.

My Pregnancy 2014

This fourth edition published in 2013 by White Ladder Press, an imprint of Crimson Publishing, The Tramshed, Walcot Street, Bath BA1 5BB

First, second and third editions published by White Ladder Press in 2010, 2011 and 2012.

© Crimson Publishing 2013

British Library Cataloguing in Publication Data
A catalogue record for this book is available from the British Library

ISBN 978 1 90828 171 5

Typeset by IDSUK (DataConnection) Ltd
Printed and bound in Malta by Gutenberg Press Ltd, Malta

Contents

Introduction

Congratulations, you're pregnant! Whether this was a well-planned occurrence or a happy surprise, this book will guide you through this exciting new chapter in your life.

In addition to the excitement, pregnancy can be daunting, frightening and often downright uncomfortable, and sometimes you really don't know who to turn to for reassurance or information. This book aims to be your pregnancy 'big sister', dishing out friendly advice when you need it most.

We have the latest medical practices and policies 'delivered' by two brilliant experts to help you feel informed when you discuss your pregnancy with your midwife or doctors. We've also included lots of practical lifestyle advice from shopping to swimming; top tips from mothers on surviving pregnancy, birth and beyond; and what you can expect to feel physically and emotionally during the coming months. From birth plans to birth control and bumps to budgeting, we hope to keep you informed and amused during your 40-week journey. We won't blind you with medical science, preach at you about the odd sneaky glass of wine, or bore you with too many statistics: pregnancy should be fun and we hope to entertain you as well as inform you.

With all the latest information on every aspect of your pregnancy – from the practicalities and the big decisions, to the emotional rollercoaster and lifestyle changes you'll face – this book includes everything you need to guide you through your pregnancy.

Authors' notes

We've referred to baby as a boy throughout and to midwives as female and doctors and partners as male. This is pure literary licence and we apologise to all baby girls, male midwives, female doctors and female partners for any sexism...

About the authors

My Pregnancy 2014 is written by a team of experts, and is thoroughly updated every year. The team includes parenting journalist Kate Street, gynaecologist and obstetrician Dr Joanna Girling and midwife Pippa Nightingale. Our experts share with you their own tips and advice in *Words from the professionals* which you'll find throughout the book.

Thanks go to Jo Wiltshire, Hollie Smith and the new mums who share their pregnancy and birth stories with us so honestly and openly.

1

I'm pregnant! Now what?

Whether this is a planned pregnancy or a pleasant surprise, this chapter will help you deal with all the wild and wonderful thoughts that are rushing around in your mind. We'll cover how to improve your chances of getting pregnant (if you're still planning), what to do when you find out you are pregnant and how to prepare yourself for what happens next.

UNDERSTANDING CONCEPTION

If your knowledge of the 'science' bit of conception was gleaned from a biology lesson in your first year of secondary school, you'll probably need a quick refresher on how the miracle of creating a new life actually happens.

For a pregnancy to take place, an egg has to be fertilised by a single sperm. A man can ejaculate as many as 300 million sperm but most simply fall out of the vagina or fail to swim up to meet the egg. Successful fertilisation usually takes place in the fallopian tube. The fertilised egg changes from being a single cell into a rapidly dividing group of cells called an embryo that travels down the tube to the uterus. When it gets there, it embeds itself firmly into the lining of the uterus – a process called implantation – and at that point the embryo starts the miraculous journey of becoming a baby.

PLANNING TO GET PREGNANT

Many sexually active women of child-bearing age spend a considerable amount of time and energy trying *not* to have a baby, so for some women it can be a surprise to discover that getting pregnant isn't as easy as they thought.

Cycles, tracking and planning

Research shows around 80% of couples in their twenties and early thirties conceive within a year of trying. This figure rises to 92% within two years. Fertility does decrease after the age of 35, although around 94% of women of that age will conceive within three years.

When they begin planning a baby, many women make a note of when their period is due and start tracking their cycle so they can work out when they are most likely to get pregnant. The average menstrual cycle is 28 days, although the length of a cycle can vary between 21 and 35 days. Ovulation – when the egg is released from the ovary – typically takes place 14 days before your period is due to start. For women who have regular periods, then, it can be quite easy to pinpoint their most fertile period. However, rather than calculating dates rigorously, many couples choose to adopt a relaxed approach, and only after a year or so do they begin taking a more methodical approach.

If you do start tracking your cycle, it is worth bearing in mind that some women can detect ovulation through bodily changes, like vaginal secretions becoming clear and stretchy like raw egg white, or by experiencing abdominal pain. There is also evidence that a woman's waking temperature increases by at least 0.2°C after ovulation, although NICE (2013) advises against keeping a daily record of your temperature to track these changes. You can also buy a fertility prediction kit that tracks hormonal changes in your urine to highlight your most fertile days.

Actively trying to get pregnant

If you're actively trying to get pregnant you don't need to plan your sex life with military precision and take all the passion out of it. However, you are most likely to conceive if you have sex on alternate days around the time of ovulation, so some planning can be useful! Sperm can live for three to seven days in a woman's body and an egg lives for 24 to 48 hours. It takes two days from ejaculation for a man's store of sperm to build.

You may have skipped this planning stage, as recent research shows that around 40% of all pregnancies are unplanned.

START LOOKING AFTER YOURSELF

The most important thing to do if you are planning a pregnancy or have just found out you are pregnant is to eat a healthy, well balanced diet; stop or at least reduce smoking if you smoke (reducing the amount you smoke now will make it easier to give it up when you're pregnant); avoid or reduce alcohol intake to no more than one or two units of alcohol once or twice a week; and take 400 micrograms of folic acid every day. This is a vitamin supplement which comes in a tablet that you can buy at all supermarkets and pharmacies. Women at risk of being low in vitamin D should take a supplement of 10 micrograms (see page 132). If you have any health conditions or are on any medications you should discuss them with your GP before you get pregnant or, if your pregnancy is unplanned, as soon as you find out you are pregnant.

BOY OR GIRL?

It's a question you'll probably be asked countless times and a question you'll no doubt ask yourself. Throughout your pregnancy you and your partner will probably talk about who this little person growing inside you will be and what they get from each of you. So let's have a quick look at how the sex of your baby is determined. Every human cell in the body has 46 chromosomes except the male sperm and female egg, which only have 23 chromosomes each. When they join, the chromosomes total 46.

Chromosomes are tiny structures that each carry around 2,000 genes, and these determine our characteristics like hair and eye colour, blood

Whilst there are a number of legal grounds for termination of pregnancy in the UK, gender selection is not one of them.

group, etc. Both the egg and the sperm contain a chromosome that determines the sex of your baby. The mother's sex chromosome in the egg is always an X chromosome, whereas the man's spermatozoa can contain an X or Y chromosome. If the egg is fertilised with a spermatozoa with an X chromosome the baby will be a girl (X + X = girl). If the egg is fertilised with a spermatozoa containing a Y chromosome the baby will be a boy (X + Y = boy).

Can you maximise the chances of having a boy or girl?

There are many old wives' tales out there which range from having sex on the quarter moon (for a boy) or a full moon (for a girl), to douching with vinegar (girl) or bicarbonate of soda (boy), and drinking lots of milk (girl) or caffeine (boy). One of the most popular (but again unproven) theories is that Y-chromosome sperm are faster swimmers but die sooner, so if you want to have a boy you should aim to have sex as close to ovulation as possible. X-chromosome sperm are said to be slower with more staying power, so if you want to have a girl it's best to have sex a couple of days before ovulation. As long as you have fun trying, it's probably best to just wish for a healthy pregnancy and birth and not become too fixated about whether you want a boy or girl.

The *British Journal of Obstretics and Gynaecology* recently reported new research that suggests IVF treatment increases the chances of having a boy.

If you are really desperate to find out the sex of your baby you can ask at your anomaly scan (see page 25) but it's worth bearing in mind that these aren't always 100% accurate!

There are arguments for and against finding out the sex of your baby; some people like the surprise element, while others find it helps with their planning and preparation.

Science steps in

Advancements in reproductive technologies mean that fertility specialists are now able to screen embryos for some inherited disorders and then select only embryos without these genetic defects. Mostly this is used in families who have already had a baby affected by a severe genetic condition, and who do not want to wait until tests at around 12 weeks show if this baby is also affected and then face the decision whether to terminate the pregnancy or continue. This technique is called preimplantation genetic diagnosis.

'We know our baby is going to be a little girl. I really wanted to find out, although Paul wasn't bothered. I felt like I wanted to know everything I could — I couldn't bear the woman doing the scan to know something about my child that I didn't!'

Nichola, first pregnancy

MORE THAN ONE?

'My husband and I hadn't been using contraception since the birth of our son, but it was a surprise when I became pregnant again when he was only four months old. It was an even bigger surprise though when the first scan revealed we are having twins! It was quite a shock so it took a while to get used to the idea!'

Katy, mum to twins Thomas and Evelyn

There has been a marked increase in multiple births in the past 30 years. It is believed that this is due to an increase in the number of older women conceiving and the rise in assisted conception, including IVF (since more than one fertilised egg is often returned to the uterus in order to increase the chances of successful pregnancy). It is illegal in the UK to return more than two fertilised eggs per cycle because of the increased risk to the mother and babies of higher order multiple pregnancies, such as triplets or quadruplets.

 Recent research shows that returning only one (and not two) egg to the uterus improves the chance of having a healthy baby.

The latest research shows that in the UK around one pregnancy in 65 will result in twins . . . but how does it happen?

How twins are conceived

The majority of twins are non-identical twins. Non-identical or dizygotic (meaning two fertilised eggs) twins occur when you release more than one egg at ovulation, and both are fertilised by separate spermatozoa. The babies may be of the same sex or different sex, and they will look no more alike than other brothers and sisters.

Two-thirds of all twins are non-identical. Identical twins are rarer, and account for about one-third of all twin pregnancies. Identical twins come about when one egg is fertilised by one sperm and then splits into two embryos shortly after conception. When this happens, the twins will be of the same sex and have the same genes so they will look alike. The medical term for identical twins is monozygotic.

The timing of the split of the fertilised egg determines how separate the babies will be during pregnancy. If it is within three days of fertilisation, the placentae and pregnancy sacs are completely separate (28% of monozygotic twins); four to eight days, the placenta is shared and the amniotic sacs are separate (70%); nine to 12 days, the amniotic sac is also shared (2%); beyond 12 days the babies are also joined together (conjoined or Siamese twins are very rare).

One in every 65 pregnancies in the UK today is a twin pregnancy and triplets occur naturally in one in 10,000 pregnancies.

What increases the likelihood of having twins?

- If you have non-identical twins in your family your chance of having twins increases. This is also true if you are a twin yourself.

- If you are an older mother. The latest research shows that women in their late thirties are more likely to conceive twins.

- If you already have children.

- If you are taller and heavier than average.

- Assisted conception. Your chances also increase if you conceive using treatments such as IVF.

- If you are from Africa or Asia.

'It's a magical moment when you first see the tiny, fresh, new life and I feel honoured that we will get that experience TWICE in one birth!'

Katy, mum to twins Thomas and Evelyn

Multiple births

Higher numbers of multiple births are rare. They usually occur when more than one egg is fertilised; identical triplets are very rare. Sextuplets occur only once in every 3,000 million pregnancies, though, so don't get too concerned about having six nappies to change! In April 2013, a family from Berkshire beat the odds of 70 million to one by welcoming quadruplets made up of two sets of identical twins.

CONFIRMING YOU ARE PREGNANT

Whether you've been trying to get pregnant, or even if you just have your suspicions, confirming you are pregnant is the first important step you need to take. So what are some of the signs that you are pregnant?

Around 700,000 babies are born in the UK every year.

These are some common first signs of pregnancy:

- an increased sense of taste or smell
- tender, bigger or 'tingling' breasts. Some women also have painful nipples or even find that the skin around their nipple (the areola) gets darker.
- feeling tired
- needing to pass urine a lot
- an aversion to certain foods or drinks, or a craving for certain foods or drinks
- nausea
- feeling more emotional than normal.

For most women, though, the first sign that they might be pregnant is a missed period. If you find yourself thinking you might be pregnant, then you should try to have it confirmed as soon as possible so you can start looking after yourself (although ideally you are already in perfect health before you conceive!).

When can I test and what testing options are available?

When you become pregnant, the embryo (and later the placenta) produces a pregnancy hormone called human chorionic gonadotrophin (HCG). It plays a vital role in your baby's development, as it causes the follicle in the ovary from which the egg was released to produce the hormone progesterone, which itself prepares the lining of the uterus to feed the embryo and also causes the cessation of periods. The levels of this hormone can be measured in your blood and urine. Most home pregnancy kits measure the level of this hormone via a sample of your urine and usually recommend that you take the test on the day your period is due.

Some new tests claim to give you a result five days *before* your due period, but the problem with this is that even people with regular periods can't be absolutely certain when conception and implantation occurred, and testing too early might lead to a false negative result.

A recent health study showed in up to 10% of pregnancies the embryo hadn't implanted or wasn't generating enough HCG by the time the period was due.

If you take a home pregnancy test and the indicator is very faint, wait a couple of days and test again, as it's possible that the embryo isn't generating sufficient amounts of HCG to register properly.

If you are undergoing fertility treatment it is advisable to wait up to 14 days after treatment before you take a pregnancy test because the hormones used can give you a false positive if the test is done early. Your IVF clinic will tell you when to perform the test.

Where should I take the test?
Most people choose to buy a home testing kit and see those results before going to the doctor. Home testing has advantages because your partner can be with you and you can do it at a time to suit you. However, if you prefer, you can have your first test done for free at your GP, family planning clinic or pharmacy.

If you do a test and the thin blue (or pink) line appears, then warm congratulations are in order – chances are you really are pregnant.

If you have good reason to suspect you are pregnant but have had a couple of negative pregnancy tests, it's probably a good idea to see your GP and arrange for a blood test, which should give you a definite answer.

I'M REALLY PREGNANT!

Even if you've been trying for a baby, discovering you are pregnant can still be quite a shock and it's totally normal to feel a range of emotions, from intense excitement to panic or fear. If the pregnancy wasn't planned, you might need longer to adjust to the news. Whatever your personal circumstance, don't be afraid to give yourself a little time and space to get used to the idea.

'When I found out I was pregnant, I was lying in the bath and stared at the positive pregnancy test for about five minutes, my mouth open in shock. My husband was remarkably calm. I said: "I've got something to show you," and gave him the test. He just said "OK ...". He did end up very drunk that night though – partly my fault as I was giving him all my wine at a friend's house for dinner as it was way too early to tell anyone our news!'

Ruth, first pregnancy

Do I need to buy anything yet?

Hold off on buying the cot or booties for now, as it's more important that you start taking care of your health and well-being. Ideally you should already be taking 400 micrograms of folic acid daily, but if you're not, go to your local chemist or supermarket and buy some straight away, as it can reduce the risk of having a baby born with a spinal cord defect such as spina bifida by up to 70%. There is some evidence to suggest that taking folic acid supplements lowers the risk of having a baby born with a cleft lip or palate as well as lowering the chance of going into premature labour.

If you haven't done so already, contact your GP surgery to arrange your booking appointment.

 The most recent research from Holland suggests folic acid reduces the chance of the baby having a congenital heart defect by 20%.

What should I be feeling?

There's no definitive answer to how you will be feeling in the very early stages of pregnancy: for some women, the hormones kick in very quickly and they experience strong symptoms almost as soon as the pregnancy is confirmed; other women can feel a bit anxious because they do not feel pregnant at all. Remember that every pregnancy is different and you'll have your own unique set of symptoms – lucky you!

'I had four months of morning sickness. Some days, just walking into the kitchen made me sick. It was hard, but I took comfort in the fact that the sickness was a sign that baby was growing well.'

Vicky, first pregnancy

In Chapter 2 we explore in detail all the changes you can expect over the coming 40 weeks but the symptoms you are most likely to experience in the early stages (if you haven't already) include:

Around half of all pregnant women experience some form of nausea or vomiting, with symptoms beginning around six weeks after their last period.

- a missed period. Although this might sound somewhat obvious, some women do experience a light bleed, also known as spotting, at or shortly before the expected time of the period. This can occur after implantation, when the uterus lining is disturbed as the fertilised egg buries into it. This isn't necessarily anything to worry about, but if bleeding is painful, persistent, recurrent or occurs after your period was due, you should get it checked out by a health professional, in case you are having an ectopic pregnancy (see page 38).

- nausea. Some women experience 'morning sickness' in the morning but it can happen at any other time of the day, and some women find they begin experiencing nausea almost immediately.

- needing to pee more often, especially at night

- exhaustion

- a strange 'metallic' taste in the mouth

- going off certain foods or drink. Some people can't stand the taste of coffee or alcohol once they are pregnant, and one of the theories is that it is your body cleverly rejecting food or drink that isn't good for the growing baby.

- a heightened sense of smell

- tender, tingling or swollen breasts and darkening of the areola (the skin around the nipple)

- increased vaginal discharge. This is normal as long as it is not associated with itchiness or soreness. If it is you should see your GP or midwife.

- feeling weepy or emotional

- being hungry all the time (despite the nausea).

'I couldn't get through the morning without some biscuits, so all my workmates knew I was pregnant!'

Joanna, first pregnancy

'I felt like someone was constantly poking me in the tummy button for the first few weeks.'

Catherine, second pregnancy and mum to Joe, 15 months

WORKING OUT YOUR DELIVERY DATE

Only around 5% of babies arrive on their EDD (estimated delivery date) but the vast majority are born between 37 and 42 weeks from the beginning of your last period, so you'll probably still want to work out as soon as possible when your baby is due. Once you see your doctor or midwife they will confirm the date for you, but if you can't wait until then it's pretty easy to work it out by yourself. Using Naegele's rule, just add seven days to the first day of the last period and then take away three months. So, if your period started on 18th April, the EDD is 25th January. The average pregnancy lasts 266 days but to make it easier, you can just count from the date of your last menstrual period and add 40 weeks – the two weeks before ovulation count as the first two weeks of pregnancy, even though you haven't even conceived at that point!

If your cycle is regular but lasts less than 28 days you will need to subtract the number of days that it is less than 28 from your EDD; if it is longer than 28 days you will need to add the difference.

WHO AND WHEN TO TELL

Telling your partner, your family and your friends can be one of the most exciting parts of your early pregnancy. However, it can be wise to hold off on spreading the news. You might not want to read this bit, but one in seven confirmed pregnancies ends in miscarriage – so you might want to wait until the 'risky' period is over (after your dating scan, see page 24) before you tell your loved ones, because it will be hard enough for you and your partner to cope with the loss without managing the disappointment of others.

Telling your partner

If you are married or in a stable relationship, you will probably want to share the news with your partner as soon as possible if they're not with you when you take the test.

> 'I loved those first few weeks when no one knew except us; it was our own magical little secret.'
> Catherine, second pregnancy and mum to Joe, 15 months

90% of babies are born from three weeks before the due date to two weeks after – it might be better to get an EDM (estimated delivery month)!

Latest ultrasound guidance is that all EDDs should be based on scan measurements of the baby. So be prepared for your due date to be adjusted. IVF pregnancies are excluded from this.

If your pregnancy was unplanned or if you're not in a stable relationship, you might be feeling more anxious about sharing your news and what the future holds. It's up to you who you tell and when, but the best thing you can do is get support from people you trust and who can be there for you.

Telling your family

Many women want to share the news with their family straight away too; there's nothing nicer than telling your own mother that you're going to make her a granny. As mentioned before, it can be wise to hold off on spreading the news, but if the worst should happen it may be that you will need their support. It's up to you whether you tell your entire family, just the prospective grandparents, or keep it a secret as a couple for a while.

Telling your friends

Another big dilemma is when to tell your friends. Sometimes this is one of the hardest secrets to disguise, particularly if your friendship is regularly sealed by a large glass of wine on a Friday night. Many women hate lying to their mates, but if you are worried about telling them for whatever reason, the following excuses have come in handy.

- 'I'm on antibiotics' can be good, especially if you follow up with,

- 'I'm on those awful Flagyl tablets', because you *really* can't drink on those and by quoting the brand it makes the whole thing more plausible.

- 'I'm doing that Gwynnie/SJP/Jen detox for a week.' If you are normally the 'health freak' of your social group the idea of you abstaining for a week might not be too surprising.

- Are you the Sporty Spice of your social circle? Then an impending marathon might buy you a few weeks of non-drinking time, particularly if you give it a charity angle to make you sound all the more pious.

- Try telling just one close friend and see if they'll 'drink for two' and drink both your drinks! A tip if you go down this route – pick a mate with a good constitution who isn't planning on driving home!

- 'I'm driving.' An oldie but goodie, as no one can argue with you.

The important thing is to know that people will be happy for you whenever you decide to tell them.

Some women also find telling certain friends can be difficult. There are those who might not seem overly thrilled as they realise that this will change your friendship forever, or there can be the awkwardness of telling those friends who you know have been trying for a baby of their own. The best thing you can do is be honest and ask people how they're feeling. If you understand where they're coming from it can help you to understand a perhaps less than perfect reaction.

The average age of a first-time mum in the UK is 29.7, with 49% of women over the age of 30 when the baby is born.

Telling your work

We cover all the legal and practical aspects of your working pregnancy in Chapter 5, but officially you don't have to tell your employers until you are 25 weeks pregnant (but by that time they might have guessed!). It's probably not a bad idea to keep quiet until you have got through the first trimester of your pregnancy – unless you are experiencing such obvious pregnancy symptoms that they can't fail to notice.

> 'Almost everyone has been very positive towards my pregnancy. There were a couple of work colleagues who were a bit off as they had been trying for a very long time to conceive. I've found this hard to deal with as I almost feel guilty that I got pregnant so fast.'
>
> Becky, first pregnancy

HOW YOU MIGHT BE FEELING

Your conception might have been planned with military precision or you may be one of the 40% of women whose pregnancy was a happy accident. Whatever the circumstances, don't feel bad if you are not as ecstatic or excited as you think you should be. Having a baby is undoubtedly a life-changing experience, and it's completely normal to have feelings of anxiety about the health of your growing baby, the delivery, and how it will impact on your life and relationships. If you are experiencing a range of emotions about your pregnancy, remember your partner will probably be feeling the same. This is a perfect time to share all your hopes and fears together so that you can deal with anything unexpected that pregnancy might throw at you.

If the baby wasn't planned, you might have practical considerations to take into account, like the stability of your relationship, your finances or maybe your career. If you are in this position, you and the baby's father might need longer to come to terms with your situation and work out how having a baby can work for you.

With pregnancy hormones raging around their bodies it's little wonder that many newly pregnant women find themselves inexplicably in tears over the smallest things.

If you're feeling overwhelmed by the news, just take it a day at a time and remember that women have been having babies for thousands of years without scans, epidurals, or even doctors around. It really is the most natural thing in the world!

What you might be worrying about

All of your fears are normal and natural and you should take solace in the fact that millions of people have worried about the same things. Here are a few common concerns and some advice to help you calm your fears.

'I got drunk before I knew I was pregnant'

This is a very common worry, as a glass (or three) of your favourite tipple is often what gets us in the mood for baby-making in the first place. Try not to worry if you did overindulge because a one-off boozy session is unlikely to have done any damage to the fetus, although it does increase the chance of miscarriage. Try not to beat yourself up about it, but once you have confirmed that you are pregnant it is advisable to cut out regular drinking. An occasional glass is unlikely to harm your baby but you should always read up on the latest medical advice. See page 112 for more info on drinking and pregnancy.

'I went to a music festival, got stoned and found out a week later I was expecting'

There is clear evidence to show that taking drugs during pregnancy can pose a risk to your baby's health and development, so even if you are an occasional recreational user it is strongly advised that you stop before you conceive or once you discover you are pregnant. If you did take drugs before you found out you should discuss it with your midwife or obstetrician.

'I smoked two packets of fags on a girl's night out'

If you or your partner are a smoker it's time to stub out your habit, because studies have shown that smoking (and passive smoking) is detrimental to the unborn child. Smoking slows down the growth of the baby, reduces the baby's brain development, makes premature delivery more likely, and increases the chance of cot death (sudden infant death syndrome) after the birth. Recent evidence from Scotland suggests it may increase the chance of ectopic pregnancy.

It is really important that both you and your partner try to stop together, as this will help your determination and reduces the effects of passive smoking. You can use nicotine replacement gums and patches, or try the NHS Stop Smoking counselling service – your midwife or GP should be able to direct you to them. Smoking also increases the chance of getting thrombosis (blood clots) in your legs or lungs, so that is another reason to stop. Always talk openly with your midwife and GP and seek their advice and support. A lot of people struggle to give up smoking, so do ask for the guidance you need to help you through. A study is taking place to see if increasing exercise in pregnancy helps women to give up smoking.

'I'm addicted to...'

It's easy to advise you to stop all your guilty pleasures when you are pregnant, but some people are addicted to nicotine, alcohol or drugs and even though you know you should give up for the sake of your baby, you can't. If you do have an addiction and find out you are pregnant, go to your GP straight away to seek help and advice.

'I'm really overweight; how will I manage when I'm pregnant?'

Although a lot of people think that being pregnant is the best excuse ever to put on weight, they soon find that you shouldn't gain as much weight as you might think and that you need to monitor your diet carefully. Being seriously overweight while pregnant can cause problems such as miscarriage, diabetes in pregnancy, thrombosis and pre-eclampsia (see page 81). Before you start trying to conceive it is advisable to try to lose some weight so that you are in good health to start your pregnancy. This will also help your fertility. You should talk with your doctor about starting vitamin D (page 132) and taking a higher dose of folic acid (5 mg) (page 133). When you are pregnant your doctor or midwife will advise you on how to maintain/start a healthy eating and exercise regime during your pregnancy, and will usually advise that you gain as little weight as possible. If you're particularly worried about your weight, speak to your doctor or midwife and try to start eating as healthily as you can.

If you suffer from asthma, you have a higher chance of giving birth early, evidence suggests. Tell your doctor and make sure you are monitored monthly.

ANTENATAL CARE

Antenatal care is designed to help make sure you and your baby are both as healthy as possible during pregnancy and delivery. Even if you are very healthy, you still need careful check-ups as the extra burden of pregnancy can occasionally cause problems. If you already have some health or lifestyle issues, or have had problems in a previous pregnancy, then antenatal care will help support you and your baby.

Your care options may include:

- shared care between your GP and a midwife

- midwife- or GP-led care

- hospital-based consultant-led care if your pregnancy is likely to need extra monitoring for you or the baby

- private independent midwife for antenatal care and delivery

- private maternity care with an obstetrician/midwife such as www.thebirthteam.com. The whole package can cost around £5,000–£10,000.

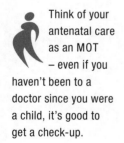

Think of your antenatal care as an MOT – even if you haven't been to a doctor since you were a child, it's good to get a check-up.

Some women have a nominated midwife they will see at every appointment and hopefully at the birth too; other women will see a different midwife each time they visit – some health authorities run what's called a 'Domino Scheme', where a team of community midwives look after you. Systems vary depending on where you live and your antenatal care will also depend on the type of birth you are planning. If you have any chronic health conditions such as diabetes, epilepsy, high blood pressure or inflammatory bowel disease, ideally you will be able to see your GP, obstetrician or hospital doctor to discuss the issues relevant to the pregnancy before you conceive, and plan the antenatal care you will need. Many hospitals run special antenatal clinics for women with medical conditions such as these. Similarly, if you take any medication you should talk to your GP, obstetrician or hospital doctor. If you are at increased risk of delivering pre-term your hospital may offer you an appointment at the Pre-term Birth Clinic.

Thinking about your options

Before you go to the doctor it is useful to have some idea about where you would like to give birth, as this will help to ensure you are booked into the right kind of hospital for you. A really useful website to help you with this is www.birthchoiceuk.com; it takes you through all of your birth options and has a really helpful section with statistics about maternity units in your local area, so you can make informed choices about where you want your baby to be born and have some ideas about the care you might like to receive. Do remember though that some of the differences relate to different populations, and not just hospital attitudes.

Your birthing options may include:

- NHS consultant-led hospital maternity unit
- NHS midwife-led birthing centre – freestanding or alongside a hospital
- home birth
- private maternity unit attached to an NHS hospital
- private hospital like The Portland (celebrity favourite) that exclusively deals with maternal and child health.

The pros and cons of each are outlined in detail in Chapter 7. Some hospitals are in such demand they get booked up very quickly.

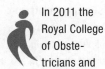 In 2011 the Royal College of Obste- tricians and Gynaecologists announced that it felt too many women were choosing to give birth in hospitals, and called for more midwife-led birthing centres to be established.

EXPLAINING YOUR BOOKING APPOINTMENT

When you visit your doctor or midwife they will organise a 'booking' appointment for you, although many units allow you to arrange this directly yourself. You might have your booking appointment at the hospital you have chosen or in a community clinic or at home. If you pick a hospital that is not local, bear in mind that you might go into labour during rush hour and a trip across town in heavy traffic might not be the best idea! Also, postnatal midwifery is organised by the hospital in whose catchment your address falls, not the one where you delivered, so you could miss out on continuity of care.

What is a booking appointment?

It is believed that the term 'booking' originates from a time when women literally had to 'book' their hospital bed for labour. (In some parts of the country it could be argued that the same applies now.) This appointment may take place at the hospital – if you have already decided where to give birth – a clinic, specialist maternity unit, GP's surgery or at home.

Latest figures show that almost 4,000 women didn't manage to give birth in a maternity ward last year; women gave birth in ambulances, A&E departments, in cars on route to hospital, minor injury units, and even in a hospital lift!

Why do I need to go?

It's your first official check-up during your pregnancy, and should provide the medical team looking after you with valuable background information about your health that may have an impact on your baby.

When do I need to go?

It is recommended that you have your booking appointment no later than week 10 of your pregnancy: the reason for this is that you might need some tests that should be done in the first trimester of pregnancy (ie 13 weeks) and they are organised once you have completed your initial consultation.

What to expect at your first appointment

Questions, questions and more questions . . . at the end of it you might feel that applying for a job at NASA would be an easier option but don't worry: none of the other antenatal appointments is as detailed as this one. What questions will the midwife ask?

- **The date of the first day of your last period.** This is so your due date can be estimated. You may be offered a dating scan at this first appointment to give an accurate picture (literally) of how pregnant you are and how many babies you've made. There are more details on antenatal scans on page 23.

- **Your obstetric history.** Details of all previous pregnancies, including terminations, miscarriages and still births. This helps to plan the type of care you will need.

- **Your general health.** This includes any significant medical problems, especially those that require you to take medication or visit a doctor regularly. The pregnancy might influence the medical condition (often improving it!) and the medical condition might influence the pregnancy (for example, women with high blood pressure are more likely to develop pre-eclampsia and might need to take low-dose aspirin to prevent it). You may need to be seen by a doctor to discuss this. Your midwife will also assess the chance of you having a thrombosis in pregnancy (see page 81) and may refer you to a doctor to discuss this.

- **Your (and your partner's) family history of genetic conditions.** You can now screen the baby for certain genetic conditions like cystic fibrosis or sickle cell disease, which the midwife will organise for you if appropriate.

- **Your (and your partner's) family history of illnesses.** These include heart disease and diabetes, amongst others. These conditions could also have an effect on your pregnancy.

- **Your mental health.** If you are prone to depression or have ever had any mental health problems, it is important that you make the midwife aware of this because you may need extra help or support during pregnancy or after the birth. There are some mental health problems that have high chances of recurring after delivery, so treatment to prevent this may be considered. If your mother or a sister has had a serious postnatal mental health problem, you should tell your midwife.

- **Your lifestyle.** The midwife will want to find out how many units of alcohol you drink and whether or not you smoke cigarettes or use recreational drugs. She might give you advice about how both can affect your developing baby, and point you towards services that help you quit if you are having trouble giving up or cutting down.

- **Your sexual health.** Whilst it may seem intrusive to ask a pregnant woman about her sexual history, chlamydia is increasingly common in young women, and if you are under 25 you might receive information on screening for this as the disease can be passed on to the unborn child.

- **Your smear history.** If you are over 25 years old you should have a cervical smear every three years to test for signs of cervical cancer – sadly, we all remember Jade Goody's premature death. Whilst routine smears are not usually performed in pregnancy, a repeat smear after a previously abnormal one should be done in pregnancy. If you have had treatment to your cervix after an abnormal smear you may be at increased risk of premature delivery and you should ask your midwife whether you will need any extra care.

- **Your preferences regarding delivery.** If you haven't decided where to have the baby, the midwife will go through all the birth options available to you in your locality. It's really important that you ask lots of questions about the type of care on offer because it may affect where and how you give birth. Ask if you will see the same midwife each time, if that's important to you, or whether you need to see a consultant.

NICE now recommends that women at high risk of developing pre-eclampsia are offered a low dose of aspirin from 12 weeks.

Some people don't get on terribly well with their GPs and might prefer midwife care, whereas others may be happier having appointments with a doctor they already know. You should be aware though that some people need to have care from hospital doctors because of problems with their health or the health of their baby.

If you have any anxieties don't be afraid to ask at this early stage – and if you think you have already developed 'baby brain' (see page 94) make a list beforehand so you don't forget!

What will the midwife 'do' to me?

Blood tests

If you are worried about needles, take your partner or friend to distract you, as you will need to give a sample of blood. Your blood will be checked for immunity to rubella (German measles) and if you are not immune you will be offered a vaccination after delivery. You will also be tested for syphilis, HIV and hepatitis B – if you have any of these you will be offered treatment for yourself and to reduce the chance of your baby becoming infected too. You will be checked for anaemia (usually caused by low iron levels) and for sickle cell disease and thalassaemia. These are inherited forms of anaemia that are mostly very mild, but if you or your partner both have a mild form (or 'trait') you could have a baby with a more serious form of the illness. You will get to know your blood group – this means that if you need a blood transfusion, the right blood can be prepared more quickly. If you have a religious or other objection to blood transfusions it is important that you discuss this with your midwife early in the pregnancy. If your blood group is rhesus (Rh) negative you will be offered an anti D injection at around 28 weeks to reduce the chance of having a baby with anaemia due to blood incompatibility.

Blood pressure

The midwife will take your blood pressure. This reading will act as a baseline for future checks. It will also allow her to tell if your blood pressure is already high – if it is she will probably ask you to see an obstetrician. It will be measured at all your antenatal appointments. Usually your blood pressure is lower in pregnancy than before you conceive.

A rise in blood pressure in the second half of your pregnancy might indicate that you are developing pre-eclampsia (see page 81), which can be dangerous to you and your baby.

'Weirdly, I have very low blood pressure (lower than a normal person let alone a pregnant one!), which has made me very tired. I had a few *drops in my sugar levels which have given me the shakes and a cold sweat, but it's easily solved with a chocolate bar and a lie down.'*

Virginia, first pregnancy

Urine testing

You will need to produce a fresh urine sample for the midwife at every appointment. She will dip a chemical strip into it to check for signs of a urine infection. If an infection is suspected, the sample will be sent to the laboratory where it will be possible to make a definite diagnosis. Urine infections are much more common in pregnancy, and are treated with antibiotics to decrease the chance of getting a kidney infection (or that you will go into premature labour). In the second half of your pregnancy the midwife will also be looking for protein, since this can be another sign of pre-eclampsia (or sign of urine infection, vaginal discharge or not catching the sample cleanly). Recent advice from the National Institute for Health and Care Excellence (NICE) advises using an automated urine stick reader for protein, so you may see your sample going into a machine!

Weights and measures

Your weight and height will be recorded at this first appointment and your midwife will calculate your BMI (body mass index). This determines if you are underweight (BMI less than 19), normal (BMI 19–25), overweight (BMI of 25–30) or obese (BMI more than 30).

If your BMI is between 19 and 30 you probably will not be weighed again. If it is over 30, you will need to see a doctor to look into why this might be and what extra care you might need, since women who are obese are more likely to have pregnancy complications. If you are underweight you will also need to see a doctor to explore why this is. For more information on weight gain during pregnancy see page 135.

Your antenatal notes

You might be given the antenatal notes that your midwife has been studiously filling in by the end of your booking appointment or they might be given to you when the blood results are in. You should keep them with you at all times – unfortunately you never know when you might feel unwell or have an accident, and you must always show them to any doctor looking after you so that they understand your pregnancy. You must bring them to each appointment you have during your pregnancy.

If you go on holiday, particularly towards the end of your pregnancy, it's important to take them with you in case you go into labour early or have an urgent medical problem and need to visit a doctor or a hospital.

What information is in the notes and how do I decipher it?

Initially the notes will contain much of what you have told the midwife on that first antenatal visit, such as your name, address and hospital number; ethnic group and religion; past and present illnesses; current treatment/medicines taken etc.

The midwife will also record test results, or you will be given computer-generated reports and scan details such as the size of your baby's head and length of his femur. As your pregnancy progresses, the measurement of your bump, the position of the baby, and the baby's heartbeat will also be recorded. Pregnancy problems/complications or additional unscheduled visits to the antenatal clinic will be also be noted. There will probably be a birth plan section where your preferences regarding labour and birth can be completed but you don't have to do this right now. You're quite likely to change your mind by the time the baby arrives and it's probably a good idea to give yourself time to read up and discuss all the options available to you. Practical information such as phone numbers for your GP, midwife, NHS Direct, the hospital switchboard and delivery ward will also be included.

Your notes will also contain advice on what to do in a potential emergency situation in pregnancy.

DECIPHERING YOUR NOTES

In case your midwife doesn't explain, or you can't remember what she said, these are some of the most common abbreviations you might find on your notes:

GA (gestational age or pregnancy length). If it says you are 10+ 2 it means you are 10 weeks and two days pregnant (counting from your period, not from when you actually conceived).

Urine. NAD indicates nothing abnormal detected.

BP. Ideal blood pressure is less than 140/90, and generally the lower the better. If either figure is higher you will probably need extra monitoring to see if pre-eclampsia is developing; if the upper figure is more than 150 you may need treatment.

Height of your uterus. Once your pregnancy is well underway, your midwife will be measuring the height of your uterus. Also known as fundal height, this measurement is taken from the top of your pubic bone to the top of your bump, and the length in centimetres should roughly correspond to the number of weeks pregnant you are: = D or = dates means you are measuring the correct size for your pregnancy dates.

FH (fetal heart). The midwife will either record the number of beats per minute of your baby's heart, or write the following abbreviation: FHH = fetal heart heard.

FM (fetal movements). This refers to whether you or the midwife have felt the baby move.

Baby's position. Towards the end of your pregnancy the midwife will record your baby's position, using the following abbreviations:

- Ceph stands for cephalic. This means the baby is head down and in position for birth.
- Br stands for breech. This means the baby is bottom down.
- LOA stands for left occiput anterior. This means the back of the baby's head is on your left hand side and towards the front of your stomach

- LOP stands for left occiput posterior. This means the back of the baby's head is on your left, and towards your back.
- ROA stands for right occiput anterior. This means the baby's head is at the right side of your stomach at the front.
- ROP stands for right occiput posterior. This means the baby's head is on the right side of your stomach towards the back.

When is my next appointment?

You will have a scan at around 12 weeks to date the pregnancy and, if you choose, to screen for Down's syndrome (see below), a fetal anomaly scan around 20 weeks, and another routine appointment at 24 weeks. From 28 weeks appointments will become fortnightly, and weekly from 40 weeks. However, this schedule will depend on how well you and the baby are, whether it is your first baby, whether you are having twins and what type of care you have chosen/been offered.

If you're expecting your first child, you'll have up to 10 antenatal appointments. If you've had a baby before you'll have around seven.

PUTTING YOU IN THE PICTURE ABOUT SCANS

Until you have the scan it is sometimes difficult to believe that you really are having a baby – even if you are throwing up every 10 minutes! The scan makes the whole thing very real. When you go for your scans it is advisable to bring someone with you if you can, as there is a possibility that the sonographer might pick up a problem and if that happens it's better to have someone to support you if the news is bad. About 3% of babies have structural problems, many of which can be detected by the scan. Sometimes a miscarriage is unexpectedly diagnosed at the scan.

According to guidelines from NICE women *should* be offered two routine ultrasound scans during pregnancy: a dating scan at around 10–14 weeks and an anomaly scan at around 18–22 weeks. However, if you have pain or bleeding you may need an earlier scan. There is no evidence that extra scans or 3D or 4D scans help in a normal pregnancy.

At this stage the crown-rump measurement is the most accurate way to determine the baby's age – from the top of his head to his bottom.

There is evidence that some health authorities still don't offer both scans, so it's useful to log on to fetalanomaly.screening.nhs.uk/localscreening, which has an interactive map that shows you what tests are available in your local area. There are many private clinics offering pregnancy ultrasound screening, so you might have to go down that route if your authority doesn't offer what you want – but do make sure that the private set-up is reputable before you hand over lots of money!

Dating scan: 10–14 weeks

You will be seen by a sonographer: this is a radiographer or midwife or doctor who is specially trained to conduct and interpret ultrasound scans. You might be asked to attend the appointment with a full bladder, as this helps push up the uterus and give a clearer picture. Probably the most painful aspect of the whole process is sitting with your legs crossed in a packed waiting room with a bladder fit to explode. When you go in, you'll be asked to pull your top up and your bottoms down and gel will be wiped across your bare tummy – it may be freezing or it might have been beautifully warmed, so be prepared for both. The sonographer will glide a probe across your stomach and an image of the fetus will appear on a small monitor beside you. Don't be frightened if they work in silence – it takes a huge amount of concentration to scan well. They look at the fetus from every angle, taking the vital measurements that will give an accurate picture of the 'date' of your growing baby. Once they have all the essential information, they'll talk you through the image on the screen, and point out the baby's heart beating and different parts of the body.

What else does the scan tell me at this point?

The dating scan isn't just to give you an idea of when your baby is due: it also confirms how many babies you are carrying and can detect some severe structural problems in the baby. Sadly, the scan can also pick up the news that no expectant mother wants to hear: that the pregnancy is no longer viable and the baby has died or is unlikely to survive.

If you have a scan at 10 weeks your baby will only be 3cm long.

Most hospitals will give you a print-out of an image of your baby at this first scan for a nominal charge. Buy at least two copies: one can go straight into your newborn's memory box and the second can live in your wallet to be whipped out at every opportunity . . . yes, the moment has come . . . you now have the weapon to become a fully-fledged baby bore! Mostly the photos are similar to Polaroids and will fade – so take more permanent copies if you can.

Vaginal scan

If you are overweight, your uterus is in a certain position or if the length of your cervix needs to be measured it may be difficult for the sonographer to get a good look at your baby with a trans-abdominal scan, so they might suggest a vaginal scan. If this happens they will gently insert a transducer – a thin probe – into your vagina. It doesn't hurt and won't harm you or the baby, so don't panic if you have to have one: it's about as uncomfortable as inserting a tampon and does give a much clearer picture. If you need this type of scan you are usually asked to empty your bladder first, which is a great relief!

Nuchal translucency (NT) scan:
what is it and why might I choose to have it?

The nuchal translucency scan is when the sonographer measures the collection of fluid within the skin at the back of your baby's neck (all babies have some fluid present). It is performed between 11 and 14 weeks, and there is strong evidence to suggest that if there is a large accumulation of fluid present there is an increased chance of your baby having Down's syndrome. The sonographer may also look to see if the baby's nasal bone is visible: if it is not, this is another marker indicating risk of Down's. However, not all medical professionals agree that examining the nasal bone is helpful, so it is not widely done. This scan can be performed along with a blood test, testing for hormone levels in the maternal blood. When this is done, it is called the combined screening test, and is the most accurate screening test available and is available to everyone free of charge on the NHS.

It's a good idea to photocopy any scan photos you have, as scan paper fades after about 10 years.

Fetal anomaly scan: 18–22 weeks

Around this time in your pregnancy you will be booked in for your second scan: the fetal anomaly scan. This does exactly what it says on the tin, ie looks for anomalies (things that differ from the norm) in your growing baby. The procedure is very similar to the dating scan, except that the scan takes much longer because the sonographer has many more things to look at now that your baby has grown. There are some abnormalities that will be very apparent at this scan and some that cannot be detected until after birth, so you must be aware that, even if you are told everything appears normal, this is no guarantee of your baby being born without any health problems (autism or cerebral palsy, for example, cannot be seen).

The scan will also measure the size of your baby's head (head circumference), waist (abdominal circumference) and leg (femur length), and these measurements are plotted on a chart showing their size in relation to other babies of the same gestational age. This allows final confirmation of your EDD; occasionally if the baby is unusually small, extra tests may be offered to see if there may be a problem causing this.

The scan also measures the amniotic fluid, referred to on the scan report usually as AFI (amniotic fluid index) or liquor volume. This fluid is made by the baby's kidneys (ie it is his urine) and the placenta, and circulates through the baby as he swallows it and then pees it! Too much or too little may indicate or cause a problem.

It's not just the baby the sonographer will be looking at: the position of the placenta will be noted, in case it causes difficulties later on (see below) and you may be asked to come back to be scanned nearer your due date if it is lower than expected.

The placenta will be described as being anterior or posterior (ie at the front or back of the uterus) and either high (ie away from the cervix) or low (ie over or within 2cm of the cervix). Latest advice from the Royal College of Obstetricians and Gynaecologists (RCOG 2011) suggests that looking at the placental site using a trans-vaginal probe will give more accurate localisation, and as many as 60% of women may be reassured that their placenta is not too low. You should also be offered another scan at 32–36 weeks, depending on how low your placenta is.

If you do have placenta praevia (see box below) you should have the opportunity to discuss this with a member of staff and be given an information leaflet. You may be advised not to travel, to abstain from sex and to take iron tablets. If you do experience any bleeding, you should get to the hospital straight away.

Finally, if you have an increased chance of pre-term delivery, you may be offered a trans-vaginal scan to measure the length of your cervix.

There are new gender testing kits on the market which claim 95% accuracy from as early as seven weeks, but you have to ask yourself the question – unless there was a valid genetic reason – why you would want to know so early into your pregnancy.

LOW-LYING PLACENTA OR PLACENTA PRAEVIA

The placenta is the organ that acts as a life support system to your fetus. It is the conduit which passes oxygen and nutrition from mother to baby.

Sometimes, though, the placenta implants low in the uterus and covers – or nearly covers – the cervix (the entrance to the uterus). After 20 weeks of pregnancy this is called placenta praevia. In 90% of cases it moves out of the way before the baby is due but in 10% of cases it doesn't. This is a potentially risky condition, as it can cause severe maternal bleeding, and if it is blocking your baby's exit route you'll almost certainly need to have your baby by planned Caesarean section (see page 234).

Pink or blue: which one for you?

The sex of the baby can often be detected at the anomaly scan, but do bear in mind it may not be the policy of your hospital to tell you. The sonographer's determination of the sex of your baby is also not 100% accurate, as the umbilical cord can be mistaken for a penis, and some Buddha babies like to cross their legs and make it difficult for the sonographer to see. If you do want to know, it's advisable to tell the person scanning you at the outset so they have a chance to have a look in the time allotted for your appointment. If your hospital cannot tell you and you can't wait another 20 weeks to find out, you'll need to go for a private scan or test to confirm the sex. If you do find out, you then have the tricky decision about who to tell.

In a recent study, sonographers could identify the sex of only 46% of babies at 13 weeks and 80% at 20 weeks.

'We didn't find out the sex of our baby. Life has few enough surprises and we wanted this to be a very special one!'

Becky, first pregnancy

TESTING FOR DOWN'S SYNDROME

Medical facts

Down's syndrome is named after John Langdon Down, the doctor who first identified it. Down's syndrome is a genetic disorder that affects around one in 1,000 babies. We know that babies with Down's syndrome inherit an extra copy of the number 21 chromosome, but it's not known exactly why this occurs. When your egg is being prepared for release (and therefore for pregnancy) the chromosomes separate, so that instead of being in pairs (as they are in all cells apart from egg and sperm), they are single. At conception, the chromosomes in the sperm and those in the egg join together to form pairs again, meaning that the genes of the baby are a mixture of the mum and dad's. However, sometimes the chromosomes in the egg do not separate correctly and both of the chromosomes – in this case pair number 21 – join with the number 21 in the sperm, meaning that the baby has 47 chromosomes instead of the usual 46, resulting in Down's syndrome.

A study at Birmingham University revealed that fathers are more likely to bond with their newborn quickly if they know the gender of the baby before birth.

Appearance and outlook

Babies born with Down's syndrome will typically have a flat facial profile and the back of their head will be flat. Their eyes slant upwards, and they have smaller ears and a protruding tongue. They are likely to have floppy joints and poor muscle tone, and other problems may include impairment of their sight, hearing, heart or digestive system. Down's syndrome children tend to develop at a slower pace and are likely to have learning difficulties.

Prognosis

There is no cure for Down's syndrome but modern education and therapeutic services have progressed to the point where a Down's syndrome diagnosis is not the devastating blow it once was. Instead, people with this disability are able to integrate into society almost as easily as anyone else. For more information on the condition visit www. downs-syndrome.org.uk.

Chances of having a baby with Down's syndrome

For more information on these tests log on to www. fetalmedicine.com.

We may not know exactly why Down's syndrome occurs but we do know that the risk increases with maternal age. A girl is born with all her eggs already inside her, meaning her eggs age as she does. Older eggs are less able to separate their chromosomes than younger ones, so the risk of having a baby with Down's syndrome increases proportionate to the mother's age. By way of illustration, consider that pregnant women aged 20 have a risk of one in 1,500 of having a baby with Down's syndrome, while a woman aged 30 has a risk of one in 900, and a 40 year old woman has a risk of one in 100.

Should I take a test to see if I am at risk?

All pregnant women who book before 20 weeks should be offered a test to screen their pregnancy for Down's syndrome. You do not have to have the test and you should consider if there are any ethical, moral or religious reasons why it might not be right for you. If you do decide you don't want to take the test, just tell your midwife and she will ensure your wishes are complied with.

About 750,000 women are offered the test annually and 60% take up the offer. In 2011, 725 babies were born with Down's syndrome.

If you feel you might not be able to continue the pregnancy if your baby is given a diagnosis of Down's syndrome, or would like more time to adjust to the idea of having a baby with the condition, you should probably take the test. But remember that these tests do not diagnose Down's syndrome – they only show if there is a risk. If the test results show that your baby has an increased risk of Down's syndrome then you will be offered a diagnostic test, which is discussed in more detail below.

What tests are on offer?

There are two stages to this process: the first is a screening test, which indicates the *likelihood* of you carrying a Down's baby, and the second stage is a diagnostic test, which will give you a *definite* answer. The reason that not every woman is offered a diagnostic test is because the chance for most women of carrying a baby with Down's syndrome is low, and as the diagnostic tests do have a small risk of miscarriage, they are only done if the screening test has indicated there is a likelihood of the baby having Down's syndrome.

Single blood test

There are several screening tests available. Which one you are offered will depend on whether you are less than 14 weeks pregnant or not and what your particular hospital has available. Some health authorities will offer blood tests that show an increased risk of Down's through markers in the blood. They may measure two (double), three (triple) or even four (quadruple) substances – the more they measure, the more accurate the test. This test is done between 15 weeks and 20 weeks. The results of the test analysis, combined with the mother's age and the stage of the pregnancy, are fed into a computer and the result will give a statistical risk of Down's syndrome. If the risk is between one in two and one in 250 you will be offered a diagnostic test.

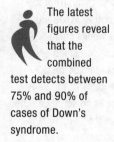

3%–5% of all women will have a 'positive' screening test. For many of these women, the baby will not have Down's syndrome.

Combined test

Some hospitals will also perform an NT scan (see above), and combine the blood test results with the NT measurements to get an even more accurate assessment of risk; this is called a combined test, and is done between 11 weeks and 13 weeks plus six days.

If you want a combined test and the NT scan isn't offered in your area, you can choose to visit one of the 100 private screening centres in the country. It costs between £100 and £200 depending on where you live. You can ask your midwife for details of local centres or call the Fetal Medical Centre for a list of accredited centres.

The latest figures reveal that the combined test detects between 75% and 90% of cases of Down's syndrome.

LOCATION, LOCATION, LOCATION

There is evidence to suggest that there is a postcode lottery when it comes to Down's syndrome screening. London hospitals currently have the most accurate screening tests, while the lowest detection rates are occurring in the North and Midlands area. If your local hospital relies on just a single blood test or NT scan you may consider going private for peace of mind. Some hospitals miss up to a third of Down's syndrome cases and give mothers false negative results, whereas in other areas 20% of women go through needless diagnostic invasive tests that could risk them losing the baby.

WORDS FROM THE PROFESSIONALS: Be aware. Recent research indicates that two healthy babies are miscarried, as a result of the diagnostic tests, for every three Down's syndrome babies detected, so it is important that you are aware of the risks of having an invasive test.

Latest evidence shows that within a few years a simple blood test taken from the mother at around 9 weeks could replace the screening and diagnostic tests – enough of the baby's cells could be detected so that his chromosomes can be counted.

What happens if your risk is high?

The RCOG recently estimated that around 30,000 women are offered a diagnostic test each year in the UK, or 5% of all pregnant women. You will be offered either chorionic villus sampling (CVS) or an amniocentesis test. CVS can usually be performed between 11 and 14 weeks, whereas amniocentesis is carried out from 15 weeks. There is an additional risk of miscarriage with amniocentesis of 1% and a 1%–2% additional chance of miscarriage with CVS, although the risk varies from hospital to hospital.

In both procedures a fine needle is inserted into the uterus; this can be done vaginally for CVS or trans-abdominally for CVS and amniocentesis. Don't panic that your baby will be stabbed by the needle: an ultrasound probe will be guiding the doctor to ensure that he has a clear picture of the position of the needle and your baby.

Latest RCOG guidance also ensures that doctors only continue to do these tests if they have sufficient experience each year – set at 30 cases. Therefore, you may find that you are asked to go to another hospital for the test, since some units are combining their resources to ensure the best levels of experience for their doctors and fewer complications.

A sample of tissue from the placenta (the chorionic villi) will be removed if you undergo CVS and a sample of the amniotic fluid is extracted if you undergo amniocentesis. The actual test only takes a couple of minutes and you should have the results back within a couple of weeks. Many hospitals now offer rapid testing for chromosomes 13, 18 and 21, with results being available in three to five working days.

Ask your hospital which tests it uses and how it will inform you of the result – usually a phone call to your preferred number.

Does it hurt?

Most women describe the procedure as uncomfortable as opposed to painful. CVS has been likened to having a smear test and amniocentesis can make your tummy a bit sore afterwards. Slight cramping and very mild vaginal bleeding afterwards are considered normal, although if you have heavy bleeding, clear vaginal fluid loss or flu-like symptoms you should seek immediate medical assistance.

> **WORDS FROM THE PROFESSIONALS:** 92% of women choose to terminate if they get a positive confirmation of Down's syndrome. If you have a high risk screening test result, you might want to opt for CVS because it can be done earlier in your pregnancy.

If you want more information about these tests, or need help and support after taking them, check out www.arc-uk.org (Antenatal Results and Choices).

GOING PRIVATE

Private scan options

We have outlined the scans you can expect to receive on the NHS unless there is a potential problem with you or the baby that your midwife or consultant wants to keep an eye on. There are other scans available if you want reassurance and have the money to pay for them, but you need to realise that outside the NHS the standard setting and auditing of results may be different, and so the quality not so good. You also need to think through why you want a scan – and discuss it again with your doctor of midwife. Women commonly ask for a scan to reassure themselves that the 'baby is OK', but unfortunately the scan cannot do that. It is usually better to talk about what is worrying you, rather than pay large sums of money for a scan that may not be helpful.

Costs for scans if you go private

The number and type of scans you can pay for vary widely from region to region. Below is an indication of what prices you can expect to pay.

- Cost of a private appointment: £80 to £150

- Cost of a nuchal translucency scan (2D Imaging) (11–14 weeks): £135 to £200

- Cost of a Soft Markers/Detailed Fetal Anatomy scan (2D Imaging) (16–22 weeks): £150 to £250

- Cost of reassurance and anomaly scans, including sexing (20–36 weeks): £95 to £250.

Take a deep breath . . .

All this talk of scans can sometimes turn an already emotional pregnant woman into a complete nervous wreck, but remember: in the majority of cases your baby will be completely normal, and the purpose of these scans is to give you the chance to identify any potential problems and make informed choices about how best to prepare for or deal with them.

Private tests

Group B Streptococcus (Group B Strep or GBS) is a common bacterium that's carried in the vagina of around 25% of pregnant woman. It is usually harmless, but it can be passed from mother to baby during birth, and occasionally this causes very serious health problems in the baby.

Around 75 babies die annually from neonatal Group B Strep, and 40 sustain longterm health problems. If GBS is detected incidentally during other antenatal tests, you will be offered antibiotics to significantly reduce the chance of your baby contracting GBS. However, GBS is not routinely tested for in hospitals in the UK. This is because if you are a carrier today, you might not be tomorrow and vice versa; there is not an accurate bedside rapid response test available and the risks of antibiotic use may exceed the benefits. It is of debatable value knowing if you do or do not carry GBS, and so there is not a UK screening programme for it. There are, however, several labs offering screening for around £35.

There's lots of information on the Group B Strep website: www.gbss.org.uk, and a patient information leaflet, 'Preventing Group B

SCAN SCARE! UNNECESSARY 'SOUVENIR' PICTURES MAY BE HARMFUL TO YOUR BABY

There isn't any evidence to show that two or three scans will harm your baby, but having unnecessary scans to fill your family photo album may not be the greatest idea. According to the latest research from the Health Protection Agency (HPA), there can be risks associated with an unnecessarily large number of scans. If there isn't a medical reason for having a scan you might want to think twice about having one.

4D scans

Technology has improved enormously over the past few years and recently we have seen a move towards colour scans and 3D scans. A step up from a 3D scan is the newly emerged 4D scan, which is rapidly growing in popularity. A 4D scan is a 3D scan with the added dimension of time – as in a film or video – so the baby can be seen to be moving; therefore, if you book a 4D scan, you not only get to see your baby in all his 3D glory on screen during the appointment, but you get to take home a DVD keepsake (and in some of the luxury packages you also get a video for your iPhone or iPod, as well as photos and a fetal growth report that gets sent to your hospital). The hospitals offering this service will also tell you the sex of the baby, which they can hopefully see in all its 3D glory! If you google 4D scans you will find a wealth of companies offering this service for around £200.

Streptococcus infection in newborn babies', on the RCOG website (www.rcog.org.uk).

ANTENATAL CLASSES

Antenatal classes can be one of the most exciting parts of your pregnancy. You have a few options available to you: you can either sign up for NHS-run classes, or try to go to classes run by the National Childbirth Trust (NCT). Either way it is something you'll have to consider early in your pregnancy as classes can fill up remarkably quickly.

NCT classes

If you fancy joining the NCT and attending its fabled antenatal classes, you need to get your name down quicker than you can say 'natural birth'.

The NCT is a membership charity that provides information, support and classes for parents, families and health professionals, and its classes do get booked up very early. There are a variety of courses on offer, including weekends and evenings for couples, and daytime women-only sessions too. Prices start at around £6 an hour – depending on the session and time.

One of the benefits of joining a local NCT class is that you may forge friendships with local mothers who are giving birth around the same time as you, as the classes are organised around due dates. You probably won't get on with all the women there, but then again, do you like every woman you work with in the office? If you find just one like-minded kindred spirit, it'll be worth it for all of the support and cappuccinos you can enjoy together once you both have babes in arms.

'NCT classes have been great for meeting other "bumpy ladies". They've definitely been informative, and made my husband feel involved and clued up. But as someone who is going to have to have quite a "medicalised" birth, I'd say it's good to get a balance by attending the NHS classes or talking to your midwife. Otherwise you might feel like you're "failing" to do things the "natural" way.'

Vicky, first pregnancy

If you do want to sign up to NCT classes, go to its website: www.nct.org.uk

Another bonus with the NCT is that it has classes at convenient times, so that working parents can attend without having to take time off work. Some people find there is a distinct bias towards natural childbirth and a 'breast is best' attitude towards feeding, although this does depend on the views of your particular teacher.

NHS parentcraft classes

The NHS provides 'parentcraft classes', usually in the last 10 weeks of your pregnancy. These take place either at the hospital where you're due to give birth or at a health centre. The number you get varies from hospital to hospital. Recently many hospitals have combined the classes into a smaller number of more detailed sessions, rather than a large number of short classes. The NHS now offers classes in the evenings and at weekends, and involves partners in all or some of the classes. Some people find these classes a bit basic. You are allowed to take paid time off to attend antenatal classes, but your partner is not, so you might want to look at what your local hospital offers as soon as you can in case you need to look at alternatives.

Private classes

If you want, you can also go down the private route. Some women choose this route if they can't get into an NCT class near them. Googling 'private antenatal classes' brings up a host of options, including one company in London that offers a six-week antenatal course with a cupcake at every session and a 35-minute facial on completion of the course! The course costs around £295, from www.cupcakemum.co.uk.

Other companies offer small group sessions and even one-to-one private evening classes in your own home. Check out www.theknowledgeantenatal.com for more information. There are even antenatal packages online for women who are just too busy to attend classes, such as www.antenatalonline.co.uk. However, you might want to reflect on why you are so busy and what is more important – your priorities may be changing!

WHAT COULD GO WRONG

Before you start reading this section, you need to know that we're going to discuss miscarriage, ectopic pregnancy and stillbirths. This isn't to scare you or worry you – it's here so you're fully informed. If you'd rather not read this section, skip ahead to Chapter 2.

Miscarriage

If you saw the film *Marley & Me* (2008), you'll probably remember the scene when Jennifer Anniston goes in to have a routine dating scan and the monitor looks like a mini snow storm. The happily married couple – played by Jennifer Aniston and Owen Wilson – are blissfully unaware there is anything wrong, until the sonographer goes off to find a colleague who confirms that the baby is no longer alive.

This is not just a fictional occurrence: one in seven confirmed pregnancies ends in miscarriage, but in reality the figure is much higher – as many as one in four – because many women miscarry even before they know they are pregnant. Early miscarriage is the loss of a baby before 13 weeks, while late miscarriage is considered to be between

13 and 24 weeks. If you lose a baby after 24 weeks it is called a stillbirth (see page 39).

Why does it happen?
If you have a miscarriage it is likely that you will never know the cause of it. Chromosomal abnormalities in the fetus are believed to cause around 50% of early miscarriages; this is often described as 'nature's way' of dealing with a baby that wouldn't have survived until full term or would have had severe health problems. Other factors that can influence miscarriage include certain hormone imbalances, physical problems such as a weak cervix or fibroid, your health and lifestyle, and certain blood clotting disorders. Very occasionally the baby might get an infection in the uterus and die.

Miscarriage risks
Your age has quite a significant influence on your miscarriage risk: women between 25 and 29 have a 12% chance of having a miscarriage, whereas the risk rises to over 50% in women aged 40–44.

If you have already suffered a miscarriage, you are slightly more at risk of experiencing another in a subsequent pregnancy. Ninety-nine percent of miscarriages happen in the first trimester (13 weeks), so the longer your pregnancy progresses, the less likely it is that you will miscarry.

What happens during miscarriage?
You might experience cramping and blood loss like you would during a normal/heavy period. If you experience bleeding with low abdominal pain, contact your GP or midwife as soon as you can. They will probably arrange for a scan to check whether you have miscarried and, if you have, that there is nothing left in your uterus that could cause infection.

Often you experience no symptoms and only discover your baby has died when you go for a routine scan, when the sonographer may not be able to detect a heartbeat or may discover an empty pregnancy sac with no baby inside. The doctor may recommend that you go home and let nature take its course, or they may recommend you have an 'evacuation of retained products of conception' or ERPC. This is a surgical procedure normally carried out under general anaesthetic that will remove the pregnancy. It is a simple procedure and will usually be performed as a day case. Alternatively, 'medical management' may be offered, whereby you are given tablets, usually two days apart, to make the pregnancy miscarry completely.

Miscarriage is a devastating thing to happen, but remember that most women go on to have successful pregnancies and that there is lots of help and support out there to help you get over your loss, including the charity Tommy's and The Miscarriage Association.

It is recommended that you have at least two periods following a miscarriage before you try to get pregnant again. Emotionally, though, you may feel you need to wait longer before trying to become pregnant again.

Threatened miscarriage

Some women will experience bleeding in early pregnancy. If a scan shows that the pregnancy is developing in the uterus their doctor may advise them to 'wait and see'. This is called a threatened miscarriage. Whilst it's absolute torture wondering whether your baby is going to make it or not, it is quite common to experience light bleeding in the first 12 weeks of pregnancy. If it is not accompanied by pain it might well be your body 'settling down' to being pregnant, and in around 50% of cases the baby will be fine. It is important not to rest completely, but you should stop working while you are bleeding and take life slowly.

Is there anything I can do to avoid miscarriage?

If you do experience a miscarriage, don't beat yourself up about it and wonder if it was anything that you did when you didn't know you were pregnant. There is some evidence to show that smoking, drinking, recreational drug use and excessive caffeine consumption do increase your risk of miscarriage, which is why it's advisable to quit or severely cut down when you are pregnant. Similarly, women who are seriously overweight and those with some health problems should get advice before trying to conceive again – it may be that losing weight or improving control over diabetes will improve the chances of a good outcome next time.

In 2010 a 33 year old woman from Brighton gave birth to a perfect little girl after 18 miscarriages.

Stress has also been shown to play a part, so worrying about what you did or didn't do may put your baby at just as much risk as that daily double shot latte from Starbucks. Just make sure you look after yourself and always follow your doctor's advice.

Ectopic pregnancy

Another tragic reality of pregnancy is the occurrence of ectopic pregnancies. This is an uncommon occurrence, although the incidence seems to be increasing, possibly because of tubal damage caused by sexually transmitted infections such as chlamydia and by delayed childbearing. Records show there are 11,000 ectopic pregancies in the UK each year, but this is thought to be an underestimate.

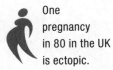

One pregnancy in 80 in the UK is ectopic.

Ectopic means 'in the wrong place', so an ectopic pregnancy is when the pregnancy develops outside the uterus. Ectopic pregnancies can occur in several places – in the ovary, the abdomen, the cervix, the scar from a previous Caesarean section, or the join between the uterus and the Fallopian tube, but most often it occurs in the Fallopian tube. As the pregnancy develops it can cause pain and bleeding, and if it is not recognised quickly enough it can cause the tube to rupture, causing internal bleeding. This can be fatal if it is not treated quickly enough.

Other symptoms of an ectopic pregnancy include pain at the top of the shoulder, pain when you open your bowels or pass urine, diarrhoea, vomiting and dizzy spells. Clearly none of these is specific to ectopics, but if you are pregnant and have not had a scan yet, you should seek medical advice if you experience any of these.

Ectopic pregnancies are usually found between week 4 and week 10, and it is thought that they are caused by a problem in either the Fallopian tube or embryo.

How to recognise an ectopic pregnancy
There are a number of ways in which an ectopic pregnancy can be recognised.

- Most commonly, a woman experiences abdominal pain (normally on one side) and some irregular bleeding. She may or may not know she is pregnant.

- Increasingly, ectopic pregnancy is diagnosed by scan in a woman who has no symptoms but is at risk of having an ectopic pregnancy – eg someone who has previously had one.

- Finally, presentation may occur when a woman collapses and, at the hospital, a positive pregnancy test and further testing reveal a ruptured ectopic pregnancy.

How ectopic pregnancies are treated

Some ectopic pregnancies are absorbed naturally back into the body, while others can be treated with a drug which causes the cells to stop dividing, meaning the pregnancy shrinks away. However, the majority of ectopic pregnancies will require surgery, where either the pregnancy or the whole Fallopian tube is removed. Sadly, an ectopic pregnancy can never survive.

Around 65% of women who have an ectopic pregnancy go on to conceive again within 18 months, but for many women having an ectopic pregnancy is associated with reduced fertility. This may be because previous damage to their Fallopian tubes caused the ectopic pregnancy, or because the ectopic pregnancy and its surgical treatment damaged the tube.

Much like a miscarriage, the emotional drama and potential danger caused by an ectopic pregnancy can be a traumatic experience and will often require a similar grieving process to a miscarriage. If you need any help or advice about ectopic pregnancies, ask your doctor or midwife, or check out www.ectopic.org.uk.

Stillbirth

While we are discussing the tragic things that can go wrong in a pregnancy, we also need to acknowledge that not all pregnancies end with a live baby and that stillbirth is a reality. There cannot be a harder birth to prepare for than one when you know that your baby has already died in your uterus, or know that your baby will die within hours of birth.

Around one in 200 babies is stillborn. The term 'stillbirth' means death at, or before, the birth of a baby that is more than 24 weeks. There is not always one single factor that causes a baby to die in the uterus: often it can be a combination of factors, like congenital abnormalities (that may not always be picked up on a scan) or low birth weight, or sometimes the placenta can start failing towards the end of pregnancy. Some women will already know that their baby is ill or unlikely to survive, as many problems are detected through antenatal tests and scans; other women will stop feeling their baby move or go for a routine scan to be told the devastating news that their baby has died.

What will happen if a stillbirth is detected

One of the things that many women find surprising is that you normally give birth to a stillborn baby vaginally. This is much safer for you (and for any pregnancies you may have in the future) than a Caesarean section, as all surgery has associated risk. You should discuss the best option for delivery with your midwife or obstetrician; you may be given the choice to have your labour induced or wait for it to happen spontaneously. Some women want to get it over with as soon as possible; others want some time to get used to the idea and would prefer nature to take its course.

When you deliver, you should be treated with the utmost care and compassion by the medical team, who will know your circumstances and ensure that the birth is as calm and stress-free as possible. Most units will have a particular room where women anticipating a stillbirth or early death after delivery are managed. This will usually be a bit quieter and a bit larger than the other rooms, and have facilities for you and your partner to stay together throughout the delivery and until you are ready to go home. There will usually be a bed for your partner, an en-suite shower and toilet, and probably a television. All the usual forms of pain relief are also available to you. You may want to include something that makes you feel a little sleepy and calm – a patient-controlled analgesia (PCA) of diamorphine can be good for this, as you can press the button and get a small boost of painkiller as you need it.

You will be allowed to spend as long as you need with your baby after he is born, and will be encouraged to hold him, take photographs of him and take imprints of his feet or hands. If you have other children, and maybe even grandparents, they may want to come and spend time with the baby – obviously this will depend on your personal circumstances and your family: the midwives can guide you, as they are used to supporting families in this situation. Although this might be incredibly difficult and painful for you and the baby's father, it may give you comfort in years to come.

Your body may not immediately work out that the baby has died. This means that your breasts will probably fill with milk, which can be very upsetting and uncomfortable. Your midwife will usually offer you a tablet shortly after the baby is born to reduce the milk supply. You should wear a good supporting bra, and leave your breasts alone as much as possible – don't be tempted to squeeze out some milk, as this can encourage the supply to continue for longer.

Your midwife will help you to understand all the paperwork required for registering the baby's death and the options for funeral arrangements. Many units will have a team of midwives who specialise in supporting bereaved families – and this will include helping older brothers and sisters understand why the baby isn't coming home and why all the grown-ups seem so sad.

If you wish to have your baby blessed or baptised, there are usually hospital chaplains on call who can perform a ceremony for you in the religious denomination of your choice. The chaplain may also be able to offer you spiritual help and guidance at this very difficult time, so if you feel you would like this type of support, do mention it to your midwife.

If a baby dies in the uterus or shortly after birth, a number of tests including blood samples, urine analysis and swabs, plus a post-mortem, are usually offered to try to establish the cause of death. The concept of a post-mortem might be very distressing at the time, but it might help you understand how your baby died and therefore come to terms with the loss, or help the doctors treat you during subsequent pregnancies. In nearly half of cases it is not possible to work out why a baby has died. This might be a source of frustration or sadness at the time, but you can take comfort from the fact that this often means that you will have a successful pregnancy if you decide to try for a baby again.

Sands (the stillbirth and neonatal death charity) offers a confidential helpline to provide support – 020 7436 5881.

Around eight weeks after a stillbirth, you will be offered an appointment to discuss the results and the events surrounding the loss of your baby.

As your grief might be still raw and you may still be feeling very emotional, it can be useful to prepare a list of questions that you would like to ask your consultant. Try to take the baby's father if you can, because you might not be able to remember all the details of the discussion afterwards, although usually you do get a letter confirming what was said at the appointment. Possibly, one of the things on your mind will be if and when you can try for another baby – this will depend on whether you need further investigations and the emotional well-being of you and your partner, as well as your general physical health.

There are many excellent organisations that can help you cope with your grief and loss through counselling and advice; they are listed at the back of this book.

2

My baby's development and how I'm feeling: week by week

Imagining your baby growing inside you is one of the most amazing parts of being pregnant. In this chapter we go through a week-by-week account of your baby's progress in your uterus, and what these changes will mean for your body, both inside and out! We'll cover both the physical and emotional aspects of being pregnant, and also look at some tips on how to stay stylish during your pregnancy. We'll also look at some suggestions on how to make your pregnancy truly 'memorable'.

TRIMESTERS EXPLAINED

Trimester is a word you will see and hear regularly during your pregnancy. It is believed that 'trimester' evolved from the Latin word *trimestris*, meaning 'three months old' ('tri' meaning three and 'mensis' meaning month), and that's what it roughly means in English, too – three months. So your first trimester is weeks 1–13, your second trimester weeks 14–27 and your third trimester weeks 28–40. However, as you'll soon discover, it's weeks rather than trimesters which are regularly used to monitor the progress of your pregnancy.

WEEKS NOT MONTHS

Ask anyone how long it takes to have a baby and they'll say nine months, but once you are pregnant you will find that everyone will refer to your pregnancy in weeks. The reason for this is that, from a medical perspective, so much happens from week to week that it's important to pinpoint exactly where you are in the process. This is why everyone, including you, will refer to your pregnancy in weeks and days.

THE FIRST TRIMESTER

The first trimester is probably the most amazing in terms of your growing baby: one minute you're having a night of passion, six weeks later there's a fuzzy little life you can marvel at on ultrasound, and by your 12-week scan there's a tiny form that's easily recognisable as your baby. The rate at which the cells multiply and change into a growing baby and support system is nothing short of miraculous, and it's fascinating to know what's happening (particularly as you can't see or feel much at this stage).

Week 1

The date of the first day of your last menstrual period (even though you are not even pregnant yet, this still counts as your first week of pregnancy).

Week 2/3

Conception takes place and the fertilised egg (or zygote) implants into the lining of the uterus. After implantation, the zygote is termed the embryo.

Week 4 (the week your period doesn't start)

The embryo is now nestling nicely in the uterus lining; the outer cells are branching out like roots to link into the mother's blood supply to nourish the embryo. The inner cells now divide into three layers that will form the baby's body. One layer will form your baby's brain, nervous system, skin, ears and eyes. Another layer forms the lungs, stomach and intestine, and the third will form the heart, bones, muscle and blood. A sensitive urine pregnancy test is usually positive at around this time.

Week 5

You may have just found out you are pregnant, but already your baby's nervous system is developing. By the end of this week the top layer of cells have formed a neural tube, which has a 'head end' for the brain and a 'tail end' for the spinal cord. This is why it's advisable to start taking 400 micrograms of folic acid before you conceive, to give you the best chance of preventing neural tube defects such as spina bifida.

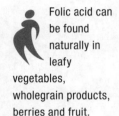

Folic acid can be found naturally in leafy vegetables, wholegrain products, berries and fruit.

The heart is also beginning to form, and blood vessels connecting mother and baby are the beginning of the umbilical cord.

The embryo now becomes safely encased in a bag called the amniotic sac and is just 4mm–6mm in size (about the size of a pea).

> **MUMMY MATTERS:** Are you feeling sick this week? There are tips on how to deal with morning sickness in the next chapter (page 87), but if you are feeling distinctly queasy here's a crumb of comfort: a recent study suggests that women who suffer badly from morning sickness are more likely to give birth to a baby with a high IQ, as the hormones that cause a woman to vomit are also those that assist in the baby's mental development.

Week 6

Bulges appear showing the position of the heart, and the developing brain and the heartbeat can be detected on an ultrasound scan.

Week 7

The eyes, ears and limb buds are already starting to form, as are the muscles and bones.

> **MUMMY MATTERS:** If you are suddenly resembling a spotty teenager with lank greasy hair and zits, don't despair: this phase is usually short lived and is thanks to those hormones running amok in your body.

Week 8

At this point the embryo is now around 15mm–20mm (1.5cm–2cm) long and prawn-shaped (about the size of a small bean). The foot and hand areas can be recognised, as can the fingers and toes, but these may still be webbed.

The eyes are now becoming visible, the mouth and tongue have formed, and the major organs are developing.

> **MUMMY MATTERS:** Having trouble keeping your eyes open past 9pm? Feeling exhausted is very common in early pregnancy, and is just your body reacting to the effort it takes to set up the life support system for your baby.

River Cottage chef Hugh Fearnley-Whittingstall once pan-fried a placenta with shallots on TV and served it to the baby's parents and 20 guests.

Week 9

The embryo is now between 20mm and 30mm long, measured from head to bottom. This is called the crown-rump length, and is a very accurate way of dating the pregnancy between 7 and 12 weeks. When you have your first scan, it is very likely that you will see the abbreviation CRL, indicating the length of the baby and therefore his gestational age. At nine weeks your baby is approximately 22mm long, and at 10 weeks, 31mm. This measurement is used since the baby is usually in a sitting position, with the legs bent at the hips and knees, so getting his full length (including the legs) is almost impossible.

The placenta

The placenta forms from part of the group of cells that implanted into the lining of your womb shortly after conception. It is the organ that joins you and your baby together via the umbilical cord, and it supplies your baby with all the resources he needs to grow. It allows for the transfer of oxygen, nutrients and antibodies from the mother to the baby, and for the baby to get rid of waste products. It also means that your baby is born with some immunity against many serious infections that will protect him in the first few weeks of life before he gets his own vaccinations. The circulation of blood for the mother and baby are kept completely separate, though. This is a really important part of the placenta's role, particularly if you and your baby have different blood groups, or you need to take certain medications – many drugs have molecules that are too large to cross through to the baby, so you can be reassured that they won't harm him. Problems with the way the placenta works can sometimes cause the baby to be smaller than expected (because the supply of food is less than usual), or can be linked with pre-eclampsia (see later).

The placenta grows throughout your pregnancy, and by the time the baby is born it will weigh a whopping 1.5lbs! It normally detaches itself after birth (sometimes called the afterbirth) and is usually delivered less than 30 minutes after your baby is born via the birth canal. Sometimes the placenta does not deliver spontaneously, and then you might need to have it removed (see page 341) or you may be given an injection to speed up the process. Occasionally the placenta seems to have delivered completely, but small pieces remain that might come away later, or might cause bleeding or infection – this is why the person who delivers your baby always inspects the placenta to check that it seems complete.

The placenta is considered to be very important in certain cultures and there are many stories stemming from old traditions surrounding it. Filipinos are said to bury a child's placenta with a book to encourage a bright child. In Cambodia some people wrap the placenta in a banana leaf and place it next to the newborn for three days before burying it for luck. In Indonesia the placenta is regarded as the baby's twin, to act as a guardian angel, and has to be cleaned, wrapped and buried according to traditions by the baby's father on the day of birth. In some African countries the placenta is swaddled and buried beneath a tree to symbolise ongoing life, and other cultures, such as the Maori, bury the placenta to bind the baby to the ancestral land.

In China some people view the placenta as having life-giving properties – even after the baby is born – and it is dried and added to food to enhance energy and activity. Apparently, eating the placenta can also protect you against postnatal depression, but don't feel a failure if you decide not to pursue that piece of advice!

You will probably be having your first midwife appointment at this stage.

During pregnancy your sense of smell is often heightened and certain smells can be quite repulsive, and, equally, strange smells can become quite appealing.

Week 10

From this stage the baby is referred to as a fetus. At this stage, your baby's head is still disproportionately large, but the body is starting to straighten.

MUMMY MATTERS: Feeling snuffly? You've not got a cold on the way: it's just another random pregnancy symptom you might experience during the coming weeks. There is an increase in blood supply to many parts of your body during pregnancy, including your nose, and this tends to make you produce more mucus. This extra blood supply also explains why your hands might be warm and red! Overall, your blood volume has already increased from 5 litres to 8 litres. That's a lot of extra blood, but it is really important for supplying your body with what it needs for the pregnancy. Obviously, a lot of the extra blood goes to your uterus, but there's also a lot more in your breasts and in your kidneys – which is one of the reasons why you pee so much when you are pregnant.

Week 11

Your baby's sense of hearing is now developing; his eyes are fully formed but still closed.

Week 12

Incredibly, the fetus is now fully formed, with all the internal organs, muscles, bones and limbs present. The sex organs are also well developed, although they are not visible.

Your baby can now suck, yawn and swallow, but although he is moving around a lot you won't be able to feel it yet.

By this point your breasts will be bigger, so it might be time to invest in a supportive bra.

If you are slim, your doctor or midwife may be able to feel the top of the uterus in your lower tummy, and that means they may be able to hear your baby's heartbeat. Needless to say, this is a very exciting moment, and tangible evidence that something special is really happening inside you!

First trimester summary

What has happened so far:

- You have found out the amazing news you are having a baby.

- You should have visited your doctor or midwife and had a booking appointment with a midwife.

- You may have had a dating and a nuchal fold scan at around 12 weeks, or a different screening test for Down's syndrome.

Reasons to be cheerful even if you're feeling rough:

- This is a real milestone for pregnant women, because the chances of having a miscarriage after 13 weeks drop to around 1%.

- Your morning sickness symptoms *might* subside: fingers crossed!

- You're creating your own family. Many couples find having a baby brings them even closer together.

- You can feel confident about sharing the news with work colleagues and friends.

- Soon you'll stop looking just a bit porky and actually look pregnant!

- Free dental treatment. You won't get glam new veneers like Cheryl Cole on the NHS, but any check-ups and essential work won't cost you a penny.

- Binning the diet. You shouldn't eat for two, but you certainly should eat properly for one.

- Contraception- and period-free for up to a year.

- You've only got 27 weeks to go.

Looking good: fashion tips

By the end of the first trimester, you may notice that your waistline is thickening and you can no longer squeeze into that slim pencil skirt any more. Many pregnant women find that their shape starts changing as early as eight weeks, and dislike their appearance at this stage because instead of looking a pregnant vision of loveliness, they just look like they've been eating too many doughnuts. On the flip side, many women who are flat-chested start to enjoy their newly expanding chest.

Although you'll notice your growing belly, you may not have to buy any new clothes yet. If the waistband on your bottoms is getting tight, you can buy a waistband extender such as the Belly Belt, or you can just use a piece of elastic if you want to save the cash for a truly essential maternity wardrobe staple.

MY NOSE OR YOUR MOUTH: GENETICS AND APPEARANCE

How do genes work?

Our looks are determined by our genes. The proof of this comes from identical twins, who look exactly alike and have exactly the same DNA. But why do our children inherit some of our traits and not others? This is one area of baby 'science' that still remains a bit of a mystery, as human genetics experts struggle to explain why some genes dominate or manifest themselves several generations later.

We know we inherit two copies of every gene from our parents (one from our mother and one from our father) but what can't be predicted is how those copies interact with each other, and it's this interaction that determines how your baby will look

Eye colour

Eye colour is probably the simplest characteristic to predict, as the brown-eye gene is *usually* dominant over the blue-eye gene – so if one of the parents has brown eyes, it is likely that their baby will have brown eyes, too. But don't panic if the baby's eyes turn out to be blue, since the term 'dominant' means just that – ie the brown dominates over the blue – so even if you both have brown eyes, you

might also both have a hidden recessive blue gene, and if your baby gets a blue gene from both of you, his eyes will be blue. Caucasian babies tend to have blue-grey eyes when they are born, which normally change to their permanent colour between six months and a year. Darker-skinned babies usually have brown/black eyes when they are born.

Hair colour

Hair colour can skip a generation, which is why the old 'milkman' jokes get trotted out when two dark-haired parents suddenly spawn a platinum blonde baby. It's not unusual for children to have very fair hair for the first two or three years and then become very definite brunettes.

Skin colour

Skin colour can be very difficult to predict because you don't know how much melanin (the colour pigment) your child will inherit from each parent. At birth, though, even the babies of two very dark-skinned parents will usually be quite pale – in July 2010 a British couple of Nigerian descent had a white, blue-eyed daughter.

As you can see, it's difficult to predict what your little bundle of joy will look like, but it's quite fun wondering!

THE SECOND TRIMESTER

You should have had the incredible experience of 'meeting' your baby via a scan by now, and suddenly the whole pregnancy/having-a-baby concept should be a reality. One thing you can't really glean from the scan is what your baby is going to look like – it's been described as looking at a storm report!

Week 13

By this stage your baby should be between 6cm and 8cm in length. He will also have started to develop a fine covering of downy hair called lanugo. Doctors believe the purpose of this hair is to regulate temperature in the uterus; this hair disappears before birth or shortly afterwards. Babies that are born premature are often still covered in this fine, silky hair.

By this stage of pregnancy most women can stop taking folic acid supplements, as the time for formation of the baby's spinal cord and heart is over. It is worth checking with your GP or midwife, though, since some women need to continue a foliate supplement throughout the pregnancy – this might include you if you have anaemia, are a carrier of sickle cell or thalassaemia, or if you take certain medications (typically for epilepsy and some bowel disorders).

This a good time to get your GP or midwife to complete form FW8, which should be readily available in the surgery – this confirms that you are pregnant and gets you a Maternity Exemption Certificate (more like a credit card in appearance), which allows you to have free prescriptions and free dental treatment until 12 months after the baby's due date. This only applies to NHS dentists, though, so if you have a private dentist you may still have to pay. If you don't do it now you can get around to it at any point, including after the baby's birth. But as prescriptions cost £7.85 per item (and a trip to the dentist much more) and you never know when you might need something, it's worth getting on with it!

Week 14

By now you'll not only have had the first glimpse of your baby, you'll also get the opportunity to hear him too. From around 14 weeks your doctor or midwife can use a Doppler – a handheld monitoring machine – to locate and listen to your baby's heartbeat.

Although you can now buy Dopplers that you can use at home to listen to the baby's heartbeat, the current medical advice is not to be tempted to buy one. Spend your money on something more useful, as it is often

It is advisable that you do not wear an underwire bra during your pregnancy, as your breast tissue is very delicate and expanding fast.

If you need a prescription before your card arrives, don't panic. Many pharmacists will accept other evidence that you are pregnant, such as your maternity notes.

difficult to tell the difference between your heartbeat and the baby's – it's also quite difficult to find the heartbeat unless you are trained how to do so.

A normal fetal heart rate (FHR) can be anything between 110 and 160 beats per minute (BPM), but on average it's around 140. This is twice as fast as a normal adult's. The old wives' tale says that a faster heart beat is a girl and a slower heart rate is a boy, but who knows how true that is!

Week 15

At this stage your baby weighs around 50g (1.7oz), and his fingernails have started growing. Meconium (or 'baby poo') is made in the intestine, but not released yet.

Take a photo of your profile every week to capture your growing bump.

> **MUMMY MATTERS:** Are your boobs feeling even bigger? From week 15 you might start producing colostrum: the yellow fluid that is meant to nourish your baby during his first few days before the breast milk comes in.

Week 16

Your baby's limbs are now moving around quite freely, and he might be able to suck his thumb.

> **MUMMY MATTERS:** Your skin can become quite dry during pregnancy, and if you are worried about getting stretch marks it's probably a good time to start moisturising your bump and body. There's no concrete evidence to prove this will prevent you from getting these annoying permanent marks, but at least your skin will be lovely and soft!

Week 17

Your baby is now around 13cm long – roughly the same size as a pear. Weirdly, the baby and the placenta are around the same size at this point.

Good news is that at 17–20 weeks your hair may start looking thicker and shinier.

> **MUMMY MATTERS:** If you haven't treated yourself to a pair of maternity jeans yet, now might be the time! It's probably the one maternity 'must-have' every pregnant women needs as they are soooo comfy, and if (like most of us) your body doesn't magically ping back into shape after you have given birth, they will continue to be a tried and trusty friend.

Week 18

If you were able to shake your baby's hand, you would feel a strong grip. The facial features have now also developed, making him look more human: he can even pull faces! The hands have developed lines, creating individual fingerprints.

Week 19

Hair is now appearing on your baby's head, and the eyelashes and eyebrows are growing too. The milk (first) teeth buds have also formed.

A mother's voice is the most powerful sound as the baby can hear it both internally and externally – natural surround sound!

Week 20

Your baby is now around 18cm long and weighs around 280g (9.8oz). By now he can hear noises outside the uterus, and shortly will be able to recognise your voice and that of your partner.

You might feel your baby's movements now but most women don't until they are past 20 weeks. If the placenta is located at the front of your uterus (which you will find out at your anomaly scan) it may take longer to feel movements, and it may be difficult to feel them at all as the placenta acts as a sponge at the front between you and your baby. This is not a cause for concern at all, it just makes it harder to feel movements.

'The only way I can describe the movement of my baby is as though a wiggly worm is working its way round my tummy – it's not unpleasant, but very odd and bit ticklish!'

Sophie, first pregnancy

Your baby will now have adopted a sleeping cycle, with peak movements in the afternoon and evening. Once you have established these movements you'll be able to recognise when he is awake or asleep (hopefully at the same time as you!). He sleeps for only 20 to 40 minutes at a time.

Around this time you will probably have an anomaly scan, which checks the structures of your baby and the major organs, as well as the position of the placenta. It also confirms the dates of the pregnancy. See the box on page 54 for more on this scan.

THE ANOMALY SCAN

The anomaly scan is usually done between 18 and 23 weeks' gestation, and will check the structures of your baby and the major organs. It can identify many (but not all) of the potential health problems a growing baby may develop. However, it can't tell you how well anything will function, so a normal scan, whilst being reassuring, is not a guarantee of a completely healthy baby. Approximately 3% of babies in the UK have a structural problem identified either at the scan or soon after delivery. If the scan does show a possible problem, then this should be discussed with you. You may need further scans, either in your own hospital or at a referral centre, and you might be introduced to some of the team who will give care or treatment to your baby after delivery. Obviously this can be a really difficult time, so, if possible, make sure you take someone with you when you go for this scan, and ask as many questions as you need to.

If your baby has a serious problem, you may be told that it is unlikely he will survive the full term of your pregnancy/after the birth, or will be very seriously disabled. This may lead to a discussion about the possibility of terminating the pregnancy. If you are in this situation, it is really important not to rush your decision, and to make sure that you fully understand all the issues and are making the choice that seems right for you and your baby. If you do decide that ending the pregnancy at this stage is the best course, you will probably need a lot of support as well as advice about planning for and care during any future pregnancy. Most hospitals will offer you an appointment at some point in the six to eight weeks afterwards to discuss these and any other questions you have. There are also some really good support groups that you might find helpful (see the list of useful contacts at the end of the book).

Week 21

Your baby has now started to practise his breathing skills in preparation for birth, by inhaling and exhaling amniotic fluid – this ensures his lungs develop normally.

The taste buds are also developing; it may be an old wives' tale, but apparently your baby can develop a taste for things you eat in your pregnancy (maybe stay off the caviar then…).

At this stage you can collect your form Mat B1 from a doctor or midwife. This proves you are pregnant, and is needed by your employer when arranging maternity leave and benefits (see below).

MUMMY MATTERS: If you get the odd tummy twinge, don't worry: it's just the ligaments around the womb stretching to accommodate the increase in size. This feels a little like twitching muscles after you have exercised.

'I'm now 21 weeks and, at last, actually look pregnant rather than fat. I found the early stages a bit depressing in terms of body image, as I just looked like I had eaten a lot of cake!'

Becky, first pregnancy

Week 22

Your baby's immune system is now developing by forming white blood cells to protect against infection.

The head and body size have evened out, so the fetus is now a small but perfectly formed version of the baby you are going to meet in around 18 weeks' time.

The top of your uterus is now around level with your navel and, if you lie down with your head on a pillow and press gently, you may be able to feel it. You will also notice that, as your bump enlarges, your belly button will change shape – this is normal, and caused by the stretching of your skin.

Week 23

Your baby now measures around 18cm–20cm. He may now be covered with a waxy coating known as vernix, which coats the skin and is believed to protect it from the watery uterus environment (it is your baby's own wet suit!).

He may get hiccups, which you can feel!

> **MUMMY MATTERS:** Want to give birth to a mini Mozart? If you play music to your baby from this point, he should respond to it when he is born.

Week 24

This is a key week, as from 24 weeks it may be possible for a baby to survive if born early, although the chances are slim and unfortunately many of the survivors have significant disabilities. So if you get any symptoms that might be labour – like pain in your lower tummy, vaginal bleeding, or leaking of water from the vagina – you should get to your hospital as soon as possible. If you do start to go into labour around this stage of pregnancy, the team looking after you may suggest treatment

There are now lots of phone apps (many of them free) which specialise in soothing music for pregnant women.

to try to stop the labour or give you medication to prepare the baby's lungs for breathing. You should have the telephone numbers for your midwife, antenatal clinic and labour ward easily accessible – on the fridge door, stored in your mobile and written in your diary – as you never know when you might need some advice.

Week 25

You might think you have a karate black belt in the making, as your baby somersaults, kicks and generally makes his presence felt!

Food with strong flavours like vanilla, garlic, aniseed and mint can be transmitted through amniotic fluid. This taste memory makes babies more receptive to those flavours in their diet later on.

MUMMY MATTERS: If the area around your nipple – the areola – becomes bigger and darker, this is completely normal and is just your body preparing your breasts for breastfeeding.

Week 26

Your baby may now be able to open his eyelids for the first time, and his fingernails may develop. His lungs begin to produce surfactant, the substance that allows the air sacs in the lungs to inflate, and stops them collapsing and sticking together when they deflate.

MUMMY MATTERS: As your baby gets bigger, there will be more pressure on your lower back and legs, so ask a loved one to give you a gentle shoulder massage or foot rub. Alternatively, you can have a long soak in the bath to relieve any aches or pains.

Week 27

Your baby is now around 30cm long and his brain is developing quite rapidly, so make sure you are following the best diet you can. It is believed that babies start to dream around this time, although it's impossible to know about what!

Second trimester summary

What has happened so far:

- You will have had a second, more detailed, anomaly scan to check everything is progressing well.

- You can now know the sex of your baby if you want to.

Reasons to be cheerful:

- You should now have quite a pronounced bump, and hopefully strangers are giving up their seats for you on public transport.

- Shopping: it's a good time to start buying essentials for your baby, in case you do slow down a bit towards the end of the pregnancy.

- Your baby has a reasonable chance of survival if born after 28 weeks.

- If you want to, you can go on maternity leave in just a couple of weeks.

Looking to the future

By this stage there's no going back: you will have your very own baby in a matter of weeks, so don't be worried if your emotions range from, 'I'm so excited I think I'm going to explode' (although that might have more to do with the size of your tummy) to, 'Oh my word, what have I done?' You are bound to be anxious about the birth and how you are going to cope, and these feelings are both natural and understandable.

Worries and fears

Many expectant mothers worry about the world they are bringing their children into: because your hormones are all over the place, you may find yourself sobbing when you see pictures of starving children on the television, or developing an irrational fear of travelling on public transport in case some lunatic blows you up (unlikely). To keep these feelings in check, you need to tell yourself that people have been having babies in war zones and famines for centuries, and you will give your baby the best and most secure upbringing that you can.

Planning your baby's upbringing

Thinking about the way you will bring your child up might also be occupying your thoughts at this stage in the pregnancy; it's a good time to talk over issues with your partner, because you might find that once you have had the baby you haven't got the time or energy to discuss such matters. For example, different religious beliefs can cause conflict when it comes to raising a child, so it's good to iron out any potential conflicts before they become insurmountable problems within your relationship.

You and your partner might want to talk about your own childhoods and figure out the things that made you happiest, as undoubtedly you will want the same things for your child. There might also be things in your own upbringing – like never sitting down to dinner as a family – that you look back on with regret, and you might vow not to make the same mistakes as your parents (though once you become one you will quickly learn that *nobody* is perfect).

'It wasn't until I was three months pregnant that I suddenly thought about having a chat with my hubby about our child's upbringing. We'd spent so long focusing on getting pregnant and were then so wrapped up in the excitement that I forgot to really think beyond the pregnancy, until a friend made a jokey comment about my hubby as a dad!'

Claire, mum to James, 15 months

Considering how your relationship will change

The end of the second trimester is a brilliant time to really look at how a baby is going to change your life, and how you are going to have to adapt to accommodate this new person in your relationship.

Talk about the aspects of your life that you think will change. The more you have prepared yourself for the kinds of adjustments and sacrifices you may have to make, the less of a shock it will be. Plan to make time for each other as a couple and to be honest about your feelings.

'It has been hard for us to find time as a couple, but I think that's just part of the package of having a baby. You're no longer a couple; you've become a family. On the whole, though, I don't think our relationship has changed that much. I can't say we're happier than we were before because we've always been a very happy couple, and it would almost undermine what we had before. I guess having Eloise has enhanced our relationship.'

Julie, mum to Eloise, 6 months

If you're happy and you know it...

Did you know that scientists in Japan have discovered that babies respond to emotions in the uterus? Twenty-four pregnant women watched a happy clip from *The Sound of Music* (though they listened to the soundtrack through headphones so the baby couldn't be influenced by the sound), and during the extract the babies waved their arms around. Then the women watched an excerpt from a sad film, *The Champ*, and the babies became quiet and still. No one knows exactly why this happened, but the suggestion is that babies respond to hormones released by the mother that are triggered by emotional responses to things she sees or feels. So that's another good reason to stay happy and positive in pregnancy!

THE THIRD TRIMESTER

You've reached the last trimester, where you'll be preparing for your baby's arrival, and coping with your ever-growing bump.

Week 28

Your baby's eyes are now moving around in their sockets, and if you were to shine a bright light on your bump he would probably turn to look at it.

Your baby should weigh just over 1kg, so he now weighs the same as a bag of sugar (about 2lbs)!

You might start feeling Braxton Hicks contractions (an irregular tightening of the uterus lasting 30 to 60 seconds) at this stage. Normally they last no more than two minutes and don't become stronger or more frequent, like proper contractions. They are nothing to worry about unless they become more painful or occur often, or if there is any vaginal bleeding or leaking of fluid, in which case you might be at risk of pre-term labour and should seek medical advice. If you're at all concerned, contact your doctor or midwife.

Now is a good time to have the whooping cough vaccination, to make sure your baby is born with high enough levels of immunity that he doesn't catch it whilst he is very young. Ask your GP for the injection.

Week 29

Your baby's translucent skin is beginning to turn opaque. His bones are fully formed, although still very soft.

Many hospitals have Special Care Baby Units, which look after sick or premature babies born from this stage onwards. If there is a chance that your baby might be born early, it might be worth finding out from your hospital how early it can look after premature babies, and where the nearest unit is if your baby needs to be transferred. About 7% of all babies are born before 37 weeks, but only 1% before 28 weeks.

Week 30

By now your baby is about 33cm long and gaining weight, making him look smoother and less wrinkly. The hair on his head should be growing.

> **MUMMY MATTERS:** If you are at risk of varicose veins (if your mum got them in pregnancy it's likely you will too), it might be worth investing in a pair of support tights – particularly if you are on your feet all day. You may feel like Norah Batty but it might keep the varicosities and mild ankle swelling in check.

Week 31

Your baby's lungs are fully formed and are capable of breathing air, but need more time to mature. If he is a boy, his testicles are moving through the groin toward the scrotum.

Now's a good time to start making a 'birth plan', if you haven't already done so. This can include anything that is important to you during the labour and delivery. There is probably a section in your hospital notes giving you an idea of the types of questions you should be asking yourself: 'Who do I want to be with me?', 'What type of pain relief might I want?', 'What positions do I think might be comfortable for me during labour?', 'Am I happy to have a student midwife or doctor involved during my delivery?' Make some notes about what you think might be good for you and discuss them with your midwife – she will talk through with you what will work and what might not.

We look at birth plans in more detail on page 224.

Week 32

Your baby begins to lose the lanugo hair.

Around now, you may be having trouble sleeping. Having a big tummy can make it quite difficult to get comfortable at night, so try propping a couple of pillows under your bump or between your knees as you lie on your side. You could also treat yourself to one of those V shaped pillows: they're great for breastfeeding and can help support babies when they first sit up, so we think they're worth every penny! It's better not to sleep on your back – the weight of your bump can squash the main blood vessel (the vena cava) taking blood back to your heart, and this in turn can reduce the supply of oxygen to you or even your baby. If you do wake up and find you are on your back, don't panic, but do ease a pillow or bit of duvet under your hips and back so that you roll slightly to your left. Also, always try to make sure you get out of bed slowly and carefully – you may feel that your days of jumping out of bed in a lively fashion are over for a while, but even if they are not, you should aim to get up in stages, so that you don't get too dizzy.

 A large UK study in 2011 found the peak time for experiencing depression during pregnancy is 32 weeks. It can affect about 15 out of every 100 women, so see your doctor if you feel you are struggling.

Week 33

Your baby may turn around and face downwards in preparation for birth.

Feeling your baby move

Don't be worried if you feel less vigorous movement from your baby, as space is getting a bit tight in there. However, the frequency of movements should be much the same. If you are not sure whether your baby's movements have reduced, the latest advice from RCOG is to lie on your left side for two hours and focus on the movements. If you don't feel 10 discrete movements, you should contact the maternity unit immediately. Usually there is no particular reason why the movements are less frequent, but you should always check it out, since occasionally it is your baby's way of indicating that he is not as well as he should be. Usually it's because he has rolled into a position where the limbs are facing towards you rather than away from you, or perhaps you have had a busy or stressful day and not noticed them as much as usual. Most maternity departments will have a Day Assessment Unit, which does as the name suggests – usually a friendly and relaxed place, where you can see a midwife (and if required, a doctor) without a formal appointment for a 'non-emergency' query – so it's not the place to go if you think you are in labour or you are bleeding. But if you need an extra blood pressure check, some advice about your backache, or the baby's movements are not as frequent as usual, it's ideal. You should add the telephone number to the list of useful numbers on the fridge and in your mobile.

> **MUMMY MATTERS:** During pregnancy, it takes a while longer for the blood to overcome gravity and get up to your brain when you stand up. This can include when you have been sitting down on the bus, in the cinema, at a meeting, or when you're getting out of bed, so take it easy. If it becomes a recurring issue, support stockings help to compress the legs and prevent too much blood pooling in them, leaving more for your brain!

UK scientists have recently embarked on a study to map how babies' brains develop in the womb and after birth.

Week 34

The development of the brain and nervous system is now much more advanced, and most babies born at this stage will survive and be healthy. The baby's head has two soft areas called fontanelles, which allow the skull bones to overlap each other as the baby's head changes shape during its journey through the birth canal. These fontanelles close by the time your baby is two years old. In labour, they are used by the midwife or doctor examining you to work out which way the baby's head is facing.

It is at this stage that baby boys' testicles become visible as they descend into the scrotum.

> **MUMMY MATTERS:** Started tidying obsessively? This nesting instinct is incredibly strong, and we've yet to meet a pregnant woman who didn't admit to having the urge to put her whole house in order.

Week 35

Your baby is becoming a little 'chubster' by building up fat deposits under the skin, which help him keep warm after he is born. He can gain up to half a pound a week at this stage.

His hearing is fully developed by now, so you might like to sing nursery rhymes to your bump.

Week 36

Your baby will now be about 48cm (19in) long and weigh nearly 2.8kg (6lbs).

Your baby might 'engage' this week. This is when the head drops down into the pelvis in readiness for birth. It happens earlier in first babies than subsequent ones, and later in women of African descent than women of other races, due to the typical shape of their pelvis.

If your placenta was lying low at the anomaly scan, you will probably be offered another scan around this stage to see if it has changed position. In fact, the placenta itself does not actually move. In the second half of the pregnancy, the lower section of the uterus begins to grow: this means that if the placenta is attached to the upper part of the uterus (which it frequently is), it can be carried higher and away from the cervix. If it is still low, then your doctor will talk though your options with you. If the placenta is blocking the way out for the baby, then you usually need to deliver by Caesarean section. But, occasionally, even at this late stage there may be enough growth in the uterus to allow the head into the pelvis – the guideline is usually that the placenta should be at least 25mm (1in) away from the cervix, so if your placenta is almost that far away you may be lucky!

Week 37

Your baby is likely to be born any time from 37 weeks onwards. You should have packed your bag (see page 307 for further information on what to pack) so that you are ready for when you go into labour.

Don't worry too much about religiously watching the calendar for your due date. Some say it would be better not to give a 'due date', but rather a 'due period' – it raises too many expectations, and, as you are probably about to find out, is only occasionally the day on which the baby actually arrives!

> 'I tried to tell as few people as possible the due date of my first baby as I really didn't want too many people "fretting" when he was "late" – in the end he came two weeks "early", so I need not have worried!'
>
> Charlotte, second pregnancy and mum to Oliver, 20 months

Your baby will probably have lost all the lanugo and vernix by now.

 Expect your baby to arrive between 37 and 42 weeks: that is, three weeks before and two weeks after the so-called due date.

Cover your mattress with a towel or protector just in case your waters break during the night.

Your midwife, GP or obstetrician will be keeping a close eye on the position of your baby, as he should be head down from 37 weeks and ready for when labour starts – which could be any day now. But 5% of babies are not head down by this stage, so be prepared for some poking! If the baby is lying bottom or feet first (breech) there are various methods doctors and midwives can use to try to make him turn (see page 300). If the baby can't be turned, or decides to flip back, then the team looking after you should discuss the pros and cons of a breech vaginal birth or a Caesarean section with you, and help you make the safest choice for you and the baby. Many babies are breech until the day before labour starts and decide to turn at the last minute, so don't fret too much if your baby isn't where he should be at the moment.

If your baby is lying sideways after 37 weeks, your doctor will want to find out why (for example, something else in your pelvis may be taking the space meant for the baby's head – such as the placenta), and may suggest you stay in hospital. One of the important things about your baby's head or bottom being in the pelvis at the time that labour starts is that, if the waters break, it can act as a 'plug' and stop the umbilical cord washing down into the vagina and out of your body before the baby does.

One of the benefits of your baby moving down into your pelvis is that you might be able to breathe more easily, as there is more lung capacity now he has moved down a little! Also, your heartburn might not be quite so bad. On the other hand, there will be even more pressure on your bladder and pelvis, so getting a good night's sleep won't be any easier as you will need to go to the toilet more often. Some say that is all good preparation for the sleepless nights of new parenthood!

Week 38

Your baby should weigh around 3kg (7lbs) now.

Make sure your hospital bag is packed and you're ready to go, in case your little bundle of joy decides to make an appearance!

Week 39

If you need a planned Caesarean section, this is the most common time for one to be booked – it is a balance of minimising the chance of you going into labour and maximising the baby's chance of staying out of the Special Care Baby Unit.

Week 40

Hopefully, the waiting is nearly over and you'll give birth pretty soon, although less than 5% of babies arrive on their due date and only 30% in the week around your due date, so don't fret if he doesn't make an appearance just yet.

> **MUMMY MATTERS:** Many pregnancies go on to 42 weeks and beyond. If your baby is late, put your feet up, relax and make the most of those extra days of peace and quiet: you're going to need them!

Week 41

At this stage your midwife might suggest doing 'a sweep'. This isn't part of the nesting activity we discussed earlier; it's a way of encouraging labour to start naturally. It involves having an internal examination, which allows the midwife to stretch the cervix (the neck of the uterus) and sweep the membranes of the amniotic sac away from the cervix, thereby releasing the natural chemicals called prostaglandins which are involved in the initiation of labour. It can be a bit eye-watering, but it will be worth it if labour starts spontaneously.

If the sweep doesn't do the trick, then towards the end of week 41 you will usually be offered induction of labour. There is evidence to suggest that women who labour after 42 weeks are less likely to have a vaginal delivery than those who labour earlier. There is also evidence that the placenta is less likely to function normally after 42 weeks, and this slightly increases the (small) chance of stillbirth. Most units will have an information sheet about induction for you to read, and will be happy to talk it through in as much detail as you need to. Some women are so exhausted by the pregnancy at this stage that they welcome the opportunity to finally get things going, while others are reticent to disturb a natural process.

If you are told you may need to be induced, make sure you get all the information you need and feel comfortable with what the procedure will involve. See page 321 for more on induction.

Third trimester summary

You've done it! You've got through the past 40 weeks and, if you haven't delivered by now, you will do so imminently; it might have been a struggle at times but boy, it will have been worth it... we promise.

Now that you know how your pregnancy progresses, it's time to look at the various ailments which you might encounter during that time. This information is provided to prepare you for all eventualities, not to worry you. A lot of women have very few ailments – so you might be one of the lucky ones!

3

My aches and pains during pregnancy

You'll find your support during pregnancy will be really important, because unfortunately having a baby can have alarming, embarrassing and downright amusing side effects. This chapter isn't a substitute for the expert advice of trained health professionals, but by taking you through the most common problems it'll hopefully inform you so you can judge whether you need to seek further help from your doctor or midwife. There are some intimate issues that can arise which make you squirm just thinking about, let alone talking about, but one thing's certain: your doctor and midwife will have seen and heard it *all* before, so do talk through any health issues – however cringeworthy – with them.

THE UNCOMFORTABLE TRUTH

The good news is that most of the pain you experience in pregnancy is completely normal and harmless; indeed, it would be quite surprising if you didn't experience pangs or twinges, given the weight and complexity of the cargo you are carrying. Below, we take a look at the different areas of your body that may be affected and suggest ways to make you feel more comfortable.

We know that certain factors, such as age and general health, will affect how your body reacts to pregnancy, but a great deal is down to genetics, hormones and good (or bad) luck!

It's worth bearing in mind while you're reading through all the various afflictions that can strike during pregnancy that, for every 'bad' element of pregnancy, there's a 'good' one too – glossy hair, fabulous bosoms, beautiful belly – so we also have a section celebrating the fantastic 'side effects' of being pregnant: looking at how your body changes shape and the other bonus features of having a bun in the oven!

SOS

At the end of this chapter is a list of symptoms that might need urgent advice or attention. If you are very worried and you can't get through to a midwife – your hospital emergency number should be on your notes – call NHS 111 or NHS Direct, get to A&E if someone can take you, or dial 999 for an ambulance.

Abdominal pain

It is not unusual to experience some abdominal pain in pregnancy and, although it might worry you, generally there is no cause for alarm. Wind and constipation are common and so is a loosening of the pelvic bone where it joins at the front. Some women find that they experience a period-like pain at the beginning of pregnancy as the embryo implants in the uterus. This is often a constant dull ache and feels a little like a muscle strain.

From the second trimester onwards, you might feel a sharp twinge in your side or groin area as the muscles and ligaments around your uterus stretch and contract.

In the third trimester it can be normal to experience Braxton Hicks or 'practice' contractions as your body prepares itself for labour. Remember that you are probably much more in tune with your body now than you were before you were pregnant, and so what you are feeling may be normal, but you just didn't notice or respond to it before!

Comfort zone
If you are experiencing pains in your tummy, the best advice is to sit and rest until they subside.

Doctor's orders
If you have a severe or persistent abdominal pain you should get yourself checked out immediately, especially if you experience vaginal bleeding. If it happens in the first 12 weeks, it could be the sign of miscarriage or an ectopic pregnancy (where the pregnancy is growing in the Fallopian tube, not the uterus – although if you have already had a scan this should have been ruled out); up to 20 weeks, it could be a late miscarriage; and from then on, it could indicate you are going into early labour. It's also possible that the pain might be due to another cause unrelated to pregnancy – like appendicitis – that needs urgent medical attention. The most common cause unrelated to pregnancy is a urine infection. You should contact your GP, midwife or labour ward straight away if you experience persistent pain, especially if it is associated with bleeding.

Back pain

Back pain will affect as many as 75% of pregnant women at some point during their pregnancy. It tends to get worse in the third trimester, as the body releases a hormone called relaxin to make the joints and ligaments in the pelvic region more flexible in preparation for birth. The downside of this hormone is that it makes the body more susceptible to pain and injury, and as you are carrying a lot of extra weight at the front your posture is affected, meaning your back curves more (to stop you toppling forward!) and tends to take the strain. Protecting your back is another reason not to gain too much weight while you are pregnant and a really important reason to lose it again after delivery.

The good news is that, for most women, back problems do ease after birth, although labour itself can sometimes be a strain on your back – make sure your midwife helps you to look after it in labour. Relaxin can stay in your system for some time, so you should protect your back by learning the best way to pick up your newborn. Always bend at your knees and hips, keeping your back straight, and don't twist.

 A firm mattress can help ease or prevent back pain – if yours isn't firm enough, try putting a piece of hardboard underneath for that extra support.

Local leisure centres often run specialised classes for pregnant women. Anything in the pool is great if you suffer from back pain as the water will help support your weight.

Comfort zone

- Gentle exercise like swimming, yoga and Pilates can strengthen muscles and prevent or ease backache.

- If you sit at a desk all day, make sure that your computer and chair are at the correct height (it may need to change as your bump expands).

- Pay attention to your posture and try not to stand for long periods. You should also ditch your heels and switch to flats.

- Avoid lifting anything heavy, and if you do need to pick up anything weighty make sure you bend your knees.

- Try a maternity band or belt – a stretchy fabric band that sits underneath the bump and supports it. Not the most glamorous of accessories, but it does the job very effectively.

'Luckily I haven't had any major health problems during my pregnancy, but I have had a really bad back – which worries me, as I still have two and a half months to go! I've also had a lot of pain when the ligaments and scar tissue from a previous surgery have been stretched in the lower abdomen, but that only happens when I or my baby is going through a growth spurt, so it's fine most of the time.'

Virginia, first pregnancy

Doctor's orders

- Paracetamol can be used safely in pregnancy if your back pain warrants it, but avoid ibuprofen, Nurofen and other painkillers from the same group (which are called nonsteroidal anti-inflammatory drugs), unless you have discussed it directly with your doctor.

- Physiotherapy can be helpful: ask your doctor whether a referral might help you.

- If you get any signs of sciatica (that is, compression of one of the nerves to the legs as it leaves the spinal column), such as shooting pains in the legs or buttocks (most commonly on one side only and not on both), weakness, or numbness in part of the leg, you should discuss this with your doctor.

Pelvic/pubic pain

One in five women will suffer from PGP during pregnancy.

When you give birth your pelvis, which is normally stable, widens slightly to make more room for the baby. Sometimes a combination of the weight of the baby and the loosening of the pelvic ligaments means that this widening, or separation, of the pelvic bones occurs prior to delivery, and sometimes this is painful – referred to as symphysis pubis dysfunction (SPD) or pelvic girdle pain (PGP). Usually the pain is in the lowest part of your tummy, in the midline: if you gently press with two fingers in that area, through the triangle of pubic hair, you should feel the bone. This is where the two sides of the pelvis join together (called the pubic symphysis), and it is unusual movement in the joint that causes pain. If you press too hard, it may feel tender. When your midwife or doctor examines you, they may measure the size of your bump, and the discomfort that you feel when they press at the bottom of your tummy is due to softening in the pubic symphysis. This can occur any time in the second half of your pregnancy, and the pain may vary from mild to very troublesome. It is likely to be particularly uncomfortable when you open your legs wide apart, such as when getting out of bed or out of the car; you may also find sex a bit tricky! It can involve your buttocks, thighs or hips, and some women report that they feel a clicking sensation when they walk.

When it is severe it can make everyday activities, such as walking, driving and climbing stairs, really torturous. This does not always affect how you give birth, but you should talk to your midwife about it if you are concerned. The good news is that the pelvic bones normally go back into their proper position after birth and the pain begins to improve.

'Halfway through my pregnancy I felt like I had a footballer's injury: my groin was killing me. The doctor asked me when it hurt most and I said when I was standing or when I crossed my legs. He looked deadpan at me and said, "Bit late for that, my dear, isn't it!" My husband and I nearly died laughing!'

Jane, first pregnancy

Comfort zone

Keep your knees together ALL the time and keep gently mobile if you can, even if it is at a slow and cautious pace. You may have to stop work earlier than you had planned. A pelvic support belt can also help to relieve the pressure on the pelvis.

'I had a friend with this condition during both her pregnancies, and she never went anywhere without her trusty V pillow. She used it to support a painful back when driving and sitting, and slept with it between her knees.'

Charlotte, second pregnancy and mum to Oliver, 20 months

Doctor's orders

Obstetric physiotherapists will teach you exercises you can do to ease the symptoms of SPD, and, even more importantly, positions to adopt and avoid. They may give you a 'girdle', rather like a massive tubigrip over your pelvis, which can help stabilise the joint. Sometimes safe painkillers such as paracetamol are helpful. If things get really bad, your doctor will offer advice on how to manage the discomfort. A few poor women need crutches.

Sometimes, SPD can drive women to beg for induction of labour. If it gets that bad for you, do talk with your doctor or midwife. However, usually it is not necessary to do this, and certainly the extra vaginal examinations that are required for induction as compared with spontaneous labour can be very difficult for you.

If you have SPD, your midwife will be used to looking after your pelvis and supporting your hips appropriately in labour. You may need to review your thoughts about pain relief, since the combination of SPD pain and labour can sometimes be quite wearing. Epidurals and SPD can go very well together!

Cramp

It is common to experience leg cramps during pregnancy. They can be intensely painful, and occur when a muscle or group of muscles go into spasm – you will find that the offending muscles have gone rock hard, and might pull your leg or foot into an odd shape.

There isn't a clear medical explanation for their occurrence, although theories include muscle fatigue, dehydration, mineral deficiency, and pressure on the nerves caused by the growing uterus.

Comfort zone

- If you do get an attack of cramp, stretch out your leg or foot to counteract the way the muscle is pulling. For example, if you have cramp in the bottom of your foot (a really common site) you will probably need to pull your foot up towards your body, – as your bump gets bigger, this is not as easy as it sounds, so you may need to engage the help of a supportive partner or best friend.

- Sometimes you can 'walk' off cramps, like you might with pins and needles.

- Avoid sitting with your legs crossed.

- Give your muscles a firm rub if they go into spasm, or ask someone to do it for you.

Doctor's orders
If the cramps are really bothering you, it might be worth chatting to your doctor or midwife, because you might be missing some minerals in your diet – but don't take a supplement without their advice.

If you have persistent pain, or other symptoms such as leg swelling or reddening of the painful leg, contact your GP as it could be a sign of something more serious like deep vein thrombosis (pages 81–82).

Hand pain

Carpal tunnel syndrome is caused by a buildup of fluid in the wrist which means the nerves passing through to the hand are compressed. It can affect as many as one in three pregnant women. Symptoms include numbness, pins and needles, stiffness and varying degrees of pain in your hands and fingers, which is often worse in the mornings. When you have been lying down overnight your ankles will usually become less swollen. This is because the fluid that collected in them under the influence of gravity by day has redistributed by night, and some is now in your wrists (although usually you cannot see the swelling in the wrists, unlike the situation in your ankles!).

In general it begins to get better after delivery, but may take quite a few weeks – if there is no improvement by the time your baby is ready for his six-week check-up, ask your doctor about it at the same time.

Comfort zone
If you are suffering you can try these ideas:

- Curl your fingers into a fist and then straighten them out several times; bend your hand to and fro at the wrist repeatedly to try to ease away the fluid.

- Bend your hands at the wrist so that the backs of your fingers extend up towards your forearm.

- Stretch out and relax your fingers several times.

- Raise your hands whenever you can and try to sleep with them on the pillow.

- Don't handle the family heirlooms – you may have turned into a butterfingers!

Doctor's orders

Your doctor may refer you to physiotherapy. They may give you a support brace to wear on your wrist at night, holding it in the extended position described above – it is quite hard to sleep with these on, though, so you may choose just to put up with it!

Headaches

There are a myriad of reasons why you might suffer from headaches in pregnancy: hormones and changes in blood supply are considered to be the most likely culprits, but other factors such as dehydration, nausea, insomnia, nasal congestion and stress may also play a part.

Comfort zone

- If you have a headache or feel one coming on, try taking a rest in a darkened room.

- You are probably aware you should avoid painkillers such as ibuprofen whilst you are pregnant, but it is safe to take paracetamol. There are also non-medication treatments such as 4 Head that may be worth trying.

- If you are prone to headaches, take preventative measures by keeping yourself hydrated, following a good diet and getting as much rest and sleep as you can.

- It's a good idea to cut your caffeine consumption when you are pregnant, particularly if you get headaches regularly. (It is recommended that you drink no more than two cups of caffeinated drinks a day when pregnant, or try some decaf tea or coffee.)

Doctor's orders

Headaches are not normally serious, but if you experience severe or frequent head pains/migraines or if they are accompanied by blurred vision, vomiting or swelling, you should see your midwife or GP straight away as it could be a sign of pre-eclampsia (page 81).

Rib pain

It is quite normal to experience some rib pain, especially in the third trimester. You may feel it at the sides or where the ribs join the breast bone at the front. The ribs move upwards in pregnancy: partly pushed by the expanding uterus, and partly because of the deeper breaths that you automatically make in order to take in extra oxygen for the baby. You might also feel some discomfort when your baby gives you a swift left hook in the rib cage as space gets really tight.

Comfort zone

Try to maintain good posture and support yourself with cushions when sitting for long periods of time.

Doctor's orders

The good news is that once your baby's head engages, pressure on the rib area subsides.

Treat yourself

Why not treat yourself to a massage? Find a qualified therapist who has specific pregnancy experience, or talk a loved one into doing it for you. If they need some hints or tips see below:

- Find a comfortable position. If you have a sizeable bump you're probably best lying on your side supported by cushions either on the bed or on a bean bag or, if you can, straddling a chair so you are facing the back of it.

- Apply gentle but firm circular strokes with the heel of the hand over the muscles of your lower back.

- Your shoulders and neck should be rubbed gently too, as tension in these areas can cause or worsen back pain lower down.

- Use aromatherapy oils with caution: many are unsuitable in pregnancy, so if in doubt, stick to baby oil.

THE 'BLOODY' PROBLEMS

Some pregnancy symptoms are caused by changes in the blood as it works overtime to support both you and your growing baby. Here are some of the most common problems you might encounter and some tips on how to relieve your discomfort.

Anaemia

Anaemia is a lack of haemoglobin in the red blood cells in the body. Haemoglobin carries oxygen around the body, and in the placenta it passes oxygen across to the fetus. Pregnant women increase their production of both haemoglobin and red blood cells during pregnancy, in order to carry the extra oxygen needed by the developing fetus and to provide the mother with the oxygen needed for the growth and development of her body. To produce these new red blood cells, the body needs extra iron, vitamin B12 and folic acid, and if there is a deficiency of any of these ingredients anaemia can develop. Pregnant women also pass iron to the placental tissue and to the fetus, which can lead to anaemia.

Don't worry – it is very common for pregnant women to suffer from an iron deficiency. Many will require supplements from around the 20th week.

Often anaemia has no symptoms: this is one reason why you will be asked for a blood sample both at your booking appointment and around week 28 of pregnancy. The signs of anaemia include tiredness and paleness; you might also experience exhaustion, dizziness and palpitations, although these are common in pregnancy anyway.

It is really important to prevent and/or treat anaemia in pregnancy. There is some evidence that babies of mothers who lacked iron during pregnancy have less well-developed brains. Blood loss at delivery is also relatively common, and if you are anaemic before you go into labour, you are much more likely to need a blood transfusion after delivery.

Comfort zone

To help you avoid or alleviate anaemia, try to:

- eat foods that are particularly rich in iron (such as wholemeal bread, cereals, spinach, eggs, dried fruits and lean meat).

- eat a diet rich in vitamin C (oranges, lemons and raw veg) as it helps your body absorb iron. Try to avoid tea and chapattis with your iron-rich foods, since they prevent absorption of the iron from your gut.

- eat beans, broccoli, asparagus, peas and brussels sprouts, as these are all are a good source of folic acid.

- eat meat, dairy products and yeast extract (such as marmite), as these are good sources of vitamin B12.

Doctor's orders

If you think you might be anaemic, your doctor or midwife will confirm the diagnosis with a blood test and may prescribe iron tablets. Unfortunately they can cause constipation or diarrhoea, so you might need to try a couple of brands until you find one that works for you. You can also buy natural forms of iron supplements such as Spatone and Floridix. It is commonly said that they don't cause these side effects, but that is only because they don't contain as much iron! You need to take very large volumes to get enough iron. If you are taking iron supplements you should take them with fresh orange juice, as vitamin C helps the body to absorb the iron. You also shouldn't have caffeine or milk within an hour of taking them as calcium and caffeine stop the absorption of iron. If your anaemia is severe, your doctor may suggest that iron is given directly into your blood, as an infusion.

WORDS FROM THE PROFESSIONALS: Severe anaemia can increase the likelihood of you needing a blood transfusion if you suffer heavy bleeding after birth, so expect your doctor or midwife to keep an eye on your iron levels if you do become anaemic. Severe anaemia can also cause developmental problems for your baby. If you have a fundamental religious belief against blood transfusion (eg Jehovah's Witness) discuss this with your doctor as early as possible in pregnancy.

Fainting

The pressure of the uterus on blood vessels which take blood from the legs back to the heart and lungs means that standing up quickly after sitting or lying can make you dizzy. The blood is still in your legs and takes a while to overcome gravity and get up to your brain, which is why lying down again, on your side, can help. It is also a good idea, when you can, to rest on your side or in a partially supported position, rather than lying flat on your back, because then the weight of your baby is not compressing your blood vessels as much.

When you are hot, dehydrated or standing still for too long, you can also get dizzy – the blood vessels in the legs accommodate too much blood and there is not enough left to be pumped up to your brain. Again, lying down can help, as can flight stockings. Try to walk on the spot if you have to stand in a queue or on a bus, as the muscles in your calves help to keep the blood flowing around properly.

Although fainting can be quite frightening if it happens when you are out and about, it's not unusual to have a wobbly moment or even a full-on swoon during pregnancy.

Comfort zone
To avoid feeling dizzy or faint:

- make sure you stay well hydrated.

- dress yourself in layers that you can peel off when you find yourself getting too warm.

- in the later stages of pregnancy, ask to leave work earlier so you're not battling public transport when you are tired and hungry.

- if you get that hot flush at the back of your neck and feel yourself about to 'go,' sit or lie down immediately. If you are at home, you should lie with your legs raised or sit with your head between your knees (only suitable in early pregnancy as your bump will get in the way later).

Doctor's orders
If you are fainting or feeling dizzy regularly it could be a sign of anaemia, so mention it to your midwife or doctor. Sometimes wearing flight stockings to compress the lower legs is helpful as it stops blood collecting there.

Hot flushes

The increased blood flow around the body and greater metabolic activity of pregnancy produce a lot of extra heat that needs to be dispersed. This can be quite comforting in the chilly winter months; suddenly you've got warm toes in bed. But it can be downright miserable if you are heavily pregnant in the middle of a summer heat wave. Some pregnant women feel warm all over, whereas others suffer classic hot flushes where the face in particular becomes a rather fetching shade of puce.

Another rather unwelcome side effect of overheating is that you may find yourself becoming a 'sweaty Betty'. Perspiration is the body's way of getting rid of excess heat, so you might want to slap on the deodorant more vigorously than usual.

Comfort zone
To help you keep cool try to:

- wear natural fibres as they keep the body cool.

- wear loose clothing.

- layer up so you can add or remove clothing easily.

- keep windows open so you can have some fresh air – much healthier than air con – and if you are cooped up in an office all day make sure you pop out at lunchtime (though sit in the shade if it's summertime).

- drink lots of fluid – ideally water – as your thirst levels rise with your body temperature.

Doctor's orders
It is known that a severe rise in body temperature can be harmful to your baby, which is why you are advised to get your temperature down quickly if you have a fever. You are advised not to take saunas when pregnant, but this is as much because of the dizziness that can come on in hot places as because of the heat itself. However, there doesn't seem to be anything to suggest that 'normal' pregnancy warmness or heat waves have a detrimental effect on your baby. If you're at all worried, though, speak to your midwife or doctor.

Itching

Mild itching can be normal. It is caused by increased blood flow to and the stretching and dryness of your skin, especially over your belly. In late pregnancy your tummy can become itchy because the skin is so stretched over your bump, and sometimes hormones can make your stretch marks more sensitive and more prone to rashes and itchy patches.

Comfort zone

- If your skin is itchy, wear loose soft clothing such as a cotton jersey, and use pure cotton bedding.

- If you do have patches of inflamed skin, use something gentle and soothing, such as calamine lotion.

- If you have dry skin, use a water barrier cream such as Diprobase before you bathe or swim to protect your skin from the damaging effects of water.

Doctor's orders

Persistent or severe itching, particularly on the palms of the hands and soles of the feet, can indicate a potentially serious liver condition called obstetric cholestasis, where the liver temporarily works less well. Other symptoms include mild jaundice, dark urine, pale stools, appetite loss and tiredness. If you experience itching, particularly in the third trimester, contact your doctor or midwife. You will usually need a liver blood test to try to determine if you have obstetric cholestasis or just itchy dry skin. As obstetric cholestasis is associated with a small increase in the rate of stillbirth, your baby will need to be carefully monitored and you may be offered an earlier induction (see rcog.org.uk for a useful patient information leaflet on obstetric cholestasis).

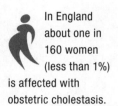
In England about one in 160 women (less than 1%) is affected with obstetric cholestasis.

Nasal congestion and nose bleeds

The increased blood supply driven by those raging hormones puts pressure on the blood vessels inside your nose and causes the sinuses to produce more mucus. This makes your nose more prone to bleeding, congestion and (unfortunately) snoring too.

Comfort zone

- If you get a nosebleed, sit upright and pinch the top of your nose gently but firmly for up to 10 minutes. This should stem the bleeding; if not, repeat the process.

- Blow your nose gently to avoid nosebleeds.

- Steam inhalation can help with congestion. Carefully fill a bowl with boiling water, point your face down towards the water, place a towel over your head and the rim of the bowl so you effectively seal in all the steam, and take a few deep breaths. Be warned, though, this technique can make an already flushed face even hotter!

Doctor's orders

If you are so blocked up that you are finding it hard to breathe or sleep, you may need a safe, prescription decongestant.

Nosebleeds are harmless, but if they are frequent or very heavy you might be at risk of developing anaemia, so do mention them to your doctor if you are suffering badly.

PRE-ECLAMPSIA AND THROMBOSIS

There are two important disorders that can be extremely serious, even fatal, in pregnancy: pre-eclampsia and thrombosis. Read up about them so you know what signs to look out for, but don't scare yourself stupid, because your doctor and midwife will be on the lookout for them at every routine appointment.

Pre-eclampsia affects up to one in 10 pregnant women and almost always develops after 20 weeks. It usually involves high blood pressure, protein in your urine, and sometimes a smaller than expected baby. Often it is mild, but sometimes it can be very serious and make you or the baby unwell, necessitating early delivery. It is often detected during an antenatal appointment – this is why you always have your blood pressure measured and urine tested.

Most women have no symptoms. Sometimes intense headaches, rapid and aggressive swelling of the hands, feet and/or face, blurred vision, upper stomach ache and new vomiting occur. If you develop any of these you should usually phone the hospital for their advice.

If pre-eclampsia is diagnosed you will usually be admitted to hospital. This is so that you and the baby can be monitored more carefully, and so that, if either of you gets suddenly unwell, you are in a place where the right care can be given by your doctor or midwife. Whilst the chance of this happening is small, and being stuck in hospital can be boring, it is really worthwhile listening to the advice you are being given. You may be prescribed medication to lower your blood pressure and you may need extra scans or blood tests. You may also be told you need to be delivered earlier than nature was planning.

Many women are offered low-dose aspirin tablets to take every day from 12 weeks of pregnancy to reduce their chances of getting pre-eclampsia. You should mention this to your midwife if you are at increased risk of getting it.

Less than two women in 100 will develop a severe form of pre-eclampsia, which might include convulsions, stroke, kidney failure, liver damage and blood clotting problems in the mother; and intra-uterine growth restriction, placental haemorrhage and possible oxygen starvation in the baby, so its risks should not be underestimated.

Thrombosis is the clotting of blood within a blood vessel. This occurs when a blood clot blocks a vein or an artery and obstructs or stops the flow of blood.

Less than two women in 1,000 develop a blood clot in the vein during pregnancy or just after birth; the risk is around five times higher than normal because blood clots and flows differently during pregnancy. Some women are more at risk because their parents or siblings have had a clot, or because they are overweight, older (which sadly is defined in this context as over 30!), less mobile, smokers or have certain medical problems – especially involving the kidneys. If you have any of these risk factors you may need to take some form of prevention against thrombosis during the pregnancy. Your midwife will ask you questions about clotting when you attend your booking appointment, and your risk of getting a clot will be reviewed if you are admitted to hospital and when you have the baby. If you have had a thrombosis before you are very likely to need extra advice during the pregnancy, so make sure your midwife and GP are aware.

Deep vein thrombosis (DVT) is the most common type of thrombosis in pregnancy and is a blood clot that occurs in a deep vein, usually in the leg.

Symptoms include pain, tenderness and swelling in the leg, and it may turn pale blue or reddish-purple in colour.

If you develop a DVT you will be given heparin to thin the blood, and you'll probably be advised to wear compression stockings to reduce the swelling and improve blood flow. You will probably need treatment for three months or even longer.

If you suspect you have a DVT you should seek immediate medical advice. It has a very dangerous complication called pulmonary embolism, when the blood clot or a piece of a blood clot breaks off and travels to the lungs where it can block one of the blood vessels. **Potentially life-threatening, pulmonary embolism may cause chest pain, shortness of breath, or the coughing up of blood – if you get any of these symptoms you should get immediate medical advice, as prompt diagnosis and treatment are essential.**

Bleeding in pregnancy

In the first three months:

- implantation bleeding. Also called 'spotting', happens a couple of days after conception as the embryo implants itself in the uterus.

- breakthrough bleeding. Light bleeding or spotting when your period would have been due (and occasionally subsequent periods).

- bleeding can also, sadly, signal that the pregnancy is no longer viable; this might be because the pregnancy was ectopic, molar or the embryo did not develop properly. For more details on miscarriage see page 35.

Very rarely bleeding is due to vasa praevia, where one of the baby's blood vessels runs across the cervix.

After the first three months bleeding is much less common, and tends to have a different list of possible causes. Important causes of bleeding in the second half of pregnancy include:

- placenta praevia. When the placenta is positioned low down in the uterus over the cervix, it more likely to detach and cause severe bleeding, which is typically painless.

- placental abruption. A rare complication where the placenta detaches itself from the implantation site. Can be life threatening to mother or baby and often necessitates delivery by an emergency Caesarean. Typically very painful.

- a bloody 'show' could indicate that labour is imminent. After 37 weeks this would be considered normal; before 37 weeks you might be heading for a premature delivery, so you should get to hospital as soon as you can.

There is also a long list of fairly harmless causes of vaginal bleeding, including:

- cervical ectropian (previously called an erosion). This doesn't mean it is damaged or eroded, but that cell changes in pregnancy make the cervix more prone to harmless bleeding. If you experience light bleeds after sex this could be the cause.

- vaginal infections, such as thrush, can cause bleeding as well as discharge.

- benign growths such as cervical polyps.

 Always contact your midwife or doctor if you experience vaginal bleeding so that they can decide if any further action is needed.

HORMONAL HORRORS

There are times during pregnancy when you could be forgiven for thinking that you have morphed back into a teenager with spotty skin, greasy hair and raging mood swings. And yes, as in teenagers, hormones *are* responsible for those unattractive aspects and several more besides. Here are some more symptoms caused by hormonal havoc.

Bleeding gums

Changing hormone levels cause your gums to swell and become more sensitive than normal; this can lead to bleeding gums and soreness, sometimes called pregnancy gingivitis. Some women develop little outgrowths of their gums, which occasionally bleed. These growths (known as pregnancy epulis) often appear early on in the pregnancy and usually disappear towards the end.

DENTIST'S DRILL

Gingivitis can cause permanent gum damage and lead to gum disease. Studies have shown that gum disease in pregnancy may lead to lower birth weight and pre-term babies (birth before 37 weeks), so it really is important that you look after your teeth and gums and get any problems assessed by your dentist.

Comfort zone

- Plaque can exacerbate the problem, so ensure you brush properly twice a day with a fluoride toothpaste, floss and use a mouthwash.

- Don't panic if your gums bleed when you brush; you need to get rid of plaque to ensure you don't develop gum disease.

Boobs: a tender tale

One of the most striking aspects of pregnancy is how quickly you could give a page three girl a run for her money. For girls who struggle to fill a B cup this can be a most positive thing, but if you have fairly big breasts to start with it can be a tad alarming, and quite uncomfortable.

Hormonal activity, increased blood flow and the beginning of milk production all contribute to an increase in bust size in the first trimester, and regrettably this can have some more unwelcome side effects in the form of tenderness or discomfort.

Try holding a cool damp flannel over your breasts to relieve tenderness.

Comfort zone
Earlier in the book, we suggested that you should go and get yourself measured and fitted for a new bra as soon as you feel your breast size increase. If you ignored that, now is the time to go!

- You should get properly measured several times during your pregnancy as you may go up as much as three cup sizes.

- If you are really uncomfortable at night, try sleeping in a non-wired cotton bra.

- Some women can't bear to be touched when their breasts hurt; others find massaging them helps, so find out what works for you. Undoubtedly you'll have a willing volunteer in your partner if you opt for the latter form of relief!

'During the first four months I hated the pain I was getting in my oversensitive boobs – I had to wear a sports bra at night to support them when I turned over in bed, and it hurt to hug people – but that's stopped now.'

Ruth, first pregnancy

Doctor's orders
If you are suffering, mention it to the midwife because she may have some tips to help you.

Food cravings: a taste of what's to come…

Why we get cravings for wonderful and downright weird foodstuffs in pregnancy is a bit of a mystery, but what we do know is that they are real and most women get them to a greater or lesser degree.

There's the evolutionary theory that it's just the body craving what it needs to sustain the pregnancy, or it may be triggered by your body demanding certain foods to cover nutritional deficiencies.

Some women start wanting weird combinations like mackerel and yoghurt, whereas others crave food they usually hate, like beetroot or jellied eels.

Comfort zone

You don't need us to tell you that a diet of baked beans and ice cream is not ideal for your baby or your waistline, so our best advice is to try to follow a balanced diet.

Eat your food slowly so you don't get indigestion and heartburn, and remember that a little of what you fancy will do you good… (unless it's inedible – see below).

> 'My biggest food craving has been cold custard. I had mini trifles for breakfast a few times. I couldn't stand the smell of leftover food, or food left out in the kitchen, or washing up. I used to try to tidy up but just started convulsing when I picked up some peppers or beetroot to put them in the fridge. Jim pretty much ruled the kitchen for a month.'
>
> *Corinne, first pregnancy*

Doctor's orders

You may find this hard to believe, but craving something that is not food (like coal) is a recognised medical disorder called pica. Munching sand, chalk, talcum powder, soap, rubber, wood or plaster isn't a great idea. (Google 'weird pregnancy cravings' if you want a laugh.) If you do feel the urge to chomp a non-edible object, try to distract yourself; remove it from the house if possible and discuss it with your doctor.

Hair: the long and the short of it

Fluctuating hormones can play havoc with your hair: some women shed it, some women grow it, some women report glossy locks and others lanky locks, so it's difficult to predict what will happen. And it's not just the hair on your head that's affected. Pregnancy can affect your body hair as well: some find it stops growing, while some find they start developing facial hair. Unfortunately there's no way to influence what will happen to you.

Comfort zone

You can wax, pluck and shave all you like, but seek advice if you want to use laser treatment or electrolysis to remove hair, as some practitioners don't encourage it. If you are using a hair removal cream do a patch test first, because skin does become more sensitive in pregnancy.

Tackling your bikini line post 30 weeks is not a breeze! Being pregnant is the time to relax about your usual beauty rituals and concentrate on your bump, rather than your hairy bits.

Doctor's orders

Unfortunately there isn't a medical cure for this one. Once your hormones settle down after the birth so will your hair. Don't be alarmed if it comes out in handfuls after the birth; you're very unlikely to go bald. It's just your body shedding those glossy thick locks everyone commented on while you were pregnant!

Heartburn and indigestion

Pain in the upper chest and tummy, a burning feeling or the sensation that something is stuck at the top of your tummy are all signs of heartburn or indigestion. It's not necessarily something you ate, but those dreaded hormones causing your digestive system to relax, leading to excess acid collecting in the stomach and backtracking into the gullet (oesophagus). Towards the end of your pregnancy the growing uterus puts pressure on your stomach, and this too can cause pain and discomfort in the tummy.

Associated with heartburn is also the old wives' tale about hairy babies. The worse the heartburn, the hairier the baby, supposedly – so take some solace in the fact your little one might be born with a full head of hair.

Comfort zone

Many pregnant women swear that their best friend during pregnancy was a bottle of Gaviscon. If you are really suffering, go and see your pharmacist, and get them to recommend an over-the-counter antacid remedy suitable to take during pregnancy.

Here are some tips to avoid indigestion.

- Eat smaller meals and chew them slowly.

- If certain foods bring on an attack (spicy and greasy foods are the usual suspects), eliminate them from your diet.

- Drinking a glass of cold milk helps some women.

- Don't lie down for at least two hours after your last meal, and then try sleeping propped up on a pile of plump pillows.

Doctor's orders

Indigestion and heartburn are uncomfortable, but there's no need for you to worry: it will go away once the baby is born. Occasionally a heartburn-type sensation can be a symptom of pre-eclampsia, though, so if your indigestion is unusually severe, persistent and troublesome, seek advice.

'So far I've liked the changes to my body but I do feel like my body isn't my own anymore. I now have lots of little ailments, like eczema and heartburn, which I never had before.'

Jenny, first pregnancy

Morning sickness

Firstly, the name 'morning sickness' is misleading because, for many women, the feeling of sickness goes on all day. Around 85% of women suffer from nausea and sickness to some degree during their pregnancy. The 'lucky' ones will feel mildly nauseous, whereas some women will physically retch and vomit all day.

Doctors aren't 100% certain what causes it, but it's pretty likely that the fluctuation in hormone levels is to blame.

There is an evolutionary theory that it is nature's way of putting you off potentially hazardous foods. This may be true in the case of wine: many pregnant women find they can't even stand the smell of it, let alone the taste; but when you can't even keep a healthy breakfast down, the theory wears a bit thin.

Early in her pregnancy, the Duchess of Cambridge was admitted to hospital with hyperemesis gravidarum (severe morning sickness), proving that no one is immune from this debilitating condition.

If you are afflicted in the mornings, try getting up slowly and making your routine as leisurely and relaxed as possible. Leaping out of bed and snatching some toast on the hoof isn't going to help. It's also important to eat as soon as you get up, because nausea is often worse on an empty stomach.

Comfort zone

Here are a few methods to try to help you alleviate nausea and sickness.

- Ginger is an 'alternative' remedy that is considered effective. Try infusing a ginger root in boiling water or use ginger tea bags for a soothing hot drink. You can even nibble on ginger nuts whenever you are feeling nauseous.

- Eat little and often if you can.

- Cut out things that make the problem worse – usually greasy and spicy food – and be prepared to experiment to find things that you can stomach. Bland food, such as mashed potato, white rice or bread, often does the trick.

- If you really can't face food it is essential that you keep yourself hydrated; drink plenty of fluids, particularly if you are actually vomiting.

Sea sickness bands can be helpful for alleviating nausea. Homeopathic remedies can also help.

Doctor's orders

We are all aware of the importance of a good diet even when we are not pregnant, so it can be very worrying when you feel you are not nourishing the new life growing inside you because you're living on a diet of mashed potatoes and ginger biscuits. Please don't fret about this: your baby will be able to get enough nutrients from you, however 'bad' your diet is. To reassure yourself you only have to think about women in developing countries who have very limited access to nutritious food, and who still manage to have surprisingly healthy babies, given their restricted diets.

Sickness tends to decrease after the end of the first trimester, because the placenta is now functioning fully and providing your baby with all the nourishment it needs. Until this point, the hormone human chorionic gonadotrophin (HCG) is responsible for your baby's growth, and morning sickness is believed to indicate that you have high levels of it in your system (there is even a theory that says that you are less likely to suffer a miscarriage if you have morning sickness).

Vomiting in itself is not a worry, but if it is accompanied by fever or pain you should seek medical advice. If you vomit excessively, you could be suffering from hyperemesis gravidarum, which essentially consists of persistent vomiting, usually with weight loss, needing intravenous rehydration. Your baby will probably not be affected by this condition but you may have to be hospitalised if you become severely dehydrated. Recently more and more hospitals are offering outpatient care for this condition, so do ask! There are anti-sickness medications that you can take safely, so do seek advice from your doctor or midwife if you are really suffering.

If you have had hyperemesis gravidarum, you are quite likely to get it in another pregnancy, so talk to your doctor before you next conceive – the best plan is to be ahead of the nausea.

Mood swings: a crying shame

Pregnancy is quite tough emotionally and there's no getting away from it. You know you should be on cloud nine and super happy, but half the time you're weeping at some soppy movie on TV or wondering why you ever thought that having a baby with HIM was a good idea. Wanting to throttle your partner or cry for England is all totally normal and is a result of your raging hormones. To further compound the problem, if you are not feeling great physically, this can make you feel more vulnerable emotionally.

Comfort zone

It's those damn hormones doing their worst and there's nothing you can do to prevent it happening, but there are things you can do to lift your mood.

- Talking is always good. Discuss your anger, frustrations or worries with a friend or your partner, as a trouble shared really can be a trouble halved.

- Go and see a feel-good chick flick with your mates. Cinema trips will be harder once the baby is born, so treat yourself and have a good night out with the girls.

- Even in the depths of winter the sun's watery rays can cast a little bit of sunshine on us all. Go for a walk, as it can make you feel better physically and emotionally.

- Join a pregnancy yoga class. Not only will it keep you fit and supple for labour, but it's a great stress buster too.

- Sleep, sleep and more sleep. If you are feeling good physically you'll feel better emotionally.

'To begin with, things were a bit difficult with my husband. I was very moody and irrational and would take it all out on my nearest and dearest. Now my hormones have settled down and we are getting on fantastically. He is really looking after me and is constantly touching my bump and talking to "Jelly Bean".'

Becky, first pregnancy

Doctor's orders

There is evidence to suggest that women who are low or depressed during pregnancy have a greater chance of developing postnatal depression. If you are prone to this problem or have prolonged periods of depression during your pregnancy, do speak to your doctor, because he can prescribe something to help you or refer you for counselling.

Skin changes

Hormones can literally have a 'marked' affect on your appearance during pregnancy. Even if your teenage years were Clearasil-free, you might become a spotty mama-to-be. This is because your hormones release more sebum: an oily substance to keep the skin supple. Hormonal changes can even alter the pigmentation in your skin, causing dark patches on fair skin and light patches on dark skin.

Some women develop eczema for the first time during pregnancy, particularly over the bump, where the skin becomes very taut. Others who are already prone to the condition, may have more flare-ups or find it disappears completely. To try to prevent the occurrence of eczema, keep your skin as well moisturised as possible, use very gentle soap products or get your doctor to prescribe you special emollients for the bath or shower to stop your skin drying out.

You might also notice that the area around your nipples (the areola) darkens and a dark line running down the centre of your tummy appears. This is known as the linea nigra. Moles may appear darker and you may develop skin tags anywhere on the face and body.

The increased blood flow to the skin can give you a lovely rosy glow; it can also give you spider naevi – small clusters of tiny capillaries usually over the upper chest or arms – which are somewhat less attractive!

Given the number of changes hormones can cause in your skin, it's no surprise that it isn't a good idea to sunbathe while you're pregnant. Your skin will be more sensitive than normal, so if you are out in the sun make sure you use a high factor sun protection.

Comfort zone

The good news is that your skin normally fades back to normal once the baby is born. However, there are a few things you can to do alleviate the changes.

- Review your beauty regime if your skin becomes oily and go for a medicated cleanser if you're getting unwelcome outbreaks.

- You can buy a green-coloured concealer at a chemist or The Body Shop that takes the redness out of your complexion and also covers up those pesky broken veins.

- If you are feeling like the ugly sister rather than the belle of the ball, treat yourself to a facial or a makeover to give your image a boost.

Doctor's orders

If you are worried about any moles that start growing or changing color during pregnancy, see your doctor to get them checked out.

Smell

You may find that your hormones make you incredibly sensitive to smell from virtually the moment you confirm your pregnancy. For some women, this kicks in almost immediately, and the smell of the fridge at work is so repugnant that they can't even get the milk out!

Just like morning sickness, the theory goes that you are repulsed by the smell of things which you shouldn't consume during pregnancy: so, in some cases, women can't stand the smell of beer.

'I remember during my first pregnancy one morning my husband and I were on the train into work together. He had been out the night before for beer and curry, and I had to ask him to stop talking to me as his breath nearly made me sick! Not sure he's ever got over that one!'

Nicola, second pregnancy and mum to Callum, 18 months

Comfort zone

Your sensitivity to smells may subside with your morning sickness, or it may continue throughout your pregnancy. Try these tips if you are suffering.

- Good food hygiene is common sense and if you wrap things properly in the fridge they shouldn't smell.

- Avoid crowded public transport in summer if you can: sweaty bodies in a confined area is enough to make anyone retch!

Doctor's orders

Unfortunately, there isn't much your doctor or midwife can do. Tell them if you find you are particularly sensitive, though, as they might have some tips to help you.

LET'S GET PHYSICAL

Breathing, walking, sleeping and thinking are all things we take for granted but they can all be negatively affected in pregnancy.

Breathing

We normally take breathing for granted, which is why it can be a bit worrying when you become breathless and tight-chested in pregnancy. Your lungs need to work harder to provide extra oxygen for your baby, which can make you breathless. Towards the end of your pregnancy the uterus might be pushing on the diaphragm (the muscle that regulates your breathing) and this will also cause breathlessness.

Comfort zone

There's no need to panic if you have an attack of breathlessness, but it's probably worth sitting down and resting if you can.

Doctor's orders

If you have palpitations or chest pains, do seek medical advice urgently, as it could be a sign of something more serious.

Exhaustion

It's incredibly common to feel exhausted in the early stages of pregnancy as your body works overtime to set up your baby's support systems in your uterus. Towards the end of your pregnancy, you are carrying the equivalent of around seven bags of sugar in your tummy, so it's no wonder you feel exhausted. Morning sickness, poor diet and lack of exercise can also contribute to feeling shattered.

Comfort zone

- It goes without saying that you need to get as much rest as you can. If you are still working, try to have many early nights during the week and lie in at the weekends.

- Listen to your body: if it is telling you it is tired, give in and have that afternoon siesta or power nap.

- To make life as easy for yourself as you can, hire a cleaner to do the housework or get your local supermarket to pick, pack and deliver your shopping.

Doctor's orders
Exhaustion can also be a sign of anaemia, so make sure you get checked out.

Insomnia

Sometimes insomnia is caused by other physical pregnancy symptoms such as heartburn, backache or an overactive bladder. It could be that your baby is literally kicking you awake or you might be mentally overactive: baby anxiety has kept many a pregnant woman wide awake into the wee small hours.

Some women have strange dreams and even nightmares during pregnancy – talk to your partner or midwife to dispel any anxiety.

Comfort zone

- Avoid caffeine in the evening, as it can keep you awake and necessitate a night-time trip to the loo.

- Make yourself as comfortable as you can in bed, with comfy pillows supporting your back and your bump.

- Pop a little lavender bag under your pillow; it makes the room smell heavenly and has restful qualities.

- Don't over-stimulate your brain watching TV in bed.

- Try not to lie awake worrying about everything. Anything you need to do can be done in the morning. You need your rest!

Doctor's orders

If you're really worried you're not getting enough sleep, talk to your doctor or midwife. However, sleeping tablets are not recommended, not least because they cross through the placenta to the baby. Some cynical people say the altered sleeping pattern is preparing you for life after the baby is born.

Baby brain

No one seems to know why pregnant women develop 'baby brain', but what we do know is that many pregnant women do seem to become extraordinarily forgetful during pregnancy. A recent study by scientists at Bradford and Leeds Universities seems to support the theory that hormones are to blame for short-term memory loss, but another study in 2009 claimed that 'baby brain' is actually a myth – at least physiologically. It seems that the only explanation for any memory trouble you're having is that your pregnancy is occupying so many of your thoughts that everything else gets pushed to the side.

Comfort zone

It can be frustrating and embarrassing when you keep forgetting things, so try these tips to help your memory.

- Try carrying a large diary around so that you can write down all your appointments and work meetings.

- Keep a small pocket notebook handy for lists.

Doctor's orders

Unless you do something really stupid – like go to work and leave the front door wide open, or drive the wrong way up a motorway – there isn't any need to worry if you do become more absent-minded; your brain should be delivered back to you with your baby!

THE LEG-ACY OF PREGNANCY

For some reason your poor old legs can take a pasting during pregnancy. Let's stroll through a few of the most common problems.

Oedema

Swelling, or oedema, is extremely common in pregnancy: it can affect your face and hands and invariably makes its presence felt in the legs.

It is caused by fluid leaking out of blood vessels with sluggish flow, and gets worse if you have been standing for long periods of time or in hot weather.

Comfort zone

- Invest in a pair of Crocs. Love 'em or loathe 'em, they are brilliant when you are pregnant. They are loose enough to accommodate pudgy swollen feet, and if you buy the proper ones they have 'nibbles' on the bottom to massage your soles. They are also the *perfect* shoes to venture into dreaded hospital bathrooms. If you are a germa-phobe like we are you can even shower in them.

- Support tights are fantastic if you are on your feet all day. Granted, they are not the sexiest of fashion accessories, but they really do what it says on the packet.

- Literally put your feet up whenever you can.

- Practise foot rotation exercises when you are sitting down.

 Your feet may actually grow during pregnancy and not return to their original size!

Doctor's orders

Swelling of the body can be an indication of pre-eclampsia and your doctor and midwife will be alert to the signs, so if you are worried or suddenly balloon out, get some advice as soon as you can.

Restless leg syndrome

If your legs feel as if they are tingling, burning, 'crawling' or you have an uncontrollable urge to move your legs, you may have restless leg syndrome (RLS). This affliction tends to strike at night when you are sitting down or sleeping, which makes resting or snoozing really difficult.

 One in five pregnant women develops RLS during her pregnancy.

Comfort zone

Cutting down on alcohol and caffeine helps, but hopefully you've pretty much knocked that on the head anyway.

A recent study suggested that women who took gentle/moderate exercise regularly in pregnancy were less likely to suffer from RLS, and doing gentle stretching exercises in the morning and evening will also help.

Doctor's orders

RLS can be a sign of anaemia, so do visit your doctor. If an iron deficiency is detected, iron tablets will be prescribed by your doctor to alleviate your symptoms.

Varicose veins

Swollen bulging veins that may ache or itch are a common feature of pregnancy. Your hormones cause your blood vessels to relax and your body's increased blood flow and growing uterus put pressure on your veins, causing them to swell.

Varicose veins occur most commonly on the legs, but also around the anus (known as piles) and in the vaginal area (see page 101). They are partly hereditary, and being overweight and carrying multiple babies also increases your risk of getting them.

Comfort zone

- The advice is very similar to that given if you're suffering from swelling: keep your feet raised on cushions or on the arm of the sofa when you are resting; wear support tights during the day; and if you are on your feet all day, make sure you have regular rests, as you have a legal entitlement to do so.

- If they are hurting, you can pop an ice pack or bag of frozen peas on them to soothe the pain.

- Make sure you take regular exercise to boost your circulation.

Doctor's orders

We'd love to tell you that they go away after birth, but this is not always the case. The bad news is that unless they are causing you real pain removal is considered to be a non-essential cosmetic procedure; therefore you are not entitled to have them removed on the NHS. If you have private health insurance and a sympathetic GP you might be able to get them done on your policy for free. If you do need surgery, try to wait until you have had all your babies, as pregnancy after surgery can make new ones appear!

UP CLOSE AND PERSONAL

There are certain problems you might suffer from during pregnancy that you would prefer to keep mum about. However, pretty much anything you're going through is completely normal. Don't suffer in silence – get help if you need it.

Constipation

Pregnancy hormones relax the digestive system, causing the movement of food to slow down – so if you were prone to constipation before you became pregnant, it is likely you are going to suffer now. The pressure of the uterus on the bowels also restricts their ability to function properly, so there are two reasons why doing a number two may be problematic for you now.

Comfort zone

- Drinking lots of water is a must, and following a fibre-rich diet of wholemeal bread, fruit, vegetables and pulses should get things moving.

- Regular exercise such as swimming and walking can 'wake up' a sluggish system.

- If you are prescribed iron tablets for anaemia, consider switching if they make you pass pellets like a rabbit (quite common, honestly!).

Doctor's orders
If you are completely bunged up, you might need a mild laxative to get you going. Consult your midwife or pharmacist, as some are too strong to use in pregnancy.

Incontinence

Your pelvic floor (which supports the bladder) comes under a lot of stress during pregnancy as your uterus grows. The hormone relaxin, which makes your muscles relax in preparation for birth, can make the problem even worse. For some pregnant women the problem can be so bad that they leak when they laugh, sneeze or cough.

Comfort zone

- We're not going to recommend you give up laughing, coughing or sneezing, but you do need to start doing pelvic

 When you go for a wee, rock back and forth slowly to make sure your bladder is completely empty.

floor exercises – also known as Kegels – ideally as soon as you discover you are pregnant.

- Use a panty liner or pad to protect your clothes (and your dignity).

Doctor's orders

Giving birth can sometimes damage the pelvic floor and make it even weaker, leading to long-term incontinence problems that might require surgery. Therefore it really is of paramount importance for you to get going with those Kegel exercises. The good thing is that no one can see you doing them, so you can practise at the bus stop, in the hospital waiting room or sitting at your desk (see www.nhs.uk and page 141).

Piles

Probably the least favourite pregnancy symptom (and one of the most common). Piles (or haemorrhoids) are like little bunches of grapes that protrude around your back passage area (that's probably the most polite way of putting it). They are caused by your hormones making the veins in that area swell, and if you're are having problems with constipation, straining on the loo will exacerbate the problem further. They can itch, ache and sometimes bleed, which can be quite alarming the first time you see it because any blood 'down below' immediately makes you think, 'Baby on its way: SOS!'.

Comfort zone

- Drink lots of water and eat fibre-rich food to keep everything moving in that department, so you don't have the extra difficulty of constipation to contend with.

- Sitting on an ice pack can numb the pain and soothe the area.

Doctor's orders

You can ask your pharmacist to recommend an ointment to alleviate the symptoms, or, if they are really bad, you can ask your doctor to prescribe some suppositories.

Piles normally shrink back or disappear after childbirth; however, if they persist there is a medical procedure you can have (don't ask… google it if you're that fascinated). Fingers crossed they'll go of their own accord.

Stretch marks

These purple and pink lines can appear anywhere you gain weight during pregnancy, including your thighs, hips and bottom, as well as your tummy. They fade to a silvery-grey in time, but once you have them they won't go away of their own accord. It's difficult to know whether you will be affected: a great deal depends on your skin type and it doesn't seem to be hereditary.

Comfort zone

There are many brands out there that claim to help prevent stretch marks but there's no concrete evidence that any of them actually work. Cocoa butter is supposed to be effective, is cheap as chips, and smells quite nice so it might be worth giving that a go, but feel free to splurge as your budget allows. Logic says that you should probably start early, before your bump becomes too pronounced.

> Stretch marks affect up to 80% of women.

Doctor's orders

There is no magic cream or potion your doctor can prescribe, so just learn to accept them as a triumphant baby battle scar! They do fade a little with time!

Thrush

You are 10 times more likely to develop thrush (also called candida) in pregnancy, because hormones affect the natural balance of bacteria in your vagina and allow this annoying yeast infection to develop.

Comfort zone

- Natural yoghurt is said to contain active bacteria that can combat thrush, so you can eat it (preferably) or apply it directly to soothe your vaginal area.

- Wash carefully with unperfumed soap not more than once daily, and wear cotton knickers.

- You're probably not feeling much like having sex if you have thrush, but it can be passed on through sexual contact. If you think your partner might be affected they'll need treatment too.

- When you pass urine make sure you dry from 'front to back', not the other way – thrush lives in the back passage, and it's very easy for it to hop out into the vagina if you drag it forwards with the loo roll!

Doctor's orders

Thrush is not dangerous for you or the baby. It only needs to be treated if it is troubling you, with an antifungal cream or pessaries. Some brands are not suitable for use in pregnancy, so ask your pharmacist or doctor to recommend or prescribe a suitable one for you.

Urination

Needing to pee more often can kick in almost as soon as you confirm your pregnancy, and annoyingly the urge often strikes in the middle of the night. Hormones are normally responsible in the early weeks, but as your pregnancy progresses your kidneys step up a gear to rid your body of excess waste products. In the third trimester the pressure on your bladder from your expanding uterus means you'll be visiting the loo more than usual as well.

Comfort zone

- Don't restrict your fluid intake to minimise trips to the loo, as both you and your baby need plenty of liquid to keep healthy during pregnancy. You'll just have to grin and bear it!

- Avoid caffeine, particularly in the evening, as it has a diuretic effect.

- Try to empty your bladder completely when you go. Tipping your pelvis back and forth a little can help ensure you get rid of everything properly.

- Find out where the loos are when you're somewhere unfamiliar to avoid feeling desperate.

Doctor's orders

If your urine is cloudy or bloody or it's painful to pee, you probably have a urinary tract infection. This can trigger premature labour, so seek medical advice if you have these symptoms.

Vaginal discharge

You may experience an increase in vaginal discharge during pregnancy. It is believed that this is nature's way of protecting against infections that could travel up into your uterus, but it can also be a sign of cervical ectropion. It may be clear, white, grey, yellow or even greenish!

Near your due date you may experience a thick show of discharge, tinged with blood, that normally indicates labour is imminent. If this happens, you should prepare yourself for the fact that you might be about to go into labour.

Comfort zone
As with thrush, wash carefully with unperfumed soap and wear cotton knickers with a panty liner (not a tampon) if you feel the discharge is particularly heavy.

Doctor's orders
If the discharge changes colour, smells, or stings, mention this to your midwife. If you start leaking a watery discharge in late pregnancy this should be reported to a doctor immediately, because you might be losing amniotic fluid as a result of premature rupture of the membranes.

Vaginal varicose veins

These form in the same way as varicose veins in your legs or piles, but obviously they're in a slightly more delicate place!

Comfort zone
You can buy something called a V Brace, which resembles a large pair of padded support pants. Hardly Agent Provocateur, but they do keep everything safely gathered in.

Doctor's orders
There's nothing your doctor can do about them except tell you they'll improve after you've given birth (thank goodness!). But he might want to look at them if they are very extensive to ensure they won't get in the way or become damaged during delivery.

Wind

Wind has the same cause as constipation and is often related.

Comfort zone

- Specific foods (such as spicy food like curry) can trigger the condition, so try to eliminate them from your diet.

- Don't overload your system with big meals – particularly late at night – and eat slowly, ensuring you chew your food thoroughly.

- Keeping active can stop wind from getting trapped in your stomach.

Doctor's orders

There are products such as Wind-eze on the market that may relieve the symptoms of flatulence and trapped wind, but it is important that you consult a pharmacist or your midwife before you take them to check they are safe for use in pregnancy. Some women also find mints, peppermint oil or peppermint tea can alleviate symptoms.

WHEN TO SEEK MEDICAL HELP

If you are experiencing any of the symptoms below, call your maternity unit or request a same day GP appointment, as they *may* indicate a serious problem that could threaten the health of you or your baby.

- Severe, persistent abdominal pain
- Disturbance of vision
- Sudden or severe swelling on your face or hands – particularly if you have a headache
- Raging thirst and lack of urination
- Severe vomiting accompanied by pain or fever

- Fluid leaking from the vagina
- Severe headache that persists for more than a few hours
- Pain or burning on urination
- Severe itching all over your body
- Lack of fetal movements
- Vaginal bleeding
- Frequent dizzy or fainting spells
- A heavy fall (although your baby is well cushioned in his amniotic sac, it's best to get yourself checked out if you take a tumble)

PREGNANCY PREENING

We hope the previous section hasn't horrified you too much: very few pregnancy illnesses or problems are serious or long lasting, and the prize you get at the end should make any short-term suffering worthwhile.

Pregnancy doesn't just affect your health; it affects the way you both look and feel, and in this next section we suggest ways to make you feel more beautiful on the outside *and* on the inside.

Hair

Limp and lanky or gloriously glossy? Your hair may become luxuriously thick and fabulous or come out in handfuls, and it's notoriously difficult to predict what effect your hormones are going to have on your hair follicles. Your hair might become drier than normal or much greasier, and some women report that it changes texture too. You might also find your hair grows more quickly than normal.

A trip to the hairdresser's is a great pick-me-up, and in the first trimester, when you might be feeling a bit sick and grotty, a new hairstyle or even a wash and blow dry will give you a much-needed injection of glamour.

Dyeing your hair

Experts cannot say for *certain* that chemicals in hair dye are completely safe for use in pregnancy, which is why some recommend that you avoid colouring your hair in the first trimester, when your baby's brain and nervous system are developing at the most dramatic rate. There are no studies that say with absolute certainty that it does your baby any harm, though; so if changing your hair colour is fundamental to who you are as a person, then 'carry on colouring' and don't lose any sleep over it, because modern hair dyes are probably safer than they have ever been.

If you do like to give your hair colour a boost and are worried about using chemicals on your scalp, you can always use a semi-permanent rinse which isn't as strong; henna-based dyes; or consider highlights or low lights to give your lacklustre locks a lift.

If you want to take a more natural approach to hair colour, here a few 'recipes' that might do the trick.

Blondes

Try steeping chamomile tea bags in boiling water and then mixing the liquid with a small pot of natural yoghurt. Apply to dry hair, wrap your hair in plastic and leave for half an hour, rinse and shampoo.

In the summer, just put lemon juice on your hair and sit outside in the sunshine, as it has proven hair-lightening properties.

Brunettes
Make up a pot of very strong black coffee and, once it's cool enough, rinse washed hair in the solution several times. Leave the final 'rinse' on for half an hour and then wash off with cold water.

Redheads
Mix half a cup of carrot juice with half a cup of beetroot juice and apply to damp, washed hair. Wrap hair in a hot towel and leave to dry in the sun, or dry on a medium heat hand dryer.

Changing life, changing style

In the third trimester it's not a bad idea to assess your current hairstyle and consider whether it is going to work when you have a newborn. However much you'd like to think your life isn't going to change when you have a baby, the reality is that you probably won't have as much time to spend on your personal appearance as you used to pre-baby, and there's no point in having a fancy hairdo if it only looks good after half an hour of blow drying. If you don't want a new image but want to look respectable in those post-birth photos, book a hair appointment a week before your due date for a cut and blow dry, because it might be difficult to go for a snip with a newborn in tow.

Hands and nails

Some women find that they grow fabulous talons in pregnancy, while others find their nails become brittle and split. If you fall into the latter camp, the best advice is to keep them short, and protect them with gloves if you are doing stuff like gardening or cleaning.

If you do think your hands need a little TLC, you could treat yourself to a manicure or pedicure (a virtual necessity by the end of your pregnancy, when getting anywhere near your toes is nigh on impossible). Nail bars are becoming a common fixture in the high street now and many don't require you to make an appointment in advance; you can just stroll (or waddle) in. It's worth remembering, however, that nail varnish is usually removed before surgeries – including Caesarean sections. During surgery, levels of oxygen in the blood are measured via a red light that passes through tissue. A device is placed on the fingertip and monitored by the anaesthetist. Nail varnish can reduce the effectivness of the equipment.

You can also lavish your hands daily with your favourite hand cream to make them super soft and silky.

Chemical considerations

The smell of nail polish is pretty horrible even when you are not pregnant, so it's not surprising to learn that these enticing bottles of pretty coloured liquid are jam-packed with chemicals. As with hair dye, there isn't any conclusive evidence to prove that nail varnish is dangerous, but if you are worried about this check out the Karpati range of nail lacquers. Australian mother Eva Karpati developed a range of nail varnishes that are chemical-free.

Facial skin

You will have read earlier in this chapter that your skin can be adversely affected in pregnancy. It becomes more sensitive, can be prone to spots and can develop pigmentation marks or rashes.

Chloasma, otherwise known as 'pregnancy mask', is relatively common during pregnancy and is thought to be due to hormonal changes in the body. Chloasma is the development of darker pigmentation marks, usually on your face, and can be quite distressing to acquire. There's not a great deal that can be done for you medically, but you can use foundation or concealer to even out the skin colour, and the good news is that it usually disappears within a few months of giving birth.

In terms of beauty treatments, you should avoid anything that involves chemicals (such as peels); as your skin is more sensitive, also avoid micro-dermabrasion, as you might experience adverse reactions like redness and itchiness.

If you become very spotty, check with the pharmacist before you slather your face in zit cream, because some of the stronger products on offer contain chemicals that could be harmful to your baby.

So what can you do to make yourself look more gorgeous when pregnant?

- You *can* have a facial, ideally in the second trimester (working on the theory that if you are feeling really rough in the first trimester no amount of lotions and potions will improve your appearance). There are many beauty therapists that advertise pregnancy-specific pampering. If you already have someone you use and trust, do let her know that you are pregnant, because it may affect what products she chooses.

■ Have a makeover at a department store. Maybe you need some help covering dark circles or newly acquired blemishes, or some new make-up products to brighten up your look. You don't have to buy anything; it could give you some good ideas, and as long as you don't end up plastered in slap like a drag queen what have you got to lose?

Bathing beauty

There is nothing like a long, leisurely soak in the bath to soothe aching muscles and make you feel sweet smelling and gorgeous (not to mention clean!). Some experts claim that bubble baths in pregnancy make you more prone to infection, but there isn't any hard evidence to support this.

What *is* known is that excessively hot (as opposed to warm) baths can raise your base temperature and that of your baby, and there's a slight chance that exposure to excessive heat in the uterus in the first trimester can cause neural defects. Always check the temperature of the water with your elbow. (It's also good practice for when you have the baby because this is the recommended way of doing it before you bathe him.)

If you want to properly pamper yourself, treat yourself to some yummy expensive bath oil (think of the money you're saving on wine and justify it that way!).

There are some essential oils you can drop in the bath, but this can be quite complicated. Some can't be used early in pregnancy but are safe later on (rose); some can be used throughout pregnancy and beyond (lavender); and some should be avoided at all costs (herb oils such as rosemary and thyme). Like any oils or lotions, it might be safest to stick with baby bath products.

Brilliant bosoms

Make the most of your newly acquired assets and wear a low-cut top if you fancy it; it's the perfect time to celebrate your breasts before they are put to a completely different purpose! There's no reason why you shouldn't celebrate your new curvaceous shape in all its glory.

Pregnancy is fantastic if you have small or average-sized breasts, but if you were busty to start with, it can be difficult to keep them under control. Do get yourself measured regularly and, if your budget allows, buy something a bit lacy and frivolous (but supportive, obviously) to make you feel glam.

'I now really love the way my body looks with a definite bump and bigger boobs. I was on holiday last week in the Caribbean and wore a bikini and for the first time actually felt comfortable in one, which is strange as I weigh more now than I ever have in my life.'

Becky, first pregnancy

Eating for two

You don't need to be pregnant to know that the old adage 'eating for two' needs to be taken with a pinch of salt (but only a pinch, as excess sodium in your diet's not great either). It's not just down to what you eat and how much, but also your pre-pregnancy weight, age, height and even your race. We tackle healthy eating and food in the next chapter, but it is important for you to know how much weight you can expect to put on.

- Your weight will not be monitored throughout your pregnancy unless you are underweight or overweight or have certain medical conditions in which weight loss might indicate a problem (eg Crohn's disease). At your initial booking appointment your midwife will weigh you and work out your BMI (body mass index). This is your weight in kilograms divided by your height in metres squared: normal is 19–25; underweight is less than 19; and the more your BMI is over 25, the more obese you are. Being overweight or seriously underweight can be a cause for concern for you and your baby.

- You will put on between 9 and 13kg (20lb and 28lb) during your pregnancy, with most of it being gained after 20 weeks. If you are overweight, you should seek advice from your midwife about pregnancy weight gain. Your midwife will be able to offer guidance to ensure you don't gain too much weight.

See Chapter 4 for more information on the medical aspects of weight gain during pregnancy and how important it is to follow a healthy, balanced diet.

A 2012 study assessed 4,000 women 16 years after they gave birth, and found those who had gained more than the recommended weight during pregnancy were now three times more likely to be overweight or obese.

YOUR BUMP

Like the population in general, bumps come in all different shapes and sizes. Thin people often have very prominent bumps, whereas larger people have less obvious ones; some women carry very 'high' and others 'low'; and some tend to carry out front, whereas other women go 'wide' and carry on the hip area. The shape and size of your bump depends on the following factors:

- the size of your baby and placenta

- the amount of weight you gain

- your height and general posture

- the strength of your tummy muscles (if they are strong your bump will initially be less noticeable; in subsequent pregnancies women often show earlier, as their muscles are not as strong as they were)

- the amount of amniotic fluid

- the position of the baby in the final trimester

- the number of babies you are carrying.

Making a show of yourself

Most women don't show until they are at least 12 weeks. From this point your uterus begins to push out beyond your pubic bone and, depending on your weight, size and strength of your abs, your bump will make itself known to the world.

Whilst many women (and their partners) love their bodies when pregnant, there are some of you that won't enjoy having a bump, massive boobs or the other wobbly bits that you may acquire. Don't worry if you have feelings like this; it is more common than you think. If you feel fat and frumpy rather than fabulously fecund, layer up to disguise your shape and wear dark, flattering hues. A killer hairdo, vampish lips or cool shades might make you feel more glamorous, and if you resent spending money on clothes, why not treat yourself to a frivolous handbag to lift your mood and update your look?

Your beautiful bump

There's something really nice about rubbing something sweet-smelling into your baby bump, but don't take our word for it; über super-mama Claudia Schiffer swears by it too: 'I do like to put a lot of cream on my tummy, as long as it's natural. I think it really works to help stretch marks and make the skin really nice and soft.'

There are heaps of oils, lotions and potions that are specially developed for use in pregnancy, and it is very important that you check the provenance of anything you use on your body, because certain essential oils can be very harmful. **Never** massage them directly on the skin.

If in doubt, you can always resort to baby oils and lotions: if they are safe enough to use on a newborn, they will be fine for you to use.

Don't touch me!

One of the oddest things about being pregnant is that as soon as you have a sizeable bump it suddenly becomes public property, and people you don't know feel totally at ease with touching your tummy. This can be most disconcerting, particularly the first time it happens – and if you are shy you will probably find this intrusion torturous. How you deal with it depends greatly on your mood; people are generally well meaning and don't want to freak you out, but if you really hate it you might just have to murmur, 'Excuse me,' and make a swift exit!

'I think I give out "don't touch" vibes, so not many people try to touch my bump, and anyone that does tends to be a close friend so I don't really mind. I had a horrible experience when I was heavily pregnant on the tube sitting next to an Asian lady. She started getting a bit fidgety and suddenly reached out to touch my bump ...it was really odd and I felt very protective, but I found out afterwards that in parts of Asia it's meant to bring some kind of fertility-good-luck if you touch a pregnant lady's bump. I was still very uncomfortable, though!'

Nicola, second pregnancy and mum to Callum, 18 months

Meet bump

There is an emerging new trend of couples naming their bump (but not using the same name they intend to call the baby). Naming your growing bump can make your pregnancy and impending parenthood all the more real, and saves you always saying 'the baby'. Some of the names our new mums and mums-to-be named their bump include Smurf, Bumpette/Bump/Bumpy, Wiggler, Beanie and Winchester!

Even though you might feel a bit terrified having read about the myriad ailments that you can experience during pregnancy, don't panic! Pregnancy does bring some odd, unpleasant, uncomfortable and even mildly amusing side effects, but most are normal and your body will adjust to these changes. Always seek medical advice if you are concerned about any symptoms or side effects. Never feel embarrassed to ask for help.

We'll now go on to look at how you can adapt your life to suit your pregnancy, and still feel like yourself.

4

My lifestyle and body during pregnancy

In this chapter we look at your lifestyle and how you might have to adapt it now that you are pregnant. We give you the latest info on the hazards of modern-day living during pregnancy, and try to balance this with statistics and anecdotes to reassure you that unless you are still living life to excess, a little bit of what you fancy in pregnancy is (probably) not going to do you or your baby any harm. You're a grown-up now who is about to bring a new life into the world, and you should still be able to enjoy your pregnancy and your life without giving up everything: you should just make informed choices about how much and how often.

ALCOHOL

Until 2007, official advice on drinking during pregnancy was that it was perfectly safe for women to drink one or two units of alcohol on one or two occasions in any given week. Since then the Department of Health has revised its stance, and the latest advice is to abstain from alcohol completely during pregnancy. This is not based on any new evidence proving that small amounts of alcohol in pregnancy are harmful, but as doctors can't be *certain* that it doesn't have a detrimental effect on the baby, they are playing it safe and recommending you don't drink at all.

The National Institute for Health and Care Excellence (NICE) has slightly more relaxed advice, recommending that women abstain from alcohol in the first trimester and then stick to the pre-2007 guidelines of not more than one or two units a week after that.

Why did the guidelines change?

Statistics reveal that women are drinking more than they used to and standard measures in pubs and bars are larger than before. It is possible that officials are worried that women may unwittingly do their baby harm by exceeding the recommended amounts without realising – so a blanket ban recommendation on alcohol is the safest option, however patronising it sounds.

To drink or not to drink?

There has been much in the press recently about Britain becoming a 'nanny state', telling us what we should and should not do, and you only have to look on the forums of UK parenting and baby websites to see that many pregnant women are confused, worried and bewildered by the bombardment of advice they get from officials, doctors and others. We cannot tell you whether you should drink or not; but we can give you the information so that you can make an informed decision.

You probably know by now that the 'riskiest' time in terms of the baby's development and risk of miscarriage is the first trimester, so many women choose to abstain during that period and then have the odd tipple after that.

A survey by the charity Tommy's revealed that 40% of women in the UK drank in pregnancy and that 28% drank more than the previously recommended two units a week.

Sobering facts?

We do know that alcohol passes from a woman's blood stream into the baby's through the placenta, and that the baby's liver is very immature, so excessive drinking is very likely to harm your baby. This includes binge drinking – more than 7.5 units on one occasion. Women who drink more than six units a day have babies who are at significant risk of developing fetal alcohol syndrome, a condition that causes facial deformities, restricted growth and learning and behavioural difficulties. Research in 2010 revealed that children with fetal alcohol syndrome are also much more likely to suffer from epilepsy.

If you drink heavily in pregnancy you are also more likely to:

- have a miscarriage in the first trimester
- suffer a stillbirth
- have a low weight baby
- have a baby prone to illness.

 The latest figures show that, for every 1,000 live births, between one and two babies are born with fetal alcohol syndrome. This means of the 700,000 babies that are born annually in the UK, between 700 and 1,400 have this condition.

> **WORDS FROM THE PROFESSIONALS:** You would have to be drinking three very large glasses of wine every day to put your baby at risk of fetal alcohol syndrome, so don't scare yourself unnecessarily if you have the odd one or two in your pregnancy, or if you had a drink before you knew you were pregnant.

If you are usually a heavy drinker, you should tell your midwife so she can provide you with the support and advice you need to reduce your alcohol intake and monitor your baby closely.

Having given you all the bad news, here's something to make you feel better: a large 2008 study by UCL in the UK revealed that boys born to mothers who drank lightly in pregnancy (one or two units a week) were better behaved (40% less likely to have conduct problems) and were able to recognise more letters, shapes and numbers at the age of three than children born to mothers who abstained during pregnancy. Girls born to light-drinking mothers also fared 30% better.

A 2010 Danish study found that women who drink more than 4.5 units of alcohol a week in pregnancy were more likely to give birth to sons with a lower sperm count, so you might think about that second glass of wine if you want to become a granny in future.

Your choice

There is plenty of research on this topic, and whilst there is conclusive evidence that heavy drinking will have a detrimental effect on your baby, there doesn't seem to be any hard evidence proving that the odd drink will do your baby any harm.

If you are going to spend your whole pregnancy fretting after the occasional indulgence, it's probably best if you do give up booze, because we know that worry and anxiety are not good for you or your baby.

If you want to have the odd glass and promise to stick to one drink, once or twice a week, there doesn't seem to be a definitive reason not to allow yourself the odd treat, but ultimately the decision is yours.

If you do want to give up or cut down on alcohol, consider these alternatives.

- Switch to low-alcohol or alcohol-free versions of beer or cider. Served chilled in the summer they can as refreshing as the real thing.

- Many companies specialise in alcohol-free wines. www.alcoholfree.co.uk has a big selection, including mixed cases, so you can try them all and find your favourite.

- If you are pregnant in the winter, there are some nice mulled drinks and teas that are alcohol-free and quite warming for the body and soul.

'I have started drinking the odd half a Guinness occasionally now I'm six months, and have a small glass of red wine once a week, but haven't missed alcohol.'

Ruth, first pregnancy

Know your limits

If you do decide to enjoy the odd tipple during your pregnancy, it's essential that you know how many units you are having each time. Measures are definitely getting larger, so study the table below to check that you are not consuming more units than you should. You also need to take into account the strength of the wine: there is definitely a trend for more 'powerful' wines from Chile, South Africa and the USA, so check the alcohol by volume (ABV) on the back of the bottle before you quaff.

WINE	ABV 12%	ABV 14%
Small (125ml) glass of wine	1.5 units	1.75 units
Standard (175ml) glass of wine	2.1 units	2.45 units
Large (250ml) glass of wine	3 units	3.5 units

From this table you can see that you are exceeding your daily unit allowance just by drinking one standard glass of wine, and that gets even higher if the wine is strong.

DRINK	UNITS
330ml bottle of 5% strength lager	1.7
Pint of 5% strength lager	2.8
25ml of spirit	1
35ml of spirit (usual pub measure)	1.4
Double (50ml) measure of spirit	2
275ml bottle of alcopop	1.4

Stick to one bottle of beer or a pub measure of spirit and a mixer to stay on the safe side.

When to worry

On page 14 we've already mentioned that if you went out and drank alcohol before you knew you were pregnant (even if you exceeded six units in one sitting) it is unlikely that you have done your baby any lasting damage. It is prolonged heavy drinking and binge drinking in pregnancy that does the harm. If you are having trouble giving up or cutting down, do seek help from your GP or midwife, who can refer you for specialist help. Your baby will thank you for it.

SMOKING

In England in 2013 13% of women smoked during pregnancy, ranging from 6% in London to 20% in the North East. Among the under twenties it's fallen from 45% in 2002 to 25% in 2011.

Research in 2012 suggests that women who smoke during pregnancy are more likely to have a child with high functioning autism.

If you didn't manage to stop smoking before you conceived, once your pregnancy is confirmed you should make every effort to quit for the sake of your unborn child. Take a look at the risks below: if they don't convince you to quit – or at the very least, cut down drastically – nothing will.

- According to research by the Health Education Authority, if you smoke during your pregnancy your risk of miscarriage increases by around 25%.

- You have a 50% increased risk of stillbirth if you smoke throughout your pregnancy, but if you quit during the first trimester your risk drops to the same as a non-smoker.

- Latest health figures show that babies born to smokers are on average 8oz lighter than babies born to non-smokers. (Some women see this as a positive thing, wrongly thinking giving birth will be easier, but just remember the baby may be lighter because his brain is lighter due to reduced brain development.) New Canadian research from 2012 shows they are also more likely to become obese teenagers.

- Smoking has been shown to increase the chance of birth defects such as a cleft palate.

- You're more likely to suffer a placental abruption – the partial or complete detachment of the placenta – if you smoke.

- Babies born to smokers are more likely to be born prematurely at any time from 24 to 37 weeks.

- Your baby is more likely to have respiratory problems (such as asthma and chest infections) after birth.

- According to The Foundation for the Study of Infant Deaths, if you smoke one to nine cigarettes a day during pregnancy, you are four times more likely to have a baby die as a result of cot death than is a non-smoker.

- A study in Denmark in 2010 found that smoking increased your risk of having a baby born with crossed eyes by 26%.

- A leading reproduction biologist has recently discovered that smoking in pregnancy can reduce your baby boy's sperm count and affect his future fertility.

Stubbing out the habit

It isn't always easy to give up smoking: according to ASH (Action on Smoking & Health), in certain areas of the UK as many as 33% of pregnant women continue to smoke. However, it can be paramount to the health of your baby that you try to quit. If you want to give up, make sure you see your GP or ask your midwife to put you in touch with a health professional who can help you safely quit for good. You can also check out the NHS website at www.smokefree.nhs.uk, or call the NHS smoking pregnancy helpline on 0800 169 9 169. You can use any of the cigarette substitutes such as gums, patches etc.

'I do miss smoking, but that's easier to deal with since people can't smoke inside public places anymore.'

Virginia, first pregnancy

Sometimes your body gives you the helping hand you need to quit: many women who were committed smokers pre-pregnancy found it quite easy to stop in the first trimester, because they were so queasy and sick that the last thing in the world they wanted was a ciggie. However, quitting cold-turkey can also leave both you and your baby stressed out, so make sure you wean yourself down to a bare minimum as soon as possible, and then aim to quit completely as you adjust. Research is currently underway to see if exercise can help women to quit.

> **WORDS FROM THE PROFESSIONALS:** If your partner smokes, you need to encourage him to give up too. Not only can you support each other, but your home will be smoke-free, making it a much safer environment for your newborn. Passive smoking, including toxins from his hair and body, are dangerous for you and the baby.

The risk of having a baby with missing or deformed limbs or a cleft lip is over 25% higher if you smoke during pregnancy.

Research shows that passive smoking (ie smoke products on hair, clothes and skin of people who smoke as well as in the air around them) is harmful to children, so try to persuade friends and family to quit too, rather than just going outside for a fag.

DRUGS

Although it's fairly obvious that illegal recreational drugs will be harmful to your baby, you also need to realise that if you take a regular prescription drug you may need to change your dosage, and even if you have a simple headache you will need to reconsider the type of painkiller you might normally reach for.

Prescription drugs

If you have a chronic or long-term condition that requires regular medication, ideally you would have discussed the condition and its treatment with your GP, the doctor you see at the hospital or an obstetrician before you conceived. Assuming you didn't quite get round to it, then you must tell your GP that you are pregnant as soon as it's confirmed, in case your drugs need to be changed or the dosage needs to be altered. Do not stop taking prescription drugs without seeking medical advice first. If you are advised to start on a prescription drug while pregnant, always remind the prescriber that you are pregnant – many drugs are safe, including, for example, most antibiotics.

Over-the-counter drugs

Pregnant women should avoid over-the-counter medicines and drugs that you normally buy from the chemist or pharmacy. If you do buy over-the-counter drugs, you must first check with the pharmacist that they are safe to take in pregnancy: they are trained to know what is safe to take. If you have a pain that will not go away, you can take paracetamol as long as you stick to the recommended dose (but not ibuprofen as this can cause birth defects), and if you suffer from heartburn, a common pregnancy ailment, Gaviscon is perfectly safe to swig in moderation.

Remember it's not just products you take orally that could be risky: some creams you put on your skin could also harm your baby, so read the instructions of any product carefully before you use it. If it does not clearly state that it is safe to use in pregnancy, make sure that you ask a pharmacist, your GP, midwife, or call NHS 111 before you use it.

Homeopathic drugs

Homeopathy can play a very useful part in pregnancy as *most* of the remedies are safe to use (although not all). If you buy anything homeopathic over the counter and there isn't a qualified homeopath to advise you, do check with your midwife before you take it, because some 'natural' remedies do carry risks and it won't have been carefully scrutinised for safety in the same way as conventional medicines. You need to remember that even though something is herbal, it might still be harmful. For example, essential oils can be very dangerous in pregnancy, so double-check everything before you use it.

Illegal drugs

If you continue to take recreational drugs once you know you are pregnant, you will undoubtedly put your health and that of your baby at risk.

There is plenty of research to show that taking illegal drugs in pregnancy is a bad idea, and here are some of the reasons why you should stop before you conceive, or, failing that, as soon as your pregnancy is confirmed.

- Regular use of cannabis during pregnancy may cause fetal growth restriction and low birth weight.

- Amphetamines (speed) can cause heart problems and congenital deformities.

- Ecstasy use can result in low-weight babies.

- Half of the babies born to heroin-using mothers will be born early, and there is also an increased risk of stillbirth. If a baby is born alive he will still be addicted to heroin, so he also will need specialist care while he goes through withdrawal.

- Cocaine can trigger miscarriage, early labour or placental abruption, give your baby physical disabilities or brain damage and may cause a baby to die in the uterus.

If you were using drugs on a one-off or occasional basis before you knew you were pregnant, do mention it to your doctor or midwife in case they want to run any additional antenatal checks. They won't judge you and it's best that they have a clear picture of your health and lifestyle. If you have an addiction to drugs, we cannot stress enough the need for you to seek professional help immediately to minimise the risks to you and your baby. If you want to speak to someone in confidence you can always call the National Drugs Helpline (0800 77 66 00), and it will put you in touch with people or organisations that can help you.

X-RAYS

The risk from diagnostic X-rays is low, but if it's essential to have one in your pregnancy the radiographer will still do everything she can to protect your unborn child. If an X-ray is non-urgent, she'll probably wait until your baby is born. For example, a chest X-ray has the same amount of radiation as 10 days of background radiation in the general atmosphere, or a one-way flight from the UK to New York. If you need an X-ray at the dentist's he will provide a special protective apron to cover your bump.

CAFFEINE

You'd think, with all that abstinence, you'd be allowed to stick your feet up and enjoy a cuppa whenever you felt like it, but sadly you can't, because too much caffeine during pregnancy can cause low birth weight in babies. There have also been some studies indicating that excessive caffeine consumption can lead to miscarriage. There's not only the health of your baby to consider: excessive caffeine intake can also trigger or worsen a range of general health problems in the mother, such as insomnia, headaches, high blood pressure and dehydration, so think before you drink!

'I found Mother Nature to be very helpful when it came to caffeine. I used to have at least three Starbucks skinny cappuccinos every day at work, but the minute I knew I was pregnant even the smell of it made me want to heave, and it cured me of a lifelong addiction as I still barely drink the stuff now.'

Jane, first pregnancy

The Food Standards Agency (FSA) advises 200mg of caffeine a day as the safe limit for consumption during pregnancy. That's just two mugs of instant coffee or even less if the coffee is strong. Caffeine is also found in lesser amounts in tea, cola, chocolate and some medicines.

How much caffeine does it contain?

- Mug of instant coffee = 100mg

- Mug of filter or ground coffee = 140mg

- Mug of tea = 75mg

- Can of cola = up to 40mg

- Can of energy drink = up to 80mg

- 50g bar of plain chocolate = about 50mg

- 50g of milk chocolate = about 25mg

How to keep your caffeine consumption within safe limits

Here are a few tips to help you live without your daily cuppa:

- Switch to decaf versions of your favourite hot drinks.

- Try fruit teas: they have no caffeine in them and can be quite refreshing served hot or iced.

- Switch to caffeine-free cola.

- Try having a glass of water instead.

WORDS FROM THE PROFESSIONALS: Watch your consumption of herb teas: green tea has been linked to birth defects and might contain unfamiliar ingredients that may be harmful in pregnancy. For example, red raspberry leaf has been linked to inducing contractions, so only drink it if you're full term and trying to get labour started!

Finally, if you do exceed the safe limit occasionally, don't beat yourself up about it; it's unlikely to do your baby any damage as long as it's an occasional thing.

FOOD

In pregnancy your immune system is suppressed, which means you have a greater chance of picking up certain types of infections, and there are certain bugs that can have a harmful affect on your unborn child. If you suspect you have contracted anything potentially dangerous from food you should contact your GP as soon as possible, as he may be able to treat you quickly and prevent the infection spreading to your baby.

Before we start . . .

In this section we go through the reasons why some foods aren't recommended during pregnancy, but you mustn't get too hung up about what you ate before you knew you were pregnant, or worry about an occasional lapse during pregnancy: normally, the chances of your baby being harmed are minute. We've included the most commonly avoided foods here, but it's not a definitive list.

Meat

Undercooked or raw meat can harbour the toxoplasma parasite, which causes the illness toxoplasmosis. In the UK, it is relatively uncommon and most of us have not had it – it normally causes mild flu-like symptoms in a healthy adult – but if contracted by an unborn child it can cause illness or birth defects, miscarriage or stillbirth.

Around 800 women a year contract toxoplasmosis during pregnancy and around 80 babies are seriously affected. Given that over 700,000 babies are born in the UK each year, you can see that this figure is very small. If you contract toxoplasmosis in early pregnancy your baby is less likely to be affected (although you are more at risk of miscarriage).

> **WORDS FROM THE PROFESSIONALS:** The toxoplasma parasite can also be found in cat poo, so if you have a cat be careful when you're changing the litter tray, and wear gloves while gardening.

If you suspect you contracted toxoplasmosis in the three months prior to pregnancy or during pregnancy itself, you should see your doctor as soon as possible. The blood tests for toxoplasmosis do not make it easy to tell whether you have recently caught it or whether you got it some months ago and are no longer infectious. In the UK, therefore, the blood tests are not carried out very often in pregnancy, as the test can cause more confusion than it resolves. If it seems you have had toxoplasmosis in pregnancy, then you may be prescribed an antibiotic drug to reduce the chance of the infection being passed to your baby. Amniocentesis can confirm whether it has passed to your baby, and if this is the case you may be given treatment to reduce the possibility of, or prevent, your baby being born with problems.

How can I prevent it?

- To eliminate the risk entirely, ensure all meat products are well cooked, particularly poultry and barbeque items such as steak, sausages and burgers.

- Heat ready-meals or convenience food thoroughly, ensuring it is hot all the way through.

- Pay attention to food hygiene – in particular, the storage and preparation of raw meat.

- Avoid raw meats such as salami, Parma ham and pastrami. These are fine if they are cooked (as a pizza topping, for example), but not in their raw form.

- Delegate changing the cat's litter tray to someone else if possible, and always wash hands very carefully before any food preparation or eating.

- Wear gloves when gardening and wash your hands thoroughly afterwards.

Cheese

Cheese is a fantastic food to eat in pregnancy because it is a good source of protein and calcium. However, you should not eat soft cheeses such as Camembert or Brie; blue veined cheeses such as Stilton or Dolcelatte; or soft cheeses made from unpasteurised milk, as these cheeses are more susceptible to bacterial growth such as listeria – a bacteria which can cause an infection called listeriosis.

Listeriosis is an incredibly rare infection occurring in three in 25,000 pregnancies, although it is 15 times more common than in the non-pregnant population. It causes mild flu-like symptoms in healthy adults but can lead to serious illnesses such as meningitis, pneumonia, jaundice, premature birth or even death in an unborn baby. If you contract listeriosis in pregnancy you will be given antibiotics, and if your newborn is affected he can be treated in the same way.

How can I prevent it?

Listeria is found in unpasteurised milk, soft cheese, soil and some animal faeces. If you stick to the list below and maintain scrupulous hygiene standards in the kitchen, you should minimise the chances of catching this infection.

 There seems to be conflicting advice on whether you should eat feta cheese or not, so unless you're truly addicted it's probably best to give it a miss for the next few months.

Cheeses you should avoid
Mould-ripened soft cheeses: Brie, Blue Brie, Camembert, Chaumes, Chèvre (goat's cheese with a white rind), Pont l'Eveque, Taleggio, Vacherin

Blue-veined cheeses: Bleu d'Auvergne, Blue Wensleydale, Cambazola, Danish Blue, Dolcelatte, Gorgonzola, Roquefort, Shropshire Blue, Stilton, Tomme

Soft, unpasteurised cheeses: Goat and sheep's cheeses

Cheeses you can safely eat
Hard cheeses: Babybel, Caerphilly, Cheddar, Cheshire, Derby, Double Gloucester, Edam, Emmenthal, Gouda, Gruyere, Halloumi, Havarti, Jarlsberg, Lancashire, Manchego, Parmesan, Pecorino (hard), Provolone, Red Leicester

Soft and processed cheeses: Boursin, cottage cheese, cream cheese, Mascarpone, Mozzarella, Philadelphia, processed cheese (eg cheese spread), Quark, Ricotta

Getting around the rules

If you can't live without your blue or soft cheeses, cooking them will destroy the bacteria. So if you fancy a goat's cheese and Parma ham pizza, Brie in breadcrumbs, or Stilton soup, as long as you serve them piping hot there should be no risk to you or your baby.

Eggs

Undercooked eggs and poultry may contain salmonella – a bacterium that causes very severe food poisoning. If you contract salmonella while you are pregnant you are unlikely to harm your baby, but it can cause severe dehydration that can lead to complications and possible hospitalisation.

You should always cook your eggs properly and avoid food that contains raw or partially cooked egg. Look out for eggs with a lion stamp on them: the hens have been inoculated against salmonella so in theory the eggs should be safer to eat.

Foods containing egg you should avoid

- Homemade ice cream

- Hollandaise sauce

- Fresh mayonnaise

- Certain uncooked puddings such as chocolate mousse and tiramisu

WORDS FROM THE PROFESSIONALS: If you are at a restaurant or having dinner with friends, it is a good idea to check that the food you are eating doesn't contain raw or partially-cooked egg.

Foods containing egg you can eat
Shop-bought versions of all of the above should be fine because they will have been made with pasteurised eggs – ie heated to a point where the bacteria are destroyed.

You can also eat slightly runny boiled or fried eggs, as long as the white is cooked through properly and is no longer translucent.

Ice cream

You can still eat ice cream while you are pregnant, but only shop-bought varieties: not soft ice cream (like a Mr Whippy). Soft ice cream that comes from a machine is kept at a higher temperature and there is a danger that the machine could also be harbouring germs. (Ice cream vans never strike us as the most sanitary places, and as they are powered by generators you don't know whether the power to the machinery is consistent.) So if you get the urge for an ice cream when you are out and about, stick to a tub or visit an ice cream parlour.

Liver

In the 1960s and 1970s pregnant women were encouraged to eat buckets of liver, and as it was a fairly cheap form of protein they dutifully obliged. These days liver seems to give most people the shivers, which is just as well as it contains quite a high amount of vitamin A – which can cause birth defects if taken in an extreme quantity.

Official guidance is to avoid all liver products, including liver pâté and sausage, but please don't worry if you ate some before you knew you

 Not all bacteria are harmful: those probiotic yoghurts and drinks that contain 'friendly' bacteria are perfectly safe in pregnancy, as is sour cream.

were pregnant; you'd need to be eating a tonne a day to have done any damage to your baby.

> **WORDS FROM THE PROFESSIONALS:** Cod liver oil tablets also contain vitamin A, so stop taking them as soon as you know you are pregnant, to be on the safe side.

Raw (unpasteurised) dairy products

Unpasteurised dairy products can harbour bacteria such as listeria, salmonella and toxoplasma, so you should avoid them in pregnancy.

Most milk products you find in the shops are pasteurised (unpasteurised milk is normally only found in specialist shops and has a green top), but if you have an intolerance to dairy and usually drink goat's or sheep's milk, you need to check before you buy as they can often be unpasteurised. Soy milk is a good alternative.

Check the labelling on cheeses before you buy, as quite a few are made with unpasteurised milk, though you only need to worry about the soft ones: hard unpasteurised cheese, such as parmesan, is considered safe.

Fishy tales

If you're looking to follow a healthy diet while you're pregnant you might think that fish is a good source of protein. You need to be aware, though, that there are some risks attached to different types of fish, so don't break out the salt and vinegar just yet.

Shellfish

It is sensible to avoid raw or undercooked shellfish, such as mussels, oysters and prawns, because they also harbour salmonella and another, rather wonderfully named, germ: campylobacter.

You can eat cooked shellfish as long as you are satisfied it has been cooked properly, but it's probably best to avoid it at a buffet when you don't know how long it has been hanging around. It's also advisable to give fish stalls a miss unless you are sure of the standards of hygiene and quality of the food.

Raw fish

The Food Standards Agency's advice on eating fish such as smoked salmon, mackerel and trout is that the risks are negligible, but as it is smoked rather than cooked it is classified as partially raw. If you can't live without it you're probably best buying it pre-packaged from a reputable supermarket, refrigerating it and eating it within the sell-by period.

Supermarket sushi is considered to be safe because it is normally frozen beforehand, which will kill any parasites. If you are making it at home, freeze it for 24 hours before consumption, and if you are eating it at a restaurant do check that it has been frozen before you tuck in.

Oily fish

Oily fish is very nutritious and contains omega oils that can boost the development of your baby's nervous system, and vitamin D, which is good for both your and your baby's bones. The Food Standards Agency (FSA) advises that you have only two portions a week of mackerel, salmon or trout, though, as they have been found to contain pollutants.

Fish with high mercury content

Shark, swordfish and marlin may contain high levels of mercury – which has been shown to damage a baby's nervous system – so you should not eat it at all.

Tuna is considered safer, but even so the FSA recommends no more than two fresh steaks or four cans of it a week.

Fresh pâté

There's a tiny risk of listeria in fresh pâtés, which is why official advice warns against eating even the vegetable varieties. If you can't live without it, pâtés in vacuum packs or tins are considered to be safe, but you should avoid liver pâté entirely because of the vitamin A risk.

Nuts

The latest advice from the Department of Health is that eating peanuts during pregnancy is not putting your baby at risk of developing a peanut allergy – indeed, there is some evidence to show that eating peanuts during pregnancy might protect your baby from developing such an allergy himself.

Having said that, guidelines also state that if you or your partner are in a high risk group, ie either of you has a peanut allergy or other allergic reactions such as eczema, you might want to steer clear of peanuts and peanut products during pregnancy.

If you or the baby's father are allergy sufferers, you might want to chat to your midwife or GP about it before you make any decisions.

All other nuts are safe and an excellent source of protein in pregnancy.

Bagged salads

You are advised to re-wash salads that have been washed and bagged, as bugs can breed in the bags in the chiller cabinet. It goes without saying that you should also wash all vegetables and salads thoroughly to remove any traces of dirt, as toxoplasmosis is transmitted through soil.

Barbeques and buffets

We've already stressed that undercooked meat is a breeding ground for bacteria, so ensure that anything you eat from the barbeque is not only properly cooked but also fresh, as bacteria can breed on food that has been left uncovered in a warm place.

If you go on a picnic, make sure that you put plenty of those ice blocks in your cool bag, place the bag in a shady spot before you eat, and don't leave it festering in the hot sun for hours whilst you snack. If you are at a party and suspect the food has been hanging around for a while, stick to hot food if possible and avoid prawns and cold meat platters.

Deli foods/takeaways/restaurants

Don't buy sandwiches from a deli where all the sandwich fillings look a bit tired and crusty: chances are they have probably been in the shop too long. If the eating area in a restaurant or café looks unclean, the chances are the kitchen hygiene is not up to much either (the state of the toilets is often a very good indication of the cleanliness standards of any food establishment). The best advice is: if you don't like the look of the place, don't eat anything.

Don't buy food from market stalls (even from farmers' markets) if it is sitting around in the sun all day with no refrigeration.

The rule of thumb is that if something is freshly cooked and hot it should be fine, and if you did buy a slice of cold quiche from the local deli and are a bit worried about it, a blast in the oven for 15 minutes should certainly kill off any harmful bugs.

Just remember: if you wanted to minimise any risk of food poisoning or contamination you'd never eat out during your pregnancy, but that's not realistic or feasible, so it's best to use common sense and follow your instincts.

Eating on holiday

If you go abroad while you are pregnant, it can be very difficult to control what you eat. It can be tricky if you are staying in a hotel that operates a buffet service at lunch or dinner; the best advice is to stick to hot food whenever possible, as in warm climates cold buffets are a breeding ground for bugs. If you can, eat food you know is freshly cooked to order, like crêpes or pizza. Sometimes it's a good idea to eat popular local food because it's more likely to be made fresh/have a quicker turnaround than some obscure Westernised dish on the menu.

Safety first

To minimise the risk of getting food poisoning during your pregnancy, follow the simple steps below:

- Keep your kitchen clean.

- Wash your hands thoroughly before and after handling food.

- Wash fruit and vegetables properly.

- Defrost frozen food thoroughly, preferably in the fridge.

- Store raw and cooked food on different shelves in the fridge. Raw food should be kept towards the bottom as it is colder there, and also so it can't drip juice or blood onto the food below it.

- Cover food in the fridge.

- Make sure the fridge and freezer are at the correct temperature: 0–4°C for fridges and −18°C for freezers.

- Chill or freeze food as soon as you get home. If you buy food in your lunch hour, store it in the fridge at work; don't leave it by your desk.

- Have separate chopping boards for raw and cooked foods.

- Eat food within the sell-by date.

- Keep pets out of the kitchen if possible and definitely off the work surfaces.

You don't need to go on a special diet – just make sure it's balanced, with plenty of variety.

HEALTHY EATING

A study in 2007 indicated that pregnant women who ate junk food were more likely to have offspring with a sweet tooth, and another recent survey showed that children born to mothers who ate lots of junk food were more likely to suffer health problems such as heart disease and diabetes in later life, so it makes sense to adopt a healthy diet when you are pregnant.

Here's a quick summary of the foods you should be eating in pregnancy and the reasons why they are beneficial to you and your baby.

Eat regularly

It's important to eat three 'balanced' meals a day – with a combination of food groups at each – to keep your blood sugar levels steady and to cope with the demands that pregnancy puts on your body. You may also have to top that up with healthy snacks to boost flagging energy levels. Ideal snacks to keep in your drawer or bag include bags of dried or fresh fruit, carrot or celery sticks and crispbreads or rice cakes.

'Being pregnant has made me look at my diet more closely. Both my husband and I are pretty poor cooks so we tend to eat a lot of convenience food. With my job I'm often at the office until the early hours, so we normally just get pizza or a curry delivered. I'm trying to be much healthier now and include more fruit and vegetables in my diet, as well as trying to make sure I eat proper meals – not just grabbing snacks.'

Amanda, first pregnancy

Drink lots (of water)

It's really important to keep yourself well hydrated when you are pregnant, so make sure you drink lots of fluid. Water is the healthiest choice, and it's a good idea to keep a small bottle of it with you at all times in case you get stuck travelling or in a meeting. You can supplement it throughout the day with teas, juices, milk and smoothies, but keep an eye on your caffeine levels and watch the sugar in some squashes and fruit juices, as they can be 'empty' calories.

Fruit and vegetables

Given the explosion of recent government advertising, you should be well aware that you should be aiming to eat five portions of fruit and vegetables a day, and that they can be fresh, dried, frozen or tinned. If you are not a real fruit or veggie fan, juices and smoothies are very palatable ways of getting a fruity fix, and they're also good if you are finding food hard to stomach in the early days of pregnancy. Tomato-based sauces are great with pasta, and you can also purée other vegetables into them to get the nutritional benefits without them tasting overly veggie. (You'll get very adept at that at weaning time too!) Eating lots of fruit and vegetables also keeps your system 'moving' as they are full of fibre, and that's important because pregnant women are prone to constipation.

Protein

Protein is very important to keep you fit and healthy and plays an important role in the development of your baby, so you need to ensure that you have plenty in your diet.

Protein-rich foods include lean white and red meat, fish (aim for two portions a week), eggs, nuts and pulses. Protein-rich foods are also rich sources of iron – another vital nutrient for your developing baby.

Dairy

Dairy products such as cheese, milk and yoghurt are great sources of calcium, which is important in the development of your baby's teeth and bones. You don't need to eat any more than usual in pregnancy, though: the recommended amount for women is 700mg a day, which is a glass of milk (230mg), a pot of yoghurt (225mg) and a matchbox-sized piece of cheese (288mg).

Carbohydrates (starch)

A balanced diet should include starch in the form of bread, rice, pasta or potatoes. You should try to include a portion at each mealtime, and preferably opt for wholegrain versions, as they are a better source of fibre and contain more nutrients.

VITAMINS AND MINERALS

Having covered the main food groups you should be eating, you also need to address whether your intake of vitamins and minerals is sufficient to meet the needs of you and your growing baby and decide whether you need to take additional supplements.

Iron

Iron is important for healthy blood and, as you also need to keep your baby well supplied during pregnancy, it's important to eat plenty of the following: red meat; leafy green vegetables such as spinach, watercress and broccoli; eggs; dried fruits such as apricots or figs; pulses or beans; wholemeal bread and fortified breakfast cereals; and (yippee!) dark chocolate. Your iron levels will be checked during your antenatal appointments, as anaemia is very common in pregnancy, so it's worth trying to follow an iron rich diet (anything to avoid those constipation-inducing iron tablets!). See page 76 for more on anaemia.

Vitamin D

Vitamin D ensures your baby's bones develop properly and also boosts the content of your breast milk, which is already in production during pregnancy. Food sources that are rich in Vitamin D include fortified margarines, meat, eggs and oily fish.

Sunlight is the greatest provider of vitamin D, meaning dark-skinned women and those who cover their skin or don't go outside often are more at risk of vitamin D deficiency, as are those who wear strong sun block.

The FSA recommends that all pregnant women take a 10-microgram supplement of vitamin D daily, beginning when they start trying for a baby through to breastfeeding. Pregnancy vitamins have folic acid and the vitamin D supplement in them, although they are often expensive and contain substances you don't need. It is important not to take 'normal' vitamins as these will contain vitamin A, which you should not take whilst pregnant.

Calcium

We have already mentioned that calcium is also important for the development of teeth and bones. If you are not keen on dairy products, other good sources include canned sardines, wholemeal bread, baked beans, nuts (such as almonds) and green vegetables (such as broccoli). Certain cereals, juices, soy products and tofu are fortified with calcium, so do check the labels of these products when you buy them.

Folic acid

Women planning on becoming pregnant are advised to take 400 micrograms of folic acid as soon as they start trying for a baby until week 12 of pregnancy. Folic acid has been shown to reduce the chance of your baby developing a neural tube defect such as spina bifida, and therefore it is advisable that you take this supplement and also eat a diet rich in folates. Folate-rich foods include green vegetables, brown rice and fortified bread and cereals.

Latest advice shows that folic acid also reduces the chance of cleft lip and heart defects in the baby, and even halves the chance that he will have autism.

Omega 3: essential fatty acids

Omega 3 is thought to boost your baby's brain and eyesight development. Oily fish is the best source: mackerel, sardines, kippers, salmon or fresh tuna. Canned fish is not as good, as most of the 'healthy' oils are removed in the canning process. If you're not keen on fish you can get some omega 3 from nuts and seeds. Some pregnancy vitamins also have omega 3 in them as well.

ANTENATAL SUPPLEMENTS

In theory you should get the nutrients you need from the food that you eat, so if you are following a healthy diet like the one outlined above you should not need to take extra supplements. However, the current Department of Health guidelines recommend that all women take 400 micrograms of folic acid for 12 weeks and 10 micrograms of vitamin D throughout a pregnancy.

If you do decide to take other supplements as well, make sure you buy a supplement developed specially for pregnancy.

Some vitamins can be quite expensive, but bear in mind that supermarket and chemist own brand labels will be just as good as those in fancy bottles, and if you are on benefits the government's Healthy Start programme (www.healthystart.nhs.uk) will provide them for free, so if you think you are eligible speak to your midwife.

If you take a mix of supplements, rather than a single pregnancy-specific dose, do ensure that you are not exceeding the recommended daily allowance (RDA) of anything (the RDA will be given on the bottle), as it could be harmful to your baby.

EATING FOR TWO

As we already saw in Chapter 3, the well worn cliché, 'I'm eating for two', is sadly a bit of a myth. You actually only need an extra 300 calories a day (max) to cope with the demands of pregnancy, and that's only in the third trimester, so if you had visions of stuffing your face with cream buns every day, think again!

The recent Centre for Maternal and Child Enquiries (CMACE)/RCOG guideline on obesity in pregnancy (2010) lists a depressingly long list of serious adverse outcomes that occur more frequently in obese pregnant women, and strongly encourages weight loss before conception, and healthy eating and appropriate exercise during pregnancy to minimise weight gain. These outcomes can include miscarriage, congenital anomaly in the baby, thromboembolism, gestational diabetes, pre-eclampsia, difficult labour and delivery, post-partum haemorrhage, stillbirth, neonatal death, wound infection and Caesarean section. Even more recently, the CMACE report (2011) shows that of the pregnant women who die, more are obese than the national average. So if you are overweight it is really important that you get advice on diet and exercise before and during your pregnancy.

You are also more prone to varicose veins, heartburn and breathlessness. Therefore, no matter how much you're craving chocolate cake, you need to maintain a healthy diet not only for your future health but for that of your child as well.

Be careful not to go the other way, though. Kate Moss may have said, 'Nothing tastes as good as skinny feels', but take it from us, nothing feels as good as a gorgeous, healthy baby in your arms. Only restrict your calorie intake or diet during pregnancy under strict guidance from a doctor – if you are overweight a diet may be advised, but you will be supported and monitored. There's real pressure on women to be slim these days, and it doesn't help when we see pictures of Gisele Bunchen and Heidi Klum striding down the catwalks in bikinis a month after giving birth. You are *supposed* to gain weight in pregnancy; after all, you have a growing baby and placenta to support. The box opposite shows the average distribution of weight gained during pregnancy.

Distribution of weight gained in pregnancy

(ON AVERAGE):

Baby: 7.5lb (3.4kg)

Placenta: 1.5lb (0.68kg)

Extra fluid: 3lb (1.36kg)

Increased blood: 2.5lb (1.25kg)

Amniotic fluid: 1.5lb (0.8kg)

Uterus: 2lb (0.9kg)

Fat deposits: 7lb (3.18kg)

Breasts: 1lb (0.5kg)

Total weight gain: 26.5lb (12kg)

How much weight should I gain, then?

In an ideal world you should be your ideal weight before you conceive; many overweight women are advised to lose weight before they become pregnant so they don't encounter the types of problems outlined above. If you are seriously underweight you may need to put on weight to improve your chances of conceiving – especially if your weight has affected your periods, as this will probably mean you are too underweight to ovulate. You may need to see a doctor to look into why you are underweight.

There are no official guidelines on this subject, but here are some figures to give you an idea of how much weight you should gain.

- As a general rule of thumb, most women gain an average of 12.5kg (about two stone).

- If you were a healthy weight before you got pregnant, you should expect to put on around 11kg (just under two stone), but there is no need to weigh yourself.

- If you were underweight before you got pregnant, you should aim to put on around 16.5kg (around three stone).

- If you were very overweight before you got pregnant, you should aim to put on no more than 6kg (around a stone), and ideally have a weight neutral pregnancy.

'I can't believe how wrong I was about what you can eat while you're pregnant. I always thought pregnancy meant you could eat as much as you wanted, but not only is there no such thing as eating for two, you don't get to eat whatever you want either! I miss goat's cheese, seafood (oysters, smoked salmon), saucisson, foie gras, pâté etc, so much – maybe if I wasn't French it wouldn't be so hard! It's so ironic that being pregnant means I get to eat fewer things than I used to.'

Virginia, first pregnancy

Gestational diabetes (GDM)

Diabetes occurs when the body doesn't make enough of the hormone insulin or when the body is resistant to the effects of insulin, resulting in high levels of blood sugar. Gestational diabetes is the same condition but is brought on by pregnancy. In pregnancy you need to make twice as much insulin to sustain both you and the baby, and many women are unable to do so. This is when the blood sugar levels rise and gestational diabetes develops. With gestational diabetes there is a risk that you will have a very big baby, meaning a complicated birth and Caesarean section are more likely.

Units will test either all or just some women for GDM at around 26 to 28 weeks gestation, so ask your midwife if you need a test. NICE recommends screening if:

- your BMI is greater than 30

- there is diabetes in a first degree relative

- a previous baby weighed more than 4.5kg at birth

- your ethnic origin is Afro-Caribbean, Asian or Middle-Eastern

- you are older than 30 years.

Healthy eating and exercise should keep your blood sugar levels under control, but you may need tablets or insulin injections if you develop this condition. You must make sure you get a check-up when the baby is around six weeks old, as in some women the diabetes doesn't go away. It also means that you have a much higher chance of getting diabetes in later life, so you should try to stick to the healthy living regimen you learnt in pregnancy, and make sure your GP checks your blood sugar every couple of years.

HEALTHY LIFESTYLE

Modern women are well aware of the health benefits of good diet and exercise. We have already outlined the advantages of eating well in pregnancy, but you should also be aware that even a moderate amount of exercise will do both you and your baby good.

What are the benefits of exercise in pregnancy?

If you exercise during your pregnancy you will find these benefits.

- It can improve flexibility, which may help during labour and birth.

- It will boost your general fitness and health, which will help you cope with the demands of a new baby.

- It will build muscle tone, which may help you regain your pre-pregnancy figure. Core muscle strength will also help you retain your posture and balance during pregnancy.

- It can help you sleep.

- It can improve circulation.

- It can alleviate constipation.

- It boosts your immune system.

- It will help keep your weight under control if you are finding it hard to resist those cream buns!

 Studies have shown that you may have a shorter labour time and fewer delivery complications if you keep fit during pregnancy.

What kind of exercise to do

Some women reading this will be committed gym bunnies; others will be committed couch potatoes. Whatever your level of fitness, you should be able to find that exercise is to be enjoyed rather than endured in pregnancy.

If you have never exercised regularly before, this is not the time to embark on a rigorous fitness regime, but there are several gentle options that will increase your fitness without you feeling the strain. If you want to join a class, make sure you join an antenatal fitness class: not only is it a great way to meet other pregnant women but you'll also be sure that the exercises are suitable in pregnancy. The NCT runs a Yoga for Pregnancy course that combines a normal antenatal class with yoga. If you need help finding a suitably qualified practitioner in your area, you can check out the website of the Guild of Pregnancy and Postnatal Exercise Instructors: www.postnatalexercise.co.uk. If you don't like the idea of classes or are too busy to attend them, there are heaps of pregnancy-specific DVDs out there for you to follow at home, but check with your doctor or midwife first if you are in any doubt about exercising.

EXERCISE AND BABY WEIGHT

A 2010 study from New Zealand showed that women who exercised for 40 minutes on an exercise bike up to five times a week had babies that were 143g lighter on average than babies born to mothers who did not exercise. There is a suggestion that babies born to exercising mothers may be less obesity prone, and by regularly exercising the mothers are keeping their babies 'fit in the womb'; however, more research is required to prove this theory.

If you are very fit and exercise regularly, you can continue to do so until your body tells you to slow down. It's OK for you to try to maintain your level of fitness, but don't try to improve it – even the mighty marathon runner Paula Radcliffe had to reduce her training when pregnant.

You may have to accept that you are not going to be at your peak of physical fitness and find new, gentler ways to exercise, but remember this is only temporary and your body will thank you for not overdoing it while it is trying to grow a new life.

A good tip to check that you are not over-exerting yourself is to do the 'talk test': if you are able to continue a conversation while exercising without catching your breath your body is coping with the activity.

Walking

This is the easiest and cheapest exercise option, as you don't have to pay to do it. Try to incorporate a half hour walk into your daily regime. If you have to drive to work, make sure that you take a walk at lunchtime. If you normally take public transport, consider getting off at an earlier stop to walk the last bit of the way or walk all the way if you can. You might find walking in the mornings easier (after the first trimester when you have got past all that sicky stuff) because the growing baby can take his toll on your energy levels.

Swimming

Swimming is ideal pregnancy exercise as the buoyancy of the water will support you and your bump; if you are not very fit you can take it at a gentle pace, or pound up and down the training lanes if you want to up the pace somewhat. The leg action used in the breaststroke can put strain on your lower back and pelvis – particularly if you swim with your head out of the water – so switch to front crawl if you suffer pain in that area.

Cycling

Cycling can be a nice gentle way of getting exercise, particularly in the early months. You should always wear a helmet for safety reasons, and the moment you start feeling unbalanced because of your bump or feel vulnerable cycling in traffic – which can be stressful even when you're not pregnant – switch to brisk walking.

Pilates

Pilates is a low-impact form of exercise and is considered one of the best forms of exercise for a pregnant woman. Pilates helps maintain and improve the condition of both your abdominal and pelvic floor muscles, meaning it can be most beneficial in pregnancy and birth. It also helps you with your posture, which can be a problem when you are waddling around with a big bump. You can buy Pilates in Pregnancy DVDs to follow at home if there are no specific classes in your area. If you already do Pilates, tell your instructor you are pregnant, as some exercises may not be suitable for you. If you want to find out more about this form of exercise visit www.pilates.co.uk.

Yoga

Yoga is a great stress buster in pregnancy as the breathing techniques can reduce muscle tension, help you sleep better and generally make you feel more relaxed. Yoga also keeps you supple, which is very helpful when it comes to giving birth as you may have to try a variety of positions to deliver comfortably. It is recommended that you seek medical advice from your doctor or midwife if you have not done yoga before, as there might be physical issues that may prevent you from practising safely. If you already take yoga classes, make sure that your teacher knows you are pregnant, as some yoga positions are not safe in the first trimester and you may need to switch to antenatal-specific yoga.

'My exercise regime has changed a lot. I'd signed up to do two triathlons this year, but have taken up yoga instead. I'm finding

It might seem blindingly obvious, but if the opportunities to walk during the day are limited, try to take the stairs rather than using the lift, as it will improve your level of fitness without you even trying too hard.

not going for runs quite tough as they always used to be a great way to unwind at the end of the day.'

Becky, first pregnancy

Aerobic exercise

Aerobic (otherwise known as cardiovascular or cardio for short) exercise is exercise that raises your heart rate, and includes power walking, running, dancing and low-impact aerobic classes. These can be safely continued in pregnancy as long as you don't overdo it. If you have never done aerobic exercise before, or you used to but your body is not up to it at the moment, stick to walking briskly or swimming to give your heart and muscles a gentle work out. Pregnancy is not a time to set a new personal best either!

High impact exercise

You need to be careful with high impact exercise, even if you are super fit, because pregnancy makes you more vulnerable to sprains and injuries. You might want to swap your step class for a dance class.

Some team sports have rules or restrictions in place for pregnant players so it is worth checking this with your local league.

Team sports

If you participate in team sports you really have to judge when to give up; once you have a baby growing inside you, a protective instinct inevitably takes over and most women don't want to indulge in a sport that could harm their baby. As a rule of thumb, once you begin to show, it's probably time to hang up your hockey boots. Sports such as rowing, weight training and tennis will expose you to the risk of muscle and back injuries; anything that involves balance (not easy when you have a huge bump) and the risk of falling, such as gymnastics, horse riding or skiing, is not recommended; and you probably don't need us to tell you that any sport that results in you getting walloped or tackled, like judo, rugby or football, isn't a great idea.

Be aware

Relaxin, the hormone that relaxes your ligaments and joints in preparation for birth, also makes them more prone to damage, which is why the biggest risk when exercising in pregnancy is injury. You should be aware that if you get excessively hot in the first trimester there is a small possibility that you could damage your baby's nervous system. If you did a particularly vigorous workout before you discovered you were pregnant, don't worry too much: you'd have to have worked yourself into a sweaty frenzy to get hot enough to do any damage.

Squeezy-peasy: the importance of pelvic floor exercises

If you do no other form of exercise during your pregnancy you really should do your pelvic floor exercises, and here's why: your pelvic floor is a layer of muscles that form a supportive 'hammock' for your bladder, bowel and uterus. Inevitably it really takes the strain of supporting your baby for nine months and also plays a key role in helping the baby down the birth canal, so it's really important (see www.nhs.uk for more details).

Earlier in the book we warned that if these muscles became really slack, you would leak urine when you coughed, exercised or laughed, so it's important you learn how to do your pelvic floor exercises. The thought of being a slave to panty liners should act as a big enough incentive, but if you want another reason to get squeezing, strong pelvic floor muscles also increase sensitivity during sex and strengthen orgasms, although that might be the last thing on your mind at the moment…

Your pelvic floor muscles are those that stop you peeing mid-flow. (Don't try it when you are actually passing urine: it's damn near impossible when you are pregnant and you should be emptying your bladder every time you pee.)

To do your pelvic floor exercises:

- tighten those muscles you would use when peeing.

- don't be tempted to tighten your tummy, buttock or thigh muscles as these won't help the pelvic floor.

- once you have identified the correct muscles, try squeezing and releasing them quickly 10 times.

- next, squeeze slowly and try to hold the muscles tightly for up to 10 seconds before relaxing. Repeat this 10 times too.

- try both sets of squeezes between four and six times a day.

A tip is to put random coloured stickers around the house, in your handbag, or in the car. You don't have to tell anyone what they are for and they'll act as a reminder to do a few squeezes. The beauty of these exercises is that no one will know you are doing them!

Exercise dos and don'ts in pregnancy

- **Do** warm up and warm down before and after exercise to minimise the risk of injury.

- **Do** invest in a decent pair of trainers: they will support your feet properly and assist your posture.

- **Do** aim to do half an hour of gentle exercise a day.

- **Do** wear loose, comfy clothes when you are exercising and invest in a sports bra.

- **Do** drink lots of fluids, particularly if you are sweating.

- **Do** listen to your body: if it is tired or achy give exercise a rest or do something gentle – it doesn't have to be strenuous to be beneficial.

- **Don't** exercise strenuously in hot weather.

- **Don't** exercise flat on your back after 16 weeks, as your baby presses on your blood vessels and may make you feel faint.

- **Don't** exercise to lose weight: you need to get fit, not thin.

When to stop

If you experience any of the following symptoms while exercising you should stop immediately and seek prompt medical advice:

- dizziness or feeling faint

- headache

- shortness of breath on exertion

- difficulty breathing

- pain or palpitations in your chest

- pain in your abdomen, back, pelvic, or pubic area

- weakness in your muscles

- pain or swelling in your leg(s)

- painful uterine contractions

- fewer movements from your baby

- leakage of your amniotic fluids

- vaginal bleeding.

'HAZARDOUS' ACTIVITIES

Being pregnant can mean that you have to change your lifestyle: not only in terms of what you eat and drink, but also how you carry out your beauty routine or clean your home. Here are a few areas that you'll need to review now that you're pregnant.

Meeting other people

Small ones…

Your friends' children may pose a hazard when you are pregnant because toddlers are prone to contagious diseases such as chickenpox, measles and Pavovirus B19 (slapped cheek disease). You will be checked for rubella immunity early on in your pregnancy by your midwife, and as most of us have had these childhood illnesses you should be immune anyway, but if you didn't contract them as a child and you do come into contact with someone contagious, contact your GP or midwife so they can run tests and treat you and your baby if necessary.

And big ones…

Bird flu, swine flu (H1N1), not to mention the old-fashioned regular influenza, are all things that you might pick up from the people around you. Pregnant women are more prone to developing severe or dangerous complications from flu, so usually the advice is to have the vaccinations. The problem with pregnancy and infectious disease is that you can't wrap yourself in cotton wool and avoid human contact for nine months, but you are more likely to catch a contagious disease because your immune system is weaker than normal. Unfortunately, results published in 2011 show that infection has become a more common cause of death in pregnancy in the UK than in previous years. So, if you do get unwell make sure you seek medical advice quickly, and ensure you maintain really good hand hygiene, washing hands before and after food preparation, and before and after going to the toilet. Group A streptococcus causes a sore throat and a 'cold', but if it gets into the uterus via the vagina it can make you or the baby very unwell.

There was an outbreak of whooping cough in 2013, so pregnant women are advised to have a booster vaccination after 28 weeks – this is for the baby, to ensure he is born with enough protection to last until his own vaccines are due. Sadly, quite a few very young babies died in the UK last year from whooping cough.

It makes sense to avoid being around ill people if you can, and if it is recommended that you have a jab to protect against an infection, make sure you discuss all the pros and cons with the doctor so you don't spend the rest of your pregnancy worrying about it.

To tan or not to tan?

Some pregnant women suffer from uneven skin pigmentation during pregnancy (chloasma), and exposure to the sun or UV rays will make it worse. If you do start getting uneven brown patches on your skin, remember to wear a hat and slap on the sunscreen when you are out in the sun.

Avoid tanning pills and injections altogether while pregnant as most brands are unlicensed and untested.

Using sunbeds in pregnancy is not recommended: firstly because research has linked increased UV rays to folic acid deficiency, and secondly because you increase the risk of chloasma.

If you can't live without fake tan, be aware that your skin is much more sensitive when you are pregnant, so do a patch test first to check that you don't get an allergic reaction. Some experts recommend you don't use fake tan, presumably because of the chemical content (you only have to smell the stuff to know it's laden with them), so it's down to you whether you can bear to be 'pale and interesting' instead.

Getting hot and steamy

Carry on in the bedroom by all means, but give saunas, jacuzzis, steam baths and hot tubs a miss during pregnancy. We have already explained that overheating, particularly in the first trimester, can affect your baby's nervous system, which is why anything that raises your body temperature such as hot tubs and saunas should be avoided when you are pregnant. Later in pregnancy, excessive heat can push up your baby's heart rate and your blood pressure – making you feel dizzy or faint – so that's another two good reasons why you should give them a miss.

Likewise, although there's nothing nicer than lying in the bath having a long soak when you are pregnant, given the reasons above, do make sure it's not too hot. If the water temperature turns your skin pink, turn on the cold tap!

Aromatherapy

Aromatherapy has been shown to be very effective in alleviating certain pregnancy ailments, but some essential oils can be risky when treating pregnant women, so it is important that you see a qualified practitioner who is registered with the Aromatherapy Council.

Hair dye

We already covered this topic on page 103, but if you have forgotten, (good old 'baby brain' again) there is no hard evidence to suggest that dyeing your hair in pregnancy is harmful.

Do remember that your hormones may affect your hair's condition so you might get a different colour or texture than expected, and you may also suffer an unexpected allergic reaction, so do a patch test first.

If you do decide to dye your hair at home, make sure you wear gloves and apply the dye in a well-ventilated area to be on the safe side.

At home

Gardening

Wear gloves and wash your hands thoroughly after gardening, as soil can contain the toxoplasmosis bug. There's no reason why you shouldn't garden throughout your pregnancy, as it is good exercise, but make sure you protect your back and leave any heavy digging to someone else.

Painting

Modern water-based paints such as emulsions should be completely safe for you to use, as they are very unlikely to have a harmful effect on your baby. As there has not been extensive recent research on this type of paint, though, the NHS recommends you avoid painting in the first trimester as a precaution.

We do know that solvent-based paints, varnishes and brush cleaners are likely to cause more harm than water-based ones due to their chemical content, so it's recommended you don't use these during pregnancy if possible.

If you are renovating a property or room in preparation for your baby, make sure that you don't strip any paint off yourself. Paint dating from before 1978 contains lead, which could be harmful to your unborn child, so leave that job to the professionals or your partner.

There are lots of eco-friendly organic paints on the market that contain no nasty chemicals, so you might like to consider these for your baby's nursery if you're worried.

Electrical appliances

There hasn't been extensive study in this area but the received wisdom is that modern microwaves are safe. If your microwave is very old or doesn't work well, it might be prudent to invest in a new one.

Electric blankets should be used with caution. It is dangerous to overheat your body during pregnancy, so if you use one keep the temperature low so the bed is warm but not hot. Some people worry about the electromagnetic field arising from the electricity used to heat the blanket being dangerous for their baby, but there is no definitive evidence to prove this. If it worries you and you can't live without a bit of extra heat in bed, why not switch to a trusty hot water bottle? If you still persist in using an electric blanket, do remember that it could be dangerous close to labour if your waters break in bed, as we all know that liquids and electricity aren't a great mix…

Household chemicals and cleaning products

There isn't firm evidence on the dangers of exposure to household chemicals, but to be on the safe side it's wise to avoid powerful products such as pesticides and oven cleaners.

If you are cleaning it also makes sense to protect your hands with gloves and ventilate the room by opening a window. Most items you use daily – such as anti-bacterial spray in the kitchen and bathroom – should be fine, but try not to inhale them.

If you are anxious about chemicals you can always make your own 'natural' cleaning products as they did in the past. Baking soda is an efficient powdered cleanser for greasy areas like pots, sinks and ovens; a solution of vinegar and water is perfect for window cleaning and mopping down surfaces in the kitchen.

Household pets

It's recommended that you wash your hands after contact with pets because animal waste does tend to harbour bacteria. In our experience this isn't always convenient – as anyone who has ever owned a cat or dog would know – but it does make sense to wash your hands regularly if you have animals in the house, particularly before eating.

Computers

If you use a computer at home and at work (there's more about specific risks at work in the next chapter), you'll be relieved to know that there is no evidence of any risks associated with their regular use.

Out and about

It's not only at home that you'll have to make a few lifestyle adjustments. Pregnancy can also have an impact on your holiday and travel plans.

Holidays

Flying

Flying is generally considered safe in pregnancy, although some airlines refuse to let you fly after 28 weeks, while others insist you have a doctor's note certifying you are fit to travel. Policies vary from airline to airline, so it is important you know your dates before you make a booking. If you have diabetes or placenta praevia, or have had issues with blood pressure or bleeding in your pregnancy, it would be sensible to check with your doctor before you fly. There is an increased risk of DVT (deep vein thrombosis – see page 81) when you are pregnant and flying can increase the risk further, so ensure you move about as much as possible, rotate your ankles while you are sitting down, and invest in a pair of flight socks (long, over-the-knee support socks). You can get these from Boots or at the airport and, while they may not be glamorous, they can be a lifesaver (literally). If you are at risk of preterm delivery, take extra care when planning a trip to make sure you don't deliver away from family and friends.

Insurance and medical treatment abroad

You need to take out adequate travel insurance and make sure you know what you are covered for before you go anywhere, in case you need

US company RadiaShield has released a range of products called 'belly armor' which claim to protect your child from 99.9% of radiation. Current products include a Belly Blanket, to use while on the computer, and the Belly Tee.

local treatment at a surgery or hospital. Read the small print because some insurers won't cover care for your baby or you, or repatriate either of you if you go into early labour. If you are travelling in Europe, make sure you travel with your European Health Insurance Card (you can apply online at www.ehic.org.uk), as it entitles you to basic medical care in other EU countries (except in Switzerland).

Even in Westernised countries, the medical facilities may not be what we are used to here in the UK. Before you travel, make sure that there is a local doctor or hospital in case you encounter any pregnancy or unrelated illnesses, and make sure you take a photocopy of your pregnancy medical notes and your GP's number with you.

If you are going to an area where mosquitoes are a problem, check with your pharmacist before you buy any over-the-counter repellent, as some contain DEET, which is not suitable for use in pregnancy. It's not really advisable to go to a country where malaria is prevalent as this disease can be harmful to you and your baby. If you have to visit such a country, speak to your doctor about anti-malarial drugs that are suitable to take in pregnancy.

If you are planning a babymoon (see page 199), or are having an exotic holiday or honeymoon during pregnancy, remember that some countries require vaccinations that are unsafe in pregnancy. Your GP can advise you, or you can check out the MASTA (Medical Advisory Services for Travellers Abroad) website for more info: www.masta-travel-health.com.

Foreign travel dos and don'ts

- **Do** check with your doctor about what medical items are safe to take with you, like oral rehydration in case of diarrhoea, antihistamines in case of bites etc. It will be much easier to take a mini medical kit with you than to try to explain you are pregnant and in need of 'x' in a foreign pharmacy.

- **Do** stay out of the sun between 11am and 3pm, and always wear a sunhat and sun protection to stop you overheating.

- **Do** drink lots of bottled water to keep yourself hydrated, and clean your teeth with it if you are concerned about the quality of the tap water.

- **Do** be careful around wet pool areas to avoid a fall.

- **Don't** eat anything you think has been hanging around or is not properly cooked.

- **Don't** travel anywhere without a mini hand sanitiser in your bag to freshen up your hands, cutlery etc.

Theme parks

You might have to curb your love of thrills and spills when you are pregnant, as many rides have rapid stops and starts which could damage the uterus. Water slides should also be approached with caution. Most theme park rides and pools display clear signage stipulating their suitability for pregnant women, and our advice would be to stick to the rules; let's face it, giving birth is usually the mother of all rollercoaster rides.

Extreme sports

Thrill seekers who enjoy extreme sports such as hang-gliding, rock climbing, bungee jumping or skydiving will have to give these activities a miss for a while, and there's probably not a doctor in the land who would disagree with us.

High altitude sports

High altitude sports such as mountaineering and hot air ballooning are officially discouraged, because a change in altitude levels means exposure to lower oxygen levels and this can be harmful for the baby.

Scuba diving

Scuba diving is also a no-no in pregnancy because there is evidence that your baby could be put at risk of decompression sickness (aka the bends) and it can also increase the likelihood of miscarriage.

Down on the farm

Pregnant women are advised to avoid sheep during lambing periods, according to the latest guidelines from the Department of Health, as there is a risk of catching chlamydophila abortus, toxoplasmosis and listeriosis from aborted sheep, newborn lambs or their afterbirth. If you do go to a farm or farm park, your best bet is to avoid sheep altogether if possible. If this is impossible, make sure you don't touch, feed or milk the lambs or ewes, avoid contact with their bedding or straw, and wash your hands scrupulously after leaving.

Having said all that...

The list of dos and don'ts can be pretty daunting and cause a lot of unnecessary worry for some pregnant ladies. Try to enjoy your pregnancy: have fun, relax and listen to your body. If you are worried about doing something, don't do it. If you feel you have bags of energy, feel free to be a social butterfly! Just remember to take it easy and try to get some rest. Take life a bit slower!

DRESS TO IMPRESS

Now that you are expanding at an ever increasing rate, you might struggle to find clothes that fit but that also look good. This section will give you tips on how to look good during your pregnancy.

Fashion has been kind to pregnant women in recent years, with kaftans, smocks and trapeze styles all being key fashion pieces that happen to work brilliantly when you are pregnant too. Whilst 'body con' has made a comeback (not great if you have a massive bump), you can be pretty sure that there will be something fashionable on the high street that will work with your ever expanding shape. Shoe-wise, the trend for flat ballet shoes and slouchy boots has also continued, which means you don't need to try to squeeze your feet into sky-high stilettos to look stylish.

Style on a budget

If you haven't got a great deal of money to spend or would prefer to splash the cash on your baby, you can still look good without spending a fortune.

We recommended earlier in the book that you treat yourself to a pair of maternity jeans, and to be honest that's probably the only thing you absolutely *need*, because you can dress them up or down. However hard you try, a pair of size 12 jeans may not get round your thighs, let alone your bump, after 20 weeks.

If you have a friend who has just had a baby, try to borrow some of her maternity clothes. Many women can't wait to get back into their regular wardrobe and will happily offload their pregnancy clothes.

The NCT often holds second-hand sales where you might pick up some second-hand bits and pieces, and you could also put out a plea on Freecycle (www.freecycle.org) for unwanted maternity wear. Jumble sales or charity shops can be good sources of baggy tops etc, and Gumtree.com is also a good source for freebies.

High street chains such as New Look and Dorothy Perkins do cheap and cheerful maternity wear, and stores such as Primark and Matalan are great for inexpensive comfy stuff like joggers and tees.

Staying stylish

If you are prepared to splash a bit of cash to make your pregnancy more comfortable and stylish, you have plenty of options both on the high street and online. The day Topshop announced it was doing maternity wear, every pregnant fashionista in the land heaved a sigh of relief, knowing that they can do this season's catwalks looks even with a sizeable bump.

The Gap is fantastic for maternity jeans, and if they are your normal wardrobe staple maybe invest in a couple of pairs with different washes or leg shape, so that you can wear them for work or dress them up with heels (not too high, girls!) in the evening. Do experiment with styles, as you might find that you can get away with a skinnier leg than normal because your tummy is bigger, meaning your legs look slimmer.

If you have to look smart for work, you may have to invest in specialist tailoring: www.cravematernity.co.uk is a good online source and Next is a reasonable high street option.

If you don't need to wear a suit but need to look groomed and profes-sional, a wrap dress is the perfect item in your pregnancy wardrobe. It's always worth checking out Boden (www.boden.co.uk), as it runs a couple of lovely print styles each season and, although they are not specifically for maternity, pregnant women swear by them. If you prefer to shop online, log on to www.mothercare.com and www.jojomamanbebe.co.uk, as they both do a good selection of flattering maternity dresses.

The French do stylish maternity dressing very well, so it's worth looking at www.vertbaudet.co.uk and La Redoute (www.laredoute.co.uk).

A Topshop dress worn by the six-months pregnant Duchess of Cambridge sold out within an hour of her being pictured in it!

Not only can you shop from the comfort of your armchair, but the prices are great and you won't run into all your pregnant pals wearing the same things.

If you are lucky enough to have a T K Maxx near you, it is a brilliant source of designer goodies at knock-down prices, and it always has a great selection of dressy tops and dresses that may well see you through pregnancy and beyond.

You don't have to compromise on style and fashion when pregnant: just look at the fabulously fun maternity section on www.americanapparel. co.uk. Asos.com also has some wicked pregnancy outfits, but you have to type maternity into its search box to find them!

If you do have a special function and can't find anything suitably glam that will accommodate your bump, the following websites may be just what you are looking for – but be warned, pregnant glamour doesn't come cheap:

- www.blossommotherandchild.com. Cherry-picks the best pieces from mainstream collections that will suit the pregnant form, so expect to find delicious pieces from Temperley as well as its own brand label.

- www.isabellaoliver.com. A fantastic source of stylish work wear, with everything from cocktail dresses to maxis.

- www.seraphine.com. Also has some very nice posh pieces.

'While I've been pregnant, my main purchase has been a couple of pairs of maternity jeans from the Gap: they're lovely and very comfy. They're also really warm in the winter because of the belly support bit! I've also bought some linen trousers from Jojo Maman Bébé. It's such a lovely shop: it makes you feel like a normal person! I've bought a few maternity tops from places like Topshop and H&M and I've also started wearing maternity bras, which makes me feel a bit like I'm in teen bras again! Other than that I'm still wearing my normal clothes, and I'm excited that I'll still be able to wear my funky tops from Topshop and H&M after the birth.'

Jane, first pregnancy

FASHION TRENDS IN 2014

So how can you look 'on trend' this year? Pregnancy certainly doesn't mean you have to forget about fashion. Here's a few tips to make sure you stay on trend…

Monochrome is everywhere right now, and it's a trend that works well with maternity fashion. Bold stripes and geometric patterns can diffuse figure flaws and hide bulky parts – but equally can be used to accentuate a bump if you want to look pregnant and proud!

Colour blocking remains a key feature – bold colours or squares of colour on tops and trousers. Emerald is an 'on trend' shade, and there are some great maternity jeans out there in this colour which will give you a nod to fashion with some good sensible comfort to boot.

For those who prefer a more feminine look, floral prints and pastels are still in – pair a floral top with jeans or a plainer bottom to avoid flower overkill. Ruffles on blouses or skirts help to pull this look off, as do peasant-style boho tops in soft cotton, in neutrals or muted patterns. In fact, that hippy-chic look can be a great, stylish and comfortable look for pregnancy in general – free-flowing skirts, colourful tunics, oversized cardigans or jumpers and empire-waisted dresses with leggings.

Maxi dresses, a huge look in maternity fashion right now, suit that boho-chic look perfectly. They are also perfect for the warmer months as they let the air circulate brilliantly. Team them with flat sandals and layered necklaces.

Peplum tops are still a key look on the high street, and can work well with a pregnancy bump as the peplum sits just underneath it and balances the silhouette. The more fitted peplum styles also work for you if you need to look smart for work or for social occasions. You can also opt for the traditional suit – dress it down with a T-shirt for daytime, or add a silk blouse for the evening. The oversized blazer is a great throw-on to smarten up a pair of jeans or trousers.

If you want to follow the celebrity trends, you can take inspiration from two quite different sources. For power dressing and celebrity va-va-voom, think Kim Kardashian and go for form-fitting tight tops, skirts and dresses that cling to your bump. High fashion, bling and lots of big hair and make-up are the way to go. If you prefer something a little more subtle, try the Duchess of Cambridge's classy maternity style. Think simple wrap dresses, coat dresses and soft tailoring. Add accents like belted tops, slim belts and bows to embellish your bump and rest on top of or under it. This look is all about understated elegance.

Finally, just because you're pregnant doesn't mean you can't wear fashionable footwear. Many pregnant women find their feet grow by half a size on average during pregnancy, due to hormones causing ligaments and joints to loosen. Your growing bump also throws off your centre of balance. This means sharp stilettos aren't the best option for later pregnancy – but if you want to escape your flats for a slightly more glamorous look now and again, go for wedges, which are still a big fashion trend. They give you height and a feeling of being in heels, but provide you with more stability. Kitten heels are also an option – a feminine heel without the height.

5

My career and my pregnancy

There is no doubt that having a baby is going to have an impact on your career to some degree, but how pregnancy and birth affect your working life will depend on your type of job and personal circumstances. In this chapter we take you through the common legal, physical and emotional issues regarding work and pregnancy, and explain how best to deal with them.

YOUR RIGHTS AND RESPONSIBILITIES

It may not be quite as exciting as thinking about names or nursery décor, but it is vitally important you are up to speed on the latest government legislation regarding pregnancy, because new rules and regulations come in all the time and you want to make the most of your entitlements and be treated properly by your employer.

The main government website is a good place to start (www.gov.uk). In the Working, jobs and pensions section there is a fairly comprehensive Maternity category that gives up-to-date info on your legal rights, so make sure you check it out, as it is possible that things have changed since this book was written.

If you work for a large corporation it is probable that it will be totally au fait with any new rules, but if you work for a small company it might not be so on the ball with any changes in the law. Below is a basic guide to your legal rights as a pregnant employee, although entitlements do vary depending on a wealth of factors, including length of service, type of working contract, employer, etc so you'll need to do your homework to find out exactly what you're entitled to. If you have an efficient HR department it can take you through all the legal stuff, but it will help if you have some idea of what your rights and responsibilities are before you talk to it. Make sure that you thoroughly consider any maternity offer it makes and ensure that you are 100% happy with the terms. Don't let yourself be rushed into a decision.

WHAT YOU NEED TO DO

When to tell

Legally, you have to tell your boss by the time you are 25 weeks pregnant, but the chances are that everyone will have noticed if you leave it that late!

Many women like to keep mum about the news until they have had their first scan, but if you are really suffering with morning sickness and running to the ladies' every five minutes, you might want to share your news with a supportive boss or trusted work colleague so that you can have some moral or physical support. If you work in a female-dominated environment it's quite likely that one of the other women will notice that you are permanently green or camping out in the loo, and you might find your 'secret' more difficult to keep than you first imagined.

Why tell them earlier than 25 weeks?

Your employer has a legal requirement to keep you safe during your pregnancy and should do a risk assessment to check that you can still carry out your working duties safely while you are pregnant (see risk assessments on pages 168–169). Therefore, the earlier you let them know, the safer your baby will be.

If you work in a small company your pregnancy leave might have a significant impact on the business, so if you can give your employer plenty of notice it does give them the opportunity to make plans to cover your absence.

What you need to do and say

You should put in writing when your baby is due and when you would like your maternity leave and maternity pay to start. If you change your mind and decide you want to carry on working until nearer your due date you should give your employer 28 days' notice, but many bosses will give you some flexibility on this issue, as it may be in their interest to keep you at work as long as possible.

You also need to show your employer a copy of your Maternity Certificate (MATB1) that you get from your midwife after 21 weeks and that confirms your due date.

What will happen then?

Your employer must assume that you are going to take your full entitlement of 52 weeks' maternity leave (unless you tell them that you are planning to return without taking the full amount of leave).

Your employer must write to you within 28 days of receiving notification of your pregnancy dates, confirming the date you are due to return to work.

What if you don't know whether you will take your full entitlement of 52 weeks or not?

If you already know you can't afford to take your full maternity leave (see page 159 for advice on how to figure this out), you *can* tell your boss at this early stage that you will be returning early. If your circumstances

A study by the charity Tommy's showed that one in 10 women thought her boss was unsupportive when she announced her pregnancy, and 25% said their bosses expected the same level of work and commitment even though they were pregnant. See page 177 for more on difficult bosses.

change and you change your mind once the baby is born, as long as you give eight weeks' notice you can still take the full entitlement, even if you said you would be returning earlier. If you don't know whether you will be off for the whole time or not, it is best to hedge your bets and assume you will take your full entitlement: you can always change your mind as long as you give the two months' notice.

'One thing that I am finding it hard to get my head around is the fact that, once I go on maternity leave, there are colleagues from work who I won't see for months, having seen them every day for the past few years. That will be quite strange, I think.'

Virginia, first pregnancy

EMPLOYERS' RIGHTS AND RESPONSIBILITIES

As soon as you tell your employer that you are pregnant, they must:

- carry out a risk assessment to identify any risk to you or your child's health

- allow you paid time off to attend antenatal appointments

- ensure you are not treated unfairly by your manager or other colleagues

- plan for your leave – you can take up to 52 weeks' leave (you must not return to work for the first two weeks after the birth of your baby, or the first four weeks if you work in a factory).

Within 28 days of receiving your maternity leave dates, your employer must:

- write to you telling you when you are due back at work and how you will be paid SMP, or, if you do not qualify for SMP, send you Form SMP1 which you will need to complete to apply for maternity allowance.

During maternity leave:

- you and your employer can make reasonable contact with each other. Your employer should agree with you the kind of contact you will have during your leave, for example, how your employer will let you know about any changes happening at work, including job vacancies, and whether there will be opportunities for you to attend training or other events.

- you can work for up to 10 days. These are known as KIT (Keeping In Touch) days (see pages 180–1).

- if your employer makes contributions to an occupational pension, they must continue to make these for the whole time you are receiving SMP or contractual maternity pay.

Before you return to work:

- you must give your employer eight weeks' notice if you change your mind about the date you return to work. If you do not do this, and your employer needs more notice than you have given, they can postpone your return until the required eight weeks' notice has passed (although they cannot postpone your return to work beyond the 52-week leave period).

- if you make a request for flexible working, including part-time work, your employer must seriously consider the request. Your employer can turn down this request on genuine business grounds or agree to a different arrangement with you.

- if you tell your employer that you will be breastfeeding, they must talk to you about any arrangements they will need to make to enable you to do this, as well as complete a risk assessment and remove any risk they find.

WORKING OUT YOUR FINANCES

Sadly, for many of us, the issue about returning to work is governed by finance rather than emotion. Many women would love to stay at home or work part time, but their financial situation dictates that they continue their career to pay the mortgage and the bills. Some women can't take their full maternity leave because they simply can't afford to manage on statutory maternity pay or 13 weeks with no pay.

Before your baby is born it's really valuable to do the sums to see if you can survive for 52 weeks on statutory maternity pay, and useful to work out if you could manage on a reduced salary if you did cut your hours or days after returning to work.

You also need to factor in childcare costs (see pages 184–190 for more on this) because you will probably have to pay someone to look after your child, unless you have a willing parent or relative close by who is prepared to care for your baby for free.

Many couples spend pregnancy squirreling as much cash away as they can; this is good practice because you will still incur baby-related costs after your baby is born, as well as having to supplement your statutory maternity pay.

Take a long, hard look at your finances before you start considering your maternity leave options to make sure you make the best decision possible.

'Being pregnant at work means people try to wrap you in cotton wool, which is annoying as I am very independent. Being in a male-dominated workplace is also interesting sometimes, as they suddenly change around you. I am planning on going back to work as financially we don't really have a choice. I am the main breadwinner of the household, but aside from that I couldn't be a stay-at-home mum either. I don't think our child would benefit from that. I will try to cut my hours down, though.'

Jenny, first pregnancy

MATERNITY LEAVE

If you are an employee you will be entitled to the maximum amount of leave set by the government, called statutory maternity leave (SML). This period is 52 weeks and is made up of 26 weeks of ordinary maternity leave (OML) and 26 weeks of additional maternity leave (AML). This means you are entitled to a full year off work if you are an employee. Your length of service, rate of pay or hours of work do not affect your statutory maternity leave.

You do not have to take all your statutory maternity leave, but legally you have to take two 'compulsory' weeks off after the baby is born or four weeks off if you work in a factory.

If you are a casual or agency worker or you are self-employed, different rules apply, so you need to check out your legal employment status to see what you are entitled to. Visit www.dwp.gov.uk for more information on this.

You can begin OML up to 11 weeks before your baby is due, although most people prefer to wait so that they can afford to spend more time off after their baby is born. You can be creative with your annual leave, though, and use some of this before your maternity leave starts to make your maternity leave last longer. You are also entitled to your allocated annual leave allowance whilst you are on maternity leave, which you could use at the end of your maternity leave.

Your basic rights

There are a number of rights that pregnant women are entitled to by law. These are known as statutory rights and are:

- the right to take time off for antenatal care

- the right to work in a safe environment

- the right to claim discrimination and unfair dismissal if dismissed because of pregnancy and maternity leave

- the right to take up to 52 weeks' maternity leave

- the right of some pregnant women to statutory maternity pay (SMP)

- the right to return to work after having the baby.

MATERNITY PAY

Statutory Maternity Pay

Your work may have its own maternity pay scheme which you may qualify for. If not, you may qualify for Statutory Maternity Pay (SMP), paid by the government.

To qualify for SMP you must have been:

- employed by the same employers for a continuous period of at least 26 weeks into the 15th week before the week your baby is due (the qualifying week)

- earning, on average, an amount that at least equals the lower earnings limit which applies on the Saturday at the end of your qualifying week. (The lower earnings limit will be £109 a week

If you do not qualify for SMP your employer must give you Form SMP1. You may be eligible for Maternity Allowance instead (see page 163).

Even if you are expecting more than one baby you will get only one SMP allowance.

if the end of your qualifying week is in the 2013–2014 tax year. This is the amount you have to earn before you are treated as paying National Insurance contributions.)

To make a claim for SMP you must:

- tell your employer when you want your SMP to start
- provide medical evidence of the date your baby is due.

As of 9 April 2012, SMP is paid:

- at 90% of your average gross weekly earnings, with no upper limit, for the first six weeks
- at either the standard rate of £136.78, or 90% of your average gross weekly earnings, for the remaining 33 weeks – whichever is lower.

You must use the date your baby is due to work out your SMP for that pregnancy. If you have more than one job, you may be able to get SMP from each employer.

Your employer will usually pay you in the same way and at the same time as your normal wages for up to 39 weeks.

Returning to work while receiving SMP

You can work for up to 10 days during your maternity pay period (MPP) for the employer paying your SMP without this affecting your SMP entitlement. These are called Keeping In Touch (KIT) days. If you then do any further work for your employer during your MPP, you will lose SMP for each week in your MPP that you do that work.

If you start work for a new employer after your baby is born (an employer who did not employ you in the 15th week before your baby was due), you must tell the employer paying your SMP and your SMP must stop.

Your company's maternity scheme

Some companies will offer additional maternity pay, paid on top of SMP. Ask if you are entitled to this (most stipulate a minimum service requirement), and check the details – if you decide not to return to work, you may have to pay back some or all the money paid in excess of SMP. Some generous companies let you keep the money, regardless of whether you return to work.

What if I'm not entitled to SMP?

If you aren't entitled to Statutory Maternity Pay, you'll be entitled to Maternity Allowance if:

- you have worked for 26 weeks in the last 66 weeks (this could be in lots of different chunks or for different employers. It can include self-employed work); and

- you earned more than £30 for 13 of those weeks. (You can choose the weeks when you've earned the most, combine wages from different jobs, and it can include overtime, bonuses, or sick pay.)

Maternity Allowance in 2013–2014 gives you £136.78 each week or 90% of your average weekly earnings, whichever is less. You may get an additional amount for your husband, civil partner or someone else who looks after your children, if that person is on a very low income.

What do I need to do to get Maternity Allowance?

Maternity Allowance is paid by Jobcentre Plus. To claim it, download Form MA1 from www.gov.uk/maternity-allowance and send it to the office stated at the end of the form, along with the relevant documentation. You can do this at any time after your 26th week of pregnancy. You will need to give them medical evidence of your pregnancy, usually your maternity certificate (MATB1). If you have a job, you will also have to get Form SMP1 from your employer to confirm that you aren't entitled to SMP.

I'm self-employed – what do I get?

If you are self-employed, you are not entitled to SMP, but you will be entitled to Maternity Allowance if:

- you have worked for 26 weeks in the last 66 weeks (either for yourself or for an employer) and

- you have 13 weeks where you have paid Class 2 NI contributions or held a certificate of small earnings exemption.

If you have got 13 weeks of Class 2 NI contributions, you are entitled to the full amount of £136.78. If you have the certificate, you will be entitled to £27 a week. If you own a limited company and pay yourself through PAYE, you will qualify for SMP if you meet the conditions.

Key facts about SMP

- If you go onto www.gov.uk there is an interactive tool that can help you work out what your SMP will be.

- If you decide not to return to work after receiving your SMP, you do not have to pay anything back to your employer.

- If you take time off work because of pregnancy-related medical issues from four weeks before your due date, your employer is legally entitled to start paying you SMP and assuming you have commenced your OML, even if you had planned to work up until 38 weeks.

- If you work for two employers you may be entitled to receive SMP from both.

- If you start employment with a new company while you are still pregnant your SMP is not affected, but if you start with a new company after the baby is born you must tell your previous employer, who will then stop paying you your SMP.

- If you are ill after the birth, you may be able to claim statutory sick pay after your SMP payments finish.

- If a baby is stillborn after 24 weeks, or is born after that date and doesn't survive, his mother is still entitled to SMP.

Unpaid parental leave

Unpaid parental leave is available to each parent of a child under five. In March 2013, the amount of unpaid parental leave that could be taken increased to 18 weeks (within the five-year period). The leave must be taken in blocks of one week, with not more than four weeks being taken each year. It is intended to be used, for example, to look at new schools, or settle children into childcare arrangements. See more details of this, and how it can be used, at www.gov.uk/paternal-leave, or ask your HR department if you wish to take some. The parental leave is always in addition to any maternity or paternity leave taken.

WHAT ABOUT PARTNERS?

Your partner will be entitled to two weeks' ordinary paternity leave (OPL) if he has been in continuous employment with his employer for 26 weeks up to the 15th week before your baby is due. During this time he will receive statutory paternity pay (SPP) at £136.78 a week as long as he is earning on average £109 a week. Many employers also offer their own paternity leave schemes, so your partner should check with his employer to see what he is entitled to.

In addition, fathers now also have the right to additional paternity leave and pay (APL&P). This means your partner can take up to 26 weeks to care for your child.

You and your partner can choose to divide maternity leave between you. Since April 2011, fathers and mothers have been able to share some of the 52 weeks' existing leave, with the father able to take up to six months (beginning after the baby is 20 weeks old). It works as follows.

- Your partner can take the final three months of paid maternity leave due to you, providing you return to work and end your entitlement to statutory maternity pay or maternity allowance.

- He will then be paid the statutory maternity pay for that three-month period that you would get (also called additional statutory paternity pay (ASPP)).

- Your partner is also entitled to take a further three months of unpaid leave, bringing the total length of parental time off for couples to 52 weeks.

- Once the leave period is over, your partner will have the right to return to his old position, or, if that is not practical, he must be offered a position that is suitable and appropriate for his skills, and with similar terms and conditions – and not less favourable – to his current position.

These rights will apply to you and your partner whether or not you are married and whether you are a heterosexual couple or a same-sex couple.

At the moment, maternity and paternity leave can only be taken as a single block. There are new guidelines coming into effect in 2015 which will make taking leave more flexible.

If you want to get more information on SMP and Maternity Benefits, www.gov.uk will give you the latest government guidelines on its website. And remember, talk to your employer and find out exactly what your company offers.

The government estimates that only 2%–8% of dads are likely to take their full leave entitlement, even under the new proposals.

A look at the new shared parental leave rights

The new Children and Families Bill will be rolled out in 2015. It will mean a fully flexible system of parental leave in England, Scotland and Wales – but too late if you are having your baby in 2014, although some steps towards it are already in place.

Mothers will keep the right to 52 weeks of maternity leave and 39 weeks of pay. But as of 2015, they will be able to share leave and pay with their partner. Mothers can end maternity leave, and start work again, with their partner taking up the leave and pay. Mothers may then return to their maternity leave, and take over from their partner, who returns to work – this can happen multiple times for the 52 weeks of leave (and 39 weeks of pay). For example, after the two weeks of compulsory maternity leave, parents could work alternating months if both of their employers agreed. They will also be able to take time off together.

The parent taking the first six weeks of leave will receive 90% of average earnings. For the next 33 weeks they will be paid £136.78 a week. The remaining 13 weeks of leave would be unpaid.

This is an improvement on the current system, where dads/partners can only use such leave in a single period once the mother has returned to work.

Paternity leave will remain at two weeks but is to be reviewed in 2018.

Iceland has just announced new rules offering five months' leave each for fathers and mothers and then two months to be shared between them, all at 80% of income. Currently 84% of dads in Iceland take leave, and the number is increasing. Lucky them!

Stay-at-home dads/partners

The last 10 years have seen a dramatic increase in the number of stay-at-home dads. Current research suggests a number of different reasons for this increase.

- Many women are the higher wage earners in households, so it makes financial sense for them to go back to work.

- Traditional male/female roles in society have changed, so couples are more comfortable and, in some sense, more able to move away from the stereotype of stay-at-home mum and working father.

- Some women are more career driven than their partners, so they have a strong desire to go back to work.

There are many pros and cons to your partner staying at home, but only you as a couple can decide what is best for you and your baby. The needs of your baby will be at the heart of all your childcare decisions; the best advice we can give you is to keep communication between you and your partner open so that you are both completely comfortable with the decisions you make.

Fathers now make up 10% of those parents staying at home to look after their children.

Above all, don't feel guilty if you have to return to work; you'll be earning money to enrich all your lives and help the family as a whole, and your baby will thank you for that in the long run.

Paternity leave: who's taking it?

Recent research suggests that just one in 10 fathers takes full paternity leave.

A report found that fathers are put off playing a bigger part in childcare because of lost earnings to the family budget during the recession (Demos 2011).

Fathers who take six months' leave stand to lose almost 90% of their earnings in the year that they take time off. This is because statutory paternity pay covers less than a quarter of their salary, the study of 1,500 workers found. This compares to mothers, who would be 72% worse off if they took their full leave entitlement.

A study by Ocado and the Fatherhood Institute found that 46% of British dads felt ignored by maternity services and 57% felt antenatal classes hadn't prepared them for the task ahead.

It also found that:

- 54% of fathers did not know they could take over the second six months of their partner's maternity leave

- 50% of fathers believe that taking six months' additional paternity leave would damage their career prospects – while only 22% think that their partner's taking six months' maternity leave would damage hers

- 75% of respondents think it's easier to go to work than look after a newborn baby

- 81% of fathers support the new laws and the opportunity for couples to share the care of their baby in the first year

- 70% of fathers believe their partner's career won't be affected by taking a full year's maternity leave.

Make the most of your time off

Probably the best piece of advice is to try to enjoy your working pregnancy and maternity leave. Few women find returning to work easy after having a baby, but we all manage to muddle through somehow.

YOUR MATERNITY RIGHTS AT WORK

Antenatal care

You are legally allowed to have paid time off to attend antenatal appointments. This includes parentcraft classes and hospital tours as well as your routine appointments, but you may need to show your boss or employer evidence that you have a hospital visit and you are not just bunking off on a shopping trip.

Your partner does not have the legal right to have paid time off to attend antenatal appointments with you, but if his employer is 'family friendly' they might let him take the time off and make it up at a later date.

Health and safety at work during pregnancy

You need to take care of yourself at work when you are pregnant, and that doesn't just mean legally and financially. You need to ensure that you have adequate health and safety protection as well.

'On the whole, working while I've been pregnant has been OK, just very tiring. I had a hilarious meeting with the health and safety rep, who would have wrapped me in cotton wool and only let me stand in the corner if I'd let him! I've found that loads of people fuss if you pick anything up, which can be a bit annoying.'

Jane, first pregnancy

Once you have formally notified your employer of your pregnancy in writing, they must carry out a specific risk assessment based on your needs as an employee. By law your employer has to protect your health and safety during pregnancy, and failure to do so is classed as sex discrimination.

If any risks are identified, your employer must inform you and tell you how they will ensure you are not exposed to them.

Potential workplace risks include:

- lifting or carrying heavy loads

- standing or sitting for long periods of time

- exposure to any of the following: infectious diseases; lead; hazardous chemicals; radioactive material; excessive noise; extremes of temperature, shock, or vibration

- work-related stress

- workstation setup: seating and posture

- long working hours

- mental or physical fatigue

- threat of violence.

 If you feel that your working conditions are unsatisfactory or hazardous you should speak to your boss, HR manager, union rep or employee rep. If you get no joy and feel the need to get some legal assistance, contact your local Citizens Advice bureau, ACAS or the Health & Safety Executive (HSE).

If there is a risk to you or your baby and your employer cannot adjust your conditions or hours to protect you from it, legally they have to find you suitable alternative work on the same pay and conditions. If they cannot meet this request you can be suspended on full pay until they can.

Don't be nervous about raising the issue of health and safety while you're pregnant. You might feel like you're being pushy or making a fuss, but it is your legal right to be protected by your employer, so make sure you are being properly cared for. Your safety and the safety of your baby are paramount. You might find that you are a company's first pregnant employee or that there is already a thorough health and safety policy in place. Whatever your circumstances, make sure you keep pushing it until you are happy.

BEING ABLE TO WORK

You should also be aware that if you have medical issues arising from your pregnancy that affect your ability to do your present job, you need to make sure that you get a note from your GP or midwife explaining the problem. This ensures your employer can eliminate certain duties from your workload or accommodate you in a different role within the organisation if necessary.

Applying for a new job when you are pregnant

If you apply for a position in a new company during pregnancy, it counts as sex discrimination for them not to give you the job because you are pregnant (although proving that may be quite difficult in a court of law). Obviously, if it is early days and you are not showing, any prospective employer will judge you in the same way as any other candidate, and if they give you the job and you subsequently tell them you are pregnant they cannot change their minds and retract the job offer.

Applying for a promotion

Many women worry that once they are pregnant any chance of a promotion flies out of the window. However, your employers have a legal obligation to make you aware of any promotions coming up and invite you to apply for them. We'd love to say that your pregnancy should have no bearing on whether you get the job, but sadly this is not always the case. At least you have the legal right to be considered for any promotion, and if a candidate with less experience is offered the job over you, you may well have a case to show your employer is guilty of sex discrimination.

When you are the boss

Obviously you don't have to worry about whether you are going to be promoted or asking for time off when you're the boss, but being head honcho and pregnant is not without its problems.

Responsibility to your employees

The people who work for you may be worried about what happens to the business in your absence, so make sure you have a rough contingency plan in place before you announce the news to your staff to allay their fears.

Responsibility to yourself

You have to do your own risk assessments and ensure that you are keeping yourself safe and protected at work. For the sake of your baby and your fellow employees, make sure you don't overdo it: if your body tells you to slow down or stop you should do so; that's what you would expect the people working for you to do and you should be no different.

Responsibility for your future and that of your company
You need to sit down and work out how long you can afford to take off in the personal and financial sense, and also work out how long your company can survive without you while you take maternity leave. You shouldn't rush back to work before you're ready, but you will need to make sure you have an excellent plan in place for how the company will be run while you are away.

The benefit of being the boss is that if you want to take the afternoon off, put your feet up or spend all day in the loo with morning sickness, you can!

A COMFORTABLE WORKING PREGNANCY

Even if you don't have any specific risks involved with your job, everyday working conditions can take their toll on even the healthiest pregnant women. It's useful to think about your working day and see how you might have to adapt it now you're pregnant to make you and your baby as comfortable as possible. Some women absolutely hate working when they are pregnant and can't wait to nip off on maternity leave; others find pregnancy difficult because it impinges on their working life.

Whatever your attitude to your career and your workplace, a working pregnancy can be enjoyable and not merely endurable. Here are some tips on how to make working while you're pregnant as comfortable as possible.

Commuting

Firstly, you have to *get* to work, and that's not as simple as it sounds if you are racked with nausea or fighting to get *on* to public transport, let alone get a seat.

Driving
There are benefits to driving to work: you can open the windows easily if you need air; you can stop if you are going to be sick; and you don't have to put up with all the weird and wonderful smells (that you can't

bear with your pregnancy-heightened senses) that travelling on public transport inevitably brings. However, one of the hazards of driving while pregnant is that you may be slightly more accident-prone if you are suffering with 'preg head', and you'll need to make sure your bump is protected in case of any knocks.

If you do drive to work, make sure that your driving position is comfortable, you protect your back with a cushion and you take a break and stretch your legs if the commute is a long one. If you are worried about bumping your bump, invest in a pregnancy seat belt. There are a variety of styles on offer, from cushioned straps to contraptions that actually change the position of the seat belt so it doesn't lie directly across your tummy.

During pregnancy you have a different centre of gravity, so swap those heels for flats when commuting, to prevent trips, slips or falls.

Public transport

Obviously the stress of your commute will depend on the distance, mode of transport and how congested the route becomes. There's no doubt that a rural bus journey is likely to be more pleasant (and scenic) than a trip on the London Underground during rush hour, but if you are feeling tired, groggy or sick, both will be equally torturous.

If your commute is getting you down, you can reasonably ask for a change in start or finish times to avoid the worst of the rush hour, and it may be feasible for you to work from home for part or all of the day.

It's ironic that in the first trimester – when you feel that you need a seat most – you won't get one, because you won't be showing and no one will know you are pregnant. Even when you have a bump the size of a football stuffed inside your jumper, there's no guarantee you will get a seat.

If you feel that you need a seat, just pluck up the courage and ask. Or you could always resort to one of those 'I'm not fat, I'm pregnant' or 'Mr Bump' T-shirts. Some train companies even offer 'Baby on Board' badges for pregnant travellers, so check if your local route has one.

Top tips for commuting

- Leave for work a little earlier or a little later than usual to avoid peak travelling times. Even 15 minutes can make a difference.

- Leave your fellow travellers in no doubt about your pregnant state: unbutton your coat and stick your tummy out so they can clearly see you are pregnant and not just a little lardy.

- Ask for a seat if you need one; most people normally oblige.

- Keep a bottle of water and a snack in your bag in case of a breakdown or emergency.

Sickness

Many women find it very difficult feeling green around the gills at work, particularly when the staff loos aren't quite as nice as the ones you are used to at home. We've given you some tips on how to deal with pregnancy nausea earlier on in the book (page 87), but sadly there's not a great deal you can do to hide the problem at work, even if you are trying to keep your pregnancy a secret in the early days.

If your sickness is 'mornings only' and you have a sympathetic boss, you could spill the beans and work from home in the mornings, or change your working hours so that you come into the office once the sickness has subsided. It is likely, though, that your co-workers will cotton on to the fact that you are pregnant, and you might not want to tell them until you have had your first scan and know the baby is OK.

If you suffer severe morning sickness you probably won't be able to keep it from your colleagues; indeed, you may have to get yourself signed off to prevent you getting dehydrated. Your employer may not be very sympathetic to your condition if you need to be signed off, but legally there's nothing they can do about it.

If you are suffering, think about flexible working patterns you could do (for example, could you work at home for a couple of days a week or work flexi-time?), figure out if there is any work you could hand to a colleague and go to your boss with a solution. It will be better to present possible solutions rather than just asking to be signed off.

Reduced hours

You have a right to ask for reduced working hours during pregnancy, but legally your employer doesn't have to agree to it if it doesn't suit the needs of the business; if you do cut your workload and your salary goes down it will affect the amount of SMP you receive when you go on maternity leave.

Pregnancy-related illness

If you are ill when you are pregnant you are entitled to have this time off as paid sick leave – unless you are ill in the four weeks before your due date, in which case your employer has a legal right to start your maternity leave and pay you SMP. Any pregnancy-related sickness should be treated the same as normal sick leave, and your employer is guilty of sex discrimination if they threaten you with a disciplinary action or sacking for taking time off for illness in pregnancy. If you do need to take time off for illness or health issues during pregnancy, it is important that you get a note confirming you have a problem from your GP or midwife. Not only will it confirm your absence is legitimate, but it would also be useful if you need evidence at an employment tribunal should your employer start getting nasty about you being off work.

Baby brain

According to an Australian study carried out in 2010, 'baby brain' or 'mumnesia' is all in the mind, but evidence from a study in the UK has found that hormones were to blame for short-term memory loss in pregnancy. Whether 'baby brain' is real or in the mind, there is no doubt that many pregnant women find it difficult to keep the same levels of concentration when they are pregnant, and that can lead to problems at work.

Here are some tips to help you combat your 'baby brain'.

- Write a 'to do' list of jobs every morning when you get into work to make sure that you get all your tasks completed.

- If possible, schedule meetings when you are most alert. If you are liveliest in the morning and doziest after lunch make sure you try to have breakfast or brunch meetings.

- Eat and drink regularly to keep your energy levels up as this will assist concentration.

- If you are really struggling, enlist the help of a sympathetic colleague to get you through difficult meetings and presentations; a PowerPoint shared can be a problem halved!

Stress

The jury is out on whether stress at work has an effect on your baby – a recent study showed that a baby's development might improve as a result of moderate work stress, whereas another showed that a fetus as young as 18 weeks could sense anxiety in the mother. What we do know is that excessive stress can raise your blood pressure (which can cause problems in pregnancy), and can also manifest itself physically in the form of insomnia and headaches, so if you are really feeling the stress at work you should speak to your boss or HR manager about finding a solution. They have a duty to try to alleviate or remove the factors that are causing you grief where possible, or adjust your conditions or hours accordingly.

If things get really bad or if work stress is affecting your well-being and that of your child, you can speak to your GP about getting signed off.

Exhaustion

Exhaustion can hit you during any part of your pregnancy: your surging hormones can completely wipe you out in the first trimester, and by the third, the sheer effort of carrying round your baby can make you so tired you just want to weep.

Many pregnant women have trouble sleeping, which exacerbates the problem, and if your job is of a physical nature or involves standing for long periods of time it's bound to make the problem worse.

To help you avoid feeling totally exhausted:

- take a 'power' nap. If you are struggling to get through the day, a short snooze for around 15–20 minutes can really boost your energy levels. Try not to nap for longer, though, as studies have shown you can wake up feeling worse. In theory your employers should provide a place for you to rest, although in reality this might not be practical. As long as you have a chair and a place to rest your weary head you should be able to get a few minutes' respite.

- take regular breaks. Most employees are entitled to breaks during the day, so make sure you take yours. If you have nowhere to 'escape' to, turn your PC off, close your eyes and relax for a few minutes; if you have a rest or leisure area make the most of it and get away from your working environment to refresh your brain and boost your energy levels. Sitting in the same place and staring at a computer screen can really sap even the most motivated of employees.

Stand by me

If your job involves long periods standing up it makes sense to work in a pair of comfortable shoes; if you are surgically attached to your heels, remember that ballerina flats are also very fashionable, so you don't have to sacrifice style for comfort (you'll just look shorter!). We covered back problems in pregnancy on page 69. Standing all day can make it worse, so make sure that you sit down at regular intervals to give your body a rest; your boss should provide a chair or stool for you to do this.

Are you sitting comfortably?

If you sit for long periods of time, you increase your risk of developing deep vein thrombosis and are more likely to feel dizzy and faint when you stand up. You may also increase the risk of back or pelvic pain; therefore it is important that you create a comfortable position in which to carry out your working duties.

Here's what you should do to ensure you're sitting correctly.

- Make sure your chair is high enough: your feet should be flat on the floor with your hips slightly higher than your knees. You can raise your feet with a box or stool if necessary.

- Your computer screen should be directly in front of you, with your eyes level with the middle of the screen.

- Support your spine with a cushion placed between your chair and the small of your back.

- Keep your posture erect. Sit up straight with your shoulders relaxed and don't slouch.

- Try to keep your pelvis tilted slightly upwards when sitting.

- Take regular breaks; get up and walk around for a couple of minutes at least twice an hour.

- Don't cross your legs when you sit down: it twists your spine, restricts circulation and may encourage the formation of varicose veins.

- If you are struggling to get out of your chair, ask your boss for one with armrests.

- As your bump increases, adjust your chair height accordingly. If your current work station can't accommodate a growing belly, ask your boss to move you or change your current office setup.

DEALING WITH AN UNSYMPATHETIC BOSS OR COLLEAGUE

In an ideal world everyone would be delighted about you being pregnant, but unfortunately many pregnant women encounter some sort of hostility at work once their pregnancy is announced. You may have the law on your side, but that doesn't prevent people being mean, sarcastic or petty, and you may find that the attitudes of your boss or your colleagues change once you are pregnant.

You may find your commitment being tested, your working hours queried or your colleagues resentful of the time you take off. This can take its toll on you when you are feeling a bit wobbly and emotional, but there are some options open to you.

- Work with your boss to make sure that he or she has plenty of advance notice of absences and appointments; you are entitled

In a recent survey by Netmums, 17% of women reported that they were treated badly by their employer while they were pregnant.

to take this time off, but operations will run more smoothly if people can plan for you not being around.

- If you have a choice of antenatal appointments, try to pick one that will have the least disruption to your working day. Again, you're not obliged to do this, but if you want to maintain good relations at work it makes sense to make things easier for your colleagues, who may rely on you being around at certain times.

- Try to look at it from your boss's perspective: sometimes they get quite frightened at the prospect of losing a key worker and this can manifest itself in them behaving negatively towards you. If you think there's a really good chance you'll be returning to work, then assure them of your intentions (it might make your working life more pleasant, and there's nothing they can do if you don't come back).

- Get someone on your side: sometimes it's helpful to have a 'work friend' battling your corner and supporting you.

- Grin and bear it. You're going to have a whole year off soon with your baby, and this is only a short-term hurdle to your long-term future.

If you do feel that you are being mistreated, make sure you speak to a higher authority. You have certain rights in pregnancy, and if you can prove you are being unfairly victimised because of your 'condition' you will have the weight of the law on your side.

Know your rights!

You should know by now that you have a right to be treated fairly and safely in pregnancy. Do try to resolve any potentially problematic situations with your boss or higher authority in your company before you go down the legal route, as it can lead to a lot of stress and heartache. If you feel you have no option but to take a grievance further, we have included a list of addresses of authorities who can help and advise you at the back of the book.

DURING YOUR MATERNITY LEAVE

When you go on maternity leave, work will probably be the last thing on your mind, but it's worth knowing what rights you do have during maternity leave, and how you should go about planning if and when you go back to work.

Holidays

While you are off on maternity leave you are still entitled to any paid holiday leave that accumulates while you are away. You can add this to the beginning or end of your maternity leave if you want to extend your time off. What you can't do is carry holiday entitlement over: so if you are due to go on maternity leave in July and your holiday year runs January–December, you need to take your holiday leave at the beginning of your maternity break, as you won't be able to tag it on at the end of the following June.

Benefits

You are entitled to keep any benefits, such as gym membership, as they are a benefit to you and not to the company. If the benefit was for the business – such as a company car or a mobile phone – your employer can legally suspend it for the period of your leave (or loan it to your replacement).

Pension contributions

Your employer must continue to make your pension contributions while you are on maternity leave.

Dismissal or redundancy

If you are dismissed or made redundant it is blatant sex discrimination if it is done because you are pregnant, you are on maternity leave or are absent from the business as a result of your pregnancy, or you are looking after your baby (if they are sick, for example).

Having said that, you can still be made redundant if your employer can prove that the area of the business you work in is closing or your position is no longer viable. If this situation arises you should know that:

- if your employer is making sweeping cuts across the company, he cannot make you redundant just because you are on maternity leave

- if you are made redundant when you are pregnant, you do have additional rights: your employer has to offer you suitable alternative employment in the business if a vacancy exists (even if there is someone else in the company who might be better qualified), and you can start this job (with a four-week trial period) when you return from maternity leave

- if you are dismissed or made redundant during pregnancy, your employer must write to you giving you a full explanation for the termination of your employment and give you your normal notice period, pay in lieu of notice, or redundancy pay if you are contractually entitled to it.

Keeping In Touch days

Keeping In Touch (KIT) days are a good idea if you want to stay abreast with what's going on in your organisation or maintain contact with your colleagues. You can spend up to 10 days in your company during your maternity leave without losing your SMP. Remember that:

- you are not obliged to undertake KIT days during your maternity leave, so if you prefer not to go in your employer cannot force you

- your employer must pay you for your time. This may just be for the hours you do, or some companies will pay you a day's wages, even if you only do half a day's work!

- you don't have to do your usual job and these days could be spent training, on a course or at a seminar

- even if you pop in for half an hour it will be treated as a full day for KIT purposes

- you can do them as single days or consecutively

- once you have completed 10 KIT days, if you do any further work you will lose your SMP for the weeks when additional work was undertaken

- you can only do KIT days if your employer is paying you SMP.

Be aware that your employer is entitled to make 'reasonable' contact with you when you are off on maternity leave, and can call or email you if they have an issue that cannot wait until your return; what they cannot do is insist that you come in.

Many women find KIT days a useful way of easing back into the working environment after a long break. If you do want to take them, make sure that you give your employer as much notice as possible, so that they can plan for your visit and make the day as productive as possible for both parties.

RETURNING TO WORK AFTER MATERNITY LEAVE

Many women are now the main breadwinner in their household and they have to return to work to support their new family. Some also choose to return to work to keep their brain working! This section covers the main points you need to know about returning to work.

When you are considering returning to work you should know that:

- you need to give your employer eight weeks' notice of your return during your statutory maternity leave. If you don't, your employer can delay your return until the eight weeks have passed.

- if you go back to work before your ordinary maternity leave (OML) period is up, you are legally entitled to go back to your old job with the same pay and conditions etc. OML is the first 26 weeks of your entitlement.

- if you return to work during your additional maternity leave (AML), you should either be given your old job back or a similar position with the same pay and conditions. AML is the last 26 weeks of your entitlement.

- if you are offered a position that you believe to be inferior or with different conditions that you find unacceptable, your company may be guilty of sex discrimination.

A recent study by the NCT revealed that only 10% of women felt that they had been helped to settle back into their old job, and one in three women said her boss wasn't supportive when she came back to work.

Flexible working

For many new mothers, working part time or flexible hours gives them the work/life balance that they want, and it is always worth investigating the possibility of working fewer or shorter days or working part of the week from home. You might want to sound out your employer during one of your KIT days (if you choose to take any) to give them some notice of what would work for you.

If you or your partner have been working for the same employer for 26 weeks you have a right to request flexible working; legally (and unfortunately), your employer does not have accommodate the request, but they are supposed to give it 'serious consideration'.

Former career woman?

It's very difficult to say with any certainty how you will feel about your job after your baby is born. One of the fantastic things about extended maternity leave is that it gives you some breathing space to make decisions about your working life, and gives you time to put the logistics of having a baby and a job in place.

You already know that you are legally obliged to take two weeks off after giving birth (even in this day and age, everyone was quite shocked when the former French Justice Minister Rachida Dati went back to work just five days after having her daughter), but you cannot yet know how you will feel after you have had the baby: so don't allow yourself to be pressured by your employer, or anyone else, into making a rash decision about your future career. Some women hate being at home, find the day-to-day baby stuff quite tedious and miss the buzz of the office; others adore being at home with their baby and find the idea of going back to the office quite intolerable. Be aware that your feelings can also change as your maternity leave progresses: you might love your freedom from the office at the beginning of your maternity leave, but crave adult company and baby-free conversations by the end.

To help you make your decision, think about what kind of person you are and what makes you tick. If you thrive on pressure, targets and results, you might find staying at home really frustrating as babies don't tend to do things 'to order'. There have been stories in the press about former career women turning parenting into their new 'job' and trying to organise their baby career with the same military spreadsheet-style precision as they organised their careers. Some women find looking after a newborn quite unfulfilling, yet get terribly sad when their maternity leave finishes as that's when their babies start talking and walking and things get really interesting.

'I have found being pregnant at work quite hard. I'm a lawyer, so I'm used to working long hours with little rest in between. I know that will have to change as my pregnancy progresses. I think I will go back to work but in a different role. My current job just won't work for me as the hours are too long. I want to be there for my baby, so I need to change to a job that allows me to leave on time every day. I love my job, but already it feels less important, as my focus is on my baby.'

Amanda, first pregnancy

Some women will feel a loss of identity if they give up their career to stay at home, whereas others will feel so fulfilled by parenting they wonder why they ever worked in the first place.

Whatever you decide to do, there's only one piece of important advice: however long or short your maternity leave is, do try to enjoy it, as you'll never get that time with your baby again.

Child benefit changes: what do they mean for you?

In the 2012 budget, George Osborne announced changes to the child benefit system, with higher-earning parents losing the benefit entirely. Here's a quick guide to who gets what now:

- Child benefit is a tax-free payment that can be claimed for a child until they are aged 16, or 16–18 in full-time education. It is worth £20.30 per week for the first child, which equates to £1,055.60 a year, and £13.40 per week for each younger sibling, or £696.80 a year per subsequent child.

- Households where one or both earners earn more than £50,000 see their benefit tapered out, at a rate of 1% for every £100 earned over that threshold.

- Those with an income of more than £60,000 lose all child benefit.

- Overall, 90% of all families remain eligible for child benefit.

- The change means that a family with two parents earning £40,000 each, earning a total of £80,000 for the household, will keep all of their child benefit, whereas a family in which one parent stays at home and the other earns £50,000 will lose it.

'Initially I found my new life quite suffocating; having been an independent professional who enjoyed going out a lot, I suddenly felt like I was "trapped" at home with such a huge responsibility to care for. Put it like this: I didn't use to hang out in ball pits at soft play centres or by the swings, and now I do! Seeing Fred's smile and the way he smells after bath time are just some of the amazing parts of having a baby, and the fact that you have this little person who thinks you're great makes it all worthwhile.'

Megan, mum to Fred, 9 months

CHILDCARE OPTIONS

When you're considering returning to work, one of the biggest considerations you'll have to make concerns childcare. You'll need to decide which type of childcare will work best for you and your baby, and look at the financial aspects as well as what is available to you locally.

We discuss your main childcare options below.

Nursery

Advantages

A place at Britain's costliest nursery this year costs £42,000, which is 37% more than a place at top public school Charterhouse (£30,574 a year).

- Your baby will be looked after by a team of qualified individuals.

- Exposure to other babies and young children can build up your child's immune system.

- Some offer a reduction in fees for second and subsequent children.

- If a member of staff is ill, your child will still be looked after – it is up to the nursery to arrange suitable care.

- Nurseries are inspected by Ofsted, so you can read past inspections and, just as with any school, get a feel for the strengths and weaknesses of any facility. You can also take some comfort that Ofsted's checking procedures should ensure an acceptable minimum standard of care.

Disadvantages

- Nursery workers can be poorly paid and staff turnover can be high.

- The menu options might be limited.

- Most nurseries only cater for parents working Monday to Friday in office hours.

- If your baby is ill, he won't go to nursery and you won't go to work but you'll still have to pay.

- The cost of nursery care can be high.

Typical costs for nurseries

- Nursery costs have risen at more than 6% (along with childminder and after-school club costs) – more than double the inflation rate of 2.7%.

- A nursery place now costs 77% more in real terms that it did in 2003, although earnings have stayed still.

- The average nursery cost for a child under two has risen by 4.2% to £106.38 per week for a part-time place (25 hours).

- A full-time place costs £11,000 for a year.

- Costs for over-twos have risen by 6.6% to an average of £103.96 per week for a part-time place.

- Most nurseries charge for the days your child is set to attend, not the days they actually attend. So, if your child is ill and is excluded from nursery, you will still pay, whether or not you work that day.

Source: Daycare Trust and the Family and Parenting Institute's Childcare Costs Survey 2013

Childminders

Advantages

- Many young children like the security of the 'home from home' set-up a childminder provides.

- A smaller group of children can often mean either a wide variety of activities or activity more closely matched to their needs.

- Again, childminders are subject to Ofsted inspections; their results are published online and therefore subject to public (especially parental) scrutiny, and an Ofsted inspection should guarantee an acceptable minimum standard of care.

Disadvantages

- Childminders look after many children, not just yours, so they may not have the flexibility to offer as much one-to-one attention as you would like.

- There might be greater opportunities for outings or a wider variety of excursions, but you will probably have to fund these on top of the day-to-day childcare costs.

- If your child is ill, the childminder may not be able to care for him (depending on the other children in their care at the time).

- If the childminder is ill, there may not be scope for any continuity of care – ie you don't go in to work. (In reality, some childminders act as emergency carers for one another and this can work well, but not all childminders offer this facility.)

Typical costs for childminders

- Childminder costs rose more than 6% from 2011 to 2012.

- The typical cost of a place for 25 hours a week for a child under the age of two has increased by 5.9% to £98.15 in England and Wales.

- For a child aged two or over, the cost has increased by 5.2% to £96.67.

- Childminders are self-employed, so you won't have to pay any tax on top of their fee.

- Some childminders charge a booking fee to secure your child's place, particularly in high-demand areas or those that have a link to particular schools.

Source: Daycare Trust and the Family and Parenting Institute's Childcare Costs Survey 2013

New rules for nurseries and childminders

Nurseries and childminders in England may soon be allowed to look after more children if government proposals go ahead – but how might this affect you?

Ministers are proposing to alter the ratio of children to carers, as long as carers' qualifications meet new standards. This will mean more childcare places should become available, and costs of places might be reduced. Critics think that the changes could mean compromising the quality of care though, and that costs are unlikely to go down substantially.

At the moment in England, the ratios are 1:3 adults to children under two, 1:4 adults to two year olds and 1:8 adults to three year olds and above. The new ratios proposed are 1:4 adults to children under two, 1:6 adults to two year olds and 1:8 adults to three year olds and above.

In Wales, the maximum number of children a childminder can care for is six children under eight years of age. Of those six children, no more than three may be under five years of age and of those three children, normally no more than two may be under 18 months of age.

In Welsh nurseries, there should be one adult to three children under two years, one adult to four children aged two years and one adult to eight children aged three to seven years.

Nannies

Advantages

- Your baby is looked after in his own home.

- It costs no more for second and subsequent children – the cost of a nanny is the cost of a nanny.

- Activities are tailored to your child's needs.

- Everything can work around your baby's existing routine.

- If your baby is ill, the nanny can still look after him.

- As the employer, you get to agree when the suitable opportunities are for your nanny to take holiday days.

- You can nanny-share with friends, neighbours or other parents in the area to save costs.

- Nannies can be employed on a live-in or a daily basis. If you have a decently sized spare room and other suitable facilities (eg an en-suite or room for a TV in the bedroom etc) then you might want to consider a live-in nanny. The overall costs are cheaper. Alternatively, for those who prefer their home to be their own at the end of a long day, a daily nanny could be the answer.

When you employ a nanny you become responsible for paying tax and National Insurance on behalf of your staff.

Disadvantages

- If you are the nanny's sole employer, your child may not meet up with many other children unless your nanny is quite gregarious.

- Without other non-family children to play with regularly, your child may take longer to adjust to a school environment and to learn to take turns and fit in with the routine of others.

- There may be extra costs you have to bear if you want your child to go out and about, from playgroups to day trips.

- You are the employer, so you will need to recruit and interview.

- You will also need to draw up a contract of employment and pay employer's National Insurance contributions.

- If your nanny gets pregnant, you will have to pay maternity benefits (although the government refunds these costs) and recruit a temporary nanny to cover the maternity period.

- Not all nannies are Ofsted registered, so some may cost more than others for the same level of take-home pay. Around half of the nannies surveyed by NannyTax for its annual pay survey were registered with Ofsted.

- Those who are not registered also don't get subjected to regular inspections that give you a third-party assessment of the childcare your baby is receiving.

Typical costs for nannies

Nanny salaries have actually fallen by as much as 5% over the past year.

The best way to lay the costs of a nanny out for you is to look at average costs for both daily and live-in nannies in different geographical areas of Britain.

Central London
Live-in nannies average £389 a week (£26,017 per annum*).
Daily nannies average £495 a week (£34,124 per annum).

Outer London
Live-in nannies average £336 a week (£21,963 per annum).
Daily nannies average £428 a week (£28,995 per annum).

Other areas
Live-in nannies average £317 a week (£20,509 per annum).
Daily nannies average £389 a week (£26,017per annum).

Source: NannyTax annual wages survey
All these weekly figures are what the nanny would receive net of tax and National Insurance. The annual figures are gross. Employers (ie you, the parents) would also have to pay employers' National Insurance.

Getting the hard work done for you

NannyTax (www.nannytax.co.uk) is an agency specifically set up to help manage your nanny's payroll issues. For an annual fee (currently £276), it can manage every element of your nanny's pay (other than actually paying it on your behalf!) and it also issues payslips. It can provide sample employment contracts, which are a great starting point, and can offer advice on recruiting a nanny.

Nanny agencies

Many nannies are registered with nanny agencies. For an annual, monthly or one-off fee, prospective employers (ie you, the parents) can register with these agencies, who will advertise your vacancy for you and screen their database of nannies to come up with a shortlist of candidates. All agencies are different, yet they have one thing in common: they act as intermediaries in the same way as, say, estate agents or recruitment consultants. If the relationship works, you will find the agency saves you a lot of time and heartache and works very well for the money. If the relationship really doesn't work, you may wonder what you're paying for, as none of the shortlisted candidates fits your criteria or the agency doesn't seem to be meeting your needs in the way you expect.

Weighing up the costs

Whatever option you decide is the best for you and your child, you need to make sure that the financial cost is less than the financial benefit of you returning to work. This may also be the time to consider only working part time. For more information on childcare and the financial aspects of raising a child, check out *Babynomics* by Madeline Thomas (White Ladder, 2010).

6

My relationships: my partner, family and friends

It's how this journey began, but unsurprisingly sex can be a tad scarce in the months that follow conception and birth. The thing to remember is that you are not alone if you or your partner go off sex during pregnancy. In this chapter we look at the factors that affect your love life during pregnancy and allay any fears you may have. We'll look at the impact your pregnancy and the impending arrival of your child will have on your relationship, and how to make sure you look after your partner as much as you do your baby. Finally, we'll have a look at what having a baby can mean for your relationship with your family and friends, and how to prepare for and cope with these changes.

THE EMBARRASSING QUESTIONS

Some women find that while they are pregnant their raging hormones make them feel sexier, and report a rampant sex life during pregnancy. If that's you (lucky thing), enjoy! However, you may find that you are feeling so sick or think you look so much like a whale that sex is the furthest thing from your mind.

However you find your love life developing, you will find that sex is a different thing now you're pregnant. There will probably be several things you might be worried about but are too embarrassed to ask. In this section we'll take you through some of the most common worries women face and give you an honest answer for each.

Will love-making squash the baby in any way?
Your baby is fully cushioned in the amniotic sac and he won't feel anything going on.

Can having sex cause miscarriage?
Unless you have experienced bleeding or have a history of miscarriage, it's perfectly safe to have sex without fear.

Can my partner's penis touch or hurt the baby in any way?
It's anatomically impossible for the penis to make contact with your baby in the uterus. Your cervix acts as a barrier between your baby and your man, so you don't need to worry.

Can my baby be exposed to any infection through sex?
The mucus plug that seals off the cervix prevents bacteria getting through, meaning your baby is not at risk from infection. However, blood-borne infections such as HIV can be transmitted through your blood to the baby. If you have any concerns about blood-borne infections, you should speak to your doctor as soon as possible.

Can I engage in oral sex?
Oral sex is perfectly safe as long as your partner doesn't blow into your vagina. If he blows up there with some force there is a chance that an air bubble could form in your circulatory system, leading to a potentially fatal embolism. However, this is extremely rare, so it shouldn't put you off. It is due to this same risk of air embolism that you should not use jacuzzis during your pregnancy and postnatal period.

Will an orgasm trigger labour?

You may experience mild contractions during orgasm, but they will not be strong enough to bring on labour unless you are ready to give birth anyway. In fact, this is sometimes a recommended way to bring on labour if you go past your due date.

Does the baby know what's going on?

Well, you know now that your baby can hear your voice from quite early on in the pregnancy, so if you happen to be whooping loudly... In all seriousness, though, you needn't worry that your baby is going to be affected physically or emotionally by your love-making.

Should I avoid sex in pregnancy if my placenta is low
(placenta praevia)?

It is advisable to avoid sexual penetration and orgasm if you have a low placenta, as movement of the cervix may dislodge the placenta and cause bleeding. You will be told at your 20-week scan if you have a low placenta and if you should avoid sex after this.

SEX DURING PREGNANCY

The first trimester

If you can't face sex in the first trimester, you are not alone. Many women report that the very thought of sex in the first few weeks made them feel more nauseous than ever. Many women just feel so sick/tired/hormonal (delete as appropriate) that intimate relations don't even come into thought, let alone deed.

It can also be that there are physical aspects of pregnancy that make intimacy uncomfortable, even at this early stage. Many women report that their breasts become so tender, even in the first few weeks, that they couldn't bear for them to be touched. Some pregnant women find they have a heightened sense of smell, which makes it difficult to

 SEX AND MISCARRIAGE

If you have a history of miscarriage, you might be worried that sex in the first trimester could be risky. If you do experience bleeding any time during pregnancy you should ask your GP or midwife whether it is safe to have sex, as obviously you don't want to do anything that could put your baby at risk, however pleasurable.

be physically close to their partner, while others actually do have the proverbial headache.

If you do feel completely off sex during your first trimester just be honest with your partner about how you're feeling. He'll understand that you're feeling sick/hormonal and won't be offended.

'I am definitely not one of those people who feels more attractive when pregnant, so our sex life suffers for a few months. Emotionally I haven't been too hormonally erratic with either pregnancy, so I don't feel like I've been too bad (my husband may have a different story though!).'

Nicola, second pregnancy and mum to Callum, 18 months

The second trimester

If your bedroom activities were somewhat limited in the first trimester, things may look up in the second, when you normally have more energy, have got over your sickness and are less anxious and stressed about anything going wrong.

Here are eight good reasons why sex in pregnancy can be fun.

- You don't need to worry about contraception.
- Increased blood flow in the pelvic region can lead to increased arousal and bigger or faster orgasms.
- You have to experiment with positions to accommodate your growing bump, which can be fun.
- It will help you feel sleepy and relaxed, which is useful if you are suffering from insomnia.
- It will encourage emotional closeness.
- It's good exercise for your pelvic floor muscles.
- If you struggled with your fertility and sex was becoming a chore pre-pregnancy, you can enjoy making love for fun – not for babies.

Many women enjoy sex in the second trimester because they actually like their new curvaceous body and feel very womanly and fecund; the problem is that their partners don't always feel the same way. There is a myth (or truth – as women we'll never know) that men think about sex every 52 seconds. This trait can go completely out of the window during pregnancy, according to some women, who found their usually amorous partners rather limited in the bedroom department while they were expecting.

If your partner is unusually reticent to make love, there are a number of reasons why your love life might be lacking at the moment.

- He's frightened that having sex could hurt you or the baby.

- You've gone from being a sexual being to a motherly one, and his instincts might be to protect you and not ravish you at the moment.

- 'He's just not that into you.' Well, not at the moment anyway; many men don't really find big boobs and bellies that alluring, and whilst you might be embracing all the changes to your body shape he might be quite put off by them.

- The concept of a new life growing inside you is weird enough as it is, and adding sex to the mix just makes it even stranger.

This can be a tad frustrating if you are feeling quite up for it for the first time in months, but don't worry – even if he isn't up for it at the moment the urge will definitely return after the baby is born. You shouldn't take it personally, though: pregnancy is a hugely emotional time for your partner as well as for you, so you should respect the conflicting emotions he may be feeling.

The third trimester

Things get trickier towards the end of your pregnancy because you get very tired, and there's the logistical aspect of dealing with your bump (the missionary position's going to be out for obvious reasons!). If you do persevere, it's perfectly possible to maintain a happy, fulfilling sex life with some patience, a sense of humour/adventure, and a stack of pillows.

WORDS FROM THE PROFESSIONALS: If your waters break early, you experience leaking, have a show (when the mucus plug sealing your cervix comes away) or have placenta praevia, you should seek advice from your midwife before you have sex as it could make your baby vulnerable to infection.

BRING IT ON, BABY!

You've probably heard that making love when your baby is due is a good way to kick-start proceedings. There is some scientific basis for this: semen contains prostaglandin, a hormone-like substance that is said to soften the cervix, and the hormone oxytocin is released during orgasm, which makes the uterus contract and helps to limber up the cervix in preparation for birth. Even if you are the size of a beached whale and sex is the last thing on your mind, you might be surprised to hear yourself asking your partner for a hot session just to test out the theory.

Sex-free pregnancy

You can still enjoy an intimate pregnancy even if you do decide, for whatever reason, that celibacy is the best policy. Obviously there's a number of very pleasurable options open to you, from the sexual (oral sex) to the sensual (body massage). If you can't face full-blown sex, intimacy in the form of kissing and cuddling will make you both feel wanted and loved, and the most important thing is that you still connect with each other physically and emotionally during pregnancy.

Dealing with your new love life

In Chapter 4 we suggested ways to keep your relationship healthy during pregnancy, because undoubtedly it does come under considerable stress. If you normally find sex a great stress buster and you are not making love with the frequency previously enjoyed, you can get frustrated with each other. If this happens, it is really important that you keep talking and try to understand why sex is on the back burner. If he doesn't want to make love to you it doesn't mean that he doesn't love you; he might just be feeling scared, weird or worried, and all these emotions are completely natural. If you don't want to make love with him because you are exhausted, feel fat and unattractive or sick, that's also completely normal and doesn't mean you don't care or no longer fancy him. Just make sure that you are open and honest with one another, and take time to be with each other as a couple, without focusing on baby stuff.

'My husband has said he likes my body and has been quite fascinated by the changes my body has gone through. In terms of our sex life, I definitely haven't experienced the sex urge some women claim they get! Our relationship has changed a bit in that I've become very clingy, which is weird for me. I think the fact that I've had to change my life overnight while he has had time to slowly adjust to changes just shows how different the experience of pregnancy is for men and women.'

Virginia, first pregnancy

And the survey says . . .

Contrary to the traditional view that pregnant women do not want an active sex life, a 2010 study reports that many women feel a high sexual interest during all three trimesters of pregnancy.

The study, conducted in Lisbon, Portugal, included 188 women aged between 17 and 40 who recently gave birth. The study was published in *The Journal of Sexual Medicine*.

- Almost 45% of women said they had sex most often during the first trimester of their pregnancy, while around 36% had frequent sex during the second trimester. Only 10% reported frequent sex in the third trimester, although 80% said they had sex, albeit less frequently, in the third trimester. A game 40% had sex during the birth week!

- Around half of all respondents reported about the same sexual satisfaction during all trimesters of pregnancy. Almost 39% of women said their sexual interest did not change, while slightly more than 32% of women noticed a decline in sexual desire.

- Around 40% of women said that they felt less sexually attractive during pregnancy, while more than 75% of women reported about the same sexual interest from their partner.

- More than 23% of women were worried that sexual activity during pregnancy might hurt the unborn baby. Some men were also concerned that sex during pregnancy might somehow hurt the baby or reported the feeling of being watched by their baby during sex.

- Many also feared that sex during the third trimester of pregnancy might cause premature birth or cause other problems for the baby.

Sex after pregnancy

We can't lie and say that the urge to have sex again gets delivered with the baby because it doesn't, and if you are sore and delicate after a difficult birth, the idea of anyone going near your girly bits is pretty terrifying until everything heals. Slowly but surely, though, you will get through the post-partum baby fug and find your sexual mojo again (well, how else are you going to make baby number two?).

FOCUSING ON RELATIONSHIPS

We have looked in detail at the practical aspects of your lifestyle in pregnancy, but there are also emotional aspects that are important to cover, because your relationships with the people you love can change quite significantly when you are pregnant. It is as important to feel 'emotionally well' as it is to feel physically well, as there is evidence to suggest that the more relaxed and happy the mother, the easier the pregnancy and birth. We also know that extreme stress is not good for you or your baby, so you need to make sure you take care of your emotional well-being as well as your physical health.

Your partner

A recent study revealed that one in three men in the UK feels left out of the pregnancy, so try to include him as much as possible.

Have you ever heard that phrase, 'Having a baby brought us closer together' and thought, 'Are you mad, woman?' For most of us, there is that wonderful honeymoon period when you find out you are going to be parents, and you are so loved up and fluffy you think you are going to explode. Then the morning sickness kicks in, you start looking and behaving like a spotty teenager and the next thing you know you're having murderous thoughts as he downs his fifth pint and you contemplate driving home without him.

The point here is that pregnancy is not always going to be plain sailing, and your partner is likely to annoy you just as much as he did before – it's just you might be arguing about different things (like names, what football team the baby is going to support, how long your mother is going to stay after the birth etc).

When you are pregnant, you are often so obsessed with your health and that of your baby it is easy to forget that there is someone else in the relationship and that he is probably as scared/excited/bewildered/fed up as you!

Some men get quite paranoid in pregnancy that all your love and energy is going to go into the baby, and that they are going to take the back seat in the relationship from now on. Remember that it wasn't so long ago that it was just the two of you, and even though you are about to become three, you have to try to keep the 'couple' side of your relationship alive and enjoy the time you have together before the baby is born.

If possible, try not to keep your relationship on the back burner and make sure you consider what your partner might be feeling. He may be jealous of all the attention you and the baby are getting; he might feel like an alien has invaded his beloved's body; he might be terrified of being a dad; he might be secretly repulsed by the belly you love so much; he might hate your choice of names but feel you should have the final say as you have done all the work. There's probably 101 niggles going on in his mind, and it's important to try to get him to share his hopes and fears with you so that you both feel you're in this together.

'Being pregnant has really brought Paul and me closer, we already feel like a proper family now. I think it's been hard on him to see me worrying, but we're coming through it.'

Nichola, first pregnancy

Once he has dealt with all his myriad emotions, he'll start taking care of you and your baby. Make sure you always tell him how you're feeling: it may be that he hasn't realised what you want from him.

Keeping the romance in your relationship

Babymoons
A 'babymoon' is a holiday that you and your partner take before two becomes three. Obviously the more luxury and pampering there is the better, but even though your budget may not stretch to the Maldives or Mauritius there is much to be said for a weekend away together, even if it is drizzly Devon. As long as you spend some quality time together you'll feel the benefit, no matter where you are.

Cinema trips
Some cinemas now have those brilliant baby screenings where you can catch up with all the latest movies with your babe in arms; however, in truth they are not the most quiet or relaxing affairs, so make the most of going to the cinema together while you can. Many people find that once

 According to latest figures, babymoons are now a multi-million pound industry and can really help you bond as a couple before the arrival of your baby.

they have children the only showings they can make are late ones, by which time both parents might be struggling to stay awake!

'We tried to really appreciate the time we had before James was born. We went for pub lunches, to the theatre, and had a few weekends away. We knew once he came our lives would change dramatically, and did a lot of stuff before I got too tired to move!'

Claire, mum to James, 15 months

Dinner

If your budget doesn't run to luxurious dinners out, then have a romantic night in with some candles, your favourite food, smoochy music and (a little) wine. It doesn't matter what you have or whether you go out or not, so long as you spend some time together as a couple and not as prospective parents.

Sex

Sex is not likely to figure highly in the weeks after birth, so make the most of any intimate time you can have together.

Breakfast in bed

Make the most of your free time now, and if you want to veg out in bed or have a duvet day in front of the sofa, wallow in it, baby!

 If you set aside a designated evening per week throughout your pregnancy for 'date nights' it will give you some much needed time to talk, plan, cuddle or just be happy together.

Relationships with family

The day a woman tells her mother she is going to be a granny can be one of the happiest moments of her life. Some women are lucky enough to have a very supportive family, but some families have complicated relationships and often a pregnancy can make matters worse.

If you find that your family is proving difficult, try these suggestions to make life easier.

- Be firm with your family if you are worried they are going to 'take over'. If you don't want your mother or mother-in-law to come and stay with you when the baby is born, be firm and say as nicely as possible that you want some time at home alone with the baby (but that you would love them to come and visit for the day).

- Your mum may have seen and done it all before, but parenting styles and opinions have changed. If she is driving you mad with her views, you have the option of trying to explain that things are different since you were a baby, or just putting up and shutting up!

- Try not to get into any sibling rivalry: there can be tensions when one of you has the first boy or girl in the family, or someone has been trying to get pregnant for ages and you did it at the first attempt etc. Try to take other family members' feelings into account, as your baby joy might be their baby misery.

- Just because every boy in your family since forever took his father's name, doesn't mean that you have to name *your* son after his father; if you are happy with your family traditions then go for it, but if not, it's your baby and you can call him what you like.

If your family do become too pushy or annoying, just remember that they're excited and they're just trying to be involved in this exciting moment in your life. Always try to consider their feelings as well as your own, and don't get too stressed about family interaction.

'I've had a lot of people keen to impart their wisdom when it's not wanted or needed, but I think it's all done with best intentions, so I have learnt to smile politely and nod!'

Julie, mum to Eloise, 6 months

Relationships with friends

This one isn't always as simple as it seems either. You might be the first one in your social group to get pregnant and suddenly you might be treated like some social outcast. Alternatively, you might be the last one in your gang to get pregnant, and discover that none of your friends is particularly thrilled or excited about your pregnancy because they have seen and done it all before. You might announce your pregnancy just when one of your friends has had a miscarriage or failed IVF attempt and feel incredibly guilty about sharing your happy news, or you might (heaven forbid) become a baby bore and drive your friends away because all you talk about is your unborn baby. No matter what your circumstances, much like your partner and family, you should try to consider the feelings of your friends, but make sure that you don't let yourself become too stressed or upset by their reactions.

'My friends have been great: they're happy to indulge in my baby talk for a while before we move on to general gossip. I try to think of it in the same way as when I was getting married – people are interested to a point, but they don't want to hear every detail.'

Amanda, first pregnancy

How to sustain friendships in pregnancy

- If there is some tension between friends for whatever reason, remember that most relationships do work themselves out and, even if there is a cooling off during pregnancy, if the friendship is strong you will be able to pick it up at a later date.

- Make time for your friends: if you put all your energy into your baby and your partner, you will miss all the laughs and camaraderie that a girly relationship brings (and boy, you'll need some after the birth!). Arrange a night for 'mocktails' (non-alcoholic cocktails), silly films or coffee, and have a good old gossip.

- Have a weekend away or a pampering day out. This doesn't have to be hen-style partying in Ibiza, but if you think this will be your last opportunity to go away without a little one in tow, get a group of friends together and hit the spa or boutique hotel for some R&R (and giggling).

- Always make sure to ask your friends what's happening in their lives. Although you're going through a life changing experience, your friends want to know you still care about their lives and experiences.

'Luckily, a lot of our friends are expecting or have had their first babies too. However, I have found that some of my single friends haven't been in touch as much, and those that have, I've tended to meet up with on my own.'

Debbie, mum to Lauren, 13 months

Meeting new friends

If you find that your old friends really can't cope with the changes brought about by your pregnancy, try making new friends. You don't have to abandon your old ones, but by joining parenting or NCT classes you'll be meeting local women in the same situation, and you might discover a kindred spirit.

GOING IT ALONE

Some women choose to have a baby without a father on the scene, and other women have this position foisted upon them. Whatever the reason, it is a strong woman who goes through pregnancy without the support of a partner, and hopefully you have a close-knit community of family and friends who can give all the love and help you need. If you are in this position, try making your life easier with a few of these tips.

- Take a girlfriend or family member with you when you buy all your baby essentials, as it can be quite a daunting job to do on your own (and they can help you carry it!).

- Shop online and have your bulky and heavy food shopping delivered.

- Enlist help to do anything practical like painting, decorating, or assembling furniture, not only because you might hurt yourself, but because it's also physically difficult to climb a step ladder when you are eight months pregnant.

- There is a US website devoted to women who choose to have a baby on their own: www.singlemothersbychoice.com. You can sign up for membership and join online discussions etc.

- Parenting forums over here can be very supportive too, so check out sites like www.madeformums.com; www.mumsnet. com; www.pregnancyforum.co.uk; and post a topic: you might find other local single mums to hook up with.

There may be a silver lining to being pregnant and raising a child on your own: you get to make all the decisions! *You* get to name the baby, decide on the nursery decor and even choose how strict a parent you want to be. There won't be another person giving their opinions or telling you off when you haven't done it the 'right' way.

When your relationship breaks up during pregnancy

Going through pregnancy and birth alone is a pretty daunting prospect, which is why splitting up during pregnancy is really tough.

Pregnancy certainly puts the spotlight on your relationship and can highlight any niggles and imperfections in it; most relationships pull through, but for some couples the strain is too much to bear and they break up.

Some men freak out at the idea of becoming a father; they don't want the responsibility and use it as an excuse to leave. Sometimes couples get pregnant thinking that a baby will 'save' the relationship and then realise it won't, even before the baby is born. Some women accidentally get pregnant quite early on in a relationship, only to work out that he isn't 'the one', even if he is the father of their child. Some unlucky women are in a violent relationship and find pregnancy is the catalyst to give them the strength to leave before the baby gets hurt too.

As difficult as it is, try to remain calm. If arguments get heated or you feel yourself getting stressed, remove yourself from the situation – it's best for you and your baby.

If you do break up, it's probably worth trying to keep things friendly for the sake of your child. You may not want to ever see him again, but he is your baby's father and hopefully he'll want to have a relationship with the child in the future. He does not have to be named on the birth certificate, but if the split is amicable or you believe that he will continue to play a role in your lives, you can jointly register the birth so that he has Parental Responsibility. If you are not married, the father does not automaticly have Parental Responsibility (which is legally defined as 'all the rights, duties, powers, responsibilities and authority which by law a parent of a child has in relation to the child and his property'). If you do not want him to have Parental Responsibility he can go to court after the baby is born to apply for it and ask for access rights too, so it makes sense to try to sort things out now. You'll have quite enough to do coping on your own with a new baby, so if you can get the legal side of things straightened out before the baby is born it's going to be a big weight off your mind. If you need legal help and advice on fathers' rights and responsibilities or single parenting support, there are details of organisations to assist you in the back of the book.

Pregnant and starting a new relationship

You might be single and pregnant by choice, or newly separated from your unborn baby's father, when you meet someone new and 'ping', it's love – probably when you least expected it.

If this happens to you, you probably can't believe your good luck, as many men wouldn't be prepared to take on a woman who is pregnant with another man's child.

Every relationship is different and it's difficult to generalise, but here are a few tips to keep things sweet with a new man in pregnancy.

- Take things slowly, particularly if you are on the rebound.

- If you think he's in for the long haul, talk to him about how he'd like to be involved and let him suggest the role he'd like to play.

- Let him dictate how involved he gets in the baby preparations; if he doesn't want to attend antenatal classes or parentcraft classes, don't force him: he'll need time to get used to the idea of a baby. By the time the baby is due hopefully he'll be (nearly) as excited as you.

- Make sure he feels as loved and as important as the baby growing inside you.

- Spend couple-time together learning about each other and not talking about the impending birth.

- If he wants to stick with you when you are fat, hormonal and generally not your normal self he obviously likes you, so count those lucky stars!

If you are beginning a new relationship, you'll need to consider not only all the usual things, like whether you like him and see a future together; you'll also need to consider your baby. Any relationship you have is going to be a relationship with your child as well, so when you're deciding about whether someone is right for you, make sure you decide whether they're also right for your child.

7

Thinking about my baby's birth

There's no getting away from it: that baby has to come out one way or another, and it's best to make plans for his arrival in the world (even if it does seem a very long way off). Keep a fairly open mind about proceedings, but do give some consideration to the type of birth you want and where you want to have the baby – after all, it might go exactly as you hope!

In this chapter we'll look at the kinds of things you need to consider in your birth plan and how best to prepare yourself for the big day.

The recent Place of Birth study suggested that a home birth is as safe as hospitals or midwife-led birthing units for women having their second or third baby.

CHOOSING WHERE TO HAVE YOUR BABY

There are generally three options when it comes to choosing where you give birth:

- a consultant-led hospital unit
- midwife-led birthing unit
- home birth.

> **WORDS FROM THE PROFESSIONALS:** People who come in with a fixed idealistic birth plan often don't get the birth they planned for and feel disappointed: as if they have failed. The best situation is a woman who knows how she'd like to give birth but has considered and is informed of all possibilities so that if anything diverts from her plan she still feels in control and understands why it has happened.

According to a recent government pledge, you should have a choice of where you give birth, but a recent study by the NCT revealed that over 90% of women are *not* given birth options, and less than 5% of pregnant women were able to choose where they gave birth. This report contradicted findings from the last published study by the Healthcare Commission, which claimed that 81% of women are offered a choice. With the figures varying so wildly, it's hard to know what the real likelihood is of being offered more than one birthing option!

Check out the website www. birthchoiceuk. com if you want some impartial advice on where to give birth locally.

> **WORDS FROM THE PROFESSIONALS:** You should be given the option of delivery at home, in a midwife-led birth centre or on a hospital labour ward. Some units do not have midwife-led units and some do not offer home birth; it is something you need to find out before you book at a hospital. Some women will not be offered the choice because they have a medical or pregnancy complication, so the safest place to deliver would be a labour ward, but they should be informed of the reasons why this is being recommended.

It's well worth researching the options available to you, because your choice may well affect the type of birth that you have. You don't have to stick with your decision, though; if you want to change your mind and opt for different care, you are entitled to do so – sometimes it may mean going to a different hospital to deliver, though, especially if the hospital does not have a birth centre or offer home births.

Consultant-led hospital unit

The consultant-led unit is where you will be advised to give birth if you have any complications or concerns in pregnancy, if you are being induced, if you are having a Caesarean section or if you would like to be able to have an epidural. You will be in a room of your own and have a midwife looking after you. There will also be doctors caring for you.

Hospital units can vary enormously – from shiny and high-tech to crumbling and Dickensian – so if environment is important to you, there's a possibility you will have to travel to find what you want. Do bear in mind that although you can choose to give birth outside your local area, journey time is an important consideration because babies can arrive unannounced and unexpectedly, even first time around. Also, after your delivery, the midwives who visit you at home will come from the local hospital, not where you delivered.

Pros

- There is an obstetrician on call, should you experience complications during delivery.

- Hospitals are best equipped to deal with medical emergencies.

- You can have an epidural, should you need one, as there is an anaesthetist on hand 24 hours a day.

- If your baby is born early or with problems, there will be a specialist neonatal unit where he can be cared for, and a paediatrician can be present at the baby's birth.

- If you have problems after the birth, you will stay in hospital and be cared for by doctors and midwives.

- If you have a high-risk pregnancy, you will be seen by a consultant at the hospital.

Cons

- Hospital wards can be rather grim, unfamiliar places.

- You may not have met the midwives who'll deliver your baby.

- Your partner may not be able to stay with you if you are on the postnatal or antenatal ward at night, but can stay with you when you are in labour.

Approximately one in eight births in the UK is assisted delivery.

Before you make your decision, you might like to take a hospital tour and check out the facilities. Unfortunately, many hospitals have discontinued tours since the swine flu outbreak in 2009. If the hospital doesn't provide a tour, it is worth looking at the hospital's website; many have virtual tours so you can get an idea what the unit looks like. If you are lucky you might find that your hospital has both a consultant-led maternity unit and a midwife-led birthing centre (see below), so you can choose between the two as your pregnancy progresses.

'We're going for a hospital birth. I want all the back-up I can get. I don't want to take any risks at all. I'm going to try for a natural birth, and they have a birthing pool where we're going, but if I need drugs I'll take them. All that matters is that the baby comes out healthy.'

Nichola, first pregnancy

You need to find out what sort of care is on offer and what facilities are available. Below is a list of questions you might want to ask, to help you decide whether the unit is offering what you want. If you have no choice, it's still useful to find out as much as you can about the hospital, because it's possible that the next time you see the maternity ward will be when you are in full-blown labour, and the location of the catering facilities or the loos will be the last thing on your mind!

Questions to ask

- How many consultants are available at the hospital? Do I only see them if there's a problem? Are they on call 24 hours?

- Will the midwife I see at my antenatal appointments deliver my baby?

- If not, will I get a chance to get to know the midwives at the unit?

- How long can my partner stay with me after the birth if the baby is delivered at night?

- What birthing equipment is available (birthing balls, bean bags, etc)?

- What are your policies on induction, pain relief and intervention?

- Do you encourage active birth and different birth positions, or do most women give birth lying down?

- Do you have a birthing pool?

- How long do women normally have to wait for an epidural?

- Is there a CD player in the delivery room, or can I bring music in?

- What is the Caesarean rate at this unit?

- What type (level) of neonatal facilities are available if my baby is born early or sick?

- How long will I stay in the hospital after the baby is born?

- Will I be moved after giving birth and, if so, how many women are there in a room in the post-delivery wards?

- Will my baby be with me the whole time after birth?

- What are the visiting hours and rules?

- Can I bring food into hospital and is there a fridge to store it?

- Do you allow the consumption of food and drink during labour?

- What catering facilities are on site?

- Are there private rooms available that I can book for some privacy after the birth?

It's also useful to find out what security measures are in place. You should also try to check out the bathrooms, because they'll give you a pretty clear picture of the standards of cleanliness and hygiene at the hospital.

WORDS FROM THE PROFESSIONALS: What's the standard procedure for going to hospital when you think you're in labour?

You phone the hospital when you think you are in labour, and the midwife will either give you advice over the phone or tell you to come in to be assessed. When you come in, you and your baby will be assessed and you will be examined to see if your cervix is dilating. If you are in early labour – before 3cm dilated – you may be given advice, such as a recommendation to go home for some rest and return when your labour has progressed. If you do not want to go home, you may be kept in the antenatal ward to wait for labour to become fully established; it is generally best to go home as women tend to cope much better and can relax more in their own home. You may well be in a bay with other women on the antenatal ward, which many women don't enjoy, and would prefer some privacy. It is not until you are admitted to the labour ward and in established labour that you have your own room and own midwife.

Midwife-led units/birth centres

Midwife-led units (also commonly known as 'birth centres') provide a sort of 'halfway house' between hospital and home births. The rooms are usually more homey and comfortable than consultant-led delivery rooms and, as the name implies, there are no doctors for you or for the baby. They may be attached to a consultant-led unit at a hospital, or operate as a stand-alone centre.

The difference between birth centres and consultant-led units is that the former are staffed and run by midwives. If the birth centre is attached to the consultant-led unit, there are doctors on hand if things go wrong and you can easily be transferred to the labour ward if necessary. If the birth centre is a stand-alone centre away from the hospital, you will be transferred by ambulance with the midwife to the consultant-led unit if complications arise. Birth centres are gaining in popularity and around 10% of women delivered in one last year. More are being opened every year, but there's no guarantee you'll find one in your area, so check out www.birthchoiceuk.com if you think this sort of care is for you.

A recent report noted that only 10% of hospital births in England were midwife-led.

Midwife-led units are normally more low-tech and homey – for example, one in London has fibre-optic lights and funky bean bags and looks more like an average teenager's bedroom (albeit rather more sparse and tidy) than a room you'd expect to give birth in, which is precisely the appeal of these centres.

You should be aware that you will only be accepted for care at a midwife-led unit if your pregnancy is low risk: that is, if you have no complications and are expecting a healthy baby. Your age may be a factor with some centres too, and for most, being overweight will be an exclusion. If you have gestational diabetes or high blood pressure, or if you know your baby is going to be born early or have health problems, you will usually need some input from a doctor, so you will probably need consultant-led care. The midwives are trained in life-saving and resuscitation techniques should your baby need help, and if you are in a birth centre joined on to a consultant-led unit there will be obstetricians and paediatricians available in an emergency. If you are unsure, ask your midwife or doctor where they think you should deliver your baby.

Pros

- A relaxing environment to give birth in. Rooms are usually equipped with mats and bean bags to give birth on.

- Your partner may be allowed to stay the night with you after the baby is born, space and schedule permitting.

- You'll be provided with equipment to facilitate natural birth, like birthing pools, birthing balls, etc.

- Statistically, you have a lower chance of having an assisted delivery (and you would need to be transferred out for this).

- You are less likely to tear or have an episiotomy (when they have to cut your perineum to help the baby out), as labours are 'lower risk'. See page 336 for more on episiotomies.

- You may be offered complementary therapies such as aromatherapy or acupuncture to make the birth a less painful and more relaxing experience.

- You may have your own private en suite room after delivery.

- You will have access to Entonox (gas and air).

- Some units offer the same pain relief options that are available on the consultant-led unit, apart from an epidural; you would be transferred to the consultant-led unit if you needed one. Other units offer only gas and air, so remember to ask about this.

Cons

- If the pain becomes unbearable, you won't be able to have an epidural at a birth centre.

- You will have to be transferred to hospital if you or your baby get in trouble during labour or after delivery.

- You can't have a Caesarean at a birth centre.

Apparently around 22% of first time mothers do transfer to hospital or the labour ward from a birth centre, so if it happens to you your midwife will be used to this happening and will make the transition as smooth as she can.

- If your baby needs special care after birth, he will have to be transferred to hospital.

- If the unit is a stand-alone birth centre, it may be some distance from a hospital and transferring could take time. If it is a birth centre joined on to a consultant-led unit this is a lesser issue.

Women who use birth centres report very high satisfaction concerning the standard of care they receive, and experts believe that if women have good one-to-one care during labour they are more likely to have a straightforward birth.

Questions you might want to ask at the birthing centre

- How do you manage pain at the centre?

- What birthing aids do you provide?

- What complementary therapies do you offer?

- What can I bring with me to make the birth more pleasant (music, pillows, candles, etc)?

- How long will I stay after the birth?

- If I stay overnight, can my partner stay with me?

- How many first-time mothers have to transfer to hospital?

- Which circumstances in labour would necessitate a transfer to hospital?

- How long does it take to get from the unit to a hospital?

- How often do you update your neonatal resuscitation skills?

Midwife-led units are a very positive development in the provision of maternity services, and are definitely worth considering if you are low-risk and the idea of a 'natural' birth appeals.

'I'm hoping to give birth at a midwife-led unit, but I need to do some research into what options are available in the area. I'm worried I won't cope well and will want an epidural so I need to think carefully about my options.'

Amanda, first pregnancy

WORDS FROM THE PROFESSIONALS: What happens if there are no free beds available when I go into labour?

It's very rare that there are no beds for women to deliver in, but if this is the situation, then the unit will have an agreement with a hospital close by in which you will be able to give birth. While it is very unusual for this to happen, it can undoubtedly cause a certain amount of anxiety if this situation arises, so do ask this question when visiting your midwife-led unit. Each hospital closely monitors how many women are due each month, so it can manage its staffing and beds.

Through the keyhole

Birth centres are the ideal place for low-risk women to deliver; they have a more homey feel and often don't feel like you are in hospital. Because your baby's heart rate does not need to be monitored continuously, you can move around with aids such as active birth bean bags, mats, stools and birthing pools, all of which can make labour quicker, less painful and with fewer complications. During labour you will receive one-to-one care from an experienced midwife who is confident in supporting women through labour. Women who deliver in birth centres are usually very satisfied with the experience.

On a separate note, midwives get great satisfaction from working in birth centres, as it is rewarding to support women through the normal birth process, as well as sharing that special moment when they meet their child for the first time and become a family.

Home births

In England and Wales, 2.4% of births took place at home in 2011. The popularity of home births has seen a change over the decades: in the 1960s one third of all births were at home, but by the late 1980s, less than 1% were home births. This percentage then rose steadily to a peak in 2008 at 2.9%. These rates vary in other UK countries – 1.5% in Scotland and 0.4% in Northern Ireland – but all of these figures 'hide' local peaks and troughs, so check your local hospital. In some parts of the country, the percentage of women choosing to have a home birth is as high as 11%.

A study from the end of 2011 showed that for women having their first baby, home birth resulted in three times as many complications, but the absolute risk was still low. For women who had previously had a vaginal delivery, home delivery was not more complicated than delivery elsewhere.

All of the Royal Family were born at home until Princess Diana bucked the trend and had her sons privately at the Lindo Wing in St Mary's Hospital in Paddington, London. Davina McCall had all three of her children at home, and describing her first daughter, Holly's, birth said: 'Giving birth at home was the most fantastic experience; I have never felt so beautiful and loved.' And she's not the only one: Charlotte Church, Demi Moore, Meryl Streep and Cindy Crawford all had home births. Some women love the idea of giving birth in their own home in a relaxed environment, while others like the security of having doctors on hand. The choice is totally your own, and you should just make sure you consider all aspects of this option.

You *should* be offered home birth as an option, although a recent survey revealed that only 57% of pregnant women were offered it by their midwife at the booking appointment. However, only women with no complications and a normal singleton pregnancy would be offered a home birth, which perhaps explains this statistic. Some authorities may not push the home birth option because of the cost – you need to have two midwives in attendance if you give birth at home, and their budget may not stretch to it.

The appeal of a home birth is obvious but it is not without its risks, and you should weigh up the pros and cons and have a good chat with your doctor and midwife before you decide it's the birth option for you.

Pros

- You give birth in a familiar environment surrounded by the things (and people) you love.

- You can be tucked up in your own bed straight after the birth.

- You have complete privacy.

- You don't have to share wards or bathrooms with anyone.

- You have two midwives looking after you and it's likely that you'll know one or both of them from your antenatal appointments.

- The midwives will also stay with you for the duration of your labour, so you won't have the change of shift that can blight a hospital labour. The two midwives will relieve each other if it is a long labour.

- You can recover in the relative peace and quiet of your own home.

Cons

- You'll probably only be able to have gas and air at home (although some midwives can administer the drug pethidine).

- If anything happens during labour that the midwife can't deal with, you'll need to go by ambulance to hospital.

- If an emergency arises during labour, there will be time spent travelling to the hospital that could at best be uncomfortable, and at worst could endanger your life or your baby's life.

- You might miss the 'security' of 24-hour midwifery care that you'll get in hospital after the birth.

> **WORDS FROM THE PROFESSIONALS:** If you have complications such as pre-eclampsia, are expecting twins or your baby is breech, your midwife will encourage you to have a hospital birth as the labour needs additional monitoring.

You should also be aware that some health professionals don't support the idea of home births for first-time mothers, and other health authorities won't sanction one on the grounds of cost. If you really want to have one and you are coming up against opposition to the idea, you can always book a private midwife to look after you in the last weeks of pregnancy (for more info on private birth options, see below).

> **WORDS FROM THE PROFESSIONALS:** How do I plan childcare for my other children if I'm having a home birth, and what sort of after care will I get?
>
> Other children are often in bed or cared for by friends or family during a home birth. I have done a home birth at night with three other children in bed who did not even stir. You tend to find women who deliver at home are more rested and relaxed, and are better supported as their partner doesn't get sent home at night like in hospitals. The midwife stays and shows you how to care for the baby – you will receive the same level of care as you would in a consultant-led hospital or midwife-led unit.

PRIVATE CARE

If you are prepared to splash the cash, there are plenty of private care options you can choose during pregnancy, birth and beyond, and you might feel it is money well spent. Be aware, though, that going private won't guarantee a better, safer or more comfortable birth. You might get more attention, more pleasant surroundings and nicer food, but these do not guarantee safer or better midwifery or medical care. Every birth is different and there are only so many factors determined by the location.

Independent midwives

Independent midwives are fully qualified midwives who have chosen to work outside the NHS in a self-employed capacity, and look after you before, during and after the birth. Some women choose to hire an independent midwife because they want continuity of care throughout their pregnancy; others take on an independent midwife because they will facilitate a 'natural' or home birth if a woman wants one but has been advised against it on the NHS, or it is not available locally.

Independent midwives are fully regulated in the same way as midwives in the NHS, and must adhere to government rules and guidelines. They are also subject to annual inspection visits and equipment checks. An independent midwife can support you as a birthing partner in hospital if you need to be transferred during your planned home birth, but she cannot provide care in hospital, as she is not employed there.

How much do they cost?
A lot will depend on where you live and the package of care you choose, but ballpark figures show that, on average, independent midwives charge between £2,000 and £4,000 for their services. Normally this has to be paid in full by week 36 of pregnancy.

Pros

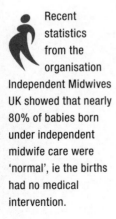

Recent statistics from the organisation Independent Midwives UK showed that nearly 80% of babies born under independent midwife care were 'normal', ie the births had no medical intervention.

- An independent midwife will build up a relationship with you before your baby is born, which may result in a better birth outcome.

- She may help you have a home birth if you have been advised against one by the NHS.

- She will stay with you throughout your pregnancy, birth and for an agreed period afterwards, so you have continuity of care.

- They work alongside the NHS, so that you can still have all your scans and tests etc done in hospital.

- They are trained to deal with emergencies and will stay with you if you need to be transferred to hospital.

Cons

- Independent midwives do not have personal liability insurance, so you can't sue them if something goes wrong. Although midwives seem to want insurance, insurers aren't keen to provide it at the moment as there are fewer than 200 independent midwives operating in the UK, meaning there is no profit in it.

- If you have to be transferred to hospital she will stay with you as your 'birth partner', but will let the midwives and doctors at the hospital take over your midwifery care.

- If your birth doesn't go to plan in any way, you can't have a refund.

- If the NHS has declined a home birth, there might be very good safety reasons for this, so be sure you aren't taking risks.

For more information on having an independent midwife, visit www. independentmidwives.org.uk.

What else can you get privately?

Earlier in the book we discussed your options regarding private scans and tests, such as 3D baby scans and Group B streptococcus testing. There are companies that offer 'enhanced midwifery' services, where you can book a qualified midwife to supplement your antenatal appointments on a regular or *ad hoc* basis.

There are also new treatments such as moxibustion (see page 301), which may not be available locally and which you can pay for privately. If there is just one facet of your NHS/midwife care that you think is lacking (from baby handling skills to aqua-natal classes), you might be able to get it as long as you are prepared to pay for it.

If you google 'private maternity care' and your location, you should easily find what's available; otherwise, you can ask your midwife.

Doulas

The word *doula* (pronounced doola) derives from a Greek word meaning servant or caregiver, and a doula will do just that during birth: attend to your needs and help you emotionally and physically, but not clinically. She is not qualified to provide medical care, but can support you as a primary or secondary birth partner.

The doula philosophy is to 'mother the mother', so you get lots of support during birth – which might be useful if you think your partner is going to be a gibbering wreck and faint at the sight of blood!

If you want to hire a doula, she will normally meet you a couple of times before the birth and then will be at your side during the big event. She can also follow up with postnatal care if you want more help.

What does she do during birth?
A doula might help you with your breathing, suggest relaxation techniques, help you get into comfortable positions, and offer continuous nurturing support. She can also be your advocate and tell the health professionals your desires for the birth.

Pros

- If you are by yourself a doula will be your primary birthing partner, instead of you labouring alone.

- She will be known to you, and that may be important if you don't know your midwife at the birth.

- Studies have shown that having a doula present reduces the need for medical intervention and can shorten labour time.

- She can focus on you while the midwife focuses on the safe delivery of the baby.

- She can help you after the birth, which is useful if you do not have support from family or friends. She will often help you around the house or look after other children so you can have time to care for your baby.

Cons

- It's important that you get on with your doula, as she has to work closely with you, your partner if he is present, and the midwife during labour, and you may struggle to find someone you like locally.

- Postnatal support is extra and will be a minimum of £10 an hour. Doulas normally want three-hour bookings as a minimum, and travel expenses may also be charged.

How much will it cost me?
An experienced trained doula will charge between £250 and £500, depending upon where you live, her travelling expenses and experience. Trainee doulas cannot charge more than £200, according to their governing body.

How do I find one in my area?
An excellent online resource is www.doula.org.uk, which has a handy section of questions you can use to vet a prospective doula to see whether she is the right one for you.

What's the alternative?
There's always family or friends who can act as doulas. Sadie Frost was Kate Moss's birth partner, and Kate returned the favour by doing the same for Sadie!

Private hospitals

The most exclusive (and expensive) option is to go for consultant- or midwife-led care in a private hospital or birth centre. The most famous is probably The Portland Hospital in London, beloved by celebs such as Victoria Beckham, Claudia Schiffer and Zoë Ball.

There are also consultants and midwives that provide private care in local NHS hospitals, such as those on www.thebirthteam.com, so it may be worth researching the private options available in your local hospital if this is the sort of care you think you may want.

So how much can I expect to pay?

It really depends on the level of care you want and where you want to give birth. You can find 'birth only' packages countrywide for around £850; independent midwife care from £2,000 upwards; private care in an NHS hospital at around £5,000; and a full-on celebrity experience at The Portland from £8,000 (but that's just for a midwife-led package – a consultant is going to set you back considerably more).

You might think that once you get out of 'celebsville' prices would drop dramatically, but research shows that's not the case, with many private hospitals countrywide charging similar rates to that of the private London birthing centres.

What will I get for my money?

It varies depending on where you have decided to give birth and what facilities you have paid for, but can feature the following.

- Full maternity packages often include four detailed scans, antenatal appointments, routine blood tests, 24-hour telephone support, postnatal checks with complementary therapies and private GP visits thrown in.

- A 'birth only' option means you have NHS care up until you go into labour. You will then give birth in a private facility and usually stay for around eight hours afterwards. If all is well, you will then be discharged into the care of your community midwife. Usually this type of birth is not recommended for first time mothers, and it's easy to see why: if something does go wrong you may have to rack up thousands of pounds in additional fees, so you need to ask yourself whether the benefits outweigh the potential disadvantages.

- You can opt to have your own dedicated consultant or midwife that you see at every antenatal appointment – but bear in mind it can cost twice as much to have consultant-led care rather than midwife-led care.

- You will have an en suite room of your own after birth – the degree of luxury will obviously depend on the hospital.

- You may well get better food than standard NHS fare, and you may even be able to order a little tipple to wet the baby's head.

- Your partner may be able to stay with you overnight and visiting times and numbers may be more relaxed.

- You should be able to expect a better level of postnatal nursing care.

Any disadvantages to private care?

- Obviously the cost: private hospitals and birth centres charge between £4,000 and £8,000 on average, but when you look at the rates at The Portland, you can see you can rack up £10,000 or more quite easily if you need surgery or a prolonged stay in hospital.

- You may find that the private hospital does not have the same array of immediate emergency staff available if there is an unexpected emergency. Check who is on call at night and whether there is an intensive care unit for your baby.

Having a Caesarean

The latest NHS guidance is that Caesareans should not be performed on maternal request alone, on safety and cost grounds. However, it is quite obvious that some women do have elective Caesareans for non-medical reasons, and some private clinics are prepared to carry them out. On the NHS, if there is no physical reason for a Caesarean but you still feel that it is what you want, talk to your midwife and doctor as early as possible in the pregnancy. They should try to understand why you want a Caesarean, and may be able to give you a clearer picture of the pros and cons (see page 236).

If you do find out late in your pregnancy that you have to have a Caesarean (if the baby is breech, for example), you can choose to go private for the operation if you wish.

There are several private clinics in London offering care, from the full maternity package from 12 weeks gestation to one-off consultations. Outside of London you may find your private maternity options more limited, particularly if you don't live near a city that has a large hospital or a private clinic. Before selecting a private stand-alone hospital, make sure it has full emergency services and work out if there is a doctor resident all the time – and if so, what, if any, obstetric knowledge they may have. No one wants a blood transfusion, major surgical complication, or to end up in intensive care, but it does happen occasionally, so check beyond the gloss of the carpets and food and make sure all eventualities are covered. Also, try to make sure your private obstetrician has an NHS appointment somewhere – chances are that, if he does not, he may not have 'made the grade' in the competitive world of NHS medicine. You may find that your chosen NHS hospital does have a private facility which runs alongside the NHS services, and that the consultants may work in both. This can be a good option if you want a high level of one-to-one care, but like the security of being in a big hospital environment with all the latest equipment and emergency facilities to hand.

Some women book to go private for the birth and are so delighted with the antenatal care offered by the NHS that they give birth on the NHS too. The head of the Ann Summers empire, Jacqueline Gold, did just that. She was set to have her first baby (at the age of 48) at a private hospital in London, but when she discovered that she could have her own room at the NHS University College Hospital she stuck with them (after they allowed her to bring her laptop and go back to work just days after the birth).

Wherever you decide to give birth, you can rest assured that statistically the chance of you having serious problems during labour and birth is very low.

Choosing to stick with the NHS is another very popular option. Many women are generally very pleased with the level of care and attention they get from their local NHS maternity unit, but like the idea of having a private room after the birth. Often referred to as amenity rooms, they are only suitable if you and baby are well enough to be alone, so are not suitable immediately after a Caesarean. When you take the hospital tour, ask if any rooms are available, how and when they can be booked, and how much they cost, as prices will vary enormously. You won't get private care, treatment or special meals, though, and some new mothers have reported that they felt quite isolated in them, so take a look before you decide to go for one; if your birth has gone smoothly you could go home the same day and won't need one.

WORDS FROM THE PROFESSIONALS: If you are unhappy with the care you are receiving or with the midwife who is looking after you, you should say so. There is always a midwife in charge of every shift, and she is the one you should talk to if you are unhappy or don't feel you are being well supported or informed. Often the problem is easily fixed, so is worth mentioning. Maternity wards are busy places and continuous one-to-one care is not always achievable, but you are entitled to a high level of care so do voice any concerns you have.

WRITING A BIRTH PLAN

When you get your baby notes for the first time you will probably find a section or dedicated space for your birth plan, which should contain all or some of the following:

- Name
- Where are you giving birth?
- Labour ward/midwife's phone number
- Birth partner's name/phone number
- Anyone else to be present/phone number
- Who will look after other children, if any?
- Do you wish to be cared for by women only?
- Do you need an interpreter?
- Pain relief choices
- Are you happy for students to attend the birth?

- What position do you want to give birth in?

- What birthing aids do you want to use?

- Does your partner wish to be present at a Caesarean?

- Do you want an anaesthetic for a Caesarean, or an epidural?

- Do you want the baby delivered onto your chest or to be cleaned up first?

- Does your partner want to cut the umbilical cord?

- Do you want an injection to contract the uterus and deliver the placenta?

- Do you want your baby to have a vitamin K injection?

- Do you plan to breastfeed?

- Do you wish to feed straight away?

If you have strong feelings about any of the above, it might be useful to use the phrase, 'I should like to avoid X and Y, but if my health or that of the baby is in danger I consent to having medical intervention to deliver my baby safely'.

You might also like to state what kind of birth you are hoping for, ie 'natural' if that is your wish. (See page 231 for more on natural births.)

> 'Did things go according to my birth plan? Not even slightly! I had planned for a natural water birth in the birthing centre. I ended up on the labour ward on a drip, with all sorts of monitors, unable to move around. The only thing that was according to plan was that I didn't have an epidural. I was screaming for one, though, but it was too late!'
>
> Amy, mum to Aiden, 11 months

Why do I need to make a birth plan?

The benefit of making a birth plan is that it does focus your mind on the type of birth you would ideally like; it also forces you to consider things you would rather avoid during birth if at all possible. Critics of birth plans say that they are about as useful as a chocolate teapot, as every birth is different and no one can predict what is going to happen. Many women find that decisions they'd made before labour go out of the window once they are faced with the pain of contractions – there's many a story of women opting for epidurals, when they'd expressly said before that they wanted a natural birth. Although in the end the birth may be nothing like the one you imagined, your birth plan can really help you to focus on what you do and do not want, and prepare for what can happen. The other benefit of a birth plan is that it does encourage you to confront the possible issues that can arise during birth, which is beneficial if you are in a state of denial about the whole thing and hoping the baby will just magically appear at the end of nine months.

Remember that midwives and doctors will always aim to discuss options with you as the labour unfolds, so you don't have to foresee every permutation, nor worry that you or your birthing partner will be excluded just because you haven't written something down.

The most important thing to remember is that you have to keep an open mind and be flexible about the whole thing. There is no benefit in putting 'I refuse to have any medical interventions' or 'I must have an epidural', because you don't know how your labour will progress and how you are going to cope.

If you are not given a printed birth plan to fill in, you can make your own using the questions outlined on page 224 to guide you. Make sure it is legible and preferably typed. If your partner is present at the birth, make sure he knows what you wrote on your birth plan, and discuss it with those providing your antenatal care too – particularly if there's something in your personal circumstances that might have a significant bearing on how you want your baby delivered, or your personal care during labour.

Make sure your birth partner is informed and aware of your birth plan, as he is often your spokesperson in labour.

WORDS FROM THE PROFESSIONALS: Many women will state their preferences regarding pain relief and intervention but indicate that they are happy for the doctor or midwife to take any reasonable steps to ensure that the baby is delivered safely.

Your birthing team

While you are writing your birth plan, it is useful to consider who you want to be present at the birth. Until the 1960s, men were actively discouraged from being in the delivery room, but these days around 90% of fathers attend their child's birth.

Recently Michael Odent, the French obstetrician who popularised water births in this country, said that having a partner or husband in the room increased the chances of having a Caesarean section, a longer labour, a marriage break up or mental illness. Odent argued that by having a man in the delivery room, the woman gets distracted by the male's anxiety, making the birth more difficult; he believes the best way for a women to deliver is on her own with just a midwife present (that's him out of a job then). There's not much evidence to prove that men are positively harmful in the delivery room, but there *is* evidence that shows women do better with a female birthing partner, so you might like to bring a female companion or family member with you. However, don't feel you should have anyone but your loved one present; it really is down to personal choice.

> **WORDS FROM THE PROFESSIONALS:** Do check your hospital or birth centre's rules about the number of people allowed to attend the birth; if you have a home birth your midwife might allow a few more people in the room, but in hospital you are unlikely to be allowed more than a couple.

If you want your current partner/husband to be your birth partner, it's handy if he knows what to expect during the birth. It can be surprisingly difficult to persuade a man to pick up a pregnancy manual, as even the most excited of prospective fathers are terrified by the idea of birth and don't want to read about it. Do ensure that he has a rough idea of what he is letting himself in for, though, because it can be very upsetting seeing someone you love in such pain or having a medical procedure you weren't expecting.

If he doesn't want to read a weighty medical tome on pregnancy and birth you could give him this chapter to read, or maybe he could watch Channel 4's *One Born Every Minute*.

Channel 4's fly-on-the-wall documentary *One Born Every Minute* first hit our screens in March 2010 and is now in its fourth series. *Call the Midwife* also launched in 2012 and pulled in huge viewing figures of up to 9 million.

Eight things your birth partner should know

- It may be stating the obvious, but childbirth is incredibly painful and it is likely that you will scream, rant or swear. Most women do!

- Prepare him for possible birth interventions: explain what ventouse and forceps delivery are and why it might be used (see page 336 for more info).

- Explain that sometimes you can't get a large head through a small hole, so occasionally women tear or need an episiotomy. The reason it's good to prepare him is that sometimes you will need stitches after birth – this can be alarming if he thinks your future sex life is literally getting stitched up, but more importantly he might be left holding the baby if your midwife needs to do some minor repairs on you after birth.

- Tell him about the kind of birth you are planning. Many men probably still imagine we all give birth lying down with our legs in the air, and he might think you really have become deranged with pain if you start wandering around or squatting in preparation for an active birth.

- There is a lot of blood, and if he is at all squeamish he probably should stay away from the 'business' end. It's not uncommon for men to faint during childbirth, and even if they don't actually faint, it can get pretty messy down there, so it's best to prepare him.

- You may do quite odd things to cope with the pain, like bite your hand or make strong, guttural noises.

- Explain what happens to the baby after birth (see page 339), and that your work isn't done until you've delivered the placenta.

- Give him the opportunity to say if he wants to cut the umbilical cord.

Useful things your partner can do as a birth supporter

Before you go into labour it can be helpful if your partner:

- stops drinking alcohol in the run-up to your due date so that he can drive you to the hospital, rather than having to call a taxi or a nearby friend or relative.

- works out the route to hospital and does a dummy run before your due date to get timings right.

- keeps an eye on roadworks and closures. He won't want to deliver the baby himself in the car if you don't make it in time.

- works out where he is going to park when you get to hospital and makes sure he has enough money to pay and display. Some hospitals allow you to park for free during labour, whereas others charge you for your whole stay.

- puts essential numbers into his phone so he can call or text family and friends. And, of course, he'll need to make sure his phone is fully charged!

- takes enough cash to pay for magazines, treats and drinks. If your labour is prolonged you will need entertainment and sustenance.

- is responsible for putting your birth bag/luggage in the car (many a bag has been left at home in the excitement).

- makes sure he know how to fit the baby car seat – you might be home in 12 hours with your baby if you are lucky – so take it with you when you head off for hospital just in case.

While you are in labour your partner can help by:

- making sure he has read and understood your birth plan in case you are not able to state your preferences during labour.

- having some idea of how active you want him to be in the birth. Some partners are physically supportive as well as emotionally; you might want to lean on him while you're pushing, or you might want him to just hold your hand or stroke your hair.

- being aware that the birth cannot be controlled, and that just because you wrote something on your birth plan doesn't mean you can't change your mind. You don't want him 'helpfully' reminding you that you said you didn't want an epidural when you are screaming for an anaesthetist because you can't bear the pain.

- having a job to do if you think it will keep him calm: it might be feeding you ice chips, getting you drinks (if you're allowed them) or spraying you with water mist to keep you cool. If he is a bit of a control freak or the dominant one in your relationship, try to make him understand that *you* need to dictate what happens during the birth.

The professionals

You will (hopefully) have plenty of help and care from a midwife, and possibly a doctor if labour isn't progressing as it should.

If continuity during the birth or knowing who is going to deliver your baby is important, we have already outlined the options available to you to try to get the midwifery care that you want. If you give birth in a large urban hospital, it is very possible that you will not have met the midwife before who delivers your baby. If you are in this situation, there's not much planning you can do in advance, but it is a good idea to prepare yourself for what might happen so it doesn't throw you on the day.

Firstly, there is the issue of shifts. In an ideal world, you would have the same midwife with you throughout the birth, and some of them are such dedicated professionals that they do stay on to help you if you are in the final stages of labour. But you have to remember that many of these women have families and responsibilities, and they can't just ignore them because *you* are having a baby. The hospital staff have rotas for a reason: to ensure there is a even level of care at all times and that staff don't get dangerously tired. Given that we can't predict with total accuracy when a baby is going to arrive or how long or complicated the labour is going to be, it is not feasible to expect continuity of care throughout your baby's birth.

It is entirely possible that you may not form a bond with your midwife: midwives are like anyone from any walk of life – some people you get on with and others you don't – but at the end of the day, as long as they are competent and deliver your baby safely, it's really not worth getting stressed about bonding with them, unless you do feel that your health or that of your baby is in jeopardy. If you are really unhappy with your midwife you should quietly tell the midwife in charge of the shift about your concerns: she may be able to change staff around if it is just a personality clash.

Don't get worried if you have a student midwife on hand either: this is quite common in teaching hospitals, and it can be very positive having an extra pair of hands helping to look after you.

The key to having a happy birth is not to worry too much about the things you can't control. If you love your midwife or hate her, if you have one midwife or 10, it really doesn't matter as long as you and your baby come out of it physically and emotionally intact.

Be prepared for anything and everything

You can make things easier for yourself by being completely up to speed about what is likely to happen on the day. Don't decide to read the chapter on giving birth as your first contractions start; you need to have a good idea of the stages of labour and, even if it does make scary reading, know all your pain relief options and learn what could go wrong (even though it's unlikely). The reason this is important is that you may have to make decisions during labour, and if you are ill-informed you may make the wrong one and end up with a birth you won't want or enjoy.

PLANNING FOR A NATURAL BIRTH

Definitions of a 'natural' birth vary, but in general it means a labour and birth without pain relief (apart from gas and air, which still counts as 'natural') and without intervention (such as forceps or surgery). For many women this is the 'ideal birth' – to deliver in the way nature intended – and indeed it is the way that many women in the world give birth, particularly if they don't have access to hospital facilities.

The issue of natural birth is an emotive one, with its advocates arguing that if women were left to their own devices with a supportive midwife, there would be far more natural deliveries than we have at present.

Plan for a natural birth by all means – there are plenty of good reasons why you should – but please don't feel that you have failed if it doesn't happen. Just remember, your goal is to deliver a healthy, happy baby who won't give two hoots about how he arrived in the world. There is always that cliché that if men had to give birth they would have invented a way to make it painless by now; well, to an extent they have – it's called an epidural, and if you want one, have one. You don't go to the dentist and say, 'I'd like an extraction without the anaesthetic because I want to feel the pain,' and the same should apply to childbirth. You are no less of a woman or a mother if you want every drug and intervention going.

'I'm going to try for a natural birth, and they have a birthing pool where we're going, but if I need drugs I'll take them. All that matters is that the baby comes out healthy.'

Nichola, first pregnancy

You're not alone

It took four years for Kate Winslet to admit that her first daughter, Mia, was born by emergency Caesarean section: 'I just said I had a natural birth because I was so completely traumatised by the fact that I hadn't given birth. I felt like a complete failure.' This shows that even celebrities aren't immune to feeling they need to have the 'perfect' delivery.

Pros of natural birth

- Studies show you are likely to suffer less postnatal pain and have a faster recovery.

- You may have a higher sense of awareness during the birth.

- You may bond better with your baby as a result of a rewarding birth experience.

- Your birth may be more enjoyable if you are in a more relaxing environment like a birthing centre.

- There are lots of nice relaxing techniques like water baths and massage to help you.

Cons of natural birth

- There's no getting away from it: birth can hurt, a lot, and many women have no idea what their pain threshold is like until they have a baby.

- Some women only increase their stress levels by worrying that they need to persevere and have no pain relief.

How to increase your chances of a natural birth

- Statistically you are more likely to have a natural birth if you give birth at home or at a midwife-led birthing centre (but this is at least partly because you have a low-risk pregnancy).

- If you're giving birth in hospital, make sure that your desire for a natural birth is written clearly on your birth plan, and make sure your birth partner knows what you want so he can speak up during labour.

- Sign up for NCT classes or active birth classes. Their focus is normally on low intervention or natural birth, and any classes on relaxation and breathing are good preparation for labour.

- Consider a water birth. Studies have shown that women who spend even part of their labour in a birthing pool are less likely to need pain relief such as pethidine or an epidural, and there's some evidence that shows it could reduce the likelihood of tearing or the need for an episiotomy. Some women choose to give birth in the water, whilst others use the birthing pool for pain relief and relaxation but give birth 'on dry land'. Even a warm bath can have therapeutic qualities during labour, although it's difficult to deliver in one. If you are giving birth at home you can hire a birthing pool; your local birth centre may well have one and many standard maternity units in hospitals have them now too, so it's worth asking when you do your hospital tour. Check any weight/size restrictions. If you are overweight, you may not be able to give birth in a birthing pool, as a hoist may be needed. If you are interested in a water birth then discuss the practicalities with your midwife.

- Look into the possibility of using 'alternative' methods of pain relief such as hypnotherapy, acupuncture, aromatherapy, massage, TENS machine and breathing techniques (for more detailed descriptions of each see pages 243 and 247).

- Have a woman as a delivery partner. Research shows that a female companion in the delivery room can improve your chance of having a birth without intervention. If you think your baby's father might be a bit upset if you tell him he can't come in, then ask your mum, a friend or hire a doula to come as well.

- After 37 weeks, if he's not there already, encourage your baby into the right position prior to birth – ie head down: do this by getting on all fours to allow your baby the space and gravity to move. If the baby is breech, you may not be allowed to deliver vaginally.

WORDS FROM THE PROFESSIONALS: Can I ask for a second opinion if the advice I'm given moves me away from my natural birth plan?

You can always ask your midwife's opinion, and if you really don't agree you can ask for a second opinion. However, if it is an emergency you may not want

Around 65% of UK women have a natural birth.

to waste time getting a second opinion. Often people feel they need a second opinion because they don't fully understand the reasons why the intervention is needed, so make sure you ask why and what other options there are, as this may make you feel happier and more involved with the decisions.

HAVING AN ACTIVE BIRTH

Active birth became popular in the late 1970s, when pioneers of this type of birth recommended that women should be free to move around spontaneously during labour, and adopt upright or squatting positions to give birth. Fans of active birth believe that it makes birth less painful, easier, and more efficient. For many women it works (you have gravity on your side for a start); they also believe it is a more 'natural' way to deliver as it is universally and culturally adopted the world over.

However, over 50% of women in the UK still deliver lying on their backs on a bed, with critics saying that it is easier for the health professionals to manage the labour if the patients are lying down. There can be patient-led reasons too, though: some women get quite embarrassed squatting or kneeling half naked in front of people they don't know and want the 'security' of a bed and sheets where they can have some degree of modesty, and some just feel that lying down is right for them.

'When I was giving birth the midwife wanted me to get on the bed to examine me, but I just wasn't comfortable. In the end I delivered standing up, leaning over the bed; I can't explain it but it just wasn't comfortable sitting or lying down. I think gravity really does help!'
Nicola, second pregnancy and mum to Callum, 18 months

If you like the idea of an active birth, there are lots of websites where you can read up about it and decide if it is the birthing style for you. If you want to give it a go, make sure you put it in your birth plan and talk to the midwife about it at the start of your labour. Even if you do give birth lying down, there's nothing to stop you having a 'natural' birth.

 About 37% of Caesareans in the UK are planned or elective.

PLANNED CAESAREAN SECTION

If your midwife suspects you will have to have a planned Caesarean section, you will normally see a doctor to discuss the pros and cons and work out what is best for you and your baby. Caesareans account for around 23% of births in this country, and if you know in advance you are going to have one it is called a 'planned' or 'elective' Caesarean. This type of Caesarean will be recommended if the health professionals believe in advance that it will be safer for you or your baby to deliver this way.

There are a number of reasons why your obstetrician might want to pencil in a Caesarean for a birth:

- if you are suffering from pre-eclampsia

- if your baby is too small (intrauterine growth restriction) or already distressed

- if your baby is breech (bottom first) or transverse (lying sideways), and attempts to turn him have failed. It is possible to have a breech baby vaginally, but for some women, a Caesarean section is thought to be safer

- if you are expecting twins there are more likely to be complications and a Caesarean might be recommended. Do keep in mind that it's not unknown for one twin to be born vaginally but for the second twin to be delivered by Caesarean section. Speak to your midwife about your options so that you can make an informed decision about your birth plan (see page 224)

- if you have placenta praevia

- if you have had two or more Caesareans before

- if you have a chronic condition such as heart disease, which could, in some circumstances, make the strain of a normal labour potentially dangerous for you

- if it is suspected or confirmed that your baby's head is too big to pass through your pelvis.

Many women do give birth to twins vaginally (around 50%), but if you are expecting more than two babies it is almost certain you will be having a planned Caesarean.

If your consultant recommends that you have a planned Caesarean section, it will be because he has the health and safety of you and your baby in mind. It is quite a major operation with an extended recovery period, so it is not something that he will suggest without careful consideration. It must be explained clearly to you why this procedure is the best option, and you should have plenty of opportunities to discuss the options. Don't be afraid to ask questions, and even ask for a second opinion if you are not sure – no one will mind! Whilst you may be tempted to 'research other options', please try to avoid the temptation to use the internet – it is so difficult to find reliable information that you can trust, and usually there will be circumstances unique to you that will only be apparent to someone talking to you.

Pros

- The birth will be quicker.

- The birth itself should be less painful.

- You know when you are going to have your baby.

- You have a good idea of what will actually happen during your delivery/labour.

Cons

- Recovery time is longer and you have to spend longer in hospital – your baby stays with you, though, and you are supported by midwives and nursery nurses to care for your baby.

- Statistically, they carry an increased risk of complications (see below).

- You might feel 'cheated' as you didn't give birth as nature intended.

- You are more likely to have complications in your next pregnancy.

Also, do remember that things change – you may be booked in for a Caesarean if your baby is breech, but he may move at the last moment. Your baby's position should be regularly monitored in case he turns head down at the last moment and you can attempt a vaginal birth.

Caesarean factfile

The 'too posh to push' myth has been busted. Research shows most Caesareans are for medical reasons and not due to women choosing to have a Caesarean.

Having a Caesarean is not the easy option when it comes to giving birth; there are many risks associated with them, which is why doctors don't recommend them on a whim and won't perform one just because you are 'too posh to push' or want to keep 'down there' intact.

The complications associated with Caesareans can mean:

- you have an increased risk of excessive bleeding and needing a blood transfusion.

- you have an increased risk of developing a blood clot (thrombosis) in your legs or lungs (see page 81) and are more likely to need to give yourself once-a-day heparin injections for seven days or six weeks afterwards to try to prevent one.

- you are more likely to suffer abdominal pain.

- you are more likely to be re-admitted after birth or have further surgery.

- you are more likely to get an infection (wound, uterus, urine, chest or blood for starters!) and will be given preventative antibiotics immediately before the operation.

- you may have complications in future pregnancies.

The points above show that having a Caesarean is not a stroll in the park, but do remember that most women who have a Caesarean don't suffer any long-term effects, and the safe delivery of your baby should override any worries about possible complications of the surgery.

Caesarean rates around the world

China 46%	USA 32%	India 18%
Canada 22%	Thailand 34%	UK 23%

FEAR OF GIVING BIRTH

Although you might be over the moon about your pregnancy and thoroughly excited about becoming a mother, it may well be that you are frightened of giving birth, but you're too embarrassed to admit it.

'I worry that [my husband] Jim was a massive baby and I was small so really hoping my baby takes after me! I'm scared about tearing or having an episiotomy. Apart from that, I feel quite relaxed about the labour.'

Ruth, first pregnancy

Don't worry: there's not a first-time mother in the land who isn't frightened of giving birth, and if that's you, you are certainly not alone.

The problem for all pregnant women is that the fear of giving birth is the fear of the unknown. You have absolutely no idea how your labour is going to go, and that's why the thought of it can be so scary. You also worry that there might be something wrong with the baby that you'll only discover once it's born. The best advice is to read up as much as you can about giving birth and prepare yourself for every eventuality; it won't necessarily influence the outcome of your birth, but it might help you make informed decisions on the day.

TOKOPHOBIA

Tokophobia is the extreme fear of giving birth and was only recognised as a medical condition in 2000. It is thought to affect as many as one in seven women. If you think you have tokophobia, ask for counselling or hypnotherapy to help you overcome it. If you are truly traumatised by the idea of giving birth vaginally, it is essential that you speak to a doctor as early as possible, who may refer you for a psychological assessment; if your anxieties are found to be genuine and serious you may be allowed to give birth by elective C-section.

MULTIPLE BIRTHS

If you are having twins, you will usually have doctor-led antenatal care, including more scans to check that each baby is growing normally, more checks for pre-eclampsia and gestational diabetes and more discussion about the options for delivery. Women having twins are more likely to develop problems during their pregnancy, although of course not everyone does! These might include:

- exaggerated symptoms of 'normal' pregnancy such as thrush, urinary frequency, heartburn, tiredness, backache and pelvic discomfort

- anaemia – most women with twins should take an iron and folate supplement routinely, to supply enough for both babies and themselves

- pre-term delivery, baby or babies smaller than expected, pre-eclampsia, gestational diabetes or thrombosis in your legs.

Caesarean sections and multiple births

Your doctor may recommend that you have an elective Caesarean to give birth if, for example, the first baby is not coming head first or if the pregnancy is complicated in some other way. It is also entirely possible to give birth to twins vaginally, especially if you are having a normal pregnancy in other respects. You are particularly likely to have a vaginal delivery if:

- the first baby is head down

- both babies are growing normally

- there are no other pregnancy problems like pre-eclampsia or gestational diabetes

- there are no other reasons why a vaginal birth might be problematic – for example, if you have a low-lying placenta or have had previous surgery on your uterus (for example a previous Caesarean section or removal of fibroids).

Occasionally during a vaginal twin birth, the first baby is born vaginally but the second has to be delivered by Caesarean section because he's in the wrong position or an emergency arises, so you should be prepared for that eventuality.

If you're having more than one baby you should also know that:

- twins are usually born earlier than single babies, probably because they stretch the uterus more. As a result of this they are smaller and lighter on average than singletons. A twin pregnancy is considered full-term at 34 weeks, not 37 weeks like single pregnancies.

- if you are having a multiple birth there will normally be more people in the delivery room, including (possibly) a paediatrician for each baby, an obstetrician or two and a couple of midwives. The anaesthetist is usually in the vicinity too. Everyone will introduce themselves and everyone will have a role to ensure the delivery of your babies goes smoothly.

- if you are planning a vaginal delivery for twins, you will be recommended to deliver in a consultant-led unit.

- you are quite often induced around 37–38 weeks if you have not gone into labour before this, and often it is recommended that you have an epidural to help with the safe delivery of each baby and in case a Caesarean is necessary.

If you are having more than two babies, it is very unlikely that you will give birth vaginally.

PREMATURE BIRTH

If your baby is born before 37 weeks the birth is considered to be premature. About 7% of babies are born before 37 weeks, including about 1% born before 28 weeks.

Sometimes you will know in advance that it is more likely to happen; for example, if you have a medical condition that means you are unlikely to carry until full term, if you are having more than one baby, if your previous delivery was before 37 weeks, or if you have had trauma to or operations on your cervix. There are several exciting trials going on at the moment trying to predict and prevent pre-term birth, so don't be surprised if you are asked to take part. If you do know that your baby is likely to be born before 37 weeks, you might want to visit the Special Care Baby Unit (SCBU), or meet some of the staff who will care for him – ask your doctor or midwife about this. Many hospitals now offer a prematurity clinic and you might benefit from this, either in this pregnancy or the next.

Sometimes you just go into labour spontaneously: you may start contracting or the membranes may rupture prematurely. This is more common if you have vaginal bleeding or if you have a raised temperature for a prolonged period, but sometimes it has no identifiable medical reason at all. If you have any bleeding after 24 weeks or if your temperature won't settle with paracetamol, then you should **always** be checked out at the hospital.

Travelling after 24 weeks

The possibility of pre-term delivery will also mean you have to reconsider travelling abroad after 24 weeks. If your pregnancy is normal, it is unlikely that you will deliver pre-term, but if it does happen whilst you are on business in Bombay, on holiday in Honduras, or visiting friends in Finland, the logistics of looking after yourself and a newborn baby in a neonatal intensive care unit overseas are worth considering carefully – is the trip really worthwhile at this stage of pregnancy? Can someone else go? Can it wait until after you deliver? If you do travel, please check your insurance policy to make sure it includes cover for you and for your baby.

What risks are associated with having a premature baby?

Many babies born pre-term are completely healthy and well. However, babies who are born before they are full term are more likely to develop health problems because they haven't had the chance to fully mature in the uterus. You should be aware that:

- in the early days they may have problems breathing, feeding and regulating their own body temperature.

- they may be more prone to infection when they are first born.

- they are more likely to develop problems post-birth, such as anaemia and jaundice.

- some are more likely to have longer-term problems, such as issues with their hearing or eyesight, and some may have neurological problems such as difficulty or a delay in walking or talking, or difficulties with cognition, co-ordination or concentration.

There is no doubt that babies born very early are more likely to suffer short-term health problems but the good news is that current survival rates are improving.

- Recent figures show that around 20% of babies have a chance of survival if born at 23 weeks, although many have long-term disabilities.

- At 25 weeks they have a 67% survival rate, and around half will have a disability.

- At 32 weeks they are likely to survive without any significant health problems.

If you go into labour early you may be given treatment to temporarily halt contractions, giving you time to get to a hospital with specialist facilities for premature babies. The doctors may also offer you two injections of steroids, which help the baby's lungs to mature and so reduce the chance of severe breathing problems by 50%. These steroids also reduce the chance of the baby having a brain haemorrhage by 50%, and improve his chance of survival. Therefore, although it may sound a bit scary to be offered steroid injections, these are in fact very well proven to help your baby.

GET CHECKED OUT

If you are bleeding, having regular contractions, your waters have broken or are leaking or if you think you may be in labour for any other reason, you should contact your delivery unit immediately – or, if you are really concerned, call an ambulance and go straight to your local maternity unit.

PAIN RELIEF OPTIONS

We have looked at the types of birth you can plan for: now we can consider your pain relief options, so you can research them and note what you think you might like (or not like) on your birth plan.

There's no doubt that giving birth hurts. But it is very difficult to generalise about it because everyone's coping mechanisms and pain thresholds are different. If you find the pain unbearable, there are several options to make you more comfortable, and our advice would be to take them!

Just remember one thing: however bad the pain, a lot of women go on to have another child – so however terrible the agony, you may soon find yourself willing to give it another go!

Entonox: gas and air

What is it?
Entonox is a mix of 50% oxygen and 50% nitrous oxide, and is administered through a mouthpiece or mask that allows you to breathe in the gas during a contraction.

When can I have it?
In theory you can have gas and air at any time during labour or birth, but let your midwife be your guide. If you are in early labour and find you need pain relief, this probably isn't the best choice.

Is it any good?
It's not the most powerful form of pain relief, but it can certainly help you deal with contractions for a while. It can take up to a minute for the effects to kick in, so it's best to take it when you feel a contraction coming on, rather than start it in the middle of one. You need to remember to stop using it at the height of the contraction, so that it wears off as the pain ends – that way you won't feel too 'spaced out' in between contractions. Partners and midwives can be quite useful for gently dissuading you from gulping down more than you really need!

You can also use it at a home birth, in the birth centre and in the birthing pool.

Are there any side effects or anything else I should know?
Gas and air undoubtedly creates a sort of 'high' that can make you feel woozy, drunk or slightly out of control. However, this feeling wears off minutes after you stop inhaling. It can also give you a dry mouth and

can sometimes make you feel nauseous. It is not harmful to you or your baby, and probably the worst thing about it is that your birthing partner will try to wrestle it off you for a go!

TENS machine

A TENS (transcutaneous electrical nerve stimulation) machine is a little box which emits electrical pulses through four wires and four sticky pads, which you fix to your back.

The theory is that it intercepts the pain signals to your brain and stimulates the release of endorphins, the body's natural pain-relieving hormones. There are dials so you can control the frequency and intensity of the pulses. You need to start off low and increase them as the contractions get stronger.

When can I have it?

As early as you like, although be aware that it takes up to an hour for your body to respond, so you need to get it on in good time. You are best to start using it at home as soon as labour starts. You will probably need help from your birth partner or midwife to put the wires on because it is a bit fiddly to do by yourself. You'll probably want to ditch it towards the end of labour, because the wires will become a nuisance and TENS machines aren't normally capable of dealing with really strong contractions.

Does it work?

Opinions vary: they seem to work for some women and not for others. They can be a great distraction from pain and help you feel in control as you press the buttons when you feel a contraction coming.

Anything else I should know?

There are no side effects when using a TENS machine, but you can't use them in a birthing pool for obvious reasons; electricity and water don't mix! You also can't have a back massage if you have the pads on and you can feel a bit constrained by all the wiring. Beware turning them too high: you can get a pulse so strong it gives you a bit of a shock. TENS machines aren't routinely available in all maternity units, but if your hospital has a stash you might be able to borrow or hire one. If not, you can hire them from places like Boots or Mothercare. They cost around £20–£30 to hire and £50–£60 to buy.

Painkilling drugs (pethidine, Meptid and diamorphine)

These painkilling drugs (also known as analgesics) are usually administered by injection into your thigh or bottom, or occasionally into a vein in your arm.

Midwives are able to give you these drugs, so there is no need to wait for the okay from an obstetrician or anaesthetist. Sometimes the maternity unit has a PCA (patient controlled analgesia) unit, so you can actually control the dosage yourself.

Pethidine

Pethidine is the most commonly used painkilling drug. Pethidine is great when you feel Entonox is not quite enough, as it just gives slightly stronger pain relief and can be used along with gas and air. It can be given in some birth centres and some midwives will give it at home births. It is the next strongest thing after Entonox, but it is not as effective as an epidural.

> **WORDS FROM THE PROFESSIONALS:** Some antenatal classes seem to discourage pethidine or similar drugs as they can make the baby sleepy, but as a midwife I think that pethidine is a great analgesia option. It is really good when someone's labour is very slow to get established and she is becoming exhausted through lack of sleep; often a dose of pethidine relaxes her enough to sleep for a few hours and lets the labour progress.

Meptid

Meptid is a strong painkiller, but it doesn't make the baby as sleepy as pethidine. Pethidine and Meptid are both injections that will be given mixed with another injection to stop you from feeling sick.

Diamorphine

Diamorphine is not used in many maternity units now as pethidine and Meptid are much safer and more effective.

If you find that the painkilling drugs are not strong enough, you can still go on to have an epidural after having pethidine or Meptid.

When can I have them?

You can have these painkilling drugs at any time until you are close to the pushing stage. If you have these drugs too late in labour they will

Around 35% to 49% of women have pethidine or Meptid at some point in labour.

not be effective, as they take about 30 minutes to take effect; they can also make the baby sleepy just before he is born, which could make him slower to start breathing and slow to feed. If there are severe problems with the baby's breathing at birth following pethidine (which is rare), there is an antidote the baby can be given to stop the pethidine effects.

Does it work?

Some women find these drugs very effective; others don't. Even if they don't take the pain away, they might make you feel more relaxed between contractions.

Any side effects or anything else I should know?

These drugs can make you feel drowsy, dizzy or sick: you will usually be given an anti-sickness injection with them to reduce the chance of you getting nauseous. If you have too much or are given them too late, they may hang around in your baby's system for a few days and could make him sleepy, slow his breathing or make it difficult for him to feed. Allergic reactions are rare, but do ensure your medical team are aware of any known allergies.

Epidural

What is it?

An epidural is an anaesthetic injection into the spine, which numbs the nerve supply serving the uterus and cervix and gives complete and quick pain relief. Some hospitals offer mobile epidurals (lower dosage injections) that give pain relief but don't numb the legs so much.

When can I have it?

As a rule of thumb, you can have an epidural as soon as you are in established labour or you feel the pain is more than you can deal with. If you are being induced you may want to have it around the time that the Syntocinon (oxytocin) hormone drip is started. The effect lasts several hours, and it can either be topped up as you require or maintained using a constant infusion – each hospital has a slightly different approach but patient controlled administration of the epidural solution is increasingly popular – you control how much you have and when, and this results in greater satisfaction and less medication being used. Most women will keep it working until they have delivered; it used to be said that you should let it wear off when the time comes to push so that 'you can

> The term 'mobile' is a bit misleading – mostly it means there is still some movement in the legs, but not usually that you are safe to walk around.

feel what you are doing' – whilst this may suit you, it is certainly not encouraged, since it can be really hard to deal with the pain again just when you need to focus on pushing, and your midwife will direct you on pushing without you needing to feel the pain. Most modern epidurals now allow complete pain relief without numbness, so you can feel a contraction coming and push without pain.

It is estimated that 20% of epidurals are given to women who don't need them.

Does it work?

In a word, yes. However, there is also the possibility that it will take only partially – some women have relief on one side of their body, and have to be positioned on a bed to assist gravity and 'move' the medication to both sides.

Any side effects or anything else I should know?

It can completely numb your body from the waist to your toes and you won't be able to walk around. If you have an epidural you will need a drip in your arm in case your blood pressure drops and you need to be given fluid quickly. Your baby will also be constantly monitored. You will need a catheter (a tube going into your bladder) to help you urinate, as you won't be able to feel if your bladder is full or not. Some women experience severe headaches, shaking, backache or fever after having one.

Around 70% of women have an epidural in the US and the UK is catching up. The latest figures show that epidural rates here have doubled, from around 17% in the early 1990s to around 33% now.

You need to have an anaesthetist present to site the epidural into your back and give you the first dose of painkillers. This can take up to 30 minutes. The midwife will then give the rest of the painkillers into the epidural site when they are needed, or you can do it yourself. Most maternity units have an anaesthetist on staff 24 hours a day just for maternity cases; however, if he is busy in theatre you may have to wait for him to become free, and occasionally the baby will arrive before the anaesthetist! In some hospitals you might struggle to get one in the middle of the night; you also won't get one in a birthing centre or at a home birth. If you think you may want an epidural it is worth asking in advance if there is a 24-hour anaesthetist.

Epidurals are fantastic at taking away the pain of childbirth, and you shouldn't feel that your birth experience is 'inferior' because you chose to have one. Giving birth should be a joy and not a competition, so if you can't stand the pain any longer you should definitely ask for one. At the end of the day there are no medals for bravery.

Alternative methods of pain relief

If drug-taking and button fiddling is not your thing, there are other pain relief options you can explore. Make sure you note them on your birth plan if you want to give them a go.

Whilst these might have been considered genuinely 'alternative' a few years ago, you may find that more and more midwives are open to the idea of different methods of pain relief, and many already practise them. Some women find that they can be very successful when used in the early stages of labour, particularly if you combine a couple of them. Other women find they don't work at all. The trick is to consider them and give them a go by all means, but if you find they are not working for you then ditch them and try something else.

Acupuncture

You are probably already familiar with the ancient Chinese therapy that involves the insertion of fine needles into various points in the body. It is said to stimulate the energy channels and release endorphins, which are the body's natural painkilling hormones. It is also thought to be quite effective at inducing labour that is overdue. There isn't any hard scientific evidence in its favour, so you might struggle to find a supportive health professional. If you decide it's for you, do find a qualified private practitioner through the British Acupuncture Council.

Aromatherapy

Aromatherapy is the use of natural 'essential' oils that are said to have a positive effect on the body and mind. These oils can be diluted and used in massage, inhaled via a burner or vaporiser, or put on a hankie or pillow as droplets. You should avoid putting them directly on your skin or into the water of a birthing pool; however, they can be used in a bath. Some oils are unsuitable for labour, so you should check with a trained aromatherapist before you use them, or do some careful homework on the subject. It's unlikely aromatherapy will do much to improve the pain of labour; however, the back massage might, and it may aid relaxation in the early stages. It can stimulate more effective contractions and, if nothing else, will make the delivery room smell good!

Breathing techniques

Slow, rhythmic deep breathing can help you relax during labour, and you're more likely to cope with the pain if you can relax into it rather than fight against it. Breathing also helps you conserve your energy and boost oxygen supplies to you and your baby.

Breathing tips

- Focus on a two syllable word (relax is actually a good one): think 'reeeeee' as you breathe in slowly and 'laaaaaax' as you breathe out again.

- Try counting as you breathe in and out, or breathing in through your nose and out through your mouth.

- Get your birthing partner to help you and join in with your breathing exercises.

Be aware that breathing techniques might help you in the early stages, but may not do the job when the pain is so bad that breathing becomes a labour in itself. Pregnancy yoga classes are often effective at teaching breathing techniques.

Heat therapy

Some women find heated pads useful during labour, in the same way that many of us put a hot water battle on our tummies to alleviate period pain. You might find that it does a job for you in the early stages of labour but probably won't hack it towards the end.

Conversely, if you find labour makes you feel very hot, ask your birth partner to wet some cool flannels and apply them to your eyes, forehead or neck. Refresh them often and suck on ice chips to cool your mouth, but do not apply ice directly to bare skin, as it can stick to you and cause burning.

Hypnobirthing

In 2011 the NHS launched an 18-month study into the effectiveness of hypnobirthing in helping women give birth without painkillers. We should see results shortly.

Some people believe that you can take the pain of childbirth away, or distract yourself from it, using hypnosis. Hypnobirthing is based on the theory that fear causes great tension and that in turn leads to pain, and it's believed that if you put your mind into a state of deep relaxation then the pain will go away. If you want to learn these techniques, you'll need to find someone qualified to teach you and then practise them before the birth. You can also buy CDs that claim to teach self-hypnosis.

Massage

Massage is another technique that is supposed to release those natural endorphins by putting pressure on the body's energy channels.

Massage definitely boosts relaxation and gives you a sense of well-being, especially if lovingly applied by a willing birth partner, so it might make you feel spiritually better even if it doesn't do much for you physically. Shoulder massage is effective to relieve tension, and a lower back massage is useful for trying to alleviate the pain of contractions. Bring along a small wooden massage tool for your partner to use if his hands get stiff. Slow, rhythmic strokes or circles, firmly applied with the fingers or the palms of the hands, are most effective, but you can be the judge and tell your partner what is working for you. Many women can't bear to be touched during labour, so warn your partner beforehand that you may rebuff him on the day, even if you have enjoyed massages throughout the pregnancy.

Reflexology

Reflexology involves massaging particular points of the feet, and is said to work in a similar way to acupuncture by tapping into the body's energy channels and releasing naturally occurring painkillers. You'll need to find a qualified practitioner to help you if you want to try it during labour.

Water

Many women report that a birthing pool of warm water can be a very relaxing, effective method of pain relief. Widely available in maternity units and birthing centres, you can also hire one if you are having a home birth. If you are giving birth in a hospital where a birthing pool isn't available, you may be able to wallow in a warm bath instead (as long as someone is with you). Many women who have had successful water births claim they are comforting, and others said they helped make birth a 'calm' and 'peaceful' process. Remember that you won't be able to have anything stronger than gas and air in the birthing pool, so if you want to hit the drugs you'll have to get out.

> **WORDS FROM THE PROFESSIONALS:** I had all three of my children in the pool and thought it was amazing; it just took away that heavy feeling, as you become weightless in the water, and it definitely dulls the pain. It also reduces your chance of tearing as your skin becomes soft and stretchy when in warm water, and at the end of it all the mess goes down the plug hole!

New age techniques

If your tendencies move towards 'new age', you can look into visualisation techniques where you 'see' each stage of labour (which apparently makes it easier to cope with), or vocalisation, when you sing, chant or grunt to relieve the pain: you may laugh now, but on the day you might do anything to take the pain away!

Birthing balls

You might also want to look into birthing balls, which you can use throughout pregnancy and at the birth. The benefit of them in labour is that they can be more comfortable than a bed, they encourage good posture and you can use them to 'rock and roll' your way through the pain.

8

Shopping for me and my baby

This chapter gives you a rest from all the medical stuff and deals with the fun stuff – like shopping and planning the baby's nursery.

In this chapter we take you through your baby essentials and desirables, looking at both budget and luxury options, and hopefully give you some good tips to help you shop in style without breaking the bank.

We'll also give you some tips on budgeting, what you should beg or borrow, and how to get the best deals and freebies.

WHEN TO START SHOPPING

Some women are superstitious during pregnancy and don't want to go shopping until the final weeks, but you should be aware that one in 10 women delivers prematurely, so there is a slight chance that you might go into labour and not have all the things you need. It also makes sense to start your baby shopping at the start of the third trimester, when you are still quite mobile and probably not as tired as you might be at the end of your pregnancy.

Of course, you don't actually need to battle your way through Mothercare any more, because the wonders of the internet mean that you could, in theory, do all your baby shopping online. If you are happy to shop from your armchair by all means go for it, but our advice is to do your research early online and then try to check out the key items in store, because you might want to properly test just how easy that drop-catch cot side is to release, or feel the weight of your favoured buggy or test how foldable it is.

CLOTHING ESSENTIALS FOR YOUR BABY

The first piece of advice is: don't spend a fortune on newborn outfits. You invariably get lots of baby clothes as gifts so, without sounding cynical, let family and friends 'indulge' your baby while you stick to the practical items. Here are the essential clothing items you should focus on.

Sleep suits and vests

If your baby is born in the colder winter months, you will need seven vests and ideally around 14 sleep suits (long sleeved body suits with feet attached). If your baby is summer-born it might be more sensible to buy 10 sleeveless body suits and 10 long-sleeved sleep suits.

It's useful to choose sleep suits with feet because they eliminate the need for socks, which get kicked off.

Because newborns often vomit up some milk and new mothers can be slow at nappy changing (don't worry, you'll soon be a pro), it's useful to bank on using two body suits during the day. You'll spend a lot of time nappy changing and feeding, so it makes sense for your baby not to be trussed up in too many fiddly layers. Keep it simple with these vests and sleep suits.

Your baby may very well live in a sleep suit during the day for a while too, and you may only bother getting him 'dressed up' for visitors or outings. There's nothing wrong with that! As a general rule it's better to have more than you need, because you'll be so absorbed in your baby you won't always remember to turn the washing machine on, and as they are available cheaply in packs of three or five it's worth stocking up.

Babies should wear natural fibres like cotton, as they 'breathe' better. Babies are not so good at regulating their body temperature, so they shouldn't wear man-made fibres that could cause them to over-heat. You are going to be soaking and washing these clothes every day, so buy good quality if you can afford it. Cotton jersey is the probably the best fabric for your baby essentials because it is soft to the touch, won't irritate your baby's skin and is stretchy, which is useful as you will be taking these clothes on and off all day. If you are prone to allergies and think your baby might have sensitive skin, organic cotton baby clothes are widely available. If you google 'organic baby clothes' a wealth of companies miraculously appear, so you'll have no trouble ordering them.

John Lewis, Mothercare and Marks & Spencer all sell good quality cotton jersey baby basics that wash and wear well. You can also try BHS, Matalan or supermarkets like Asda or Tesco for cheaper versions.

A hat

Your baby will need a hat – or most likely two because invariably one gets lost or forgotten somewhere. Babies need to wear hats to keep them warm and also to protect their heads from the sun.

If your baby is summer-born, try a soft jersey beanie to keep him warm (they are also very easy to get on and off) and a sunhat to protect his head and face from the sun's rays.

A winter-born baby might need a soft fleece pull-on and maybe a wool one if you have a knitting granny (make sure it's not scratchy, though).

You can also get sunglasses for babies, but unless you're out in the sun all the time they're not necessary. Most babies won't like wearing them either!

A cardigan

You need to dress your baby in layers when you are going out, and a cardigan is ideal: because they are short they don't interfere with nappy changing and are reasonably easy to get on and off.

Gap always seems to do nice jersey jacket-y things which do the job brilliantly, but can be expensive. You can also try Marks & Spencer, Next and supermarkets for slightly cheaper versions.

Bonnie Baby does lovely cashmere baby sweaters if you want to splurge, or if someone wants to get you an extravagant gift. It feels gorgeous to cuddle a newborn in a lovely, soft cashmere cardigan!

A coat or all-in-one suit

If you know you are going to be out and about doing a lot of walking, you might consider buying your baby a padded, waterproof all-in-one suit that he can wear over his clothes. These are a bit fiddly to get on and off, but it does ensure that he is evenly covered and warm. If your baby is mainly going to travel by car, a coat or lightly padded jacket should suffice (make sure you buy one labelled 3–6 months for a newborn so you actually get a decent amount of wear out of it), but don't put him in heavily-padded suits because they can interfere with a car seat's protective qualities. For some reason, the French are really good at outerwear, so check out brands like La Redoute or Vertbaudet: not only are they well priced, but they often do quite interesting colour combinations as well if you want to escape the inevitable pink and blue.

Mitts

Babies have quite sharp fingernails, and despite your best efforts to cut them, they can cause quite a lot of damage to delicate newborn skin. You can buy jersey mitts from Babies R Us or Boots.

Bibs

It's useful to buy some towelling or soft jersey bibs because babies dribble milk or posset, whether they are bottle or breastfed. If you pop a bib over his clothing, it obviously stops you needing to change a complete outfit. Choose ones that just pop over the head or fasten with Velcro, as they are safer and easier to get on. Silly Billyz newborn fleece bibs are very popular and widely available.

Shawl

Although it sounds rather old fashioned, you might want to consider a shawl for your baby. Research has shown that babies who are swaddled (wrapped quite tightly) in a shawl or piece of fabric settle better because they feel secure like they did in the uterus, although you must be careful not to let your baby overheat. Shawls are recommended for daytime sleeps only because babies might get too hot wrapped up all night, and some people advise that you stop swaddling at around four to six weeks anyway, because babies need to be free to move around to help their motor development.

'A good tip when you're shopping is to talk to mums of older babies about what they found useful, rather than being influenced by what the first-time mums-to-be in the antenatal group are buying.'
Belinda, mum to Harry and Adam

Where to shop

Value
If you are on a tight budget, then supermarket chains like Tesco, George at Asda and Sainsbury's should be your first port of call; the quality is usually good, and if you stick to plain white basics, you can jazz them up with other items you may be given as baby gifts.

You can also try charity shops, as some people donate unworn clothes they got as gifts, or try Freecycle (www.freecycle.org) to see if you can find any new clothes being given away for free. eBay is another place you might be able to pick up a bargain.

High street
Mothercare, Marks & Spencer, Boots, Babies R Us, John Lewis and Next are all excellent sources of reasonably priced baby essentials.

The latest research by Mintel (March 2011) found that expenditure on nursery furniture grew by 10% between 2008 and 2010 to reach £137 million.

Chain stores

Monsoon, Gap, Joules and Cath Kidston all do distinctive baby clothes; they are not the cheapest, but are usually quite special.

Mail order

Boden, Blooming Marvellous, Jo Jo Maman Bebe and The White Company are definitely worth checking out for their well-priced yet stylish babywear.

Foreign brands

Petit Bateau and Polarn O Pyret have a presence on the UK high street, and they are definitely worth looking at if you want something a bit different.

Funky fashionistas

If you want cool T-shirts, look at www.noaddedsugar.co.uk; www.nippazwithattitude.co.uk; www.sugarbullets.co.uk; or www.stardustkids.co.uk. They all do brilliant slogan vests, bodysuits and T-shirts that are sure to raise a smile.

Internet

If you want to shop from the comfort of your armchair, look at www.ASOS.com; www.vertbaudet.co.uk; or www.laredoute.co.uk. Again, Freecycle and eBay are worth checking out while you're online.

Practical tips

Many of the big-budget items you'll need for your baby will at least last a few years into toddlerhood. But clothes? If budgets are tight, it's best to rein it in and go cheaper, leaving the occasional expensive item for besotted grandparents and friends to buy as a gift.

So where do you start? Apart from the obvious supermarket and high street chains, parents these days have the option of hunting for bargains online. Internet shopping has opened up a whole range of budget-conscious brands. Try www.cheapbabyclothesuk.com for some ideas – and look for online discounts offered by baby websites such as Mumsnet. But be aware – check postage and packing costs, which can hike up prices, and have a careful look at the sizing guide before you buy.

When you're choosing designs, try not to be seduced by pretty prints or cute designs only – bear in mind that you will potentially have to change these outfits several times a day for many months! Therefore, outfits with awkward buttons, tight necks and fiddly elastic will soon be abandoned at the back of the wardrobe. Go for poppers, soft fleeces and common-sense designs.

Equally, look at the washing labels. You'll be handling mountains of washing – some babies can go through several outfits a day. Hand-wash and dry-clean-only garments are a bad idea, unless they're for a special occasion. Look for materials which wash well, don't pill and keep their shape – the best bet is for high street brands such as Marks & Spencer, John Lewis and Next, as they are at the cheaper end of the scale but still good quality. Some of the supermarkets have good quality basics, too – experiment until you find a favourite.

Remember to wash all items of clothing in a mild detergent before you put them on your baby – clothes come with various starches and chemicals in them, which will irritate your baby's skin if you put them on straight from the shop.

In terms of colour and design, avoid clothes that will look 'tired', washed out and ruined once they've been through the wash several times. Choose darker colours or fabrics with prints to disguise stains. And look for fabrics suitable for the 'dry and fold' technique – a quick blast in the tumble drier, folding and no need for the iron! Cottons and linens look cute for occasions, but you'll curse the need to iron them on a regular basis.

Colour me beautiful

One final thing to mention: if you are on a tight budget or prefer to buy quality clothing that can be passed onto a future sibling, you might want to consider buying gender neutral clothes in creams, greys, lemons etc. Obviously, if you are desperate for a pink princess, then you're going to buy everything girly in sight, but be warned: the sibling prince that may follow her won't be able to wear any of her hand-me-downs.

You will need to buy lots of other things for your baby, too; for ease we have separated them into two categories: practical (where we'll cover travel, out and about and feeding kit); and interiors (where we'll cover the items you'll need for your baby's nursery).

PRACTICAL KIT

Pushchair/pram/travel system

You could probably write a whole book on this subject alone, so we will only cover the options available and let you research and decide what is right for you. We'll take you through the pros and cons of each one and give you pointers to help you make the right decision for your lifestyle.

Before you buy, consider the following.

Where you live/your lifestyle

- If you live in the country and plan to take your baby on rough terrain, you might want a sporty three wheeler that can tackle hills and bumps with ease.

- You might live somewhere so remote that you are going to spend most of your time ferrying your baby around by car; if that's the case, you'll need a buggy that will fit easily into the boot.

- If you don't have a car, you'll be using public transport and will need a pushchair that can fold easily – ideally with one hand. Some modern buses have buggy spaces and lowering systems to help you get on easily with the buggy, but many don't, so you need something you can collapse with one hand while you hold your baby in the other.

- If you live in a congested urban area, you might want something reasonably compact, as pounding the pavements can be quite tricky with a big buggy.

- Are you planning on having more children in the near future? If you are, you might want to consider one of those pushchairs that convert to a two tier configuration, so you can accommodate two children, with the baby on the top and the toddler below. Considerably slimmer than the traditional double buggy, many women find these are a good solution for a growing family.

- Do you plan to travel a lot with your baby? If so, you might consider investing in a proper pram and a 'holiday' buggy.

A fold-up umbrella-style pushchair is a good investment for air travel, as it can usually be folded once you get to the aircraft; and you don't mind so much if it does get mangled on the conveyor belt, as it will be reasonably inexpensive to replace.

- Do you want to get fit with your baby? You can buy jogging buggies that are specially designed to let you run and push your baby comfortably at the same time. These are good if you want to regain your pre-pregnancy figure and improve your fitness.

Your budget

You can spend anything from £20 to £2,000 on a pushchair, so it is important that you set a budget. It is really important that you do your research and don't get seduced by the latest design, or buy one because you saw a celeb pushing it (celebrities usually have someone else to fold their buggies or push the pram when we are not looking, so it's not too much of an issue if it's unwieldy for them).

'We bought a full travel system, only to find that 12 months later we wanted something much lighter, so bought a MacLaren buggy. So we spent nearly a grand on something we only used for a year! In hindsight, I would definitely get a cheaper pram or buy second hand.'

Claire, mum to James, 15 months

Your baby might start walking at 12 months, but the reality is that you may still be pushing your tot around in a buggy four or five years from now, so you want to buy something you know is going to last. The pushchair is probably the most important purchase you will make, as you'll probably be using it every day and it will be subject to much more wear and tear than something like a cot. For this reason, you might want to spend as much as you can possibly afford (although make sure it ticks all the boxes as far as your requirements go).

Do you want your baby facing you?

This is quite an interesting recent development; for years babies were pushed around in 'perambulators' (which is where the word pram comes from) and they would always face the person pushing them. The benefit of this was that you could make eye contact and talk to your baby as you walked along. Pram designs changed, and as the 'buggy' style became popular, babies tended to face out with their backs to the pushers. It was argued that this was beneficial to the babies because they could see the outside world and be visually stimulated, but critics argued that they were missing out on vital contact with their carers.

In the last few years, many new pushchairs have the flexibility to face both ways, so you can have your baby looking at you or at the outside world. This is brilliant because when your baby is learning to talk it's useful to make eye contact and chat to him, and when he gets older and wants 'entertaining' he has a good view of what's going on around him to stimulate his curiosity.

If you can, go for a buggy that can face both ways – that way you don't have to choose!

Travel systems

In essence, a travel system is a pushchair that is compatible with an infant rear-facing car seat, and often comes with a carrycot that you can attach to the chassis.

Pros

- If your baby is asleep you can simply unclip him from the car and clip him onto the pushchair frame, without the need to wake or unstrap him.

- If it comes with a carrycot, this eliminates the need to buy a Moses basket; you can transfer your sleeping baby from the pram to the house with ease.

- This is a convenient and sometimes economical way of buying the car seat, carrycot and pushchair all in one.

- You can have your baby facing you.

Cons

- Your baby will grow out of the carrycot within months.

- You will need to buy another car seat once your baby is around a year old and weighing over 10kg (22lb).

- The chassis can be quite heavy and difficult to fold in some designs.

- These systems are not cheap, ranging from around £200 to £1,000.

- Not all infant car seats are compatible with travel systems, so you should check before you buy if purchasing separately, or buy everything as a complete package.

Lightweights

If you are looking for a buggy that is easy to fold and light to push, there are many models on the market. Most have the traditional umbrella-type fold, but in the last couple of years some exciting new designs have come onto the market. Improvements in design mean that they have become more comfortable in recent years, with more attention to padding and detail in the seat area.

Pros

- Light to carry.

- Traditionally easy to fold.

- Often more compact than other types of pushchair.

- Useful if you live in a flat and have to fold and carry up stairs.

- Good for urban living where space is tight.

- Usually have a carry strap or handle.

- Good budget option if cash is an issue.

Cons

- Some are not suitable for newborns.

- Some models are quite basic and don't have sophisticated suspension or braking systems.

- Not good for bumpy countryside walks or travelling on sand.

- May seem the cheapest option, but you'll bump up the price if you buy all the 'optional' extras.

Sporty pushchairs/three wheelers

If you have a fairly active lifestyle and can see yourself taking the baby on long country walks, jogging or taking a stroll in the sand dunes, you'll need a pram that can cope with all terrains. Traditionally, this type of pram was called a three-wheeler, but there are more four-wheeled versions coming onto the market. They're not just for country dwellers, though; they'll be as happy pounding pavements as hiking over hills.

Pros

- Flexible – you can use them wherever you are.

- Easy to manoeuvre.

- Suspension is normally really good.

- Phil & Teds' Sport has a 'doubles' kit, so you can convert it to a two tier buggy to accommodate two children.

Cons

- Can be bulky when folded. Sometimes you need to take the wheels off if you are attempting to put it in the boot of a small hatchback.

- Can be quite heavy.

- Can be expensive.

According to stockists such as Tesco and John Lewis, three-wheeled buggies have fallen out of favour recently, replaced by more traditional four-wheeled prams.

Designer/luxury prams

In the past few years, there have been some very exciting developments in the pushchair market: from designer collaborations to the use of new innovative materials, it seems we just can't get enough of these luxurious, super-stylish prams, and we are prepared to pay a premium for them. It helps when we see our favourite celebs out and about with these objects of desire; it just makes us want them even more. What you have to remember, though, is that celebs get them sent for free, which is why Gwen Stefani had a customised black and white Bugaboo Bee as well as a limited edition gold Mamas & Papas Ziko (one of 10, in case you were wondering – P Diddy has one as well!). She has become renowned for her buggy habit and spotted out and about pushing at least four other strollers.

New research shows that while parents may be happy to use second-hand clothes and toys, the vast majority want to buy brand new prams and buggies. At the top end of the market, the must-have Bugaboo, chosen by royal parents William and Kate, and the classic Silver Cross favoured by celebrity mums such as Madonna, Victoria Beckham, Liz Hurley and Sarah Jessica Parker have gained almost cult status.

So what are the cutting-edge designs currently favoured by the celebrity parent?

Celebrity wheels and top rides for stylish 2014 infants

Bugaboo continues to be a top brand, with the Duke and Duchess of Cambridge choosing a blue Bugaboo for their new arrival (although it's not known what model they chose). The royals have followed in many a celeb parent's footsteps, including Fearne Cotton, Peaches Geldof and Sienna Miller.

For a top-of-the-range Bugaboo option, see the **Bugagoo Donkey** at £1,200 – a flexible mono-duo-mono convertible stroller with an expandable frame which transforms with a click from a one-seater to a two-seater. Snapped up by the likes of Mariah Carey, this is the sports car of the buggy world.

For smaller budgets, the **Bugaboo Bee** at £439 plus hood £39 is a favourite of London- and New York-based celebrities, and is a great lightweight city pushchair. Sienna Miller has the All Black Special Edition Bee, while Victoria Beckham has the same model with yellow and pink hoods for her daughter Harper.

The **Origami Power-Folding Stroller** at around £560 is one for hi-tech fans. Jennifer Garner's little boy Samuel has been spotted testing it out! It boasts an LCD dashboard, phone charger, speaker, daytime running lights and a speedometer, and opens and closes at the touch of a button within 10 seconds. It also detects when a baby is in the seat to avoid accidental folding.

The **Orbit Baby G2** at £999 for the full kit is very popular with US celebrities such as Jessica Alba and Kourtney Kardashian, and allows you to rotate your baby 360 degrees as well as having a one-handed folding mechanism. This futuristic design is the epitome of celebrity cool right now.

The **Uppababy Vista** at £630 has been seen out and about with Reese Witherspoon and Sarah Jessica Parker, and has a massive basket for shopaholics and excess baby paraphernalia.

The iCandy range is still very trendy, with the latest **iCandy Peach** costing £595 – this is another one test-driven by little Harper Beckham, although iCandy made one exclusively in lilac for her that isn't available to the public! Other 'flavours' you can go for include Apple, Pear, Cherry and Strawberry.

Miranda Kerr's baby Flynn has been cruising around in the **NunaPepp** at £200 – a smart pushchair at an affordable price. More expensive is the **MimaKobi** at £950 –with their sleek look these are a newish addition to the market and Lily Allen is rumoured to have been impressed enough to get one for her daughter Marnie.

Chantelle Houghton, on the other hand, has gone for a celebrity staple with the **StokkeXplory** at £829 – this has a high seat to keep baby Dolly up close, and Bruce Willis has also been seen out with this with his daughter Mabel.

The Maclaren range is ever popular, and the **Maclaren Grand LX** at £640 has been seen out with Jennifer Garner (she gets through a few brands!). The **Maclaren Techno XT** at £235 for the classy 'champagne' colour is a perennial favourite and has been seen out with Selma Hayek and Naomi Watts, to name but two.

The **Jeep Overland Jogging Stroller** at £150 is a great urban buggy for keep-fit enthusiasts such as Minnie Driver – it has a front fixed wheel, air-filled tyres, a super grip and adjustable handle.

For those who really want to be cutting edge, though, look out for those Bugaboos again…they are launching a new Andy Warhol-inspired, pop art collection of buggy accessories beginning in May 2013 over a period of two years. The collection will offer bright, trendy and achingly cool accessories to jazz up your Bugaboo, including sun canopies and fabric sets in flower prints to go with the Bee, Cameleon and Donkey. It's all in the accessories, dahling...!

The future?

Many pushchair manufacturers are embracing technological advances and incorporating them into their designs, as we can see from these recent releases.

Want your baby to share your love of music?

A recent innovation is pushchairs with speakers incorporated in the hood, so that you can plug in your mp3 player and keep your baby entertained as you stroll. Check out the Cosatto I Spin.

Want to work out how far you've travelled?

Or do you need to know the air temperature or the time? The new Maclaren Grand Tour LX has a 'strollometer' (a wireless device with integrated sensor to measure time and distance). There is also a console on the handle with a clock and thermometer, and there are even safety lights with remote control for visibility in the dark.

Pushchair-buying checklist

- Do your research on the internet and then find a local stockist that has all the styles you are interested in. We cannot stress too much the importance of actually handling the pushchair to see if it is comfortable, folds easily and manoeuvres the way you want it to.

- Accessories are very important, but check what is included in the price, because extras can really bump up the price of a basic model. A rain cover is essential because you'll need to keep your baby dry, and a sunshade and shopping basket/ storage are desirable extras.

- Make sure the handles are easily adjustable, as your partner might be considerably taller than you and what is comfortable for you will not necessarily be comfortable for him.

- Check it will fit easily into your car boot when folded; you don't want to have to take the wheels off to wedge it in.

- Look at the seat positions on your favoured models; can it lie flat, for example? This is useful when your newborn is sleeping most of the day because it will be more comfortable for him.

- Are the brakes foot operated or operated from the handle? Test the brakes to see if they are easy to access.

- For a smooth, comfortable ride, the pushchair should have good suspension. You can test this by pushing down on the buggy; if it bounces back in one smooth movement then it's probably a goodie.

- How easy is it to handle? Can you get it through narrow gaps with ease? This is useful if you're going to be using it for shopping.

- If you are going to need to carry it upstairs (for example, if you live in a flat), or use public transport frequently, look at lightweight models.

Car seats

If you have a car, you will need an infant car seat, and if you are going to bring your baby home from hospital in a vehicle, you need to know how to fit it properly before the baby is born. Hospitals **will not** release babies without a car seat if they are travelling home in a vehicle.

Things you should know

- There are two types of infant car seat: Group 0, which is from birth to 10kg (22lb); and Group 0+, which is from birth to 13kg (28.5lb).

- All newborn car seats must be rear-facing until your baby is at least 10kg (22lb). The reason for this is that it is much safer for your baby if you have a crash, as the force of the impact is more evenly distributed if he is rear-facing.

- If your baby is going to travel in the front seat and you have airbags in the front, they **must** be deactivated as the force of the airbag could kill your baby if it inflates. If you cannot turn the airbags off, your baby must be strapped in the back.

- Since 2006, most new cars have an ISOFIX-compatible system, an internationally recognised safety standard that was launched with the backing of car seat manufacturers. ISOFIX seats clip into a base that stays in the car and are supposed to be safer and easier to use.

- If your car is older or doesn't have ISOFIX, you will have to use the traditional seat belt method. If you have a vintage car that doesn't have seat belts, you will have to have them fitted to ensure your baby has a safe ride.

- You should not buy second-hand car seats because you don't know their 'history'. If they have been in a prior accident or have a hairline crack, they could severely compromise your baby's safety if you are involved in an accident.

- Not every car seat will fit every car, so make sure you try before you buy; many stores like Mothercare, Mamas & Papas, Halfords and Babies R Us offer a car seat fitting service if you go to their larger outlets with space outside for your car.

- Your baby should preferably spend no more than two hours a day in a car seat, as research has shown that babies have low levels of oxygen in their blood if they sit in the same position for hours at a time.

Studies show that seven out of 10 car seats are installed incorrectly. The Summer Infant Prodigy Infant Car Seat and Travel System is a little gadget to ensure you get it right every time. It has a car seat base with a smart screen that gives you step-by-step instructions for levelling, tightening and installation. Available from www.summerinfant.com.

You don't need to worry about the safety aspect when you buy an infant car seat from a reputable baby goods manufacturer, because it will have been subjected to rigorous tests before it came on the market; there are, however, certain features that offer more protection, make the chair more comfortable, or the seat more user-friendly, so it's worth doing some research before you buy. Looks might be important, too: if you are going to carry your baby about 'handbag' style in a seat, you might not want one with a hideous teddy print dangling off your arm.

Car seat-buying checklist

- Does your favoured model actually fit in your car? Try before you buy!

- If safety is an issue and you have the ISOFIX system in your car, it's worth buying a compatible car seat. A recent survey showed that only 4% of ISOFIX car seats were incorrectly fitted, whereas a whopping 60% of traditional car seats were not fitted properly.

- How heavy is it? The car seat you choose may look lovely, but if it weighs a ton it won't be easy to get in and out of the car with a chubby baby inside.

- Does your baby fit in it? Very small or premature babies are too small for normal car seats and require specialist car cots to travel in. Likewise, if you're purchasing a seat for a child who has outgrown one already, make sure the weight restriction goes high enough.

- Does it have a head hugger? These removable padded supports are good for giving your newborn extra support and protection and for making him feel more secure.

- Can you take the cover off and wash it? Useful if the baby is sick all over it.

- How adjustable is the handle? Some handles go forward as well as back, so that the car seat can become a rocker inside your home.

- Does it have additional safety features? All car seats come with a three-point harness, but some new models have five-point harnesses.

- How deep are the safety wings? The deeper and more padded the 'wings' of the car seat (the sides by your baby's head), the better the protection.

- Does it have a reclining feature? Some models on the market allow your baby to lie flat, which is more comfortable for him.

- Is it buggy-compatible? It may fix to the frame of your chosen pushchair. Most car seats are compatible with their same-brand pushchairs, but the Maxi Cosi fits most pushchair options.

Slings

Sometimes it is more convenient to just pop your baby in a sling than to go out with a pushchair. You don't have to buy one new, however; it's the perfect item to borrow if you have a friend who has one lying idle. There are several types of slings: there's the traditional fabric type that you can tie in a variety of ways; there's the papoose type where your baby lies vertically against your chest; and there are some on the market that start life as a papoose and can be converted to a hip carrier once your baby gets too heavy to 'wear' round your neck.

Pros

- You can keep your baby close to you, and it is said that the sound of your heartbeat can be reassuring to him.

- This is a very convenient way to transport your baby because you have your hands free (great when you are busy).

Cons

- A recent study in the US showed that there is a danger of suffocation if the baby is curled up in the sling and his oxygen supply is restricted (more likely if you use the fabric type and the baby is cocooned rather than upright).

- If you have a bad back or a particularly heavy baby, you might find it puts too much strain on your lumbar region after a few months, or even weeks.

- It can be tricky to put the baby into the papoose if you are on your own.

- If you want to use a fabric sling you have to learn how to tie it correctly.

Celebrity fans include Angelina Jolie and Nicole Kidman, and it might be the sight of our favourite celebs out and about with their babies in slings that has fuelled a recent 100% increase in sales of the product at Mothercare.

Sling-buying checklist

- How long will you be able to use it? Does it convert for use with a toddler?

- Is it well padded, with protection for your baby's head?

- Can the baby face inwards and outwards?

- Is the fabric breathable or can your baby get too hot?

- Can you use it from birth? Some companies recommend that you use them after one week.

- Can you wash it?

Changing bag

In theory, you can manage without a changing bag, but we normally succumb to buying one because they are designed to make nappy changing on-the-go as quick and efficient as possible.

In the past the only option was a padded nylon bag, but nowadays many designers have got in on the act to produce some rather glorious bags that are so super stylish, you can continue to use them after the nappy days are over.

What you need to know

- It helps if your changing bag can function as a handbag as well as a nappy bag (meaning you don't have to carry two bags around), so it makes sense to buy one that you like the look of, as you will be using it every day.

- If you want a bag that will last you through the year, opt for sensible black or metallic that will work in different seasons.

- There are many designer/fashionable bags on the market, so do some research on the internet before you buy. Some of the most exciting bags come from the States and Italy, and if you want something different it's definitely worth logging on and seeing what's available.

- If you don't find anything you like, go the DIY route; as long as a bag is roomy, has handles you can sling over the buggy (or is a backpack), you can buy the components separately to create the functional bag you want.

Changing bag-buying checklist

- Is the bag wipe-clean? That butter-soft tan bag may look gorgeous, but if you accidently get some baby poo on it you'll be traumatised (patent would be a great choice fashion-wise at the moment).

- Does it have somewhere special to stash your mobile phone, keys, wallet, etc? You don't want to be scrabbling around in a bag containing soiled nappies to locate your essentials, and many changing bags have key clips, phone holders and special pockets, so keep an eye out for these features.

- Does it have insulated pockets to keep milk or food chilled? Useful if you are going to be out all day.

- Does it have a fold-up padded changing mat? Obviously you need to be able to wipe this clean, but it also helps if there is some padding in case you have to change your baby somewhere unforgiving, like on a hard floor.

- Does it have pockets for baby wipes and nappy bags? Useful if you need to find them in a hurry.

- Does it have a removable bag for soiled clothes or nappies? Desirable but not essential, although it does help if you have a separate bag you can wash inside the changing bag for stained clothing, or nappies if there's no disposal bin nearby.

Steriliser

If you know that you are not going to breastfeed, it makes sense to buy a steriliser before the baby is born. There are basically two different types: electronic steam sterilisers and microwave sterilisers, but both types create steam to sterilise the bottles. Many retailers sell starter packs with bottles, teats and other accessories included, which can work out cheaper, so make sure you see what deals are available before you buy.

What you need to know

- Some sterilisers keep the items sterilised for 24 hours. If you are working or have other time pressures, this feature will be a godsend because it means that you will only be sterilising once a day.

- Some models are quite big and cumbersome, so if space is tight in your kitchen, you might have to find a small model or look at the microwave options that tend to be smaller.

- Sterilising times can vary between four and 10 minutes, so if time is precious or you are worried you might have to sterilise in the night, go for one with a quicker time.

Steriliser-buying checklist

- How many bottles will it hold at once? If you have twins or your baby turns out to be hungry you'll want a bigger one.

- Does it only work with the same brand bottles? This is important if you wish to use BPA-free ones and they are not compatible with the steriliser.

You might want to invest in a bottle warmer – ideal for night feeds.

- How long do the bottles and teats stay sterilised? If it's not long, you'll be using it more often.

- Are you likely to travel a lot with your baby? Choose a model that is compact; a microwave version is probably the easier option.

UNDERSTANDING BPA

There is some concern over Bisphenol A (BPA), which is present in plastic in some baby bottles in the UK. Exposure to BPA has been linked to breast cancer and there is a possibility that it can have an effect on your baby's reproductive, neurological or immune systems. Canada has recently withdrawn from sale all baby bottles containing BPA, and an EU ban on BPA in baby bottles came into force in March 2011 and came into complete effect in June 2011. In July 2012 the USA also implemented a ban. It is possible that other governments will follow their lead in the near future. Read the latest research and make an informed judgement on whether you think the risk is significant enough to opt for BPA-free bottles; they are widely available and should be clearly labelled 'BPA free'.

Formula

If you are planning on bottle feeding, have a word with your midwife about the different brands of formula milk available; you can buy it in powdered form or ready-made in cardboard cartons. Make sure you buy the correct one – it should state it is suitable for newborns.

Muslins

Muslins are absolutely essential when you have a newborn, and are sometimes known as 'burpminas' because they are always artfully draped over your shoulder. Every baby tends to regurgitate some milk after feeding or winding, and the idea of the muslin is to protect your clothing from that vomited milk.

What you need to know

- They are going to be in the wash all the time as they are going to get covered in stains, so it makes sense to buy them in the same colour so you can soak them all together.

- If you don't like the plain white ones you can find them in colours, and for true muslin glamour check out the printed range from Aden + Anais; they are not only big enough to swaddle your baby in, but come in a gorgeous range of prints to add some glam to the daily wind!

- You're going to need a lot of these, so it's probably wise to buy one of the larger packs available from places like Mothercare and supermarkets.

Baby hygiene and grooming

We go into how to care for your baby's hygiene later in the book (page 357), but there are things you need to buy in advance to prepare for his arrival. Experts recommend that you wash your baby's face and bottom with just water for the first few weeks (a practice known as 'top and tailing'), so there's no need to buy any baby bubble bath yet.

If you want some in the cupboard in readiness, make sure you buy baby-specific products, as chemicals in some adult soap products may irritate your baby's delicate skin. If you have sensitive skin or are worried about chemicals there are lots of organic baby products on the market.

Things you need (or might want)

- **Cotton wool.** You'll need this for cleaning faces and bottoms (although obviously not with the same piece).

- **Nappies.** Many of the supermarket and chemist chains have them on offer, so stock up before the birth because you'll be getting through them at an alarming rate in the early days. Check they are suitable for newborns, but maybe buy a pack of the next size up in case you give birth to a whopper. If you want environmentally-friendly nappies, most supermarkets stock biodegradable versions, but they are slightly more expensive. If you decide not to use disposables at all, you'll need to buy fabric nappies, liners and some kind of pail to put soiled liners in.

- **Baby scissors.** Babies' fingernails can be sharp and grow quite quickly, so it's useful to have some special (round-ended) scissors to do the job. However, you should not cut your baby's nails until about four weeks after birth, as they have the skin still attached to the back of the nail, meaning you can cut the skin and cause infections. It is safer to file them with a nail file and to put mittens over them if you're worried about him scratching his face.

- **Something to bath the baby in.** You don't *need* a baby bath, and if space is tight, don't bother. You could use a washing up bowl just as successfully. If you have a bad back as a result of pregnancy or birth, though, a baby bath could be a godsend; you can buy ones on legs or one designed to fit over the top of the bath. You can get little chairs that you can use in your normal bath; these will be easier on your back because you don't need to support the baby with one arm and wash with the other. You can also buy bath beds, which is a towelling support that you lie your baby on in a normal bath. Places such as John Lewis and Mothercare sell them.

- **Bath thermometer.** Not essential, as you can use your elbow to test the water, but if you are worried about water temperature they are quite cheap and can put your mind at rest.

- **Thermometer.** Hopefully your baby won't become ill in the coming weeks; but it is useful to buy a thermometer, if you don't already have one in your medicine cabinet, to check your baby if he does seem unwell or unduly warm. You can buy thermometers that you place under the arm or on the forehead to get a reading, but usually the digital ones that you gently insert into the ear canal are the easiest to use and give very accurate results. Try any large chemist or specialist baby products retailer.

- **Baby hairbrush.** Maybe wait to see if you give birth to a baby with a full head of hair, and only get one if you need one.

- **Wipes.** You are advised to stick to soap and water for the first few weeks, but many new mothers can't wait to start using wipes because they are larger and slightly easier to use. Flushable ones are now available, and if you are worried about the environment you might like to use wipes that are biodegradable. Fragrance-free wipes are best for new babies because the chemicals in the scented ones might affect your baby's skin.

- **Nappy bins.** There's something a bit yucky about putting dirty nappies in with general household waste, so it's probably a good idea to put them in a designated bin with a sealed lid. You can buy a nappy wrapper (that looks like a large thermos flask) that you store your dirty nappies in, but this can seem like just another piece of kit you don't really need. If you have a garden you can always use a nappy dustbin that you leave outside.

- **Nappy sacks.** You will need as many of these as you do nappies. Buy the scented variety if you are worried about less than pleasant smells impregnating your home. Alternatively you can use old carrier bags instead.

- **Face flannels.** These are useful for washing any bit of your baby.

The following items are also useful but not essential:

- hooded baby towel

- baby sponge

- top and tail bowl.

'I wouldn't bother getting most of the baby stuff that's available. The amount you buy and never use is ridiculous. Plus, friends and relatives always want to buy [you] stuff, so you can end up with five playmates and seven bouncy chairs; a bit like toasters at weddings! I'd recommend buying as much as possible second-hand or even just borrowing.'

Claire, mum to James, 15 months

Cloth nappies: what do they involve?

Cloth – or 'real' or 'reusable' – nappies are an option many women are returning to these days. The benefits are that they are better for the environment, can save you money and even look cute!

The cloth nappies of our childhood – squares of terry fabric and plastic pants – are long gone, and modern reusables are easy, convenient, quick-drying and come in a range of designs.

The first task is to decide what kind of nappies suit your family. If you don't have a tumble dryer or want to avoid using one, you need quick-drying nappies. If your baby is a heavy wetter you need high absorbency. If you're planning on using childcare, nappies that go on all in one piece are good.

Get some support. There are many real nappy forums on the internet where you can swap tips and get some support and recommendations.

Once you find some you like the look of, go online and read some reviews. This will give you a good idea of what the nappies are really like to use, whether they will meet your needs and if there are any common problems.

You don't need to buy a full set of 25 nappies straight away if you don't want to. It's good to get a mixture of a few different brands and build up your collection slowly, once you figure out which nappies work best for you. In some areas you may be able to hire a trial kit from your council or local NCT branch.

As well as nappies, you will also need a nappy bucket for the dirty nappies, mesh bags to line the bucket and a wet bag for when you are out and about. Washable liners can be used to create a stay-dry layer and flushable liners can help to catch solid poo. You may also like to use a special nappy detergent to sanitise your nappies in the wash.

It's really important to read the instructions on your nappies very carefully. Most nappies need pre-washing before you use them. It's a bit like when you buy new towels – washing them makes them more absorbent. Don't use too much detergent, as this can make your nappies smell, and never use fabric softener as this will reduce absorbency.

Buying real nappies can cost a lot of money in the short term, but they will save you hundreds of pounds compared with using disposables, and if you look after them, they will last for years.

MUMMY SHOPPING

Probably the least glamorous part of your baby shopping, as it's quite difficult to get excited about a packet of breast pads, but there are things you need to buy for your hospital visit and to help you in the first few weeks post-birth, when shopping will be the last thing on your mind.

Something to give birth in

Your hospital will supply a gown, but you might prefer to bring in something from home. Be prepared for it not to make the journey back again, though, because it is bound to get ruined. If your partner has an old baggy T-shirt he no longer wants (don't nick his beloved Guns & Roses tee from uni days), that's perfect, because it'll probably be big enough to give you some modesty. If you don't have anything suitable, head to somewhere cheap and cheerful like Primark, who do some of the cheapest nighties around.

Maternity towels

Sometimes referred to as house bricks because of the resemblance. They tend to make normal sanitary towels look like panty liners, but they are necessary. Buy several boxes as you'll get through them quite quickly, and ensure you buy specific maternity sanitary towels, not just normal sanitary towels, as these are not as absorbent.

Big knickers

If you are normally a thong kind of gal, you're going to need to buy yourself some big pants to accommodate your maternity pads. Buy a couple of cheap multi-packs from a chain store and just chuck them away a few weeks after the birth when the bleeding has subsided. Much better value than disposable knickers.

Nursing bras and breast pads

Try to get measured as close to your due date as possible and buy three nursing bras. Buy *one* of them in the next size up, because your breasts will swell even more when your milk comes in and you'll need a bigger bra for a bit. Breast pads are little absorbent circles that you pop in your bra in case your breasts leak between or after feeding. They stop your bra from getting stained and save on washing.

Breast pump

If you are planning to breastfeed, it is useful to invest in a breast pump; if you plan to go back to work and want to continue breastfeeding, you can express and freeze milk that can be given in a bottle to your baby in your absence. You can also express milk and sneak off on a guilt-free date night with your partner.

 If you return to work, your employer has a responsibility to provide a fridge where you can store breast milk you have expressed.

PLANNING AND SHOPPING FOR YOUR BABY'S NUSERY

You may be planning for your baby to sleep in the same room as you for a while, but you probably have a room in the house already earmarked as the nursery. It's worth considering if you want to plan and decorate it before the baby is born, because you may not have the time, energy or inclination after the birth. You don't have to spend a lot of money to create a stylish sanctuary for your baby, and in the next section you'll find lots of ideas to suit all tastes and budgets. You don't need to buy much either: as long as you have something for your baby to sleep in, a place to change him and somewhere to stash his clothes you'll have all the essentials.

> If you have room, consider getting a feeding chair (a large rocker that's great for breast or bottle feeding), as they can prove very useful – they are comfortable for you and also rock your baby to sleep.

Sleeping

There's nothing wrong with putting your baby to sleep in a drawer (though obviously not a shut one). On the other hand, you don't need to worry about getting an extravagantly hand-carved crib for your baby either. What you choose will depend on the budget available, whether you are planning on having more children in the near future and the space available to you. According to experts, a newborn baby will spend up to 21 hours a day asleep, so it makes sense to have one (or two) sleep options in your home if finances run to it. Your baby might sleep in a carrycot downstairs and a cot upstairs, or a Moses basket in the living room and a crib in the bedroom. Research the options and see what is likely to work best in your home.

Moses baskets

A Moses basket is a woven basket with handles, which most newborns sleep in for their first few weeks.

Pros

- Newborns are said to feel secure in the cocoon-like enclosed basket.

- Easy to transport your sleeping baby from one room to another.

- Inexpensive sleeping option for a newborn.

Cons

- They only last around four months because your baby will grow out of it, so if money is tight, it might be worth trying to borrow one (for safety reasons, you need to replace the mattress if you borrow one).

- You need to put them on a stand or the floor (not on a high surface) if you want to keep your baby close for night feeds, or want to keep an eye on your baby while he's sleeping.

Buying guide: what to look for

- A Moses basket should have sturdy handles.
- There should be a removable, washable liner in the basket for hygiene reasons.
- Wicker and palm are considered the best materials.

Shopping tips

- www.thelittlegreensheep.co.uk has beautiful 100% chemical-free organic Moses baskets.
- www.naturalmat.co.uk has heirloom-quality baskets with environmental integrity.
- For classic willow, check out www.lulasapphire.com.

Cribs

Cribs usually last around the same amount of time as a Moses basket, ie around four months.

Pros

- Often made of wood, so they are sturdier than a woven basket.
- Many cribs have a rocking feature, which is useful when you are trying to lull your newborn to sleep.
- Good option if space is tight or if you are waiting to 'inherit' a cot from someone else.

Cons

- Can be quite expensive.
- Have a short life of four to six months.
- Your baby might not like the rocking motion; some don't.

Buying guide: what to look for

- Check that the crib is stable and sturdy.

- If your baby is very active, a rocking crib might move too much and unsettle them.

- Ensure you pick the correct-fitting mattress as recommended by the manufacturer.

Shopping tips

- If money is no object, try www.mumsaid.co.uk.

- If you want a co-ordinated nursery, check out www.funkykidsfurniture.co.uk.

- If you are looking for unusual brands (and some of the most over-the-top cradles in the world), visit www.vivababy.com.

Convertible cribs/cots/cot beds

Some cribs convert from cots to cot beds to chairs (the STOKKE Sleepi, for example); others convert from cots to beds to sofas (like the Simon Horn); so there are a wealth of different options available. However, some of them can be quite expensive, so it's useful to canvass opinions from friends who already have children. It's also a good idea to look around in stores and showrooms to get a feel for what's on offer and how it will fit in your home.

Things you should know before you buy

- Your baby is only going to use the cot for two years, so don't spend a fortune on one unless you really want to. If you think about it, most people aren't going to be snooping around the nursery (unless you invite them), so it's not like you are going to be judged on your choice of cot. Finally, you can be absolutely certain that your baby has no knowledge of interior design!

- The Lullaby Trust (formerly the Foundation for the Study of Infant Deaths) recommends that your baby sleeps in your room for the first six months – but *not* in your bed. It also recommends that you **always** buy a new mattress if you accept a hand-me-down cot, crib or Moses basket.

- The slats on the sides of cots should be spaced no more than 6cm apart (2.4″).

- The mattress should fit snugly and there should be a gap of no more than 4cm between the mattress and side of the cot.

- Mattresses are usually made of foam, are sprung or are made of natural fibres. Organic mattresses are gaining in favour because they are said to promote sleep, are naturally non-allergenic and breathable (Natural Mat has a good selection).

- Cots are subject to regulations, and there are strict guidelines on safety features. Beware buying a vintage cot, however beautiful it is, because it may not conform to modern safety rules.

Cots *vs* cot beds

Cot beds are cots that convert to junior beds. Fans of cot beds argue that they represent better value for money, because your child can use them for longer (usually between five and eight years). The problem is that, if you have a subsequent baby, he might need the cot around the time your toddler would be transferring to a bed. So if you want to be economical, it makes sense to buy just one cot that you can use for both babies and then two single beds, because a cot bed won't last until adulthood.

Buying guide checklist

- **Does it have a drop side?** If the cot has a drop side, check that you can operate it with one hand, as you'll probably have your baby in the other. Drop sides are good because you can get the baby in and out of bed easily. Some cots have sides that drop right down so that your baby can sleep right next to your bed in your room, at the same level as your own mattress; the benefit of this is you can keep a close eye on him and can also get him out of bed easily for night feeds.

- **Does it have wheels?** This is useful if you want to move it from room to room. If it does have castors at least two should be lockable.

- **Does it have an adjustable base?** Many cots have adjustable bases so you can raise and lower the height. This means, when your baby is tiny, you can put it at the highest position because it will be easier for you to lift your baby in and out, and as your baby grows and learns to sit up the base can be lowered.

- **How long will it last?** Even cots vary in size, and you might get a few more months out of a bigger one if you can fit it in the nursery.

- **Is the mattress bought separately?** This is normal, so factor in the cost of a mattress when budgeting.

- **Does it have teething rails?** Sometimes the horizontal bars at the top of the cot are coated with a non-toxic plastic coating because your baby might start gnawing everything (including his bed) once he is teething.

Bedding

Babies are at an increased risk of cot death if they get too hot at night; you should therefore keep your baby's nursery at a constant temperature of 18°C (65°F). A mix of sheets and lightweight blankets or a baby sleeping bag is ideal, but make sure you tuck blankets away from your baby's face to avoid suffocation. Duvets, pillows and cot bumpers should not be used until your baby is one year old.

Sheets

Most mums find fitted bottom sheets are better because they are less fiddly to put on, but you may want to buy a mixture of fitted and flat so you can just put a sheet over your baby if the weather is very warm and they don't need a blanket.

They do tend to get quite milk-stained, so buy four of each if you don't want the washing machine to be permanently on the go. Always buy cotton because it is more breathable and easy to wash.

Shopping tips

- For classic, crisp organic cottons, try www.thefinecottoncompany.com.
- For retro cool, check out www.bygraziela.com.
- For quality basics, visit www.johnlewis.com.

Blankets

Experts recommend you buy lightweight cellular blankets (cotton blankets with an open, holey weave), because air can circulate through them and they won't make your baby so hot. We would suggest you buy two cot-size and one pram-size.

Shopping tips

- For adorable organic baby blankets, visit www.lumadirect.com.

- For luxurious classics, check out www.nurserywindow.co.uk.

- For contemporary cashmere, try www.angelcashmere.com.

Baby sleeping bags

You need to make sure you buy the correct size for your baby (so he can't wriggle down the bag and potentially suffocate). You also need to get the correct tog rating, as there are lightweight summer ones and thicker padded versions for winter.

The great thing about sleeping bags is that they are perfect for travel; you may find your baby settles easily away from home because the bag feels familiar, even if the surroundings are not.

Grobag is often credited with bringing the concept of the baby sleeping bag to the UK; it has a great selection with different tog values for all-year use.

Shopping tips

- For designer sleeping bags, check out www.childrensalon.com.

- www.vertbaudet.co.uk has a fantastic array of budget designs.

- www.slumbersac.co.uk sells lovely sleeping bags that are 100% cotton.

Baby monitor

You will need a baby monitor so that you can hear your baby if he is in the nursery and you're in another part of the house. You can buy very basic models that will just alert you that your baby is awake, or very sophisticated models that measure the humidity and temperature in the room. Some act as nightlights or automatically play lullabies to your baby if he wakes; some allow you to 'talk back' to your baby if you are in a different room; some monitor your baby's breathing and movement for extra peace of mind; and some even have video monitors so you can actually watch your baby sleep.

If you want the latest in baby monitor technology, look no further than the Philips AVENT Baby Monitor with Temperature and Humidity Sensors and New Eco Mode. This monitor tracks the intensity level of your baby's cries – LED lights flash to alert you when the sound reaches a certain level – and the AVENT DECT monitor also reports room temperature, plays soothing music to hum baby to sleep and displays the time. It also has a two-way speaker to allow you to talk back to your baby from wherever you are in the house.

Make sure that you check the range of the monitor, and see if it works outside if that is important to you.

Changing table

Most people tend to change their babies in the nursery because you invariably need to do a nappy change after a sleep.

If you are short of space, it is definitely worth considering getting a cot-top changer if there's one that co-ordinates with your cot, or if you can find one that fits the cot you have chosen.

If you have the money and the space, by all means go for a changing table unit, but bear in mind you'll only need it for a couple of years; buy one with drawers or cupboards underneath, so that you can use it to store clothes or toys. You can also buy changing trolleys on wheels with shelves below to stack nappies and grooming products.

Finally, you can make your own changing unit by fixing battens onto the top of a chest of drawers (to hold the changing mat still and stop your baby rolling off).

Shopping tips

- Many companies sell changing tables that co-ordinate with your cot as part of a nursery furniture package, so if you want your furniture to match look out for these.
- If space is tight, byBOdesign sells a stunning wall mounted one (www.byBOdesign.se) and Ikea offers a great budget version (www.ikea.co.uk).
- For the funkiest changing mats, check out www.zpm.com.
- Cosatto sells a multi-functional baby bath/changing table/storage trolley at www.cosatto.co.uk.

Seating

For baby

For the first few weeks your baby will spend a lot of time sleeping in his bed or the pram, but if someone wants to buy you a newborn gift, a baby chair is a great idea. Get one that bounces, rocks or vibrates if you can. There's a huge range of choices out there, from the drop-dead stylish to more traditional chairs with toy bars to keep your baby entertained; below we've listed some of our favourites.

- The Pebble Cradle by Zoobie is funky and futuristic.

- The Coco Plexistyle by Bloom Baby has rock and roll glamour (literally): www.blooombaby.com.

- The Magic Astro Cradle combines the latest technology with classic play: www.mamasandpapas.co.uk.

- The Baby Bjorn Babysitter Balance is a nice classic design with a twist: www.babybjorn.com.

For mummy

If there is space in your baby's nursery, it can be useful to have a chair for you, as you might find it a nice, restful place to breastfeed. You can buy rocking chairs designed specifically for feeding and they are brilliant; they also happen to be incredibly expensive, very large and not the most beautiful of objects.

You could use a vintage rocking chair or any other comfy chair (and re-upholster it if you want it to match your nursery colour scheme).

GRAND DESIGNS

Your baby will soon grow into an opinionated little person with his own ideas about how his bedroom should look, so don't go overboard decorating the nursery because in a few years you'll probably want to do it again. If you have another child the younger sibling may take over the nursery, and you'll have to re-do it if it's Barbie pink and you subsequently have a boy. Also, your baby won't have a clue whether the wallpaper is from Homebase or Colefax & Fowler, so don't go overboard unless you have the time and the money to keep redecorating.

Planning a nursery is quite similar to planning a kitchen: you want everything easily to hand and to be able to move seamlessly from one area to another. You don't need a big room, as all you really need is something for the baby to sleep in and some means of storing clothes. You can do without seating or a changing area if space is at a premium or the budget is tight.

Deck the walls

If you don't know the sex of your baby you'll probably want to keep the nursery fairly gender-neutral. White is always a fresh, clean choice but it can be a bit stark, so you could opt for something warmer like cream. Don't feel bound by the traditional baby 'pastel' shades of pink, blue or lemon; you could go for some more quirky colours or patterned wallpaper instead.

Painting

We mentioned concerns about painting during pregnancy earlier in the book and recommended that you use organic paint, or look for paint with low VOCs (volatile organic compounds – solvents that get released as the paint dries).

If you are painting the room, leave the stripping of the old paint to someone else. You shouldn't strip off paint if you believe that the room was painted before 1978 in case you release harmful lead particles into the room.

Wall decorations

If you want to add interest to plain walls, wall stickers are excellent because you can remove them if you get bored or want to update the room without redecorating – www.supernice.co.uk; www.spincollective. co.uk; www.rockettstgeorge.co.uk; and www.lesinvasionsephemeres. com (a French site that ships to the UK) are all worth a look.

Borders can also jazz up a plain wall: The Designers Guild (www. designersguild.com) has some really sweet ones.

Murals can also look wonderful, especially if you create one feature wall (ensure you don't pick anything too babyish that you will all tire of, though). Funky Little Darlings has contemporary murals suitable for tots to teens (www.funkylittledarlings.co.uk).

You could also add colour to the walls by adding some prints or pictures. Belle & Boo has sweet whimsical prints (www.belleandboo.com); Bodie & Fou has some great graphic examples (www.bodieandfou.com); and www.notonthehighstreet.com and www.bouf.com both feature work by artists you wouldn't normally stumble across.

Flooring

Here are some tips on choosing the best flooring for your nursery.

- If you are putting a new carpet down, try to get it laid a couple of months before the baby is born to get rid of that new carpet smell, and the chemicals and fibres they shed.

- Don't buy an expensive carpet for the nursery because there are bound to be spills, vomits or accidents on it.

- Wooden floors can be very practical but a tad unforgiving underfoot; you can 'warm' the room up with a rug, but make sure that it has those sticky pads beneath it to stop it moving, so you don't slip.

- Vinyl flooring is gaining in popularity and you can see why: it's not only very practical, as it is warm underfoot and easy to keep clean, and you can also get it in some really funky colours and designs.

Lighting

When thinking about lighting your nursery, consider:

- installing a dimmer switch so that you can have bright light when you need to change nappies during the day and dim lighting for the night feed

- when using lamps or nightlights in the nursery you'll need to keep the wires concealed, and, as your baby grows, keep the flex away from prying fingers. A nice, varied selection are

available at www.minilinelights.co.uk; www.nubie.co.uk; and
www.whiterabbitengland.com.

Storage for clothes

Your baby's clothes will be quite small, so there's no need to get a
hulking great wardrobe yet unless you want one. A chest of drawers will
suffice, and you can either buy one new or paint an antique one if you
prefer (make sure someone sands it down first to ensure there are no
splinters or rough edges).

Safety tip: any
heavy piece of
furniture
should be
securely fixed to the
walls.

Here are some other storage ideas.

- Colourful storage boxes can be a fun way to keep clothes tidy.

- Display key pieces from your baby's wardrobe on a painted
  peg rail attached to the wall (try www.scumblegoosie.com for
  unpainted versions, or Ikea: www.ikea.co.uk).

- A free-standing rail can be practical, especially if you have a little
  girl and have lots of gorgeous items to show off.

- For interesting, funky storage, www.theholdingcompany.co.uk,
  www.gltc.co.uk and www.vertbaudet.co.uk are all worth a look.

Toy storage

You are bound to be given lots of toys, and you can either stash them
in boxes (see above) or display them on open shelves. Shelves should
be securely fixed to the wall and out of reach of the cot. Habitat always
does great funky shelving for children (www.habitat.net), and www.
giosto.com has amazing modular storage and shelves.

Window dressing

- You need to shut out the light during daytime naps. John Lewis
  stocks plain and printed roller blackout blinds (www.johnlewis.com).

- You can also buy blackout linings that you can clip onto regular
  curtains.

- If you are likely to travel with your baby, drop a hint for a 'Go
  Anywhere Blind' – a blackout blind that fits to any window with
  suction cups (www.bumpto3.com).

Nursery toys

A mobile hanging above your baby's cot gives him something to gaze at when he is lying down. You can get quite sophisticated ones that attach to the cot and can play music or rotate, or you can go for the simple hanging variety.

Remember:

- you must ensure that the mobile is properly secured, as it could be a severe hazard if it is pulled into the cot by inquisitive fingers.

- black and white pictures are supposed to stimulate your baby's brain, so you might want to find a monochrome mobile or images you can stick to the wall near the cot so he can gaze at them. Wee Gallery stocks a great selection (www.weegallery. co.uk), and the Wimmer Ferguson Infant Stim mobile from Manhattan Toy is a classic (www.manhattantoy.com).

GADGET HEAVEN

Do you love a gadget? Every year brings new products to the market which are designed to make your life as a new parent easier...and more fun! Some are kooky, some could be lifesavers. Here are a few.

Exmobaby smart suit

This is a suit with built-in 'biosensors' that let parents know why their baby is crying. It has a thermometer, heart rate monitor and movement sensor built into the fabric.

The gadget builds up a picture of the child's 'mood' – and lets parents know, for instance, if the child has been moving about rather than sleeping, updating them via email or text. The gadget can also sense moisture and tell parents when it's time to change their baby. It's currently being tested in hospitals – and Exmobaby is looking for volunteers to test the gadget at home.

Glo Nightlight with portable balls from Boon

This two-in-one interactive night light and toy transitions between colours for 30 minutes until baby falls asleep (if you're lucky). Then, during the day, you can remove the BPA-free plastic balls and let baby toss them around and play with them.

Cocoon pillow

Make sure that your baby is safe with this state of the art pillow that has noise-cancelling technology and will block any unwanted noise and dirt, owing to its HEPA air filtration system. This purifies air particles with an ionizer built inside the pillow to help prevent uncleanliness which can cause sneezing or coughing. Not yet in the shops but should be available soon.

Itzbeen baby care timer

When was the last time your baby nursed? How long did he sleep? Never over-tax your sleep-deprived new-mum brain again with this handy timer that keeps track of it all (and issues gentle reminders if you want them). Also available in pretty pink and cool green, to co-ordinate with your buggy/bag!

The MagicBath by Blubleu

This is a deluxe, Italian-made spa bath on legs, with mini whirlpool, massage bubble system and LED lights which can be set to different colour displays depending on your baby's mood. It stands at adult height on four sturdy legs and has a digital display to allow parents to monitor water temperature. With a hefty £1,358 price tag, it's the bath for the baby who has everything.

SweetPea MP3 Players

If you don't want to hand over your expensive MP3 player to your baby – even though the smallest of them seem to love reacting to music, kicking and moving around – these gadgets are specially designed to be suitable from ages 0 to 6. With no moving parts and just three buttons, the SweetPea can hold up to 32 hours of music and stories and your little one can take it safely with him wherever he is. www.SweetPeaToyCo.com.

iiamo Go Self-Warming Baby Bottle

This is a self-heating baby bottle which reaches the recommended feeding temperature in about four minutes with no electricity or cords. It works by loading the iiamo warmer, a disposable heating cartridge containing just salt and water, into the bottom of the bottle and shaking the bottle to activate the mechanism. Heat is generated from the rehydration of the salt inside, and warms the milk that has been poured in through the top. The BPA-free bottle was designed by world-renowned designer Karim Rashid, who has won awards for his product designs for companies like Asus and Samsung. It will soon be launched in UK for around £20.

MONEYSAVING TIPS

We've given you lots of food for thought in this section, but what about your budget? Here are some tips and tricks to cut down your bill.

Grandparents and other family members often want to contribute, and (without sounding mercenary) it's useful to have a wish list so that you can get some of the items you *want* rather than leaving them to choose stuff you don't. Vouchers for John Lewis or Mothercare are always useful, so put a big hint in at work if they are having a whip-round for you.

Freebies

- Most of the major supermarkets, Boots and Mothercare etc, have Baby and Toddler clubs you can join. These are usually free and will send you anything from money-off vouchers and magazines to free samples. You can sign up online, but check their privacy policy if you want to avoid being mailed by anyone else they might pass your details onto.

- Companies that actually sell baby products also have baby clubs you can join. The benefit for them is that they build brand loyalty; the benefit for you is that they will send you free stuff and coupons. Again, you can join as many as you like, and the only downside is you might find your postbox and inbox stuffed full of offers you may or may not want.

- If you don't have a Boots Advantage card, get one now. It is widely accepted to be one of the most generous loyalty schemes around, and if you have a Boots locally you'll find you'll soon rack up the points buying your baby essentials. These points can then be exchanged for more baby bits for free. Check out other loyalty schemes as well, because they often give targeted offers and discounts, too.

- Sign up to websites like www.moneysavingexpert.com and www.ukhotdeals.com. They may not alert you to specific baby deals, but if cash is tight, any savings you make on general expenditure will come in handy.

- www.kidstart.co.uk is a website that offers you cash back on all the purchases you make for your baby from over 400 online retailers. It is free to join.

Swap shop

If you have a number of friends who are pregnant or already have children, why don't you try holding a swapping party, where you swap maternity jeans for Moses baskets etc? Friends are also usually only too happy to give things away once their own family is complete and they no longer need stuff.

Gumtree and Freecycle are good sources of free baby items that people no longer need. Remember that you must replace mattresses and you'll probably want to give everything a good scrub, but as long as the item is in good condition you can make some brilliant savings.

Top tips

- Buying baby items in bulk can lead to substantial savings. You'll see 'bedding bundles' or 'all-inclusive travel system deals', so it is worth shopping around to get the best deal.

- Sometimes manufacturers discontinue a product and substantial savings can be made; keep checking their websites to see what's on offer.

- If money is tight it really is worth trawling through all the baby internet retail sites to get the best deal. It's amazing what savings you can make if you persevere.

- The NCT often runs good second-hand sales where you can bag a bargain.

9

The last few weeks of my pregnancy

The last few weeks of pregnancy can be both an exciting and an uncomfortable time. For many women the novelty of being pregnant wears off, and they just want the waiting to be over. Even though you might be getting even more excited about finally meeting your baby, there's still a lot you can do in these last few weeks to prepare for your new arrival. In this chapter we'll take you through what you can expect to happen in the next few weeks and how to have fun preparing for your new baby.

PREPARING FOR PARENTHOOD

If you have signed up for parentcraft or other antenatal classes, you'll start attending them now that you are in the last trimester. They are normally very informative, and even if you have read the books and think you know everything you need to know, you'll probably come away with some useful tips or new knowledge.

Don't be afraid to ask lots of questions if you don't understand any aspect of the class; this is the perfect opportunity to get some first-hand experience from women who are at the coal face of birth every day. These classes not only have a practical function, but a social one, too: hopefully you'll meet at least one other local mum-to-be that you'd be happy to share a coffee with after the baby is born.

FEEDING: BREAST OR BOTTLE?

Fewer than one in 100 women follows government advice to breastfeed exclusively in the first six months.

One subject that (hopefully) you'll get a lot of information on is how to feed your baby, as it is advisable to give it some consideration before you give birth.

According to a recent survey, over 70% of women attempt to breastfeed after their baby is born, but nearly half switch to bottle feeding within a month. Many of the women who gave up said they didn't feel adequately prepared to feed their baby, and many worried that their babies were not getting enough milk, because it's impossible to know when you are breastfeeding exactly how much milk your baby has taken in.

You probably already know that breastfeeding is the best nutritional start you can give your baby, but you may feel slightly intimidated by the 'breast is best' brigade. Breastfeeding is sometimes quite difficult to get the hang of at the beginning, so it's useful to read up on it; the NHS and government have produced some very informative leaflets which you should definitely take a look at.

Many hospitals provide antenatal breastfeeding classes in the last trimester of pregnancy; these are well worth attending, as it is important to understand how breastfeeding works and what you can do to ensure it happens smoothly. If they do not provide a class, ask for the *From Bump to Baby* DVD, as all hospitals have to provide it. You can also watch it online on www.bestbeginnings.info.

The NHS has a dedicated breastfeeding helpline on 0300 100 0212, and La Leche League also provides help and advice on 0845 120 2918, so give them a call before you give up, as the solution to your problems might be simpler than you think.

> **WORDS FROM THE PROFESSIONALS:** The key to successful breastfeeding is skin-to-skin contact at birth until the first feed, as the smell of his mother's milk is what stimulates the baby to feed.

Breastfeeding can be quite painful when you start: the first few sucks as your baby latches on can be wince-inducing. You might also get stomach pains, as breastfeeding stimulates the release of the hormone oxytocin, which causes the uterus to contract. Think of this as a 'good' pain, as it helps to reduce the chance of you having a haemorrhage, and it will get easier and less painful with time.

We are not going to tell you whether you should breastfeed or not, but please do read up and get as much advice from health professionals and friends as you can *before* the birth. Many women are, understandably, so focused on their labour that they don't give enough thought to what will happen afterwards.

> **WORDS FROM THE PROFESSIONALS:** If you are breastfeeding, health professionals recommend you take a vitamin D supplement to ensure you have enough to pass to the baby.

Despite valiant efforts, some women find that they *can't* breastfeed, and if you are one of them don't let yourself feel like a huge failure. If you are struggling with breastfeeding, do seek advice from your midwife while you are still in hospital, and your health visitor or GP should give you support when you get back home. If you're not embarrassed being topless in front of a good friend who has breastfed, she might be able help your baby latch on properly.

> 'I intended to breastfeed but neither of the twins took to it. They each had a minute or so straight after birth and on several occasions over the next day or so but nothing substantial. I hadn't even considered bottle feeding and had bought nothing for it.'
>
> Soozi, new mum to twins

Breastfeeding

Pros
For your baby

- Breast milk is completely natural; therefore, it will give your baby exactly the right amount of proteins, carbohydrates, fats and fluid that he needs.

- Breast milk is so rich in nutrients and so highly concentrated that only small volumes are needed.

- Breastfed babies are statistically less likely to have chest or ear infections, vomiting or diarrhoea, thanks to the antibodies that are passed from mother to child.

- Breastfed babies are less likely to suffer from eczema or asthma.

- As the milk is easily digested, your baby is less likely to suffer colic or constipation.

- Studies show that breastfed babies are less likely to develop high blood pressure, high cholesterol or obesity.

- There is evidence that breastfeeding reduces the chance of children getting leukaemia or diabetes.

For you

- Breast milk is free!

- Breastfeeding can help you bond with your baby.

- Breastfeeding makes it easier to travel with your baby as you don't have to worry about sterilising.

- You don't have to fumble around in the middle of the night warming bottles.

- You need to take less kit around with you if you are breast-feeding.

- Some studies have shown that breastfeeding can reduce your chances of getting breast cancer and osteoporosis.

- Breastfeeding speeds up weight loss because you use up to 1,000 calories a day fully feeding your baby.

- It's a good excuse to sit down and take it easy.

A 2011 study by researchers from Oxford, Essex and York, involving 10,000 mothers and their babies, has found that babies that are breastfed for four months or more are 2.5 times less likely to have behavioural problems by the time they reach five years of age.

Cons

- Breast milk is less filling in the first three days before your full milk comes in, so your baby will spend longer feeding.

- You can't delegate someone else to do the job in the middle of the night or have an evening off in the pub (unless you express).

- Whilst most medication can be taken, always check with your doctor first in case it might be harmful for the baby.

- You can't start necking the vino just because you've had the baby. Alcohol is passed into your breast milk, so you are advised to keep booze to a minimum, although you can purchase alcohol-testing strips to test expressed milk.

- You also have to watch what you eat: some spicy or strong foods can affect your baby and give him wind or colic.

- You might feel embarrassed breastfeeding in public, and a recent survey showed that even nowadays prejudices about women feeding in public persist.

What you'll need for breastfeeding

- Breastfeeding bras. These have clever clip details or fastenings that make the breast easily accessible. You'll need at least three or four, as they need washing daily.

- Make sure you have plenty of tops (and nighties) that open down the front. You can buy these really ingenious tops designed for breastfeeding that have very discreet openings (try www.mothercare.co.uk or www.jojomamanbebe.co.uk), and can be worn after you've weaned your child if you don't want to shell out for new clothes.

- Breast pads and muslins.

- A breast pump. You're encouraged not to use it for the first few weeks of breastfeeding to let you get your routine established, but sometimes, when your milk comes in, your breasts become so big and engorged you might have to try to express to relieve the symptoms. It is obviously useful for expressing milk if you have to go out and need someone else to feed your baby.

In 2011, experts from University College London announced that breastfed babies may benefit from being given solid food earlier. Current advice suggests weaning should occur at six months, but the UCL team says it can happen as early as four.

- Nipple cream. Your nipples can get very cracked and sore, so it's useful to have a tube of nipple cream on standby. Many midwives recommend Lansinoh, which is made from a pure form of lanolin.

Having listed all of the advantages of breastfeeding, we just have one more piece of advice: try by all means, but don't torture yourself if you can't manage.

'I decided to breastfeed and managed to do that until Fred was four months old. It was hard going, though, as he suffered from projectile vomiting due to reflux from six days old, so it was a bit soul-destroying to watch my hard-earned breast milk redecorate the room – especially at bedtime when your milk is running low. In hindsight I would have switched to bottles/formula way earlier rather than give myself the additional pressure, but I think I would have needed either my husband or my mother to tell me to just stop, and neither of them did. Comments such as, "Well, once you stop you can't start again" were not very helpful!'

Megan, new mum to Fred, 9 months

Bottle feeding

Before every feed the bottles and teats should be sterilised (you can boil them or use a steam or microwave steriliser). To make the feed up, you should pour cooled boiled water that has ideally been left for no more than an hour into the bottle and fill it up to the required level. As formula milk isn't sterile, the Department of Health recommends that you use water that is a minimum temperature of 70°C or hotter – though you'd need a sterilised thermometer to be sure of that – and only make up one feed at a time (though in practice many mothers make up several bottles at once and keep them refrigerated even though it is not recommended). Measure the formula powder using the scoop provided and drop into the boiled water, put the teat and its cover on, and shake the bottle well. Never add additional scoops to the recommended amount, as it can make your baby ill. Warm the bottle in a pan, jug or bowl of warm (not hot or boiling) water or use a bottle warmer. Using a microwave to warm formula milk is not recommended, as it can create hot spots in the milk that you can't detect, although in practice many mothers use this method.

Pros

- You can share feeding responsibilities with your partner, including getting up in the night!

- The father might bond better with the baby if he does his share of feeding.

- If you are planning on returning to work soon after the baby is born, it may be easier to leave him if he is used to a bottle already.

- Bottle-fed babies often sleep longer between feeds.

- Feeding is normally quicker.

- If you are taking medication that passes into breast milk in a way that is not safe for your baby, bottle feeding is a good choice.

- *You* can eat and drink whatever you like.

- Feeding in public is easier (but finding somewhere to warm your bottle is harder).

Cons

- Formula milk doesn't contain the same infection-fighting anti-bodies as breast milk.

- Preparing and warming bottles in the middle of the night can be a real pain.

- Cleaning and sterilising bottles can be time consuming.

- Making up bottles is something else 'to do', and you might become mysteriously time-poor once the baby is born.

- Formula costs money.

What you need for bottle feeding

- Bottles, teats and lids.

- Bottle brush and steriliser for cleaning.

- Formula milk: powdered or ready-made.

Whichever method of feeding you choose, just make sure you've done your homework in plenty of time before the birth, so that you can be fully prepared with everything you need.

YOUR MEDICAL CARE

You'll have more frequent antenatal tests towards your due date, although it varies from area to area. As a rule of thumb, you'll probably be seen at 34, 36, 38, 40 and 41 weeks, and if there are any problems with the pregnancy you might go weekly from 37 weeks. Your midwife will continue to measure your bump to check the baby is still growing as he should – if she is concerned she may refer you for a scan to check all is progressing well. She will also test your blood pressure and your urine to check for signs of pre-eclampsia.

THE BABY'S POSITION

As early as 28 weeks your baby may have turned 'head down' in preparation for birth, and as you get towards your due date, the position of your baby will become more important, as it could affect how you are going to deliver. From 36 weeks your midwife will feel your tummy to check which way your baby is facing. If your baby is breech (bottom first) or transverse (lying sideways) it is possible that a planned Caesarean section will be on the cards.

If your baby is breech at 36 weeks, you will be offered an external cephalic version (ECV). This is performed in hospital and is when the baby is manually turned from the outside to be in a head down position. This is often very successful: around 60% will turn to the head down position.

You're engaged!

Around 37 weeks (although it's often earlier for first babies) your baby's head may 'engage', which means it will drop into your pelvis in readiness for birth. This process is also known as 'lightening'. For many women it can be a relief, because it gives the ribs and lungs more space and makes breathing more comfortable. The downside is that it can feel like a really heavy weight pushing down on your pelvis/bladder and can make walking around more laboured (excuse the pun). It tends to occur later in women of African or Caribbean origin, and may not occur until labour has started with your second (or third, or fourth) baby.

MOXIBUSTION

A new 'alternative' treatment for turning breech babies that is gaining widespread mainstream approval is moxibustion. This is best performed around 36 weeks when there is still space for the baby to turn, but you can give it a go any time up to your due date. Moxibustion has its roots in acupuncture and involves lighting compressed sticks (the moxa) of a fragrant herb and holding it over certain acupuncture points on your feet. A moxa stick is made from the herb mugwort (very Harry Potter) and after it is lit, it smoulders and heat radiates from its point. The lit sticks should be held about 1cm away from your toes so you can feel the heat but can't burn yourself: it should **not** touch your skin. It is said this treatment relaxes your uterus and also speeds up your baby's heart rate and movements, which is why it can have a success rate of up to 70% in turning breech babies.

It has proved so useful that midwives are training to perform it on their patients, but you can do it yourself at home from 35 weeks (although someone else would have to actually perform it because you won't be able to touch your toes at that point).

Moxibustion can be attempted any time after 35 weeks once your midwife has confirmed your baby is breech, BUT it is absolutely essential that you check with your health professionals before you consider moxibustion, because there are certain medical conditions that could make this practice dangerous.

You should not attempt moxibustion if:

- you are expecting twins (it could turn into mayhem in there)
- you have had any bleeding during pregnancy
- you have had a previous Caesarean
- you are due to have a planned C-section for a medical reason other than a breech birth (ie you have had another underlying health problem during pregnancy).

Ask your midwife if you would like more information about this procedure.

WHAT YOU MIGHT BE FEELING PHYSICALLY

Late pregnancy can be a joy psychologically as you know you are nearing the end, but physically it can be quite draining, as your growing bump can really put a strain on your body. We won't dwell on the bad bits, but it's useful to list a few common concerns in case they are worrying you.

- **Backache.** The sheer physical weight of your baby puts pressure on your spine, resulting in back pain and curved posture. Rest as often as you can, ditch the heels and watch your standing position.

- **Breathing difficulties.** As your uterus expands, it puts pressure on the lungs and can restrict breathing, although this normally improves once the baby has engaged.

- **Breasts.** Your boobs may already be leaking colostrum – the golden, nutrient-rich precursor to breast milk that your baby will receive for the first few days if you choose to breastfeed. If this happens, you might want to start using breast pads to soak up any leaks.

- **Indigestion.** Your digestive organs get squashed by your baby, leading to indigestion and heartburn. Try swigging Gaviscon or cold milk.

- **Insomnia.** An active baby coupled with an anxious mummy-to-be can lead to insomnia. The only really comfortable position for napping is on your side with lots of pillows propping you up. Be warned, though: when you do finally get to sleep you might have weird dreams involving the baby – most women 'give birth' at least once during sleep in pregnancy and then wake up to find, rather disappointingly, that the bump is still there.

- **Itching.** Your tummy might become itchy over your bump as the skin stretches. You can try a non-perfumed emollient aqueous cream to relieve it. In the last trimester it could also be a sign of obstetric cholestasis (page 80), so if it occurs in areas where there are no stretch marks, let your doctor or midwife know.

- **Oedema.** Water retention is common towards the latter part of pregnancy, and your feet and hands will probably swell too. If you wear rings, take them off before they get too tight; otherwise they might need to be cut off.

- **Rib pain.** Most women find that they get quite a bit of rib pain as junior gives them a swift poke to remind them of his presence.

- **Tummy pains.** Ligament pain in the stomach area is common, as the ligaments need to stretch to support the growing uterus. You might also start to experience Braxton Hicks – the practice contractions to prepare your body for labour, which feel like a tightening sensation across the tummy. If the pains get really bad or start coming at regular intervals it is possible that you have started labour, and will need to contact your midwife without delay.

- **Waddling.** Confident strides can turn into hesitant waddles, as the weight of your baby on your pelvis can make you feel like you are about to drop at any minute.

WHAT YOU MIGHT BE FEELING EMOTIONALLY

Undeniably it can be a pretty anxious time as you prepare for D-day, but there are plenty of positive things you can be doing while you play the waiting game.

Nesting

It is perfectly natural to want to get your house in order before the baby is born; indeed, it is quite desirable, because realistically you won't get much chance after the event. However, there's a difference between doing something useful (like getting the baby's nursery ready and ensuring there's enough food in the fridge), and clearing out the loft, which is just going to make you tired and not improve your baby's life one jot.

Getting some rest and relaxation is probably the best piece of advice to help you make the most of these last few weeks, and here are some tips to help you with nesting.

- Inhaling a load of cleaning products isn't a great idea any time in pregnancy, but if the house dirt is getting you down, take yourself off for a day of pampering or have tea and cakes with a friend, and get a professional team to blitz your home. It may cost you, but it will be worth it.

- Fill the freezer. You probably won't feel much like cooking after you have the baby, but it is essential that you eat properly to keep your strength up, particularly if you are breastfeeding. Ready-made meals are ideal because they just involve a quick reheat. If you are climbing the walls in boredom, by all means cook and freeze meals yourself; otherwise get them from the supermarket. If you don't want to cook, ask your partner, parents, siblings or friends if they can make stuff for you.

- Do a big supermarket shop for bulky household essentials like toilet paper, kitchen roll etc. You'll be doing lots of washing for your baby, so make sure that you buy plenty of non-biological or

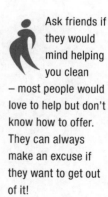

Ask friends if they would mind helping you clean – most people would love to help but don't know how to offer. They can always make an excuse if they want to get out of it!

eco-friendly washing powder or liquid. Ecover is good but pricey, so see if your supermarket does an own-brand version. If you can't face waddling round with your trolley, shop online and get it delivered: it is well worth the extra cost.

- Get all of your personal admin (aka paying the bills) sorted. This will probably be the last thing on your mind when you have a new baby, and if budgeting might be an issue it is beneficial to make a spreadsheet of your monthly expenditure. It's also a useful reminder to pay those bills on time. Sometimes you can even make savings if you pay by direct debit; this is good for regular bills like gas, electricity, council tax, etc. If you are worried you might get into arrears on your credit card (particularly if you have given it a pounding with baby shopping), avoid paying interest by setting up monthly repayments.

MAKE YOURSELF LOOK AND FEEL BETTER

You may feel like a beached whale, but there are a few things you can do to pamper yourself and make sure you feel good during these last few weeks.

The hairy bits

It may be your idea of hell, but for some women, the idea of the amount of exposure that area is about to get means they can't think of anything but making sure everything is neat and tidy.

'I worried about being in labour with hairy legs. Everyone laughed at me and said that when the time came, it would be far from my mind. Wrong! I can still recall lying there, legs spread, thinking "I'm so glad I shaved yesterday..."'

Claire, new mum

Women were routinely shaved before giving birth in the past, but these days it is really up to you what you do with your 'area' before birth. There has been research done to see if being clean-shaven reduced your chance of getting an infection if you had to have an episiotomy or tore during childbirth, but a recent trial showed that it made no difference. You'll find it difficult to get near your nether regions with a great big bump in the way, so if you want to go the DIY route, you'll probably need the help of your partner to shave or trim your bikini area (get him to do your legs while he's at it). If you don't trust him, book yourself an appointment for a bikini wax a couple of weeks before your due date, and have your legs waxed at the same time.

Paint the town, and your toenails, red

During these last few weeks, why not:

- make the most of your last few weeks when it's just the two of you, and have a night out or away with your partner.

- you'll probably have trouble reaching your tootsies by the end of your pregnancy, so if you want toenails that look gorgeous, treat yourself to a pedicure.

- get your hair cut. Make sure you go a couple of weeks before you are due; you can always treat yourself to a wash and blow dry nearer your due date too.

WORKING OUT THE PRACTICAL DETAILS

Now is the time that you need to sort out all the practical details, such as:

- working out who is going to drive you to hospital

- if you have other children, putting a contingency plan in place to ensure that they get picked up from school/nursery/their childminder and deciding who will have them overnight

- making up the spare room (if you have one) if relatives are coming to stay to help out after the birth. You could also pop a camp bed in the nursery if your baby won't be sleeping there for a while.

Spreading the news

Now is a good time to buy some birth announcement cards. We might live in a text-and-email world, but Auntie Ivy might appreciate a card. The same goes for thank-you cards. You're sure to be showered with gifts and it's good manners to show your appreciation.

RASPBERRY LEAF

Taking a regular dose of this herbal remedy in the last six weeks of pregnancy is said to stimulate the uterus and encourage a shorter labour. There doesn't appear to be any scientific evidence to support this view, but some women swear by it. You can either take it in a tablet form or infuse the dried leaves in boiling water to make a tea. You can buy both from a health food store.

One thing to bear in mind is that there is some evidence that raspberry leaf tea taken earlier in pregnancy causes miscarriage. Unless you are a herbalist and have specific knowledge to the contrary, stay on the safe side and do not take this herb before 34 weeks.

AND RELAX...

Make sure that you:

- try to get as much sleep 'in the bank' as you can in the last few weeks. Have a rest in the afternoons if you have stopped work, and get in as many early nights as you can.

- practise the breathing techniques you have learnt for labour. They'll make you feel relaxed and more prepared for the big event.

- put your feet up and spend time reading Chapter 11 of this book; it's very important you have an idea what to do when you bring your little bundle of (wailing) joy home.

A DIFFERENT TYPE OF MASSAGE

One of the physical things you can do to prepare for labour is to give your perineum a massage (yes, really). The perineum is the area between the vagina and the anus, and it does come under considerable pressure when the baby crowns – some people believe that if you massage this area daily with wheatgerm oil it really helps to stretch and soften the area, and you are less likely to tear during birth. You can buy the oil from health food shops. There's a specific technique (your midwife can explain it), and obviously you'll need clean hands and short fingernails if you want to have a go.

PACKING YOUR BAG FOR HOSPITAL

It makes sense to have your hospital bag packed and ready a few weeks before your due date, in case you are one of the 30% of mothers who give birth before their EDD. You may only be in hospital for 24 hours, but it is quite astonishing how much kit you'll need. You can break it down into three sections: labour, post-birth mummy and baby.

You should try to get it down to one 'weekend'-sized bag, as you'll look pretty silly waddling down to the delivery room with a trolley of luggage trailing behind you. In all seriousness, space can be at a premium in some wards, so from a security standpoint it's prudent to take just one bag.

Home birth

If you're having a home birth you obviously don't need to pack a bag, but it will be helpful to have everything you need ready in the room where you plan to give birth. You don't want to have to send your partner hunting round the house while you're in the middle of labour!

Things to pack for labour

- Your hospital notes and birth plan.
- Something to give birth in. (You'll be given a hospital gown, but some women prefer their own night gown or a baggy T-shirt.)

- Any medication you take regularly.

- Socks and/or slippers, as you might be encouraged to walk around to move things along. Make sure they are non-slip and expect to put them in the bin after labour. Crocs are good because you can wash them.

- Food, glorious food. Catering can be pretty hit-and-miss at the best of times in hospital, and if you give birth at night your options may be non-existent. You should pack non-perishables like crackers or cereal bars. Lollipops and chewing gum are also recommended, as you can use them during labour to focus or distract you.

- Cartons of juice and bottles of water.

- Boredom busters. Labour can be quite a long, drawn-out affair, so bring your iPod, magazines and a good book to while away the hours.

- Camera. It's up to you whether you record the event as it happens or just the prize at the end of it, but it's a photo opportunity not to be missed. Some hospitals don't allow camcorders in the delivery room, so check when you do the hospital tour.

- Music. You can use your iPod if there is a docking station; if not, bring a couple of CDs if there is a player in the delivery room. It's probably best to go for something relaxing rather than thrash metal, but the choice is yours.

- Lip balm. Gas and air can make your lips very dry, so it's useful to keep them moisturised.

- Water spray.

- Hair elastic or hairband if you want to keep your hair tied back.

- Massage tool for when your birth partner's hands get tired. Use a cheap wooden or plastic one in case it gets lost.

- TENS machine (if you have hired one). Make sure you also take spare batteries.

Get a contractions app or your phone, to log how long they last and how far apart they are. Have a play before so you know how it works!

What you need after you have given birth

- Basic toiletries such as a toothbrush, toothpaste, shower gel (though you can wash your vaginal area with water only), shampoo and a big towel.

- Hairbrush and make up. It sounds shallow, but there will be a lot of pictures of you with the new baby and it *may* be important to you to look your best.

- Maternity pads. Make sure they're the real ones, because ordinary sanitary towels won't cut it.

- Big, comfy knickers.

- A front-opening nightie or PJs and dressing gown.

- Clothing to change into to go home. Velour trackies are ideal: you may look like Katie Price (and might have the chest to match), but at least you'll feel comfy. If velour is a little too Wag-tastic for you anything jersey is ideal.

- Your feet will probably be more swollen after the delivery than before, so take some very loose fitting footwear, but make sure you can't trip over in it.

- Nursing bra and breast pads.

- Mobile phone (or money for a phone or a phone card, as some hospitals won't allow mobiles to be used). Thanks to the wonders of technology, if you have a camera phone you can send pictures of your gorgeous baby along with birth announcement news within minutes of it happening.

What your new baby will need

- Clothes. Pack a few sleep suits and vests, a cardi or warmer jacket, a hat and a blanket for the journey home.

- Nappies and cotton wool.

- A car seat to transport him home.

WHAT'S IN A NAME?

In the weeks before birth it's useful to have a serious discussion about names, if you haven't done so already. Some couples manage to narrow it down to a shortlist and wait until the baby arrives before making the final decision. Obviously, if you know the sex of the baby, it makes the process somewhat easier, as you'll only have to read *half* the baby names book.

If you think naming is likely to be a source of conflict between you and your partner, start the 'negotiations' earlier rather than later. If you find you just can't agree, compromise by each having a name you like as a middle name and choosing a name you **both** like as a first name.

> 'One of the meanings of our baby's name – Seth – is "bringer of chaos". It appealed to my sense of humour and, considering how he got here, it seemed to fit.'
>
> Claire, mum to Seth, 5 months

Keeping mum

The best advice regarding names is to keep your *real* favourites a secret. People can't resist telling you that they hate a particular name because it reminded them of their vile maths teacher or horrible uncle, or that they think it's too 'modern' or 'popular'. It's so disheartening when a name you loved and wanted to bestow on your darling firstborn is unkindly discussed over a low-alcohol shandy with your mates or a cup of tea with your mum. Keep your favourites a secret until the baby is born, and by then people will keep their opinions to themselves.

Middle names

Just because a name has been in the family for years, don't think you have to carry on with it if you really hate it – you could always slip it in as a middle name if you want to keep the family peace. Another thing to remember is that *his* mother might get jealous if you use *your* mother's name as a middle name for your daughter, so try to find a way to keep everyone happy. If you think it'll cause all-out family war, promise that you'll try to use her name next time.

It's quite common to give your child more than one middle name, but it can be a bit of a nightmare when filling in forms. It's also worth bearing in mind that some institutions only accept one middle name or an initial, so think carefully before you give your child eight middle names to keep all of the respective grandparents happy!

'Stealing' names

Sometimes you're fixed on a name and then your friend or colleague pops a baby out before you, and much to your dismay they pick the name you wanted. If this happens, consider carefully: is it *such* a problem if your children have the same name? If she is a really good friend who you'll know for life you'll definitely need to discuss it, but unless she lives really nearby and her children are likely to attend the same school, does it *really* matter?

Living up to an unusual name

Of course your child can change his name, by deed poll if necessary, but it is quite cruel to saddle him with a joke name, something out-landish, or even something as basic as a name that is very difficult to pronounce or spell. Children at school can be very cruel and will often pounce on a child that is 'different', so think carefully before you name her 'Moon Unit' or him 'Zowie'.

Names can have stereotypes attached to them, as a recent report suggested, which asked teachers about their expectations of their pupils based on their names. Children with names such as Chardonnay, Connor and Jack were listed as among the naughtiest, while Charlotte, Elizabeth and Alexander were deemed to be better behaved and more intelligent. Of course, choosing one of the 'clever' names doesn't automatically mean your child will grow up to be hugely intelligent, but it may have an impact on the initial impression people make. It might be hard for Chief Justice Bluebell or Officer He-Man to be taken seriously, so it might be better to stick to something more conventional and give him a more unusual middle name. He can always adopt it as his first name if he likes it in later life.

Sounding out

This is probably stating the obvious, but sound out your chosen first name along with your surname so you don't make the mistake of calling your child Holly Wood, Joe King or Isabella Horn.

In 2012, Dawn McManus changed her name to what she believes is the longest name in the world to raise money for charity. It comprises 161 words totalling 895 characters, and her first name is now Red.

Think about how the name might be abbreviated as well: Donald Key is fine, but Don Key… The same goes for Louis Pole, William Power and Stanley Still: you get the idea!

You also need to look at how the initial of the first name you've chosen works with your surname: if you don't, you could end up with R Slick, R M Pitt or P Brain.

Naming trends

It is interesting that trends come and go – naming your child after a place of conception springs to mind as a recent notable one – but traditional names are perennial; indeed, there has been a resurgence in popularity of old-fashioned names in recent years, especially for girls.

A trend that has emerged in the past few years takes traditional names and 'modernises' them through changing the spelling. Take a fairly conservative name like Holly. The name now appears in the Office of National Statistics registered baby names in various other forms, including Hollie, Holli, Holleigh, Lollie, Halle and Hallie. The same is true for boys' names – with some parents choosing to spell the traditional Harry as Haree, and even Arry!

Wonderful and weird names of celebrity offspring

Celebrities are known for choosing quirky and outlandish names for their children. Here are just a few of the most outrageous names from recent years.

- **Blue Ivy** (Beyoncé Knowles and Jay-Z)

- **Buddy Bear Maurice** (Jules and Jamie Oliver – also parents to Poppy Honey, Daisy Boo, and Petal Blossom Rainbow)

- **Cosima Violet** (Claudia Schiffer and Matthew Vaughn – also parents to Caspar and Clementine)

- **Rosalind Arusha Arkadina Altaluna Florence** (Uma Thurman and Arpad Busson)

- **Spike** (Edith Bowman and Tom Smith)

- **Astala Dylan** (Peaches Geldof and Thomas Cohen)

Novel names

Whilst Bella and Jacob have surged up the baby name charts over the past few years due to the hugely popular Twilight series, it is now the turn of *The Hunger Games* to influence names. The names Peeta and Gale (alternative spellings of traditional names) entered the boys' names list for the first time ever in 2012, and it might not be long before Katniss also makes an appearance in the girls' list. The name Primrose, or 'Prim', has also started to climb the charts, which supports the idea that parents are starting to choose old-fashioned names again.

THE ROYAL ARRIVAL

The most anticipated baby of 2013 was, of course, the royal baby. After his birth on 22 July 2013, the new prince was named George Alexander Louis. William and Kate did not part with tradition, and chose names of past monarchs and names with strong family ties. There have been six British monarchs called George, including the Queen's father. Alexander is the Duke of Edinburgh's grandfather's middle name and Louis is one of both William's and his father Charles' middle names.

In the latest UK baby names listing, George was the 12th most popular name, Alexander number 23 and Louis number 68. It will be interesting to see how high these three names climb up the charts this year. The little prince will be officially known as His Royal Highness Prince George of Cambridge.

Last year's names and next year's predictions

Last year, Harry knocked Oliver off pole position to become the most popular boy's name in the UK. This isn't that surprising, given its recent appearance all over modern literature (Harry Potter), pop culture (Harry Styles, from One Direction), and our affection for the Royal Family (Prince Harry). It also managed to keep the name Jack from climbing back up after at its 16-year spell at number one. The most popular name for baby girls was Amelia, pushing Olivia off the top spot. The names Ava and Isabella also climbed into the top 10.

New entries in the top 100 lists included Bella, Willow, Elsie, Kayla, Francesca, and Lydia for girls and Tommy, Blake, Frankie, Elijah, and Jackson for boys.

TOP 10 BABY NAMES

Boys	Girls
1. Harry	1. Amelia
2. Oliver	2. Olivia
3. Jack	3. Lily
4. Alfie	4. Jessica
5. Charlie	5. Emily
6. Thomas	6. Sophie
7. Jacob	7. Ruby
8. James	8. Grace
9. Joshua	9. Ava
10. William	10. Isabella

PREDICTED 2014 TOP 10 BABY NAMES

Boys	Girls
1. Harry	1. Amelia
2. Oliver	2. Olivia
3. Alfie	3. Ruby
4. Jack	4. Lily
5. Charlie	5. Jessica
6. William	6. Grace
7. Jacob	7. Ava
8. Thomas	8. Sophie
9. Ethan	9. Emily
10. James	10. Isabella

For more baby name fun and facts, take a look at *Baby Names 2014*, by Ella Joynes (White Ladder, 2013).

THE FINAL COUNTDOWN

Copy out this list and stick it on the fridge door, so you don't forget anything when the big moment arrives.

The absolutely final, definitive, 'OMG I'm going to have a baby' checklist

- Pack your hospital bag, and make sure your maternity notes and birth plan are easily at hand in the front pocket or on top of all your kit.

- Put your midwife's number/maternity unit number on a separate piece of paper, and stick it somewhere where it can be clearly seen.

- Do a final practice run to the hospital a couple of weeks before D-day to get your timings. You should also check the local traffic reports on a daily basis, in case of road works or accidents that may slow your journey if you have far to go (a job for the proud daddy or whoever else is your nominated driver).

- Make sure the car is working and has a full tank of petrol (another one for the driver).

- Make sure there's alcohol-free lager in the fridge in the run-up to the birth: you're going to need someone sober to drive you to hospital (a few dry days won't kill them).

- Put some change in the glove compartment so you know you have enough to pay for the hospital parking.

- Make sure you have some essentials in the freezer. You can even freeze milk, as long as you pour a little out of the plastic bottle before you freeze it to allow for expansion.

- Ask someone to be on cat feeding/garden watering duty if your hospital stay is likely to be prolonged.

- Install the car seat and figure out how to use it, so you're not faffing around in confusion when it's time to bring the baby home.

- Charge your mobile/iPod/camera battery.

- Now relax: all that waiting and wondering is nearly over and you're finally going to meet that little person you've been hiding all these months!

Whatever name you choose, you can be sure that most people will tell you they like the name, even if they don't. As long as you like it and it's not going to cause your child embarrassment, then go for it!

10
My labour

You have been pregnant for around 260 days, and finally
D-day is nigh. You'll probably feel so excited you want to burst
(literally) at the thought of meeting your new baby, or might
be paralysed with terror about the birth. Both emotions are
completely normal so don't worry!

In this chapter we look at what is likely to happen on the
day you give birth. We'll take you through how to get all the
information you need, what the first signs of labour might be
(and what to do if you go overdue), and take you step by step
through each stage of labour and the birth itself. Every birth
is different, but the more informed and prepared you are for
each eventuality, the better you will feel.

DO YOUR RESEARCH

While labour is undoubtedly a daunting prospect, one way to feel in control of the inevitable is to read up on it – so that when labour does come, you know very roughly what to expect, and you at least *feel* prepared. There's no escaping it: full blown labour does hurt. But we're not going to mention the pain again because you *know* it hurts – every mother you've met recently has regaled you with her birth story and, frankly, by now you're probably sick and tired of hearing about everyone else's labour. Concentrate on your own now. It won't be unbearable and you'll be just fine.

Try not to think or stress too much about giving birth; however long, however painful, you'll get there in the end, and statistically there's a brilliant chance that all will be well.

Obviously, every labour is different and hospitals have varying procedures, so our first piece of advice is to talk through the likely sequence of events with your midwife. The more aware you are of the process, the more confident you will be. Everyone has different ideas about how they would like to deliver: some go to plan, some don't, but at the end of it all the main aim is that both you and your baby are healthy.

FIRST SIGNS

If you are reading this at 38+ weeks, there is a possibility that you are in labour and you don't even know it! Your body can start gearing itself up for labour for days or even weeks (ouch!) before it finally kicks off. Those first signs can be something you didn't expect, and some women are unsure whether they're really in labour. Here are some of the first signs of labour that you should look out for.

- An increase or thickening of vaginal discharge. You'll normally have more during pregnancy anyway, but towards the end it can get very noticeable due to changes in your hormone levels.

- Backache or period-type pains.

- A show. This is when the mucus plug that seals the cervix comes away and passes out through the vagina. It often looks like a blood-streaked lump of jellied discharge (sorry, there's no nicer way to describe it). You can have a show weeks, days or hours before the onset of labour. This can be a little frightening, so if you think you have had your show, contact your midwife and she'll talk you through what, if anything, you need to do.

- Braxton Hicks. These tend to get stronger nearer your due date and can sometimes fool first-time mothers into thinking they are actually in labour. If you time them, they shouldn't be regular, but call your midwife if you are worried (or if they become regular).

- A tummy upset. Sometimes the changes that are stimulating labour can also cause loose or frequent bowel motions.

'When I went into labour I was expecting it to be like it is in the movies; I thought I would get stomach cramps. What I actually got was terrible leg pain. It was very uncomfortable, but I didn't realise I was in labour at first!'
    Charlotte, second pregnancy and mum to Oliver, 20 months

YOUR ESTIMATED DELIVERY DATE

You'll have been working towards your estimated delivery or due date (EDD) from the time your midwife worked it out for you. But in all probability, your baby's birthday will be another day. Only 5% of babies arrive on the day of estimation, with over 65% arriving afterwards. So don't stress if your EDD comes and goes without so much as a twinge. In the UK we count the pregnancy to 40 weeks, whereas in France they add an extra week, and therefore a 41-week pregnancy is 'normal'. The normal time for the baby to come is from 37 to 42 weeks, 3 weeks before to 2 weeks after the 'due date', so take your EDD as a guide and not an absolute. Easier said than done, but relax and enjoy these final days before the baby arrives.

Natural ways to get labour started

If you are keen to move things along, why not try one of these methods? They are purely anecdotal, with no medical or scientific evidence that any of them actually work, but you may have fun trying. A word of warning, though: if you have had complications in your pregnancy, steer clear of any methods to hurry things up and leave the management of your pregnancy to the professionals.

Eat me…

Curry: It is thought that the spices in a curry have a laxative effect that may also stimulate the uterus. There's no evidence to prove the theory, though, and if you are not used to hot, spicy curries, give them a miss, because you could end up with a nasty tummy upset. If you like curry, go for it – it might do the trick.

Castor oil: Taking castor oil is an old wives' favourite which seems to be based upon bowel stimulation. As castor oil tastes absolutely revolting, there's little point in taking it – at least curry tastes good! There is also a danger that taking this could upset your stomach. Always check with your midwife before trying this.

Pineapple: This tropical fruit contains the enzyme bromelain, which is said to boost the production of prostaglandin, which softens the cervix. You'd probably have to eat plantations of the stuff for it to work, though, and you're more likely to end up with a tummy ache.

Drink me…

Raspberry leaf tea: Some women swear by it, although it's a bit of a prenatal myth that just a cup will trigger labour. Don't drink it before 34 weeks, though, as it can be dangerous (see page 306). It's probably more helpful in preparing the uterus for birth than actually starting the proceedings off, but it doesn't taste too bad.

Touch me…

Sex: There is some logic at work here, as semen contains prostaglandin which could get labour started. Whether you (or he) can face it is an entirely different matter. Sex may be off the cards for a few weeks (or months) after birth, so some last-minute intimacy may be just what the doctor ordered. Don't have sex if your waters have broken, you've had your show or if you have a low-lying placenta (placenta praevia), though.

Nipple tweaking: While we are on the subject of sex, there is always nipple tweaking. The stimulation of the nipple and the areola (the dark skin around the outside of the nipple) is said to release oxytocin, a hormone that could start labour. The problem is you'd need to be pretty committed to the cause, as you need to do this for one hour, three times a day, for it to work.

Reflexology/aromatherapy/homeopathy and acupuncture: Practitioners of these therapies claim that they can naturally kick-start labour. There is no scientific basis to these claims, however. If you are interested, make sure you pick a qualified therapist who has experience of pregnancy.

Stay active!

If you have the energy, a good brisk walk might jiggle your baby further down the pelvis towards your cervix; keeping upright and moving will help too.

GOING OVER YOUR EDD

If you are getting to around 41 weeks and there's no sign of labour, your midwife will want to keep a close eye on you, because there is an increased risk of fetal distress and a (tiny) chance of stillbirth in pregnancies that go over 42 weeks. Your midwife or doctor may perform a membrane sweep (or several over the course of the week). They do this by running a finger around the inner edge of your cervix to encourage it to start dilating. It's pretty uncomfortable. You may experience a small bit of bleeding afterwards and a few cramps, so if you have one, try not to have anything planned for the rest of the day, because you might want to just go home and rest. If the sweep works, you could see labour starting imminently, or in the next few days. They'll probably book you in for a second sweep just in case, too.

Induction

If the sweeps don't work, your doctor or midwife will probably recommend that you are induced. Many women want to avoid induction because an artificially induced labour is not 'natural'. You can't be 'forced' to have an induction, but if your midwife recommends one, it is likely that she has the best interests of your baby at heart. If your midwife suspects any of the following, an induction will sound like a pretty good idea.

- You are approaching 42 weeks: induction means you avoid the post-42-week risks of fetal distress.

- There are signs that the placenta is not functioning properly or is coming away. This will affect the oxygen supply to your baby, which could be fatal.

- Your waters have broken and there is a risk of infection.

- Your baby's growth has slowed or stopped.

- You have a medical condition such as pre-eclampsia or gestational diabetes, and your doctor thinks it would be safer for you or the baby if he made his entrance sooner rather than later.

One of the benefits of knowing you are going to have an induction is that you *know* when your baby is going to be born (unless he shows up before the induction date). We go into detail about what will happen when you have an induction on page 327.

YOUR WATERS BREAKING

Sometimes the onset of labour is marked by your waters breaking, like in the movies. This is when the amniotic sac of membranes surrounding your baby bursts and the amniotic fluid inside it leaks out. It can occur without warning, which can be rather alarming (hope you're in a Mothercare shop, as there are rumours they give you £1,000 of vouchers if your waters break in one of their stores). Some women describe it as a gush, others that it feels like peeing yourself, while some women only experience a little trickle.

WHEN YOUR WATERS BREAK

If it is the waters in front of the baby's head that have ruptured, then there is usually a big gush of fluid which makes it obvious your waters have gone. It can, however, be the waters behind the baby's head that rupture, which means it just makes a small hole in the membranes above the head. This feels like a trickle of water. If you think this has happened put on a pad and re-check it in an hour. If it is wet, your waters have completely ruptured and you need to go to hospital to be checked out.

The fluid should be very pale in colour, or clear and stained pinkish with a little blood. It may have a slightly 'sweet' smell compared with urine. If there is green or brown in the fluid, your baby may have passed meconium (their first stool) into the uterus, and if this is the case you should call your maternity unit straight away, as your baby may need monitoring. If there is a lot of blood, you should also put in an urgent call to the maternity unit, because it could be a sign that your placenta is detaching.

Once your waters break you should start experiencing contractions, although they may be very mild at this point. Of the 10% of women whose waters break as their first sign of labour, one in 20 of them will experience her waters breaking and labour still not starting. If this happens to you, tell your midwife: you'll probably be called in for an assessment, as there's an increased risk of infection-causing bacteria in your vagina reaching the baby once your waters have broken. Once your midwife has seen you, there are a couple of options: you may be offered an induction (see page 327), or she might recommend a 'wait and see' approach as, in nine out of 10 cases, labour starts spontaneously within 24 hours of the waters breaking early. You might be sent home and told to be vigilant in looking for signs for infection, such as a high temperature or changes in the colour and smell of the amniotic fluid. If the contractions don't start within 24 hours, an induction is likely to be recommended, as the chances of infection will continue to rise.

'When my waters broke, it was the weirdest feeling. I thought for a moment I'd wet myself! I was shocked at how much comes out, and for how long.'

Melanie, mum to Saorise, 3 months

If your waters break very early (before 34 weeks), you may be given medication for 24–48 hours to prevent your contractions from starting. This allows time for you to have two steroid injections (see page 241) to help mature your baby's lungs and make your baby ready for delivery. You will have to be closely monitored to check you don't get an infection and may be given antibiotics.

It's also important to remember that the onset of labour is very rarely like you see on the movies: the vast majority of women experience a slow and steady progression of contractions and waters breaking, and for over 90% of women, contractions start before their waters break. So don't expect to have to hail a taxi and rush to the hospital before you deliver in the back seat.

THE THREE STAGES OF LABOUR

Labour is split into three stages, called first stage, second stage and third stage. The first stage will see your labour start (sometimes slowly), and your cervix dilate to 10cm. In the second stage of labour you will give birth to your baby, and in the third stage, the placenta will be delivered. Really it's the first two stages that you need to concern yourself with the most!

THE FIRST STAGE

The first stage is also split into three phases, which are described below. It covers the time from the beginning of labour, until you are ready to push (10cm dilated).

- **Early labour.** This is when your waters may break and mild contractions start. It is sometimes called the latent phase and it can last for many hours, and a whole day or more is not unusual. Your cervix will begin to make small changes, such as getting softer or shorter, but these may be quite subtle and difficult to detect. For some women, especially those having their second (or subsequent) baby, this phase can be very short.

- **Active labour.** This is when the contractions become stronger and more frequent, and your cervix dilates.

- **Transitional labour.** This is when your cervix is nearly fully dilated (10cm) and you are close to being ready to push and to give birth.

We'll now look at each of these three phases in turn and outline what you can expect to happen during each stage. This is not a 'medical' book and we'll try not to blind you with technical jargon, but it's useful to give you an outline of the physical things you can expect to happen to your body during labour.

Early labour

If your waters break and you start getting period-type pains, congratulations are in order: you're in labour! Inevitably your instinct is to put a call in to your midwife and say, 'I'm on my way,' but the reality is that you've probably got at least 12, if not 24, hours to go (and maybe longer). In this case you should:

- phone your partner or birth partner and get them home NOW (if only to make you cups of tea, massage your feet and time the contractions).

- if your waters have broken, phone your midwife or delivery unit to inform them and have a check-up.

- if you have other children, you should call your nominated carer to alert them labour has started and put contingency plans in place.

- if you are having a home birth, call your midwife.

- resist the temptation to call anyone else; you might be in for a long wait, and there's nothing worse than the endless 'Have you had the baby yet?' stream of texts, emails and calls. There's something rather lovely about those last few hours together, just the two of you, and a bit of peace and quiet at this stage could be just what you need.

Recently a woman gave birth on a rush hour train in Kent after being told that delivery wasn't imminent!

Your cervix

The pains you are experiencing are the uterus contracting (hence the name contractions) and as the uterus contracts, the cervix – which until this point has been shut fast to keep your baby safe and sound in the uterus – starts to shorten and open. This process is called dilation and is measured in centimetres. During early labour the cervix should go from closed to 3cm–4cm dilated and from being 2cm–3cm thick to being paper thin. It also needs to move from the back of the vagina to the front.

How far along am I?

A word of warning at this stage: some women writhe about in agony believing birth is imminent, only to discover that they are only 3cm dilated, while other women feel only minimal discomfort and get to the same stage without blinking. Like everything in labour, every woman's experience is different. You may rush to the hospital as you're in so much pain, only to get examined by your midwife and be very disappointed about how far along you are! You may even be sent home if you are not in active or established labour yet (see below). In case you were wondering, your midwife doesn't use a ruler to examine you – she does it by feel.

Your contractions

In very early labour, the contractions may come every 15 minutes or so and last for around 20 seconds. The pain is like a period cramp that slowly builds, reaches a peak, then stops until the next one comes along. The sensation of proper contractions, unlike Braxton Hicks, usually starts in your lower back and progresses round to your front, although the uterus itself actually contracts from the fundus down (the top of the uterus, just under your ribcage). Your birth partner should get the hang of timing them from the point the pain diminishes until the start of the next one. Hopefully, it shouldn't be too bad at this point – try paracetamol, a hot water bottle, your TENS machine if you hired one or a warm bath. And don't forget any breathing techniques you've learnt.

It's very difficult to describe pain, as our experience of it is subjective, but you may find you have pains in your back, your legs and obviously in your tummy. Hopefully, at this stage you will find them bearable enough to be able to walk and talk normally.

Get a contraction app on your phone for under £1 so you can time contractions really easily. Some have helpful charts and graphs which make it easy to track your progress.

One in five women in the UK has her labour artificially induced.

Coping

Labour can really take it out of you physically, and if you can manage something to eat and drink during this phase it's probably a good idea. Your body has a lot of work to do and it can't do it without energy; it is thought that you use as much energy running a marathon as you do giving birth, so load your body with as much energy as marathon runners do. Many women feel nauseous – either with nerves or with the pain – and can't manage to eat a thing, but it can give you a much needed boost if you can stomach it.

If labour starts during the day, you might feel better if you stay upright and active for as long as humanly possibly under the circumstances. Maybe go for a gentle walk or potter about the house. If you want to conserve energy, watch TV, listen to music or ask your partner for a massage. You might also try a long, relaxing soak in the bath.

If it starts at night try to lie down and doze, but if you are too excited or too uncomfortable to sleep, prop yourself up with pillows and watch a DVD in bed.

If you can stay as relaxed as you can during this period, you will definitely cope with the contractions better. It's easier said than done, but try to keep things as low key as possible because it's about to get a whole lot more exciting. Some women experience quite a smooth transition from early to active labour, whereas in other women it starts and stops. This shouldn't be cause for alarm but look at the checklist below to know when to act quickly.

EARLY LABOUR SOS

If you experience any of the following you will have to put in an urgent call to the midwife.

- Heavy bleeding. Blood from your show is normal, but heavy blood loss is not.
- If you pass green or brown fluid this could be your baby's first poo, and could be a signal he is in distress or you have an infection.

- You have a constant pain in your stomach. Contractions always come and go, so a continuous pain may need further investigation.
- You have sudden or severe headache or visual disturbances – this could be a sign of dangerously high blood pressure or pre-eclampsia.
- Your baby starts moving frenetically or stops moving completely.

Being induced

If your labour does not start naturally, or if you are over 41 weeks, your midwife may want you to be induced.

There are usually three stages of induction. Depending on your cervix and how it responds, you may need all three stages, you may be able to start at stage two, or to you may be lucky and find that labour gets going on its own fairly easily – although this is relatively unusual.

Most inductions begin with having prostaglandin inserted into the vagina. This is a synthetic version of the same hormone that is released naturally in labour (and is found in semen, if you're interested!). You may be given it as a vaginal pessary or gel; this may last 24 hours, or may need to be repeated every six hours – this will depend on the formulation, but the 24-hour version is quite popular with women and midwives, as it involves fewer internal examinations! It can also be removed easily as it has a thin string like a tampon, which is handy in the unlikely event of too many contractions or fetal distress. This part of induction can occasionally take two to three days, but be reassured this does not happen often! A new cervical-ripening balloon is now being used in some units instead of prostaglandin.

Once the prostaglandin has done its trick, your cervix will be ready for the next stage of induction – that is, to break your waters. Your doctor or midwife will do this by inserting a small, plastic, hook-like instrument (similar to a crochet hook) into the vagina and making a small tear in the membranes. It is quite uncomfortable, but not particularly painful. Sometimes the waters will break on their own, and you can skip this stage and move on to the next!

After this you will need Syntocinon, which is the proprietary name for oxytocin: the hormone that triggers contractions. It will be administered via a drip in your hand or arm. The initial dose is very low, and it is slowly increased according to your contractions until they are strong and occurring every two to three minutes. Most women have an epidural when they are given Syntocinon, as it can make contractions come thick and fast. You can have an epidural when the Syntocinon is just starting (before the contractions get too painful), or you can wait and see how it goes and how you find it. The drawback with this method is that your movement is restricted, because you are connected to a piece of equipment. Your baby's heart rate will also need to be monitored electronically to make sure he is coping with the induction.

Sometimes a Syntocinon drip is used to increase the frequency of your contractions if your labour slows down – this is called augmentation of labour.

In a first pregnancy the cervix opens on average 0.5cm per hour; if you have had a baby before it will open about 1cm per hour or more.

Active or established labour

As labour continues your contractions will get longer, more painful (probably) and more frequent. These contractions signify that you are moving into active stage, or established labour. Usually your cervix has already changed from 3cm thick to paper thin, and now it is ready to dilate. During this phase your cervix will dilate from 3cm or 4cm to 10cm, at which point it will be sufficiently open for you to give birth. These stronger contractions open the cervix more rapidly than in the first phase, but it could be some hours before it is fully dilated.

The contractions may be coming as frequently as every three to five minutes now, and lasting 45–60 seconds. As the contraction reaches the peak of its intensity, you will find that you need to start using your breathing techniques to 'breathe' through them, and usually you are not able to talk during one.

Once your contractions are coming every five minutes, it's advisable to give your maternity unit a call; you're probably still between six and 12 hours away from giving birth and your midwife is likely to encourage you to stay at home – as long as you can cope with the pain and have no other problems. Midwives are very experienced at taking these calls, and normally have a very good idea of how you are doing from the way you are breathing and the tone of your voice. If the pain is so bad that you need your birth partner to call for you, ensure he makes the timings of the contractions clear and tells the midwife that the pain is so bad you can't speak (she might still want a word with you, though, to check you don't just want to come in early!).

Planned home birth

If you have planned for a home birth you will have a midwife (or sometimes two) with you. You can deliver in any area of the house that you feel comfortable in – that is the benefit of a home birth: it's your house and the midwives are the visitors. The midwife will have all the equipment she needs to safely deliver the baby. If all is straightforward the midwife will stay for a few hours after birth to ensure both you and baby are well and that baby has fed. She will tuck you up in your own bed (yet another benefit of a home birth, being comfortable in your own bed with privacy), and will then take all the mess away when she leaves.

WHEN THE BABY DOESN'T WAIT

One of the difficulties for a midwife trying to work out over the phone where you are in labour, or for you as a first-time mother, is that one minute you are chugging along quite nicely at five minute intervals, and next 'whoosh!': you've had a baby. So now that we know that babies can pop out when you're not quite ready, here's a checklist on the minute chance (don't lose any precious sleep over it) that it happens to you.

- Dial the emergency number on your notes, tell them you think the baby is coming, and they will send someone to you. If you can't find the number, dial 999 and ask for an ambulance. Open the front door so they can get in quickly.
- If someone is with you, the operator might 'talk' your birth partner through the birth stages on the phone until someone gets to you.
- If you are alone, call your partner and then call anyone you know who can be with you quickly. It doesn't have to be family: a friend or neighbour will do.
- Try to find three big clean towels: one to give birth on, one to dry the baby with and one to wrap the baby in.
- Get on all fours, put your head on your forearms and your bottom as high in the air as you can, then try to delay things by taking three short pants followed by one long blow.
- Resist the urge to push if at all possible.
- If you can't stop the urge to push and you can feel the baby 'crowning', ie coming out,

squat, leaning back against a wall, so your baby can slide out and you can 'catch' him. (If someone is with you, you can stay on all fours and they can take the baby as you push him out.)

- If the cord is round the baby's neck, gently ease it over his head and wrap him in a towel to keep him warm. There might be fluid or mucus in his nose preventing him from breathing, so quickly but gently stroke the sides of his nose to try to shift it.
- Lay your baby across your belly with his head lower than his body to allow any remaining fluid to drain out, and firmly rub his back with the towel. Use the towel to dry him so that he doesn't get cold, then wrap him in another clean towel.
- If he still doesn't seem to be breathing, dial 999 and they will take you through infant resuscitation.
- Do not attempt to cut the cord. When professional help arrives they will do that for you. Just cuddle your baby close and put him to your breast to make him feel secure.
- A short while after the birth you may experience further contractions as your body expels the placenta. This will come away still attached to the other end of the cord, and will be dealt with when help arrives.

Remember, this happens in fewer than 1% of cases, so don't worry about it too much.

Going into hospital

Always try to phone before you go to the hospital so that the staff know to expect you; the information they give you over the phone can be very helpful. When you arrive you will be examined, and if you are not yet in established labour you may well be sent home again – it is generally healthier and more relaxing waiting at home than in a hospital environment.

It's difficult to generalise, but normally once labour is established and contractions are coming every three to four minutes, it's time for you to pick up your bag and head for the hospital or birthing centre (unless you are having a home birth, obviously).

Procedures will vary slightly depending on the type of maternity unit or centre you are going to, and you may or may not know the midwife who books you in. Here's what will probably happen.

- Your midwife will take your notes to check your antenatal history. She will ask you to confirm how many weeks pregnant you are, whether your waters have broken and how often your contractions are coming; she will then take your pulse, temperature and blood pressure and check your urine.

- She will also examine your belly to work out the baby's position and listen to his heartbeat to check he's not in distress. If you are wearing a sanitary pad because you have had a show or your waters have broken, she may check it for signs of meconium or unusual blood loss.

- She will then probably carry out an internal examination to see how dilated your cervix is. A word of warning: these examinations can be very uncomfortable. If you really don't want an internal examination you can ask your midwife not to do one, but the downside is she then won't be able to assess accurately how far gone you are in labour.

- The midwife will start recording all the events of your labour on a form called a partagram: this is a universal graphic interpretation of the progression of your labour. If the midwife looking after you has to go off duty halfway through your labour, the succeeding midwife will be able to see exactly where you are and how you are coping from reading this chart.

After 'checking in', you may go straight to the delivery suite or to the antenatal ward, depending on how far your labour has progressed.

ELECTRONIC MONITORING

When you check in with your midwife, she will probably listen to your baby's heartbeat with a hand-held monitor. Periodically during labour, she will listen again to your baby's heartbeat. If she suspects there might be a problem, or if you have an epidural, need Syntocinon or if your labour is considered to be high risk, she might wire you up to an electronic fetal heart rate monitor. This is usually called a cardiotocogram (CTG) – 'cardio' meaning heart, 'toco' meaning contraction. You are monitored using a small machine that is attached to your stomach with elastic straps and has two sensors that monitor your baby's heart rate and contractions. Your doctor or midwife can print out the information it picks up in graph form to see how your baby is coping. Sometimes a clip (called a fetal scalp electrode) is applied to your baby's head instead of the heart rate monitor to your tummy – this is more likely if the midwife is having technical problems getting a good record, or if you have twins.

CTGs are painless, but it does mean you can't move about as much, unless you are lucky enough to be offered a wireless version. You can still sit in a chair, stand or use a beanbag, but you usually can't walk long distances. It can be disconnected if you need to go to the toilet!

In the delivery room

When you are taken to the delivery suite, you'll meet the midwife who is going to deliver your baby. While you can still function fairly normally (hopefully), this is the time to give her your birth plan and go through it, so she gets an idea of the kind of labour you want to achieve. If there are any health or religious issues that may have an impact on your labour and birth, be sure to tell her at this point. If you are pretty certain you are going to want an epidural, make that known now, too, because it may take some time to get it organised. You can usually have gas and air at this stage. See page 242 for more on pain relief options.

In some units the midwife stays with you throughout labour, but if the hospital is short of staff or has a rush on, don't be freaked out if the midwife leaves you with your birthing partner for periods of time. There will be an emergency button in your room that you can press if things suddenly speed up, or if the pain gets too much to bear and you need some relief. Sometimes it is nice to be alone with your partner for short times.

Now is the time to put all those classes and plans into action and do whatever makes you feel comfortable. If you want to stand up, squat, roll on a birthing ball or a bean bag, go for it. Alternatively you might try relaxing in a pool, having a massage or simply lying in your bed: whatever gets you through the pain. If you want to crawl around on all fours howling like a coyote, that's probably (just) OK too; one thing is for certain…your midwife has seen and heard it all before.

> 'To be completely honest, the only thing that helped me to get through it all was to get naked, scream the room down, bite my lips to pieces and grab at my boobs with every contraction. I didn't expect myself to act how I did, but my body just took over.'
>
> Melanie, mum to Saorise, 3 months

This is the time to take the initiative and experiment with different positions to see what works for you. Hopefully, your birth partner and midwife will be supportive and encourage you to do this, because it is *your* body and you have a right to try to create the birth that you want. You already know that gravity will give you a helping hand if you choose to stay upright during labour and birth, so if you are told you have to lie down in bed, ask why this is – there will always be a good reason, it just might not be clear to you.

This is also the time to start considering pain relief; some hospitals won't give you an epidural until you are 5cm dilated and others won't give you one once you reach 9cm, so you need to keep communicating your wishes to your midwife so you don't miss out.

Transitional labour

This intense phase of labour can last anything between 10 minutes and one hour.

This is the end of the first stage of labour, before you get to the pushing stage. It starts when your cervix is around 8cm dilated, and ends when it is fully (10cm) dilated and you are ready to push. During this time, your contractions may become less frequent, but they will last longer and will be much stronger. Sometimes they 'double peak', meaning that you have one that reaches intensity, starts to fade and then peaks again.

You might be feeling sick, shaky and out of control during this phase of labour, and if you have decided to opt for a 'natural' birth you will need to adopt your breathing and relaxation techniques to see you through it. This is where you need a supportive birth partner to reassure you. Some women find this transitional phase quite overwhelming and exhausting, but hopefully the realisation that your baby is nearly here should be the motivation to keep you going.

What you might be worrying about

Swearing: Labour may be the most 'natural' thing in the world for a woman (it doesn't feel like it at the time), but it sure isn't ladylike, and even if you never cuss or swear you might find yourself coming out with some pretty juicy expletives. The midwives will have heard it all before – and worse!

Losing control of your bladder and your bowels: You will be encouraged to empty your bladder during labour, but even so there's a possibility you might leak some urine. Don't fret about it: you'll be giving birth on a huge absorbent sheet designed to mop up any leakages, and as there's going to be loss of amniotic fluid your midwife is hardly going to be able to tell the difference or care. When you feel the urge to push, it is very similar to needing a poo, and it is quite possible that you may pass a little faecal matter during birth – but that'll be the least of your worries at the time. If it does happen you won't notice: your midwife will discreetly remove it and you'll be none the wiser.

Being a labour monster: Being in such acute pain can also make you very crotchety or downright rude when ordinarily you are quite lovely. It's probably worth warning your birthing partner that you may well say or do things that you wouldn't normally. You'll probably contradict yourself – from 'Rub my back' to 'Get your effing hands off me' – and may well tell them you hate them, or wish the father had never got you into this mess. All these feelings of animosity will miraculously disappear once your baby is delivered, and will only return once you become a sleep-deprived, baby-feeding monster.

'I found the contractions so overwhelming I wanted everyone and everything else to go away, including my poor husband. He was all set to encourage me, hold my hand, massage me, all that stuff, but I just told him to leave me alone!'

Katy, mum to twins Thomas and Evelyn

How can such a big head get through such a small hole?

You may have had this thought a lot during pregnancy, and even when you are in labour, it can still be quite a terrifying prospect. If you have had an epidural you probably won't be able to feel the baby's head 'crowning', but if you haven't, be prepared for it to be very painful in the last few minutes when the head is about to be born. It's colloquially known as 'the ring of fire', but with the birth of your baby so imminent it'll be the last thing on your mind, and there's certainly no going back. Many women tear their perineum while pushing their baby out, but you should know that this is part of the normal process. You may tear any part of the skin surrounding the 'ring of fire', but it's more common to tear either the very bottom (the perineum) or the very top (near your clitoris), and about 70% of women having their first baby need stitches following birth. This isn't something to fear either, as most tears heal either on their own or after being stitched up following birth. If the tear is just skin deep, then there is no need for stitches. If it is a little deeper, then it does need stitching to allow it to heal quicker: you will be given a local anaesthetic by the midwife so you won't feel any of this, and the stitches will normally dissolve after a week or so.

Your birth partner can help by:

- massaging or rubbing your back

- fetching you snacks and drinks

- keeping you cool by feeding you ice chips or sponging or spraying your face

- holding your hand and offering your words of support and encouragement

- providing physical support if you need help kneeling, squatting or leaning

- speaking for you if you feel your wishes or opinions are not being heard or your birth plan is being ignored (make sure you give them the nod first)

- not getting hurt or offended by your behaviour – it's not personal!

THE SECOND STAGE

As your baby's head moves down through the cervix towards the vagina, you might suddenly feel an intense pressure in your bottom. This is described as 'bearing down', and at this point you will undoubtedly have an overwhelming urge to push. You'll probably yell something at the midwife at this point, and she'll probably calmly tell you *not* to push as your cervix isn't quite ready. You can counter the urge to push by breathing in short puffs or panting.

Your midwife will tell you to start pushing with each contraction when she believes you are fully dilated and ready to go. Trust her guidance on this and try to follow what she says, but if you feel you need to push on your own schedule, then trust your body. You'll get the urge to push through your anus even though the baby will come out of your vagina, if that makes sense. If you have an epidural and you have no feeling in the lower part of your body, your midwife will tell you when to push. She may suggest that you wait for an hour after she has diagnosed full dilation, to allow the contractions to bring the baby's head lower.

Once the first part of the baby's head appears, you can take a look at it in the mirror or feel it if you wish, or you might just think, 'Let's just get this baby out of there!' What may strike you as weird is that once she sees the baby's head crowning, your midwife might tell you to stop pushing and pant for a bit, or take small puffs so that the baby is delivered slowly and carefully: this minimises the chance of you getting torn. Also, once the head is out she may have to gently remove the cord from the baby's neck before you can push the body out.

A word of warning: for some women it is relatively straightforward to push your baby out, while for others it can be an exhausting and laborious process. It can take anything from a few minutes to an hour or more. Sometimes, despite your best efforts, you might need a little assistance.

Assisted delivery

You may need an assisted delivery if your baby is not delivering despite loads of pushing from you, or if there are signs of distress in the baby.

Ventouse

The most common method of easing your baby out is by ventouse. A ventouse is a vacuum extractor that looks like a small sink plunger. It has a plastic or metal cap that fixes to your baby's head by suction, and a vacuum pump that creates a suction effect. If you have a ventouse, you will have to lie on your back on the bed and your feet will be placed in stirrups; you will then be given a local anaesthetic if you have not had an epidural already. The ventouse will be inserted through the entrance to your vagina and placed onto the top of your baby's head. Then your baby will be 'pulled' down during contractions whilst you continue to push out. Usually it takes no more than three contractions once the ventouse is in position. The upside of this procedure is that you don't always have to have an episiotomy; the downside is that your baby might have a slightly pointy head when the cap is taken off, called a chignon (don't worry, he won't look like a relative of Mr Spock for long).

Forceps

Forceps are curved tongs that look like giant metal salad servers, which cradle and protect your baby's head during delivery. Years ago, babies were routinely delivered by forceps, but these days ventouse is the popular option because you are less likely to need an episiotomy. However, forceps deliveries tend to be quicker, so they may be used if there is a major concern about your baby's well-being. Forceps are also less dependent on your pushing than ventouse, so if there is still a little way to go before the baby can be born, or if you are totally exhausted, they may be preferred. The doctor will put first one side of the tong and then the other against your baby's head, and then when the contraction comes deliver him by gently pulling – if you can help by pushing, all the better. There may be faint marks by the side of your baby's temples after a forceps delivery but they shouldn't be there for long.

Both forceps and ventouse look like instruments of torture, but the doctor using them will know exactly what he is doing, and they will only be used if the medical team believe that your baby won't come out by himself. If you are really against the idea of an assisted birth, you have a right to question the doctor, but you will probably be prepared to undergo anything to facilitate the safe arrival of your baby.

Episiotomy

An episiotomy is when doctors make a cut from the opening of your vagina into the perineum, but this is not as horrible as it sounds, particularly at the time. You're given a local anaesthetic if you haven't had an epidural, and obviously you'll need stitching up afterwards. There is a risk of infection, and it does make the healing process 'down below' rather longer, as you may experience itching, soreness and general discomfort. Some women have to sit on a rubber ring for weeks after birth because it's still so painful down there. You do read awful stories about women getting horrible infections and suffering for months or even years afterwards, which is why midwives don't routinely perform them, but relaxing lavender and tea tree oil baths (coupled with arnica tablets) can work wonders.

There is a theory that women who tear naturally during vaginal births actually heal better than women who have episiotomies. This is due to how the two events happen: with episiotomies, all the layers of skin and muscle are cut in a straight line, which is directed away from the back passage, usually to your right. With a natural tear, only the layers that are stretched to their limit are torn, albeit in a jagged line. This can mean you experience superficial tearing in any direction, which is obviously less severe than an artificial cut through all the layers; it may, however, extend further or in the 'wrong' direction, for example into your back passage (called a third degree tear, which needs to be repaired in theatre to make sure it is all working properly again). If you feel very strongly about episiotomies and would prefer to tear naturally, don't be afraid to be speak up. However, an episiotomy is only suggested when it seems safer than allowing a tear to happen, either because it will speed things up (which might be safer for your baby) or because it might reduce the chance of you having a bad tear, so you should listen carefully to why it is being offered.

Emergency Caesarean

Sometimes your labour starts normally but you end up needing to have an emergency Caesarean. Over 60% of Caesareans performed in the UK are unplanned and therefore classed as emergency, so don't worry too much if your midwife or doctor tells you that you need to have one.

 Caesarean section births account for around one in four of all births in the UK.

Why you might need an emergency Caesarean
There are several reasons why you might need an emergency Caesarean, including:

- your labour isn't progressing, and your cervix isn't dilating

- your baby has insufficient oxygen or his heartbeat pattern becomes worrying

Caesarean rates vary widely between hospitals. A recent study showed you were twice as likely to have a Caesarean at The Chelsea and Westminster Hospital in London than you were at the Sherwood Hospital in Nottingham.

- despite pushing, your baby's head is not in a suitable position for an assisted delivery

- a dangerous complication has occurred, like the placenta detaching (placental abruption)

- you suddenly develop pre-eclampsia. This is uncommon, as often with pre-eclampsia you can still have a vaginal delivery, but if your baby is distressed or you are very unwell a Caesarean may be necessary.

What will happen?

If you have a 'normal' labour, you probably won't even catch a whiff of the obstetrician, but if something goes wrong, they will come quickly to assess the situation and make decisions about your care in conjunction with the midwife.

If a Caesarean section is recommended, the doctor must explain to you why this procedure is considered necessary and you will be given a consent form to sign. Speed might be of the essence here, so there won't be opportunities to seek second opinions or 'wait a bit longer'. If the health professionals looking after you recommend an emergency C-section, it is best to respect their judgement, however disappointed or frightened you might feel at the time.

Once you have consented to the operation you will be taken to theatre. Usually you will be given regional analgesis, such as an epidural, so you remain conscious but can't feel anything from the waist down; you can have someone with you in the theatre. You will have a catheter put in to empty your bladder, and a cannula will be put in your hand so that fluids and pain relief can be administered as necessary.

If you have to have a general anaesthetic and be put to sleep, your birth partner will not be able to join you. The need for a general anaesthetic is rare, but it might need to be administered if there is a need to deliver the baby immediately and there is not time to get an epidural/spinal block in place or working.

Once the anaesthetic is working effectively, a screen will be put up so that you will not be able to see the surgeon perform the operation (thank goodness). Encourage your birth partner to stay at the 'head' end, as you don't want him fainting at the sight of blood as they cut you open!

However, if he is brave he could look over the screen to do this, as could you if you really wanted to.

A horizontal incision is made across the lower part of the abdomen at the top of the pubic bone or bikini line. It's done here because it heals quickly, with the added bonus that the scar won't show beneath your pubic hair. Very occasionally a vertical incision is necessary, but it is very rare. Next the doctors make a cut into the uterus so that they can lift the baby out. Don't be disappointed if the baby is not handed to you immediately, as he is usually quickly checked by the midwife or paediatrician first. If he is okay, hopefully he'll be placed next to you or on your chest, or given to your partner for a cuddle while they stitch you up (this could take half an hour or so, as it is a major bit of suturing).

You will usually be given antibiotics immediately before or during the operation, assessed to see if you need medication to minimise the chance of thrombosis in the coming days or weeks and be debriefed afterwards to explain (again) why the Caesarean was needed and whether you are likely to be able to deliver vaginally next time (most women are, luckily!).

STRAIGHT AFTER BIRTH

Now that the baby has arrived, for the moment at least, it makes not a jot of difference whether you gave birth on a bean bag or had a C-section. Ask any new mother the most amazing part of her baby's birth, and she'll probably tell you that it was the moment she heard a cry and knew that her baby was alive and well. Your partner can get involved in the process at this point, and might be asked if he would like to cut the cord (after it has been clamped). Many men really enjoy this, though some do find it terrifying, so don't worry if he doesn't seem keen. Medical stuff might not be his thing, and he's going through just as many emotions as you are.

The midwife might give your baby a bit of a clean-up, as he will be covered in blood, amniotic fluid and vernix. If there are no problems at birth, you will be given your baby straight away. You will probably also be given the choice of having the baby delivered straight onto your tummy or dried off first. It is recommended that you have direct skin-to-skin contact with your baby as soon as possible following birth, as

A recent study has shown that cutting the umbilical cord immediately after birth – which is standard practice – may lead to iron deficiency in newborns. Official guidelines are being examined. Be aware that you can ask that the cord be left to pulsate for a few minutes before it's cut, so that the maximum blood passes from placenta to baby.

SKIN-TO-SKIN

Early skin-to-skin contact is important, so your midwife will be keen to place the baby on your chest as soon as possible – don't worry, you won't drop him and your partner can help to steady things. Experts believe this contact is very important because it promotes bonding, calms your baby and helps get things off to a good start if you are breastfeeding. It can also stimulate hormones that will encourage the placenta to separate. Women who have their babies whisked off to special care often report that they felt a bit let down at this point, and say that they missed out on vital bonding time. If this happens to you, please try not to fret about it. Your baby will be getting the specialist help he needs to thrive, and you will bond just as well with your baby if he has to spend the first few hours, days or weeks of life in an incubator.

this helps establish bonding. If there are any concerns with your baby (as sometimes they can come out quite shocked and forget to breathe), then the midwife will check him over first, usually still in the room, and then hand your baby to you soon afterwards.

Your baby's breathing, skin colour, heart rate, muscle tone and reflex responses will all be recorded: this is known as the Agpar score, and it ranges from 0 to 10. It's a universally adopted method of assessing the health of newborns, and your midwife may well record scores at one minute and five minutes to see how he is faring. Don't concern yourself too much with the actual number – sometimes he will get a poor score at one minute and excellent at five minutes – it just takes some babies a bit of time to 'wake up'.

The midwife will also weigh and measure the baby. You are normally told this weight in kilograms, which can be a little annoying if you only think in pounds where weight's concerned.

BABY WEIGHT

- The average weight of a newborn baby is 3.5kg (around 7.5lb).

- Full term babies normally weigh between 2.7kg and 3.7kg (6lb–8lb).

- Full term babies weighing less than 2.5kg (5.8lb) are considered low birth weight.

- Babies are normally between 47.5cm and 52.5cm (19″–21″) long at birth.

THE PLACENTA: THE THIRD STAGE

It's quite weird to think that, even though you already have your baby, your labour isn't over: you still have some pushing to do! As you cuddle your baby, you may experience some more (milder) contractions as your body prepares to expel the placenta – your baby's life support system for the past nine months.

The third stage of labour, from the delivery of the baby to the delivery of the placenta, is usually a few minutes long, but can last up to 30 minutes. Your third stage can be actively managed by having an injection of oxytocin, usually in your leg, as the baby's body is born. This reduces the chance of you having a haemorrhage from the uterus by helping it to contract, and it helps to deliver the placenta.

You can also have a physiological or natural third stage, in which no medication is given. This is only advisable if your labour and delivery have been normal, you are not anaemic and your risk of haemorrhaging is low. If you want a 'natural' delivery of the placenta, you need to note that on your birth plan and discuss it with your midwives.

After she has checked your baby, your midwife may put one hand on your tummy and gently pull the placenta out with the other. It may hurt a bit, but nothing like the birth! If it doesn't come away easily or if you are bleeding more than usual, the midwife may advise further injections or emptying your bladder, or ask a doctor to assist.

When it comes out, the placenta will be the size of a small dinner plate, and your midwife will inspect it carefully to check that it came out intact and that there's nothing left inside you. In around 2% of births, all or part of the placenta is left behind because it gets stuck to the wall of the uterus. Your midwife will try to ease it out manually, but if she is not successful, you will need to have a small surgical procedure, because if it is not removed it could lead to a haemorrhage or infection. If this happens, your epidural will be topped up or you will be given a spinal anaesthetic (similar to an epidural, but it works more quickly) and you will nip off to theatre to get what's in there quickly removed. Very rarely a serious condition known as placenta accreta occurs during pregnancy, where the placenta grows into the uterine wall to such an extent that it cannot be detached. If this happens, you may know in advance, and your doctor will discuss your options with you before your labour and delivery.

Earlier in the book we told you of the myriad things you can do with the placenta (including eat it or bury it). It's quite fascinating to look at if you like that sort of thing, but most new mums are too interested in the baby to give the placenta a second thought.

ONCE LABOUR'S OVER

I've given birth to an alien!

Just a word of warning: your baby will probably not look like one of those gorgeous chubby babies from a nappy advert. Newborns invariably have misshapen heads, squinty eyes, spots and blotches (and they're pretty slimy too). Don't worry if you don't feel an instant, overwhelming rush of love for your baby. Some women say it takes time to bond with your baby; others that they didn't think he was beautiful until a few hours later. Don't worry if you feel like this. These are completely natural feelings and you're not a terrible mother!

> 'When my baby was born I felt a very strong sense of responsibility and was relieved he was OK, but I didn't love him. That came a little later as we got to know each other.'
>
> Nicola, second pregnancy and mum to Callum, 18 months

Bonding

Don't worry if you don't fall head over heels in love at first sight. Many women are so emotionally and physically drained after the birth that they find it quite difficult to bond in the first few days. Sometimes you just need to get home and get settled into a routine before you can really relax and enjoy your baby. Some women report that 'They can't love what they don't know,' and we respect that view. It may take time, but the unequivocal love you have for your children is like no other love you will ever experience. You will form a deep, unbreakable bond with your baby: it just might take a little time.

> 'I was a bit upset because I didn't bond with my baby immediately. The first time he was placed on me I didn't really feel anything, and this lack of emotion upset me. When we were alone on the ward, though, I couldn't stop staring at him or cuddling him.'
>
> Corinne, mum to Harry, 2 months

Alone with your baby

Once you and the baby are cleaned up (that first shower is pretty amazing), you will be taken to the postnatal ward. You might feel a bit wobbly, especially if you have had an epidural, so this is usually in a wheelchair, or on a bed if you have had a Caesarean.

Earlier in the book we suggested that you find out what the hospital's rules are about partners staying after the birth. Many birthing centres let partners stay the night (and even have double beds to accommodate them), but it is worth finding out what the rules are, so you don't feel disappointed if he has to leave.

Most new mothers experience acute fear and anxiety in the days after birth; this is completely normal, as the weight of responsibility feels quite onerous once your baby is born. You might have given up booze and fags for your baby's well-being in pregnancy, but now you actually have to look after a live and kicking baby. While you are still in hospital, make the most of having a midwife 'on tap'. It can be quite an overwhelming and surreal feeling after giving birth; often you're physically exhausted but mentally buzzing. Sleep whenever you can – even a 10-minute power nap can do wonders.

BEING DISCHARGED FROM HOSPITAL

In theory you can go home as soon as six hours after giving birth, but in reality you'll probably be in for longer than that. You'll need to stay for two days if you have had a Caesarean, for example, although some units are now moving to a 36-hour discharge for planned Caesareans.

If you have had an epidural, an instrumental delivery or a Caesarean (or some combination of these), you will probably have a catheter tube draining your urine into a bag. It will usually be removed 6 to 12 hours after delivery, sometimes longer. You will be asked to do your first wee into a jug so that it can be measured – occasionally your bladder is a bit slow to get going again, so you may need the catheter back in for a few more days.

Before you leave hospital, the midwife will ensure you and your baby are well and your baby is feeding well. An examination will be performed on the baby within 72 hours following birth, either before discharge or at home. It will be performed by a midwife or paediatrician, who will check your baby's heart, eyes and whole body. A hearing test will also be performed on the baby, either before discharge or within the first 72 hours.

Once this is all organised and both you and your baby are well, you will be discharged by the midwife. Many women need to give themselves heparin injections at home for seven days to six weeks after delivery to stop a thrombosis forming. This will depend on issues to do with you and your baby's birth, and is a sensible precaution to make sure you stay healthy in the coming weeks.

A midwife will then continue your care at home, where she will check you and the baby, as well as monitor the baby's weight and perform the Guthrie test (see page 346 for more information).

11

Taking care of my baby

It's a really good idea to read this chapter before you have
your baby, because it's likely that you won't have much time
to give it more than a cursory glance once he's born.

In this chapter we'll look at your first few days at home with
your baby. This can be a very emotional and overwhelming
time for a new mother, but if you follow this advice, hopefully
you'll be able to treasure your first few days as a new family.

WE'RE HOME! NOW WHAT?

It can be quite scary when, having left the security of the hospital and expertise of the midwives behind, suddenly you are alone and completely responsible for the love and care of this little being that can't do a thing for himself.

You shouldn't feel abandoned, though: you will be under the care of the community midwife, who will be popping in on you at home for the first 10 days, and you can always call the midwives in your maternity unit. Your health visitor will be on hand once your midwife support ends as well. If you are worried that your baby is ill, you can always see your GP during the day or call NHS 111 or NHS Direct if it is out of surgery hours.

> **WORDS FROM THE PROFESSIONALS:** If you are having breastfeeding problems, there should be a breastfeeding counsellor in your area, or you can call the National Breastfeeding Helpline (see the useful contacts at the back of the book).

MIDWIFE VISITS

You will get a visit from the midwife the day after you have gone home; if it is a weekend, some hospitals may ask you to go to the drop-in midwives' clinic instead of a home visit. They will check your baby is feeding properly and that you are both feeling well. The midwife will then tell you when she will next visit, as it differs depending on the type of birth you have had. On average, if you have had a normal birth and there are no problems, you will have three visits from the day you go home to day 10. The baby will be weighed and have a blood Guthrie test taken on day five, and then be weighed again around day 10. The screening timeline can be seen online at www.screening.nhs.uk, which shows all the tests and checks that need to be performed following birth.

Save your baby's little hospital tag and first picture: you can put them in a memory box with a copy of the birth certificate.

The Guthrie test involves taking a few drops of your baby's blood from his heel and placing them onto a small filter card. This blood is tested for a number of rare but important inherited conditions, all of which are less problematic if diagnosed and treated sooner. They include cystic fibrosis, phenylketonuria, hypothyroidism, sickle cell disease and MCAD (Medium chain acyl coA dehydrogenase) deficiency.

EMOTIONAL ROLLERCOASTER

Don't worry if you get the baby blues after the birth of your baby: it's completely normal to feel a bit low after the excitement of your baby's birth, and for most of us it's short lived; you'll be back to your chipper self in no time (just a tad more tired).

All of your fears and stresses are completely normal. If you need help, just ask, and try to make sure that you relax and enjoy these early days.

Tips for enjoying the first few days

- Switch your phone off for a few hours a day and get some rest. You don't need to be rudely awoken from a much-needed doze by a text message pinging in your ear.

- Warn your partner that his role for the first few days after birth is that of a hotel concierge-cum-receptionist with chef and waiting duties thrown in. He'll probably spend the first week fielding calls, answering the door for flower and parcel deliveries, making cups of tea for the endless stream of visitors and rustling up your favourite banned pregnancy foods.

- Be strict about visiting times and **don't** offer to feed **anyone** except your baby.

- If you are too tired to have any visitors, family and friends who really love you will respect that decision.

- If you do need help physically or emotionally, don't be afraid to ask; friends and family are usually delighted to help.

Ahhhh moments

One of the most delicious aspects of being a new mother is taking pictures of your new baby. Even though most of us store our photos digitally, print your favourites and put them in an album.

- Be creative: take pictures of your baby's tiny hands or feet.
- Try taking pictures in black and white as well as colour.
- Make sure you take lots of pictures of your baby with his father.
- Take lots of pictures of the baby with family members; you can use them to make a lovely pictorial family tree for the nursery.

Memory box tip

Keep the first tiny babygrow or another favourite outfit, and put it in a box picture frame with the first pair of tiny shoes. You won't believe how cute they'll look (or how small your baby was).

Meconium is very hard to clean up, so a good tip is to smother your baby's bottom in Vaseline – then it wipes off really easily.

WEIRD BUT WONDERFUL

If this is your first baby, there are some weird and rather wonderful things you should know about your newborn, so that you don't spend the first week with your midwife on speed dial.

- The first poos (called meconium) your baby will pass are dark and sticky, and are often described as looking like Marmite! After a day or so the stools become much runnier, and are yellow or green in colour if you breastfeed. Bottlefed babies tend to have firmer, paler and smellier stools. If you breastfeed, the stools may be affected by things you are eating, so don't panic if the baby passes something very luminous. There are also sometimes 'seedy'-looking things in the poo, which are completely normal too.

- There are two soft spots on the top of a baby's head called the fontanelles, where the skull bones have yet to fuse. The skin above the front one will rise and fall (particularly when the baby gets hot). You may also worry that this part of your baby's head will get damaged, but there is a thick layer of membrane below the skin which is very difficult to penetrate (but, obviously, don't poke it).

- Babies do vomit quite a lot of milk. This is completely normal and should be a milky colour, but if it is projectile, copious or you think your baby is in pain, mention it to your health visitor.

- Babies sleep for up to 21 hours a day in the early weeks of life, but not all at once (and often only in periods of one or two hours). You should make the most of this time and try to catch a nap too.

- Your baby may be very spotty or flaky, or have rashes on his skin. It's not surprising, really, when you consider he's been hydrated by your amniotic fluid for nine months, and now he's out in the air and subjected to air conditioning, heating and so on. If you are worried about a rash, check with your midwife, but it's likely to be harmless.

- If your baby's skin is still a bit greasy, this is the remains of the vernix that protected his skin in the uterus. Don't try to wash it off because it will prevent his skin becoming dry.

- If your baby resembles a mini gorilla with lots of hair covering his body, this is the remains of the lanugo; it will drop out over the coming weeks.

- The genitals and nipples of your newborn may be swollen due to the hormones you will have passed on; if you have a little girl it's even possible she will pass a little blood into her nappy.

- The remainder of the umbilical cord stays attached to your baby's tummy for a few weeks after birth (initially he may come home with a small plastic clamp on it). It will eventually shrivel and fall off. It can become infected, so keep an eye on it and let your health visitor know if it looks sore.

- Your baby may have a squint: this is temporary while the muscles around the eyes develop.

LOOKING AFTER YOUR BABY

Now that you have another person entirely dependent on you, it can be helpful for you to have some tips and advice on caring for your newborn; these should hopefully see you through the first few weeks until you get the hang of things.

Holding your baby

It can be quite frightening holding your new baby because he is so small, delicate and, well, *new*. The most important thing to remember is that babies have no strength in their neck muscles for the first few months, and therefore their heads will flop forward and back if you don't support them.

Remember that your baby's neck muscles may not fully support the weight of his head until around six months, so make sure that you

Experiment with different ways of holding your baby, as some love to be cradled whereas others love to be held upright: you'll soon work out his favourite position.

continue to support his head and neck even after he acquires some strength in the neck muscle area.

If you are right handed, a good way to cradle your baby is to place your left hand behind your baby's head – making sure both his head and neck are supported – and place your right hand under his bottom (reverse the hands if you are left handed), lift the baby towards you and bring him close enough that he can rest his head on your chest. You should then be able to very gently shift the support of your baby's head from your left hand to your arm and then slide your left hand under his bottom, freeing up your right hand: you can then use your right hand for extra support or to continue everyday activities.

You can also lift him from lying down by putting a hand under each shoulder and supporting his head and neck with your fingers as you draw him up close to you, and then gently turn him and cradle him in your arms, with his head in the crook of your elbow.

Some babies like to lie on their fronts supported by your forearm, while others like to nestle into your shoulder; experiment with different positions and work out which ones are most comfortable for you and your baby.

If you have visitors over it is likely that they will want to hold your baby. Ideally they should wash their hands before they do so, and it's often useful to insist that they are sitting down before you pass your baby over – keep the head supported during the transition from one 'holder' to another. It may sound an obvious tip, but you are minimising the chances of actually dropping the baby.

If a child wants to hold your baby (maybe a sibling or a relative), it is imperative that they are sitting down and supervised at all times; children have absolutely no idea about health and safety and very young children are likely to imagine that your newborn is as robust as a Barbie or Action Man.

Breastfeeding

You are going to spend quite a lot of time feeding your baby in the first few weeks of his life. We've already covered breastfeeding (page 296), and must stress that how you choose to feed your baby is entirely up to you.

Even if you are committed to breastfeeding, things can conspire against you: you may have a disinterested baby or one that's not very good at sucking; you might have trouble getting your milk supply going; or your nipples might become so sore and cracked, the thought of anyone touching them makes you want to weep. But if you persevere, with the right help you will get through it and may even come to enjoy it.

You should be getting visits from your community midwife at home, and if you are struggling with breastfeeding make sure she gives you as much hands-on help as you need – and don't feel embarrassed asking for help with this.

'I found it extremely painful for the first two weeks, as he wasn't latching on properly. I found the militancy of midwives and health visitors very annoying at first, it's actually quite off-putting.'
Claire, mum to Seth, 5 months

'Once we'd both learnt how to breastfeed properly it became a lot easier, and definitely a bonding experience. I am very glad I did breastfeed, but I have to say it is not as easy as you feel perhaps it should be, and I never felt particularly comfortable doing it in public.'
Amy, mum to Aiden, 11 months

Colostrum

For the first few days of feeding you will be giving your baby colostrum, which is the rich creamy milk your breasts produce until your milk comes in. It is full of antibodies that protect your baby from infections and give him immunity. It is also very easy for him to digest whilst his digestive system gets used to working.

When your milk comes in

Your milk will normally come in around three or four days after the birth. Your breasts will suddenly feel even bigger, and may become swollen

TAKING MEDICATION WHILE BREASTFEEDING

Whilst you are breastfeeding, you need to make sure that any medication you take is not going to affect the baby. Whilst this is unusual, it is important to check carefully – unfortunately, healthcare professionals sometimes err on the side of caution; so much so that they say 'no' to breastfeeding when they mean 'don't know' or 'maybe: let's discuss the pros and cons'. If you take medication regularly for a health problem, it is a good idea to ask about breastfeeding whilst taking that treatment before you deliver. Hopefully, most obstetricians looking after pregnant women requiring medication will answer the question before it is asked, but don't be shy about raising the subject.

and tender. This may make any difficulties you've been having even more challenging, but stick with it and ask for as much help as you need. If you need tips on breastfeeding, try one of the helplines listed at the back of the book.

Cabbage: no really, cabbage!

If your breasts are really painful when your milk comes in, send out for a cabbage. Separate the cabbage into leaves and place in the fridge. Once they've cooled, place a leaf into the inside of each bra cup. Amazingly, the cooled leaves make your swollen breasts feel more comfortable – you'll need to replace them regularly as your body heat 'cooks' them, and once they are warm they no longer provide relief.

Tips for successful breastfeeding

- Are you sitting comfortably? It's important to be comfortable when feeding, so try resting your feet on a footstool and putting a pillow under your arm (or use a V pillow) so your baby is correctly positioned.

- Babies typically let you know they are hungry by turning their heads towards your breast and opening and shutting their mouths like a baby bird. If your baby seems hungry, offer him the breast whenever he wants it; it may be exhausting, but 'feeding on demand' keeps your milk supplies up. Within weeks he will feed more quickly and be able to swallow more at a time, so feeds become faster and more spaced out. In the first two weeks it is difficult to work out a feeding routine, but this will naturally happen after the first couple of weeks, so don't worry too much about it.

- Make sure your baby gets as big a mouthful of breast as possible. You need to get the whole of the nipple and areola in his mouth; if he just nibbles at the nipple end the milk won't come out and you'll be in agony.

- If your baby is wrongly positioned or hasn't got enough of the breast in, take it out and start again. Don't just try to pull him off while he's still sucking, because it will be very painful; if you pop your little finger into the corner of his mouth, you can break the suction before repositioning him.

- Let your baby drain the whole of one breast before offering him the other. You will need to go back to the first breast for the following feed. Some people like to put a ribbon or safety pin on their bra strap to remind them which breast to use, but it's normally pretty obvious which one is fuller and which one was drained last.

- Keep breast pads to hand. Your breasts can leak quite alarmingly; we've known women whose breasts started squirting like water pistols when they were taking a shower just after the baby was born.

- Breastfeeding can make you feel thirsty, so make sure that you keep a glass of water while you feed. You are also recommended to drink 6–8 glasses of water a day; it might help you to keep your milk supply up and will certainly help prevent constipation. Keeping hydrated also makes you feel better physically and less tired.

- Treat yourself! It's recommended that you take on an additional 400 calories per day when you are breastfeeding so if it's getting you down a bit, spoil yourself with a big fat cream bun!

- If you are normally quite a private person don't think you have to breastfeed in public. Request some privacy or find a quiet corner. Baby BuBu sell printed apron-type breastfeeding covers that you wear like a pinnie; your breasts are fully covered so you can hoist your top up and your baby can nestle underneath and feed without anything being on show (www.babybubu.co.uk).

- Try to stick to the same drinking limits as you did in pregnancy, as the alcohol can be passed through the milk to your baby.

- You can buy special feeding tops that help you feed discreetly, as they have little flaps or openings enabling you to just pop out a boob without your whole bosom being on show. As your baby's head is usually larger than your breast, you can feed without so much as a glimpse of the nipple. If you don't want to splash out on a specific top for the purpose, try wearing a smock-type top or loose tunic that you can discreetly pop your baby underneath, but make sure it's loose enough for plenty of air to circulate to prevent suffocation.

- You'll be advised not to smoke while you are breastfeeding, as nicotine and other dangerous chemicals can be passed on to your baby.

- Take 10 micrograms of vitamin D daily while breastfeeding for the sake of your baby's bones and teeth.

Breastfeeding premature babies

Premature babies are often not ready to breastfeed immediately. Their tiny bodies are not developed enough to get the hang of the suck/swallow/breathe reflex, and this can be incredibly disheartening for new mothers. Take heart, however, because there are things you can do while you wait for this reflex to kick in.

- If your baby isn't ready to feed directly from the breast, the hospital staff will encourage you to express milk using a breast pump. They will then administer your breast milk using whatever method is appropriate for your individual baby (this will be discussed with you before they do anything).

Some hospitals have a milk bank so your baby can have donor breast milk if you are unable to express enough of your own breast milk.

- Expressing milk is not as effective as the sucking action of a baby's mouth and tongue. Therefore, don't get discouraged if you only produce small amounts of colostrum and breast milk with a breast pump; it's perfectly normal.

- There is a 'let-down' hormone produced in a woman's body to assist with breastfeeding, and the production of it is stimulated by the smell, cry or touch of a newborn. As premature babies are often isolated and away from their mothers, this hormone takes time to get going. Try expressing milk as often as you can in the presence of your baby – you may be surprised at the difference in volume you can produce!

- Stress can play an important role in the production of breast milk, and parents of premature infants are under a colossal amount of it. Try to relax as much as possible and hold your baby whenever you can to stimulate production.

- Tiny babies may need a higher concentration of calories than full-term infants, so don't be concerned if hospital staff supplement your breast milk with artificial formula. Breast milk contains on average 20kcals an ounce, but some babies need more like 22kcal an ounce, or more. Most of the time formula is added to your breast milk, but it may be given in a separate feed if necessary.

- The most important thing to remember about breastfeeding premature infants is that even if they cannot feed directly from you, you're doing the best you can for them. If you have to stop expressing milk because it's too much stress and work, no one will blame you. It's hard having a premie!

Moving to bottlefeeding

If you choose to bottlefeed, don't feel bad or think you have failed: you are no less of a mother if you give your baby formula. For more information on bottlefeeding see page 298.

Hygiene is key with bottlefeeding: you don't want to make your baby ill because of poor preparation or cleanliness, so ensure you sterilise properly every time, and don't give your baby bottles that have been hanging around just because you can't be bothered to make up some more.

Mix and match

Some mothers reach a happy compromise by mixing feeding, and give their babies some breast milk and some formula. It may take some perseverance, but most babies will adapt in the end, and it will be useful if you have appointments, a KIT day at work or a rare night out with the girls, because it means someone else can feed the baby.

If you want to try mixing and matching, you'll need to decide which feed of the day should be formula, and stick to it because of the 'supply and demand' way that boobs work. Your breasts will adapt to this new regime and stop producing as much milk, so if you suddenly decide to switch back you might find it hard to up your milk production again.

It is recommended that you stick solely with breastfeeding for the first few weeks to get your milk supply established and your baby used to feeding. It is said that some babies experience 'nipple confusion' if a bottle is introduced too early and may then refuse to take the breast, so you might want to wait until you actually need someone else to feed your baby (for a night out or a KIT day, for example) before you introduce a bottle feed. Be aware that switching from breast to formula might be harder than you think; if your baby gets used to the sweet, filling breast milk, he might find formula milk much less appealing and refuse to drink it at first.

Changing your baby

You probably learnt to change a nappy in the parentcraft classes, so we won't state the obvious, except to say that the reality of a wriggling baby is somewhat different than practising on a dolly!

Watch out, as some babies will be affected by a rush of cold air and pee the minute their nappy is taken off, which can be quite disconcerting when this arc of wee is heading your way. Changing nappies can be incredibly messy, so make sure you have loads of wipes and anti-bacterial spray to hand because changing mats can get awfully mucky.

Practicality over style

Do not be seduced by those gorgeous towelling mats with fabric covers: after one nappy change they will look like someone has eaten a curry on them, so stick to practical, wipe-clean mats, as they are much more hygienic.

Tips for successful nappy changing

- Change your baby's nappy as soon as he does a poo, to prevent nappy rash.

- Don't let him sit in wet nappies either, as they will irritate his delicate skin.

- Clean and dry his bottom with cotton wool in the early days (alcohol-free wipes won't do any harm if you find the 'tailing' a chore).

- Apply some barrier cream before you put a new nappy on.

- Some people think that your baby should have 'nappy free' time every day to give the skin a bit of an airing; if you want to do that, lay him on the floor on top of a towel and changing mat in case of accidents.

Be alert!

- Wet nappies are an indication that your baby is feeding well, and ideally he should be doing 6–8 pees over a 24 hour period.

- Breastfed babies can have rather erratic bowels and may not do a poo for a couple of days. If three or more days go past and you are worried, or your baby seems in pain, seek advice from your doctor or midwife.

- Formula-fed babies are more prone to constipation, so if he's not going daily you might like to mention it to your health visitor.

Bathing your baby

There's no reason why you shouldn't put your baby in the bath from the word go, but if you are a little nervous you might choose to just top and tail him for the first few weeks. The best way to do this is to undress him, wrap him in a big towel to keep him warm and dip a big pad of cotton wool into a bowl of warm water. Work on the facial area first, gently wiping around the eyes, face, ears (not inside) and neck. Pay attention to the creases in the neck and under the arms, because milk tends to pool there and become 'cheese' if you don't wipe it away.

Next, wash under the arms, around the cord stump, and the hands and toes; and finally, using a fresh piece of cotton wool, clean around the nappy area – paying special attention to the folds at the top of the legs.

Tiny toes

Draw round your baby's hands and feet or make imprints of them (with non-toxic paint: any poster-type paint that is suitable for children will do). This looks particularly effective if you print or draw onto nice handmade paper; you can then frame them and put them in the nursery. Remember to put the date in the corner.

The crying game

Your new baby may cry for between one and three hours a day, and up to one in five babies is considered to be an 'excessive' crier that does more than this. If your baby is crying relentlessly, it's important to eliminate what might be the cause of his distress by checking he's not hungry, too hot, too cold, needing a nappy change or poorly.

He might be hungry, in which case offer him a breast or a bottle, or it may be something as simple as needing a nappy change; he may simply be too hot or cold – touching his hands and feet will normally give you an indication of body temperature, and it might be a simple case of adding or removing a layer of clothing. If he remains warm after you have stripped him off, it is possible that he has a high temperature (the ideal body temperature is between 36.5°C and 37°C); you can check this by using a thermometer.

Do talk to your health visitor if your baby is crying constantly, because there could be an underlying medical cause that might need investigating.

If your baby is crying excessively and you have checked he's suffering from none of the above, he may have colic. One of the popular theories about colicky babies is that they cry because their immature digestive system is causing them pain; another theory is that some babies find it difficult to be 'outside' after all that time in the womb and take a couple of months to settle down. If it is colic you'll be relieved to know that things should settle down by the time your baby is three months old (although it might seem like three years when you are going through it).

Tips to relieve colic

- There are medical preparations like Infacol that you can try to relieve colic. It doesn't seem to work for every baby, but it is worth a shot.

- 'Alternative' treatments like baby massage are said to reduce tension in the body – get a qualified therapist to show you how to do it. For more info, visit the International Association for Infant Massage (www.iaim.org.uk).

- Cranial osteopathy is a therapy that treats pain believed to be caused by the trauma of birth, by releasing tension in certain parts of the baby's body. It is gaining popularity among parents with babies who cry or refuse to settle; for more information visit www.cranial.org.uk.

Strategies to cope with crying

- If your baby is lying down, pick him up and give him a cuddle. If that doesn't work try the 'mummy jig'. All you need to do is hold your baby close to you in his favoured cuddling position and simply rock him from side to side, shifting your weight from one leg to the another.

- Sometimes a walk in the fresh air will do you *both* the world of good (keep your baby properly wrapped up, though).

- We've all read about stressed parents driving around for hours in the middle of the night trying to soothe their babies to sleep, and the car does seem to have a settling effect on some babies.

Hopefully you won't have to resort to hurtling around the motorway network of Britain, but it might be worth a shot.

- Some babies are soothed by the sound of the vacuum cleaner or washing machine; at least you can get some housework done at the same time!

Feeling frustrated

It's completely normal to feel frustration and desperation if you have a child that cries a lot, and that, coupled with a lack of sleep, can make you feel like you are really losing the plot. If you can't bear the crying any more and there's no one around to help you, just put your baby quietly and gently in his cot, put some music on to soothe him, shut the door and go downstairs and make a cup of tea. Then turn the radio or TV on loudly so you can't hear him. Then just sit and drink the tea and practise some deep breathing. It may seem cruel, but the truth is it won't do him any harm if he is left for a short period, and it will be worth it for the sake of your sanity.

'I remember once my baby was crying and crying when I was holding her, and for a very brief second I felt like throwing her down and away from me. I laid her gently down in her cot and went outside for some air, and I was fine after that – thank God. But I'll never forget that feeling and it scared me.'

Isla, mum to Lola, 10 months

(Not) sleeping like a baby

When a newborn isn't feeding he's usually sleeping – there's not much else to do at that age – but the problem is that he can't distinguish between night and day at this point, so the feeds will just continue through the night as he can't tell the difference. It's not unusual to be awoken four or more times a night by a baby wanting sustenance in the early weeks, which can be totally exhausting. The good news is that night waking does become less frequent over the coming months, and by six months many babies are sleeping through the night, or at the very least managing six hours of unbroken kip.

Get some rest

If you can't beat them, join them! Stick your jim-jams on at 8pm and snuggle down in bed. The night feeding situation really is out of your control for the first couple of months, so you might as well forget about your social life and get some much needed kip.

The risk of cot death is highest during the first six months of your baby's life.

Safe sleeping

Twenty-five years ago it was all the rage to put your baby to sleep on his front, until a study showed that it was dangerous, and the 'back to sleep' campaign was launched in 1991. This campaign advocated putting babies to sleep on their backs, and has since cut the incidence of cot death by 75%. Sadly, though, 300 babies still die of cot death annually, and no one knows for certain why. However, there are factors that increase the risk, and steps you can take to minimise the chance of it happening to you.

Tips on putting your baby down safely

- Always put your baby to sleep on his back.

- If he is a bit of a wriggler, you can buy a baby sleep positioner that will keep him on his back. There are quite sophisticated ones available in memory foam that also help prevent 'flat head' syndrome (where the back of your baby's head becomes flat from sleeping horizontally).

- Make up the bed from the foot of the cot so he can't wriggle down under the covers.

- Don't overdo the bedding; a sheet and a blanket should be fine.

- If he is an active baby, consider getting a baby sleeping bag for him to sleep in, but make sure it is the correct weight for the season.

- Don't over-dress him at night; just a sleepsuit should be fine, but you can put a vest underneath if the room is very cold.

- The room should not be heated at night and should be at an even temperature of around 16°C–20°C.

- **Never** fall asleep with your baby on a chair or the sofa, in case he rolls off you and into a gap in the cushions, or cannot lift his head off your chest. Tell your partner to wake you if you nod off together – he may think you look very sweet cuddled up together and not realise the dangers.

- If you intend to share a bed with your baby, **never** do it if you are under the influence of alcohol or drugs, a smoker, 'unusually' tired or if your baby is small or premature.

- Do not smoke near your baby, and ideally not at all, as it clings to your hair and clothes. There is a strong link between smoking and cot death, so this is the time for you and your partner to give up if you have not done so already.

- Keep your baby's cot or crib in your room for the first six months. Studies have shown that children who sleep in their parents' room for the first six months have a lower incidence of SIDS (ie cot death), but no one is exactly sure why.

Co-sleeping

The trend of sleeping with your baby has also come under scrutiny, after the science team that pioneered the 'back to sleep' research found that 50% of current cot deaths take place where a parent and child sleep together. Most of these deaths occurred when the co-sleepers were on a sofa or an armchair, but some did occur in the parental bed. In some cultures it is normal to sleep with your baby, and if you want to do it you should follow the guidelines above.

WHEN TO CONTACT THE DOCTOR

During your first few weeks as a parent you will probably (and very understandably) encounter a number of times when you are worried that something is wrong; many of these things will be completely normal and nothing to worry about, but there are a few instances when you should contact your doctor. Try not to panic, but certainly contact them if:

- he is floppy and listless.

- he is jittery: ie, very shaky.
- your baby is going longer than six hours without a feed in the first week and difficult to wake (roughly in the first week he should feed every four hours).
- all babies become a little jaundiced, but if he is very yellow and not waking for feeds.
- he is crying all the time, especially if it is a high pitched cry.

WHAT ABOUT ME?

With all this attention on the new baby, it's easy to forget that you need looking after too. You may be totally exhausted after a long labour, battle-scarred from a Caesarean or just feel like a bomb has gone off in your (big) knickers. The birth may leave its mark on you physically and emotionally, but the good news is that time is a great healer and, however difficult the labour was, you'll soon heal and recover and just enjoy being a mother. We've covered the most common body issues you may encounter post-birth and look at some of the ways you can get your body (and mind) back.

How you might be feeling

Most likely you'll be feeling battered and bruised, but give it a couple of months and any scars should have healed and bruises will have faded away (hopefully like any memory of the pain of the birth).

When the midwife comes to visit you she will not only check your baby but give you a check over as well. She'll examine your tummy to check that your uterus is returning to normal, ascertain your blood loss is not excessive, check your blood pressure and temperature, examine your legs for signs of a blood clot and look at your stitches (if you have any) to see that they're healing and there's no sign of infection. She'll also ask you if your bowel and bladder movements are OK.

Six to eight weeks after the birth you will be offered a more comprehensive post-birth check-up for you and the baby, normally conducted at your GP's surgery with your doctor or practice nurse.

Afterpains

After suffering the agony of birth contractions, you'd hope that you'd have experienced the last of any stomach pains for a while, but sadly not. Your uterus has to contract back to its normal size in the days following birth (usually by day 10) and this can be painful, especially when breastfeeding, as it releases the hormone oxytocin that triggers contractions. If they are really bad, take a couple of paracetamol or try a heated pad or hot water bottle.

Bleeding

Every new mother will experience postnatal bleeding. Its medical term is lochia and it is the uterus shedding its lining of blood, mucus and tissue.

Lochia is usually very heavy and bright red in the first few days, then becomes lighter and changes from pink to brown to yellow. The sequence is quite comparable to a period, except that it lasts around six weeks instead of six days.

If it returns and is bright red again in colour or is very heavy, do tell your health professional because it could be a sign that some placenta is left inside or you have an infection. Some blood clots in lochia are normal, but if you are getting excessive amounts or the blood is smelly, again mention it because it could indicate a problem. Any clots larger than the size of a plum should be reported immediately.

Do not try to stem the flow with tampons because they could introduce an infection into the vagina. You'll probably need maternity pads for a couple of weeks; hopefully then you'll be able to cope with sanitary towels.

Bleeding may last longer than six weeks. If it is going on for a very long time, make sure you tell your doctor.

Breasts

On day three or four after birth, the antibody-rich colostrum you've been giving your baby is replaced by breast milk. When this happens, your breasts seem to double in size and become rock hard. It's caused by a hormonal surge, and don't worry: it usually settles down after a day or so. If you are breastfeeding, you can relieve the pain and pressure by feeding your baby, but you may have to express some milk first, because they may be too full for him to latch on. You can either do this with a pump or try massaging them in a warm bath to get some milk out. If you are breastfeeding, you may also get very sore nipples, so make sure you put lots of nipple cream on them after feeds. Your midwife can recommend a good brand.

If you are bottle feeding, you will have to put up with a few days of misery. Try popping cold cabbage leaves into a snug-fitting, supportive bra and take some painkillers if the discomfort gets too bad. Your milk supply will dry up entirely within a few weeks.

If you get red streaky patches on your breasts and are suffering from flu-like symptoms you may have mastitis: a condition that causes the breast tissue to inflame painfully. Around 10% of breastfeeding women suffer from mastitis, which is usually due to a blocked milk duct or breast milk getting trapped in breast tissue. Although it can be incredibly painful, women with mastitis are encouraged to keep breastfeeding in the hope that they can 'unblock' the problem. Seek help from your GP or midwife, as it can lead to a breast abscess and the need for antibiotic treatment.

Bowels and bottoms

Passing a stool in the days after birth can become as fear-inducing as labour itself. If you have had stitches it's common to feel paranoid that they will burst, and the more stressed you get about the issue the less likely you are to go, so it all becomes a bit of a vicious circle and, next thing you know, you are constipated...

You probably won't burst your stitches, however much you strain, but for psychological reassurance it's a good idea to hold a maternity pad or a few sheets of tissue against them while you try to go. To get things moving, it's useful to keep up your fibre intake and drink lots of water. If there's no movement in that department after a couple of days, ask your midwife to recommend a gentle laxative. It might just kick-start your system again and get you going (literally). Once you have been, make sure you wash the area where the stitches are with plain warm water. Dry very carefully with a soft towel or low-power hairdryer.

If you had a third degree tear, where the muscle around the back passage is (partly) torn, you will have been given stool softeners automatically to make sure the stool slips out easily.

Piles after birth are very common, so even if you thought you got away with it in pregnancy you might find that the itchy little blighters make their presence known after labour, due to the pressure of the delivery on your back passage. You can buy over-the-counter creams, or if they are really bad you can get your doctor to prescribe a suppository for you. The good news is that they should go away of their own accord in a month or so.

Stomach

We all secretly hope that we are going to be the one in a million women who just 'pings' back into shape after giving birth (Heidi Klum, we're looking at you!), but the reality is that you will look at your tummy the day after the birth and wonder if you are ever going to get into your jeans again. Don't worry if it looks saggy and wobbles alarmingly like blancmange; it's completely normal. If you were very fit before and during pregnancy, you may have stronger muscles and revert to your pre-baby shape more quickly than others; for some of us it is undoubtedly down to luck and genetics. If you have never exercised before, this is not the time to embark on a vigorous new fitness regime, but do try to get some exercise taking your baby out for a stroll. Celebrities may look rail thin days after birth (and no doubt have had a helping hand from a personal trainer), but it's not advisable to do any strenuous exercise until at least six weeks after labour (ask if it's safe to start when you have your proper post-birth check-up at the doctor's). If you start too soon, before your stomach muscles have gone back to normal, you can cause hernias.

Most new mothers are so knackered in the first few weeks that working out is the last thing on their minds, but if you want to make a tentative start on getting some strength back in your abdomen, try just gently pulling in your tummy and holding it in for a few seconds before releasing. If you're looking for celebrity inspiration, take a leaf out of Salma Hayek's book: she bucked the Hollywood trend for whipping back into shape immediately after the birth of daughter Valentina, and allowed herself an entire year to recover.

Once you get the all clear to start exercising, start slowly and build up; you might find it difficult to sneak off to the gym or go for a long run at the moment, so focus on things you can manage easily with your baby. Going for long walks with your baby is fantastic exercise and is good for you both: you can quicken the pace as and when you feel up to it. You can also practise stretching exercises at home while your baby naps. The key thing at the moment is to listen to your body; if you start to overdo it you might find that you get too tired. You must do your pelvic floor exercises every day.

> 'To be honest – I don't like my post-pregnancy body, but I accept that this is the way I am at the moment and it won't be forever! I put on three stone and have taken off two and a bit stone now through healthy eating and lots of walking.'
>
> Debbie, mum to Lauren, 13 months

If you have stretch marks and they are still looking 'angry', don't worry: they will fade in time. It's unlikely you'll be in a bikini for a bit, but when you do get to bare your bod, apparently fake tan can conceal them successfully.

If you have had a Caesarean, you not only will have a big belly to contend with but a livid red scar as well. It may look quite alarming in the first few weeks, and may be sensitive and itchy as the pubic hair grows back around it. Although this is annoying at the time, it is a good thing because the pubic hair will cover the scar eventually – within weeks it will start fading to pink, and within a year or two it will have faded to a thin, barely visible line. You do need to keep the area clean and dry to minimise the chance of infection. If you have had a Caesarean, you will be encouraged to do very gentle pelvic floor exercises immediately after the birth and for the first eight weeks. Because you have had a major operation, you must consult with your doctor before you embark on strenuous exercise, as you don't want to rupture your scar.

Five great things about your post-baby body

- You'll have lost at least a stone in the past few days.

- You can sleep on your front again (although not when your milk comes in, as it'll probably be too painful).

- You can see your feet again.

- You won't have strangers patting your bump any more.

- You'll fit into some of your old clothes within weeks, if not days (with any luck).

Vagina and perineum

It's pretty inevitable that you are going to feel pretty sore down below, and no wonder: have you *seen* the size of your baby's head? If you were lucky enough to get away without tearing or needing stitches, you are still going to feel quite tender and bruised for a while. Make sure you wear big comfy pants and loose trousers, and if you want to give nature a helping hand you can also try taking arnica tablets – the natural remedy that is said to boost the healing process. You can buy them from health food shops and chemists, but do check the label before you take them in case you have a condition that prevents you from using them.

If you have torn or have stitches you may need to take painkillers, and warm baths with drops of lavender and tea tree oil can help too; but don't stay in for too long, as prolonged wetting can slow the healing. If things are really bad, you can try heated or chilled gel-filled packs that you pop in your knickers, hire a specially designed 'Valley Cushion' from the NCT or another private baby equipment company, or try sitting on a rubber ring.

Stitches can be an added headache, because they itch and run the risk of getting infected. Rinse the vaginal area several times a day with cool water, particularly after going to the loo. A hand-held shower is particularly good for this; otherwise you can pour a jug of water over your bits. It's really important to make sure you dry the area extremely carefully – damp stitches heal slowly and get infected. Try a really soft towel, or even a hairdryer on the lowest setting! Change your maternity pad regularly, and make sure you wash your hands thoroughly before and after.

It may sound a bit sadistic, but you really should start your pelvic floor exercises as soon as you get back from hospital. They increase blood flow to the area and can help healing. Experts recommend you do a sequence of pelvic floor exercises several times a day. If you have problems remembering to do them, use an action you do repeatedly during the day – like making a cup of tea or drinking a glass of water – as a reminder to get squeezing!

If you are unlucky enough to have a third or fourth degree tear (where the muscle around the back passage has been damaged and repaired), you will need to be reviewed by the doctors a few months after the birth to ensure it has healed well and has not damaged your bowel function. You will also be advised to start on your pelvic floor exercises immediately, and might be referred to an obstetric physiotherapist for specialist help.

Let's talk about sex

Assuming everything is healed, you will be able to have sex as soon as the lochia has stopped. If you are worried about stitches, you can wait until your six-week check-up to have them checked. You may worry that it feels 'different' down there – someone described it as a 'wizard's sleeve' (yikes) – because there may be a reduction in elasticity and you may have some raised scar tissue, but in truth most couples find these are just minor details, and things do generally get back to normal. If you have concerns that things really *aren't* right, have a chat with your GP, but bear in mind it can take months, not weeks, for everything to heal.

Don't worry if you have lost the desire to have sex in the few months after birth. You're sore, exhausted and at the moment the object of your affections is your tiny bundle of wailing joy and not the man who helped you make him. Try not to 'shut' your partner out physically and emotionally; think of lots of things he likes that don't involve intercourse (there's usually beer, for a start). Make sure you explain your feelings to your partner, and

CONTRACEPTION

When your midwife visits you to check on you and the baby she may also talk to you about contraception. The reason she asks is that in theory you could become pregnant as early as three weeks after giving birth (even when you are breastfeeding).

You may think it is highly unlikely, but you need to be aware that:

- The first egg comes two weeks before the first period – so don't assume that you can't get pregnant because you haven't had a period!
- If you are bottlefeeding or mixed feeding, your periods will probably return between six and 10 weeks after birth but as you may still have some lochia bleeding (see page 362) afterwards it's difficult to tell if it's a period or not.
- If you had a diaphragm or cap before you got pregnant, you can start using it six weeks post birth, but you will need to have it checked by a doctor to see if it still fits, because your upper vagina or cervix will probably have changed shape. If you then shed more than 3kg (7lbs) of baby weight you'll need to get it checked again.
- You can use condoms immediately after birth if you want to resume your sex life straight away (unlikely), although it is advisable to avoid sex until you have stopped bleeding.
- You can start using the combined or progestogen-only pill or implants three weeks after birth. If you are breastfeeding you should not take the combined pill, as it can affect your milk supply. Contraceptive injections

are normally administered around six weeks post birth.

If you know you don't want to get pregnant for a while, long-acting reversible forms of contraception (LARC) do what the name says – they last a long time, are not permanent and stop you conceiving. As they don't need to be taken regularly or remembered/found when you want to have sex, they are generally more effective at stopping babies – sex may happen less often for a while after the baby is born, but you want to make sure you can enjoy it without worrying about getting pregnant again. LARCs include an implant called Implanon which is inserted under the skin of your arm and lasts up to three years, a copper coil or IUD (coil) which lasts up to five years, and the Mirena IUS – similar to a coil but better at stopping pregnancies, and a great way to either stop your periods or at least make them less heavy. It lasts up to five years, too. If you think you do want to get pregnant quickly, condoms and the cap might be better in the short term.

'Natural' family planning methods like the rhythm method are quite difficult to re-establish after birth, so you might be advised to use an alternative method until your body gets back to normal. Of course, you might be happy to conceive again quickly. If you had a Caesarean section you usually need to wait at least 15 months, to let the scar develop strength. But most women can start trying once they feel ready (and are in good shape).

don't just shrug him off. You don't want him to feel rejected, and he'll understand if you explain why you feel the way you do.

When you do both feel ready to resume sex, you may find that it takes a while for you both to relax into it. You might be worried about waking the baby, you might be feeling a little self-conscious about your body if you haven't managed to shift the baby weight, or simply have a very small window of opportunity to actually commit the deed, which can put pressure on you both. Your partner may feel worried that he is going to hurt you, or feel rather embarrassed about touching your breasts if you are using them for feeding as well as sexual purposes. Your breasts may start leaking during sex, which can be a huge turn off for you both; the best advice is to take it slowly and try to retain a sense of humour about the whole thing. If you discuss these issues before you get intimate they won't be half so alien or frightening.

A wee problem

One thing you might not be expecting is how much it can sting when you pee after having a baby. You can alleviate the symptoms by pouring warm water over your urethra area when you urinate, and by ensuring you drink lots of fluid to dilute the concentration of your urine, which should make it sting less.

You might also feel that your control of your bladder isn't what it was pre-birth. Many women find that they leak when they cough or laugh, or find that, years after birth, they still need to get up in the middle of the night to pee; pelvic floor exercises will really help, so don't forget to do them, as it may eliminate any problems in the future.

If the problem is severe or persists once everything else has healed, do mention it to your doctor, because he can refer you to a specialist for treatment.

RECOVERING AFTER A CAESAREAN

A Caesarean involves major abdominal surgery, so its recovery time is usually longer than for a vaginal birth. You should be over the worst after around six weeks, but some women report that they don't feel right for months, so don't worry if you don't bounce back quickly; you have to remember you are recovering from having both a baby and an operation.

Recovery from an emergency Caesarean often takes longer than for an elective one, although that might have more to do with psychological factors than physiological ones.

Generally, if you have a Caesarean, you can expect your recovery to go as follows.

- You will stay in hospital for 36 hours or more after the birth. With any luck you might get your own room, but not for the first day, as the midwives will need to be able to check on you regularly to make sure you are okay.

- You'll have effective painkillers whilst in hospital and will have to take pain relief medication home with you, too.

- Your catheter will usually be removed the next day, and the midwife will check that you pass urine normally thereafter.

- Your wound dressing will normally be removed after 24 hours.

- Your midwife will show you how to cuddle and breastfeed your baby as comfortably as possible.

- You may see a physiotherapist whilst you are in hospital. It is important to help you to get walking again, and to do some leg exercises to keep the circulation going to prevent the formation of blood clots. You will probably be advised to wear compression stockings, and may be asked to inject yourself with heparin on a daily basis for up to six weeks to reduce the chance of getting a thrombosis.

- Your physiotherapist will also show you techniques to laugh or cough to avoid causing problems with your incision site.

- Trapped wind is common after a Caesarean, as your digestive system can be affected by the surgery. Sipping peppermint tea should help.

- Simple everyday tasks like walking and sitting up can be painful, so make sure that you have lots of help and support when you get home. If you are alone, make sure that a friend or relative comes to stay to help for a few weeks (or after your partner has returned to work).

- Keep the incision site clean and dry to minimise the chance of infection. Don't panic if your scar looks livid at the moment: it will shrink and fade to a pale line in time. The stitches may cause some itching until they dissolve or are removed.

- Wear loose clothing when you get home, particularly roomy pants, and avoid anything that has a band at the bikini line level, as it will press straight into the scar. Big bloomers are better than thongs!

- Check your insurance policy regarding driving after a Caesarean, as many companies insist you wait six weeks post-op before you drive. Physically you must be able to do an emergency stop, twist right around to see what's behind you, and of course wear a seat belt (which will press straight into your cut). In practice, six weeks is usually a safe time to consider starting to drive again, but make your first journey a short one and have another driver with you if you can.

- Even if you are feeling perfectly well physically, you should avoid carrying heavy weights or taking strenuous physical exercise until you have had the all clear to do so from your doctor or health visitor.

WHEN TO WORRY ABOUT YOUR POST-BIRTH HEALTH

There are some post-pregnancy symptoms that could signify a serious complication, so contact your GP or midwife if you experience any of the following:

- heavy vaginal bleeding

- fainting, dizziness or feverishness

- swelling, tenderness, or pain in your legs, especially if it is only one leg

- a severe headache that you can't shake off, particularly if it is accompanied by blurred vision or vomiting

- persistent stomach pains

- intense pain in the vaginal area

- extreme pain when urinating.

If you are really worried, call NHS 111 or NHS Direct or ask to be taken to A&E; your baby needs you, so don't ignore signs that could indicate you have a problem.

POSTNATAL DEPRESSION (PND)

Quite a frightening subject, but something that should be covered, because up to eight out of 10 women suffer from it to some degree.

No one is exactly sure what triggers postnatal depression (though the drop in hormones post-birth probably is a factor) but a previous history of depression, having a sick or premature baby, recent life stresses like a bereavement or unemployment, losing a parent when young or an unsupportive partner may all contribute. It can happen to anyone: Billie Piper, Gail Porter and Brooke Shields have all spoken candidly about having PND after the birth of their babies.

For many women, the symptoms are fairly mild and can be accurately described as the 'baby blues', but for as many as one in five women it can be a debilitating illness.

Signs of PND

PND usually occurs within six months of the birth but may occur at any time within a year.

Symptoms include:

- feeling overwhelmed with hopelessness
- too exhausted to do simple tasks
- unexplained anger or rages
- crying at the slightest things
- anxiety attacks
- sleeping badly
- inability to concentrate
- incapable of making simple decisions
- feeling inadequate as a parent.

Looking at the list, you can guess that most of us will experience some or all of the above in the year post-birth. For most of us it'll be down to lack of sleep, but it's important that you discuss any fears or worries about your mental health with your health visitor or GP so you can get help if you need it.

Baby blues usually go away after a few weeks once you have settled down into a routine and your baby is slightly less physically demanding, whereas postnatal depression lasts much longer. Lots of sleep, cuddles and practical support is probably what you'll need to help you get through the baby blues. Getting out of the house helps, too; whether it's a nice walk or a night out, you do need a break from your baby occasionally. If it is more serious, you are entitled to receive medical assistance; it may be in the form of an exercise programme, psychological therapy, counselling or anti-depressants (if you are prescribed the latter, ensure you tell the doctor if you are breastfeeding, because some are not suitable and could be harmful to your baby).

Birth trauma

Occasionally women can develop severe birth trauma, which is similar to post-traumatic stress disorder and usually triggered by a difficult birth. If the birth has left you truly shaken and you feel you need to talk it through with someone, seek help from a sympathetic health professional. It is believed that discussing your birth experience can be a very positive thing to do – some hospitals even offer a birth reflections service where you can go in and get things off your chest – so if you need to share your thoughts and feelings, do speak up, as there may be help or counselling available.

Feeling scared and alone

One topic that comes up over and over when you discuss post-birth experiences is how many women feel lonely, isolated or scared once their partners have gone back to work, the midwife is no longer popping in and the only person ringing the doorbell is the postie. Undoubtedly it can be a challenging time, because suddenly you have to do everything for your baby *and* cope with the household stuff, and even the smallest things can be a huge deal.

You can become quite boring, too, because your whole life revolves around your baby and you feel you've got nothing else to talk about. There are some days when it rains all day, you can't go out and you'll feel your face pressed against the front window at 6pm willing your partner to come home and take over, because frankly you have been climbing the walls. Looking after a new baby isn't all lovely walks, coffee mornings and shopping. There are days when it can feel boring, unfulfilling and downright miserable, and here are some tips to help you get through it.

Ten things to make you feel better post-birth

- Run a warm bath infused with drops of lavender and tea tree oil. There are lots of gorgeous postnatal beauty products available (check out www.mamababybliss.com and www.mamamio. co.uk, for example), and a sweet-smelling treat may be just what the doctor ordered.

- If you are feeling culturally bereft, go to the movies. The Odeon cinema group has 'newbie' screenings (where you can take your newborn to the latest film release) on weekday mornings in almost 50 locations nationwide. It's a great way to get back in touch with the outside world, will give you something else to talk about and is something you can do on your own if you are feeling bored.

- Join a class together. There are plenty of classes for mother *and* baby, from yoga to postnatal Pilates and massage.

- Get away. If you fancy a mother and baby yoga retreat, check out www.mamaheaven.org. There are spa days (the Cupcake Spa in London is very popular), and breaks for mothers and babies available in hotels countrywide (www.peelhotels.co.uk). If you want to go further afield, France is particularly good for new mummy and baby pampering.

- Go swimming. Once your baby is 12 weeks old and has his vaccinations, you could look into mother and baby swimming classes in your area: a gentle way to start exercising and bonding with your baby.

- Go to a coffee morning. The local NCT will hold them, and even if you didn't make it to the classes, there's no reason why you can't join in after birth. You might meet some new friends and have a laugh (or a cry).

- Join an online community. Post any topic regarding pregnancy or baby care, and someone is sure to come back with helpful first-hand experience or advice; most of the big parenting websites like Made For Mums, Netmums or Mumsnet have online forums you can join.

- Treat yourself. Still in your pregnancy jeans? Sick of wearing the same stuff for what feels like forever? Go somewhere cheap and cheerful like Primark, Matalan, T K Maxx or New Look, and get yourself a couple of cheerful tops to give your wardrobe (and you) a lift.

- Have a night out. Go out with your friends and enjoy time talking about things other than babies for a while. Or, if you are too anxious to leave your baby with anyone, take him with you. You may feel uncomfortable going somewhere formal, but they are incredibly portable when they are tiny because they are not in a strict routine.

- Make an effort. It sounds really simple, but just doing your hair, slicking on the lippy and hauling yourself out of your trackie bottoms may psychologically do you a world of good – particularly if you are feeling fat, frumpy and exhausted.

'I feel ok with my post-pregnancy body. I have made it my policy to be showered and dressed by 10am each morning and that helps me to get going. I have also been going for a long walk every day.'
Melanie, mum to Saoirse, 3 months

PRACTICAL INFORMATION

Registering the birth

All births in England, Wales and Northern Ireland must be registered within 42 days (six weeks) of the birth, and within 21 days in Scotland.

You can register your baby's birth at any register office, but if it is not in the district where the baby was born, you will not be able to take the birth certificate away with you, as the registrar will have to forward your details to the district where the birth took place. The birth certificate will be posted to your home address at a later date.

If you and the baby's father are married then either parent can register the birth on behalf of both parties, but if you are not married and you would like the father to be included on the birth certificate, then *both* of you must go together to sign the birth register, or submit a statutory declaration acknowledging the father's paternity (you can get the form from the register office beforehand if your partner cannot attend for

Labour leader Ed Milliband didn't register his first son's birth in 2009. As he and his partner Justine Thornton weren't married at the time, Milliband wasn't listed as the father until he went to register his second son in November 2010, when he was added as the father for both sons.

any reason). If the father's details are not registered at the time of birth registration, it may be possible for you to add them at a later date.

When you register the birth, you will need to give the registrar your baby's place and date of birth, the sex of the baby and his (or her) full name (so make sure you have decided before you go!). You will also have to give the registrar all your personal details, such as your full name, place of birth, occupation and current address.

There are two types of certificate: a short one that just has your baby's details on it, and a long one that includes your details as well. You are issued the short one for free and will have to pay £3.50 for any other certificates you order on the day (as you inevitably need them for passports/child benefit claims etc, we would strongly advise buying two more). If you don't get any additional certificates when you register the birth and subsequently decide you want some, you'll have to pay £7 per additional copy.

To find your local register office, you can look on www.gov.uk or contact your local council.

Money money money!

From 6 April 2011, the government announced that child benefits would be frozen for three years, meaning you will receive £20.30 per week child benefit for your baby and £13.40 for any subsequent child you have, before a larger review of the benefits system begins in 2013. The government has recently introduced a new tax charge for those claiming child benefits who earn over a certain amount. If you or your partner have an annual income of £50,000 or more, you will be liable to pay this new tax charge, which works out as a percentage of your earnings. You do have the option to stop receiving child benefits, and then are not liable for this tax. To read more about this controversial tax, go to www.hmrc.gov.uk.

If you are eligible for child benefit, you can claim from the day your child is born. You should receive a form in the 'Bounty' pack that's usually given to you in hospital, but if not, you can fill one in online at www.hmrc. gov.uk/childbenefit (the HM Revenue & Customs site).

You'll need your National Insurance number to hand, as it has to go on the form. You have to print the form off once you have filled it in and send the hard copy with your baby's *original* birth certificate to the Child Benefit Office (see address below). You will also need to provide details of a bank/building society or Post Office account where the benefit will be paid (some savings accounts with passbooks, ISAs or children's trust accounts cannot be used, so check on the HMRC website that your child benefit can be paid into the account you want to use). Normally it will be paid every four weeks into your nominated account, although it is possible in certain circumstances to get it paid weekly.

Forms and birth certificate should be sent to:
Freepost
NEA 10463
PO Box 133
Washington
NE38 7BR

You will receive a notice telling you that you have qualified for child benefit and when the next payment is due, and your baby's original birth certificate will be returned.

Child tax credit/working tax credit

If you have a joint household income below a certain threshold, you may qualify for child tax credit and working tax credit (which can help you pay for childcare). There is a really useful tool to help you work out whether you qualify for either form of tax credit on the www.hmrc.gov. uk website, so rather than bore you to death (and by the time you read this it might have all changed anyway), we advise you to check it out, because you may get a nice surprise!

AND FINALLY...

You've survived 270-odd days of pregnancy, got through the birth and muddled through the first few weeks (somehow), so we'll leave you with a few top tips for a happy and healthy pregnancy.

- Try to enjoy your pregnancy: it's totally amazing what you're growing in there!

- Cherish your maternity leave: it goes so fast and you'll never get that time back again.

- *Nothing* will ever beat the feeling when you gaze at your newborn for the first time.

- You don't know what love (and despair) is until you have children – but love beats the despair every time.

- Treasure each stage, because they fly by so quickly.

12

Stories from pregnant women and new mums

In this section you'll find stories from women who are currently pregnant, and stories from new mums who have recently given birth. Hopefully, their experiences and woeful accounts of aches and pains will help you prepare for your own pregnancy, and you'll pick up a few tips on the way.

PREGNANCY TALES

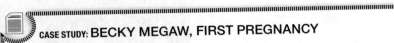

CASE STUDY: **BECKY MEGAW, FIRST PREGNANCY**

When I found out I was pregnant, I just felt complete disbelief. I ended up doing multiple tests to make sure. My husband was the same – he thought the tests were lying!

It happened within a couple of weeks of coming off the pill, which was why it was such as surprise when the test showed up positive.

We are planning to give birth in hospital – I would like to give birth as quickly and painlessly as possible! I know both are pretty unreasonable, but I'm still in denial about the whole process. I've had previous health problems which mean that it isn't a good idea I labour for too long, so I am keeping a very open mind.

I had some bleeding at about six weeks. I think I overreacted as I went straight to A&E. I had a scan the next morning which revealed a little blob of beating cells. It was the most amazing sight I had ever seen. I am not normally emotional but at the sight of our baby's heart beating, when I thought I was about to miscarry, I burst into tears.

We didn't find out the sex of our baby. Life has few enough surprises and we wanted this to be a very special one!

I'm now 21 weeks and, at last, actually look pregnant rather than fat. I found the early stages a bit depressing in terms of body image, as I just looked like I had eaten a lot of cake!

I now really love the way my body looks with a definite bump and bigger boobs. I was on holiday last week in the Caribbean and wore a bikini, and for the first time actually felt comfortable in one, which is strange as I weigh more now than I ever have in my life.

My food cravings so far have been Jammy Dodger biscuits, liquorice and sugary chewy sweets. From six to 13 weeks I felt really nauseous and the smell of coffee made me feel awful. My team at work, who I hadn't yet told, know how much I love coffee and kept bringing me fresh cups!

To begin with things were a bit difficult with my husband. I was very moody and irrational and would take it all out on my nearest and dearest. Now my hormones have settled down and we are getting on fantastically. He is really looking after me and is constantly touching my bump and talking to 'Jelly Bean'.

Almost everyone has been very positive towards my pregnancy. There were a couple of work colleagues who were a bit off as they had been trying for a very long time to conceive. I've found this hard to deal with as I almost feel guilty that I got pregnant so fast.

People have touched my bump – and I love it!! I wish more people would. It makes me feel really special when they do.

The best bits of my pregnancy so far have been the scans and feeling the first flutters of life. Also, pregnancy is the best excuse to eat all I like! The down sides are swollen ankles, a bad back, broken sleep and constant trips to the loo.

There are certain foods I really miss and am struggling with, eg sushi, parma ham, blue cheese. I also really missing having a rare steak; well done just isn't the same.

My exercise regime has changed a lot. I'd signed up to do two triathlons this year, but have taken up yoga instead. I'm finding not going for runs quite tough as they always used to be a great way to unwind at the end of the day.

I plan to go back to work. I really enjoy work and although it will be hard, I think it will be better for me and baby. We are a strong couple and have been through many ups and downs over the years so I am confident we will deal with whatever is thrown at us.

We have done quite a bit of planning, especially financially, as we want to make sure we are in as secure a position as possible.

CASE STUDY: NICHOLA CASE, FIRST PREGNANCY

I couldn't believe it when I found out I was pregnant. We had been trying for five and a half years and we had been talking about IVF. We'd even thought about adopting.

Our whole life revolved around my cycle, my periods and weeing on a stick – I think I bought the whole stock of those things from our local chemist! It sounds funny now, but it had taken over our life – looking back, I was depressed about it and pulling us both under.

I didn't just rely on the stick thing – I went for a test at the doctors too. Paul was overjoyed, just over the moon. Oddly, it was I who had a more low-key reaction. I was terrified it wouldn't last, that I'd lose it. I think I'd convinced myself my body wasn't meant to carry a baby. I still feel petrified, but after the first four months or so I started to enjoy the pregnancy more.

We're going for a hospital birth. I want all the back-up I can get. I don't want to take any risks at all. I'm going to try for a natural birth, and they have a birthing pool where we're going, but if I need drugs I'll take them. All that matters is that the baby comes out healthy.

My experience of doctors and midwives has been mixed. I suppose I've been a bit of a worrier and sometimes I feel that they're impatient with me – they've seen it all a thousand times. But I have one midwife who's been fantastic, really supportive.

We know our baby is going to be a little girl. I really wanted to find out, although Paul wasn't bothered. I felt like I wanted to know everything I could – I couldn't bear the woman doing the scan to know something about my child that I didn't!

Although I've been nervous during the pregnancy, I've enjoyed the physical changes. I've loved seeing my bump grow. It's what I've been wanting for so long.

I've had a couple of strange cravings – pickled onions, which I normally hate. And pretzels. Savoury things, basically. I had some morning sickness early on, but a friend told me to try crystallised ginger and that really helped.

We're doing NCT classes – we've made some good friends through them, although I'm not sure they'd be that great if your birth didn't follow their preferred natural route! Still, we're happy just to have made the contacts.

Being pregnant has really brought Paul and me closer, we already feel like a proper family now. I think it's been hard on him to see me worrying, but we're coming through it. My friends are all happy for me, they've seen me struggling. I picture myself with my baby, going to get-togethers with my friends who are parents, feeling like I belong at last.

A few people have commented on my bump, which I like – mostly! One woman kept trying to pat it, and I actually felt really protective and a bit uncomfortable.

I'm big now, so I've got some maternity jeans and I've bought a few other bits. I don't mind splashing out a bit – I've waited a long time for this! I haven't touched a drop of alcohol or eaten any of the things they say you shouldn't. The only exercise I've done is an aqua class, which is nice and gentle.

My hopes for my baby are that she is healthy and feels loved. My fears about the birth are all about her, not me.

I think our life will change totally when our baby is born. This is what we have been waiting for. We couldn't be more prepared – we've got the nursery ready, and we've put aside some money.

My mum took three years to get pregnant with me. She told me that the best thing I can do now is believe it – and then I can enjoy it. I feel like I'm just starting to believe it now.

CASE STUDY: **LAURA ANDREWS, FIRST PREGNANCY**

I was sitting in the bath when I found out I was pregnant. At first, I didn't really believe the positive result as I had done a test the week before which was negative. I immediately called my husband upstairs. He took a few minutes to clock, but I'd written 'Hello Daddy' on my stomach in eyeliner pencil. We went out for a curry to celebrate! I had only just come off the contraceptive pill and thought it would take a while for us to conceive. In actual fact, we appear to have conceived on the first or second attempt – so it took us a month at the most.

I wouldn't say there have been any changes to my body that I love, unfortunately – some people get blooming skin, strong nails and thicker hair…not me!

In the early days (perhaps month 4) I remember being at a stage where my 'normal' clothes didn't fit but I didn't feel that I was really showing enough to wear maternity clothes either. I remember getting ready to go out and ending up crying to my husband as I had nothing to wear that was comfortable and I felt fat, ugly and generally hideous! He calmed me down and the next day we bought some maternity clothes online.

From about 20 weeks I have suffered with itchy, irritable skin from top to toe, which is worse at night. The GP prescribed antihistamines and sent me for repeat blood tests for obstetric cholestasis. All tests came back negative. People have recommended various lotions and potions, but nothing seems to have helped ease it. At around the 6-month mark, the itching got so bad we made a 3am trip to triage at the maternity unit. Three hours later, they couldn't find any medical reason for the itching and suggested I went back to my GP to be referred to a dermatologist. The GP then concluded that it was most likely hormonal, so I've just learned to live with it.

In terms of our relationship, I think the pregnancy has brought us closer together. It's made us consider things like what sort of parents we want to be; what choices we want to make. Up until the point where he could feel that baby kicking, I think my husband felt quite detached, but as my body has physically changed, it's been easier for him to feel connected to the baby. He now rests his head on my bump, talks to the baby and regularly feels and touches it.

There were a couple of other people who used to regularly touch my bump as well. I didn't mind, but memorably one person (an adult) once expectantly kissed my bump, put an ear to it and became quite emotional. I was slightly taken aback by this, it just made me a bit uncomfortable and I remember thinking 'you're going to get lipstick on my top!'

Diet-wise I have tried to eat balanced meals, but must admit during the last two months of pregnancy I have been craving more treats! The first meal that I am looking forward to post birth is a nice medium cooked steak! I haven't completely omitted alcohol – I have had the odd small glass now and then, but less so in the first three months and last two months of pregnancy.

In terms of my birth plan, I'd quite like to labour in the birthing pool. Ideally I'd like to use gas, air and my TENS machine for pain relief as I'd like to be as mobile as I can during the birth. I have also had a course of pregnancy hypnotherapy and reflexology, so would like to be able to play music to keep me relaxed and remind me to breathe! All this said, I will be willing to do whatever is necessary to ensure baby is not in distress and ultimately I don't know how I'll cope with the pain!

We have done NCT classes, and found them useful as I had no idea about the actual process of labour. However, some of the baby-care advice given was conflicting with books I've read and at times the ideas were quite archaic (for example, there wasn't room for a lot of discussion about bottle/formula feeding).

It doesn't matter how much I've been told or read, I know that nothing is going to quite prepare us for the changes to come. I think sacrifice is going to be a word that features strongly, but not necessarily in a negative sense. While we are going to have to adapt our lives, routines and maybe even temperaments to accommodate this new little arrival, the feeling of love that we will have for her/him and the rewards that we will reap as a consequence will no doubt make it so worthwhile.

CASE STUDY: **RACHEL RHODES, FIRST PREGNANCY**

When I found out I was pregnant, my first reaction was excitement, closely followed by fear that this baby would be OK, due to a previous miscarriage, and bleeding at the time. My husband said 'I told you so!', because he had a feeling that I was pregnant – I had been resisting taking a pregnancy test as I was scared of getting a negative result.

As a couple, I feel we have become stronger through the pregnancy. We both feel very in love, but it has been a real rollercoaster. Due to our previous experiences we were both still carrying a lot of fear and worry. That's not helped by having some medical problems this time too, including bleeding on and off due to a very low lying placenta. I know my husband has been very worried about me and wondered if we've done the right thing trying again as it hasn't been a 'normal' start...whatever 'normal' is in pregnancy!

Early on, I experienced sickness but it wasn't 'morning sickness' as it started from about midday and went through the afternoon and into the evening. Several nights I would sit down to eat dinner, starving, but after two mouthfuls felt so sick I couldn't eat anymore. I was never actually sick but felt I really needed to be.

I have had a few food cravings so far, including oranges (the big navel juicy ones) and kiwi fruit. I went through a two-week phase of craving vinegar. Several times a day I was drinking cider vinegar diluted with water (until my wee started smelling of vinegar so I stopped!), salt and vinegar crisps, anything pickled – Branston pickle, gherkins etc. I found that vinegar things stopped me feeling sick.

I have totally gone off hot drinks, especially tea, which I used to drink a lot. I have still gone out a few times but find I get very tired early on and have noticed smokier atmospheres where they didn't bother me before.

We haven't found out the sex and don't plan to. It is our first baby and we don't mind what it is as long as it is healthy. We are also looking forward to the surprise. We are living in Indonesia at the moment, and it is normal for women to automatically be told the sex of their baby, so every appointment we have to remember to say 'we don't want to know what it is!' which is often greeted with a bemused expression! Hopefully any future scans won't give it away!

Work-wise I am very fortunate as I have a very supportive team – two of whom have very young babies. I was signed off work for a while on bedrest and since going back everyone has been amazing at making sure I am taking it easy. I am a primary school teacher, and am finding work much more tiring at the moment – I don't have the same energy I did!

I have had to stop exercise because of the complications so have missed running, swimming and yoga. When I was on bedrest I became very frustrated and just wanted to go out for a run but obviously wasn't allowed to!

A few months before our due date, we are returning to the UK to have the baby there. I haven't thought about the actual birth too much, but have been looking into hypnobirthing as I know friends who tried it. I like the idea of the relaxation CDs throughout the pregnancy to prepare you mentally as well as physically for the birth. We have to bring our baby back to Indonesia potentially six weeks after birth, so I hope that we are able to do this.

I am going to take three months' maternity leave. When I return to work, my husband will be looking after the baby as he works from home, so I imagine it will take a while to adjust to new routines. We haven't really allowed ourselves to think too far ahead this time yet, so are just getting our heads around everything we need to buy and budgeting accordingly for it.

The best piece of advice I have been given during pregnancy is to take one day at a time.

CASE STUDY: MARIA PAVLOU IBRAHIM, FOURTH PREGNANCY

I was excited, happy and scared when I first found out I was pregnant. We have three girls already, the youngest of whom is eight, but we had decided to try for another one. As my younger one was growing up, I felt like we didn't have a baby in the family anymore! We had been trying for two years. My husband was very happy when I told him.

I had to have an amnio at 15 weeks due to being over 40 years old. It was a nerve-wracking time for us but the results were clear. The care I've received from the hospital and doctors has been excellent.

We decided to find out the sex of the baby. It was really because we wanted to be prepared – after three girls, we needed to know if we were going to have to buy boy stuff. As it turns out, we're expecting a boy, so we are glad to have some time to get used to the idea!

I haven't been too bothered by the changes to my body – after having three children already, body changes are not a problem. In fact, I love being officially fat for a reason!

My main food craving has been beetroot – yum! But for the first 12 weeks I did feel awful. I had sickness, and strong smells made me feel really bad.

I have never done any parentcraft or NCT classes. We have just learned as we've gone along. My husband is very understanding, too, and knows how tired I am sometimes. We've been here before.

My friends and work colleagues have all been very happy and excited for me. I work at a playgroup and the staff have all been very helpful.

My own children, though, have been a bit unsure! They are eight, 10 and 14. The oldest one does not want to hear about it at all – I think she finds it a bit embarrassing!

So far, nobody has asked to touch my bump, they just want to see it! I suppose it's one of those things that just goes along with being pregnant. The best bit of my pregnancy was when the amnio test came back clear, and seeing the scans of my baby for the first time. The worst bit? Waking for a wee three or four times a night!

I haven't bought lots of pregnancy clothes yet – I will probably just buy larger-sized clothes when I need them, rather than special maternity clothes. At the moment, the only real way the pregnancy has affected my day-to-day life is regarding my social life – I've stopped drinking alcohol, and I'm going out less because I'm usually in bed by 9.30pm.

The new baby's arrival is bound to bring changes, but hopefully not too many changes for my other children. I'm sure we will all love having a new baby around the house.

I plan to go back to work after a few months. I understand that lack of sleep can be a problem, but I know it will pass and my husband and I are both good at sharing jobs. Money will always be an issue though.

If I could pass on my best advice, I'd say listen to the midwife – she knows best. Always make time for your partner and let him do things his way – don't criticise his way of managing the baby, you're not always right! And, most of all, enjoy the experience and all the young years. They pass by so quickly.

NEW MUMS' EXPERIENCES OF LABOUR AND EARLY MOTHERHOOD

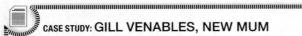

CASE STUDY: GILL VENABLES, NEW MUM

I went into labour in the middle of the night, in hospital, having been admitted to be induced the following day. The contractions woke me and quickly escalated to the point where I went out to the midwives' station on the ward. Things happened pretty quickly – I woke at 2.20am and our baby arrived just after 10am.

Quite incredibly, my birth did go according to my birth plan! I was extremely lucky to be able to deliver my baby (and placenta) naturally, just with gas and air. I put this down to the following factors: a brilliant birth partner who fully understood and shared my wishes and communicated these brilliantly to the midwives; an NCT course that empowered us with the information and confidence we both needed; a fantastic team of midwives in the delivery suite and also, I think it's fair to say, a certain amount of grit and determination from me!

I did, however, tear really badly and needed to go to theatre to have a fourth degree tear stitched back up. The maternity theatre kept being needed for emergency C-sections so I was wheeled in and out a couple of times and eventually they took me to the hospital's main theatre, which was like something out of *ER*. The epidural I now (ironically) needed proved a real problem as they couldn't get the needle in, so the procedure ended up taking a long time. Meanwhile, my partner was back in maternity with our brand new baby, worrying about why I'd been gone so long, pressing the emergency button when the baby choked on some mucus and when he needed a nappy change! Everything is scary but amazing on day one!

I really wanted to breastfeed Arthur and we did skin to skin while the cord was still attached, and he had a short feed. I am still breastfeeding him 11+ months on, and struggle to imagine stopping. It hasn't been easy all along: he was born with a very bad tongue tie that was not diagnosed in hospital. He lost 15% of his body weight in the first 10 days, so we were re-admitted and told to top up with expressed milk and formula between feeds. I literally struggled to grab a shower or sandwich between feeding and expressing sessions. It was such a relief when the tongue tie was identified and quickly cut. Things improved dramatically after that and we gradually stopped needing formula at all. He now won't take a bottle, so the whole episode is clearly forgotten, by him at least, if never by us!

Having a baby puts a huge amount of pressure on any couple. We had been together for nine years before Arthur arrived and are extremely tight, so we were fine! Our shared awe and joy in Arthur brings us closer all the time. We have an indelible connection that runs even deeper than before.

Since having Arthur, I have felt pressure from some angles and other relationships have become easier. I enjoy my mum's company more than ever before, as we now share something that has swept earlier tensions aside. The wonderful friends I met through NCT have become incredibly important to me, through sharing such a brilliant, scary life phase together.

Arthur and I started going to baby sensory classes together when he was just a couple of months old and continued until he was eight months old. The sessions were great, but the best outcome was extended coffee and chats with NCT friends afterwards, once the babies were exhausted and often asleep.

I stuck to my plan and returned to work two days a week when Arthur was 10 months old. Working part time makes me value time with Arthur even more. He gains a huge amount from being in nursery. I am extremely lucky that I have absolute faith in them and he seems to love it there.

The best advice I can give others is to trust your instincts as a mum and realise that there is usually no right answer or perfect solution to any situation. Go with your instinct and believe in it.

Life is utterly different since Arthur arrived: it is never dull and has a new, amazing purpose to it. He is utterly adorable and I feel fulfilled.

CASE STUDY: DEBBIE BECKETT, NEW MUM

I didn't know I was in labour to start with, as my contractions started in my back and not in my front, as I thought they would. It started with one big kick in my back at 3.30am, which woke me out of my sleep!

My blood pressure fell dramatically when they tried to top up my epidural and I had to have a lot of saline fluid put into my system to stabilise it.

Consequently, they had to extract blood from the baby to test for signs of distress. Thankfully, there were no complications after having a C-section in the end, as every time I lay on my back, Lauren's heart rate lowered.

I left my birth plan quite loose and just 'went with the flow'. I had some time in the birthing pool using gas and air, but with the pains being in my back (I suffered with sciatica through my pregnancy), the gas didn't touch the sides and I requested an epidural at 5cm dilated!

I'd like to have given birth naturally. You almost feel cheated by not experiencing a natural birth. I also didn't like being unable to pick my baby up, feed her or change her without assistance, or push her in her pram or drive for six weeks. I felt quite helpless at times and worried that I wouldn't bond as well with my daughter.

I stayed in hospital for two and a half days. I discharged myself early. This was due to the poor 'after care' I received.

I thought the medical staff in the labour side of things were wonderful; however, on the maternity ward it was a different story. I had to ask three nurses over four hours if I could have a shower the following day, as I was still in my blood-soaked gown from giving birth; the midwives made derogatory comments about Lauren, which I heard, when she was constantly crying on the second night; I could go on...

I think I did bond with Lauren straight away, despite my fears, and especially when she had fed from me for the first time. I am still breastfeeding Lauren and have found it all really good. However, I do find breastfeeding in public to be awkward at times, especially in restaurants/cafes etc, so I tend to express my milk and feed Lauren with a bottle as then my partner can share the feeding too.

I just love having a 'mini me'! I love seeing her little character developing day by day. Making and having a baby with your best friend is the greatest gift you can give each other, and I'm really glad I've finally been able to do this, after suffering a miscarriage last year.

Becoming a parent involves training on the job; sometimes you have to go by trial and error in order to get things right and even then, they may only be right for five minutes!

I am going back to work part time. Financially, I have to return, otherwise I would certainly like to be a stay-at-home mum. I've been really amazed at how well my partner has taken to fatherhood and how hands-on he is with everything.

Luckily, a lot of our friends are expecting or have had their first babies, too. However, I have found that some of my single friends haven't been in touch as much, and those that have, I've tended to meet up with on my own.

To be honest – I don't like my post-pregnancy body, but I accept that this is the way I am at the moment and it won't be forever! I put on three stone and have taken off two and a bit stone now through healthy eating and lots of walking.

The best advice I have been given is don't tiptoe round your baby, as they will only be used to sleeping in silence and this will make it harder for them to sleep in the long run. Consequently, Lauren now sleeps over people's conversations, the TV, the vacuum cleaner and her dad's singing!

CASE STUDY: **CLAIRE SPOONER, NEW MUM**

Unfortunately I didn't go into labour naturally. My waters ruptured at around 4am on a Tuesday morning. A community midwife came round to see me and check things out. Nothing was happening, no dilation, no twinges, nada.

So, after a lot of aggro, labour itself started at around 6pm on Friday after a huge amount of walking around hospital corridors and the grounds, two pessaries and my waters being broken by a midwife.

I was then put on a drip to speed things up (by this point I had had four nights of not much sleep and privately wondered if I'd have enough energy for the delivery). I'd wanted to avoid all of these interventions.

I was planning a home birth using a pool, as natural as possible – what I ended up with was six days in hospital and all the medical interventions you can think of. My baby showed signs of distress at each contraction – it turned out he had the cord around his neck not once but twice.

I wish I'd kept my original birth plan, as there were so many crossings out and amendments as things progressed. My baby arrived safely, though, and that's all that's important. The best piece of advice my community midwife gave me was 'be flexible on the day, your birth plan shouldn't be set in stone, things happen'.

I'm a great believer in 'you don't always get what you want, but you often get what you need' – as it turned out, perhaps if we had gone through a home birth, the complications with the cord might have been much worse.

The two doctors I encountered seemed to think of pregnancy and birth as a medical condition and not something natural, and were far too quick to want to slice and dice me. I feel that if I'd had midwife-led care it would have been better; they at least listened to me rather than dismissing what I was saying.

I bonded with my baby straight away. A smile or hand gripping your finger can so easily make up for a sleepless night.

I decided to breastfeed. It's been tough at times as my baby has wanted to feed pretty much every three hours day and night. No one tells you before you start that it's hard work, probably so you don't get put off, but I think that does you a bit of a disservice. Knowing how hard it can be would have cut out some of the worry, as I thought I was doing it wrong to begin with.

Our baby's name was one of the first ones on the list. One of the meanings for his name – Seth – is bringer of chaos. It appealed to my sense of humour and, considering how he got here, it seemed to fit.

The best things about having a baby have been joy; unconditional love; seeing small changes everyday; valuing each day; the shared experience with my partner; laughter (ours and Seth's). The hardest is the lack of sleep – nothing can prepare you for it.

I wasn't sure how I'd feel about work as I'm self-employed and have always worked. However, I now plan to have at least a year off, longer if possible, but that depends on finances. I have thought about childminding as it fits in with my work background and I will still be able to care for my little one.

I'm pretty happy with my post-baby body. I actually weigh a few pounds less than before I got pregnant (another great reason to breastfeed.) My scar is fading nicely and I didn't get any stretch marks (thanks for great genetics mum!) I have a little bit of a wobbly belly but I hope to get back to swimming and get it toned up – I'd also like to do yoga for core strength.

The best advice I have been given is to just enjoy it; to use Metanium for nappy rash (I like to keep things as natural as possible usually but I have to say it works wonders); and that you are the person who knows your baby best – trust your instincts.

CASE STUDY: AMY WATERS, NEW MUM

I was induced at 39 weeks due to pre-eclampsia so there was no mistaking whether I was in labour or not! It took them a long (and somewhat traumatic) time to get labour started (three days) but once it got going there were no further complications.

Did things go according to my birth plan? Not even slightly! I had planned for a natural water birth in the birthing centre. I ended up on the labour ward on a drip, with all sorts of monitors, unable to move around. The only thing that was according to plan was that I didn't have an epidural. I was screaming for one, though, but it was too late!

I would much rather have gone into labour naturally and not have had to be constantly monitored. Although, to be honest, the outcome is so wonderful that actually I'm not sure any of the labour stuff really matters too much.

I stayed in hospital four nights in total. I would say I had excellent care in rather shabby surroundings.

I bonded with Aidan straight away – absolutely. As soon as he was born the midwife put him on my chest and his little eyes were open. I looked at him and just couldn't believe he was there and he was mine, it's such an overwhelming feeling of love.

I breastfed him. I found it extremely painful for the first two weeks, as he wasn't latching on properly. I found the militancy of midwives and health visitors very annoying at first, it's actually quite off-putting.

Once we'd both learnt how to breastfeed properly it became a lot easier and definitely a bonding experience. I am very glad I did breastfeed, but I have to say it is not as easy as you feel perhaps it should be, and I never felt particularly comfortable doing it in public.

Without wishing to freak anyone out who is about to have a baby – it utterly changes every aspect of your life. Becoming a mummy is a big identity shift; your focus changes away from yourself and partner to the baby; your priorities are different, and your day-to-day life becomes filled with domestic chores! Oh, and you never get a lie-in.

But – it's the best thing that's ever happened to me. Watching this little person grow and develop, seeing his sleepy smile in the morning, making him laugh, hearing him say 'mama' – there is no love like it and I could go on and on!

The hardest thing is the guilt that you can feel – worrying that you're not doing a good enough job, that he misses you when you're at work etc (I went back part time).

As for my husband, having a baby brings you together, but you have to work on it. It can definitely be a strain – you're exhausted, it can be quite stressful, eg if baby is ill, and you certainly don't have much time for romance! But, you have this incredible shared experience. Plus your partner is the only other person to whom you can go on and on about how cute/clever/funny the baby is – no one else is that interested.

It does change some friendships. You inevitably become closer to your friends who are at similar life stages to you, and some friends who don't have babies can fall by the wayside a bit if they are not able to understand your changed priorities.

I'm not particularly fond of my postnatal body, but then I wasn't particularly fond of it before either. I certainly care a lot less about how I look now, though; there are too many other more important things to worry about (and a lot less money to spend). Perhaps one day my friends might take pity on me and call on Gok Wan to sort me out.

The best advice I have been given was by my friend who told me to not despair over how painful and difficult the early days of breastfeeding are, and to give it two weeks before deciding whether to carry on or not.

She promised me I wouldn't get through a whole tube of Lansinoh and she was right!

And finally. . .

We hope you have enjoying reading the advice in this book. We hope the medical information has reassured you, the birth stories have inspired you and the wit and wisdom from experienced mothers has encouraged you to treasure this very exciting period in your life.

There will be some emotional times, some scary times, some painful times and a few moments when you wonder what you have let yourself in for, but we promise you it will all be worthwhile in the end.

Cherish the time you have before your baby is born and take lots of care of yourself. Relax and look after yourself. And enjoy getting ready to meet your baby!

'The best piece of advice I have been given is to fully embrace everything about being pregnant; it's a wonderful experience and a privilege, so enjoy it.'

Amanda, first pregnancy

Useful contacts

General information and support
Bounty parenting club: www.bounty.com
For new and expectant parents: www.babycentre.co.uk
Information on pregnancy and motherhood: www.emmasdiary.co.uk
Parents' online forum: www.netmums.com or www.mumsnet.com
National Childbirth Trust: www.nct.org.uk
Pregnancy and birth helpline: 0300 330 0700
Royal College of Obstetricians and Gynaecologists: www.rcog.org.uk
Midwives Online: www.midwivesonline.com
NHS Choices: www.nhs.uk
NHS Direct (for England and Wales): 0845 4647 or 111
NHS24 (for Scotland): 08454 242424

Support for lone parents
Campaigning charity: www.gingerbread.org.uk; 0808 802 0925
Support and advice: www.bliss.org.uk; 0500 618 140

Screening and abnormalities
NHS fetal anomaly screening programme: www.fetalanomaly.
    screening.nhs.uk
Information and support for Down's syndrome parents:
    www.downs-syndrome.org.uk; 0333 1212 300
Antenatal testing: www.arc-uk.org; 0845 077 2290 or 0207 713 7486
    (from a mobile phone)
Group B Strep support: www.gbss.org.uk; 01444 416176

Medical conditions
Thrombosis: www.thrombosis-charity.org.uk; 01558 650 222
Pre-eclampsia: www.apec.org.uk; 0208 427 4217
Intrahepatic cholestasis: www.icpsupport.org
Pelvic girdle pain: www.pelvicpartnership.org.uk; 01235 820 921
Association of Chartered Physiotherapists in Women's Health:
    acpwh.csp.org.uk

Losing a baby

Ectopic pregnancy: www.ectopic.org.uk; 020 7733 2653
Miscarriage: www.miscarriageassociation.org.uk; 01924 200 799
Stillbirth: www.ukhsands.org; 020 7436 5881

Alcohol and smoking

Information and advice on alcohol consumption: www.drinkaware.co.uk
Online help to quit smoking: www.smokefree.nhs.uk
Pregnancy Smoking Helpline: 0800 169 9 169

Food safety

Health in pregnancy, including diet and nutrition: www.tommys.org;
   0800 0147 800
Food Standards Agency: www.food.gov.uk
British Dietetic Association: www.bda.uk.com

Exercise

Guild of pregnancy and postnatal exercise instructors:
www.postnatalexercise.co.uk
Suggested exercises: www.fitpregnancy.com/workouts

Employment

Health & Safety Executive: www.hse.gov.uk/mothers
Directgov, official government website: www.gov.uk
ACAS, employment relations service: www.acas.org.uk; 08457 47 47 47
Department for Work and Pensions: www.dwp.gov.uk
Working Families, helps establish home and work balance:
   www.workingfamilies.org.uk; 0300 012 0312

Childcare

Professional Association for Childcare and Early Years: www.pacey.org.uk;
0845 880 0044
National Day Nurseries Association: www.ndna.org.uk; 01484 40 7070

Relationships

Relate: www.relate.org.uk; 0300 100 1234
The Parent Connection: www.theparentconnection.org.uk

Birth

Where to have your baby: www.birthchoiceuk.com
Home birth: www.homebirth.org.uk

Association for Improvements in the Maternity Services:
www.aims.org.uk
Independent Midwives: www.independentmidwives.org.uk;
0845 4600 105
Reflexology: www.aor.org.uk; 01823 351010
Aromatherapy: www.aromatherapycouncil.co.uk
Acupuncture: www.acupuncture.org.uk; 020 8735 0400
Hypnotherapy: www.hypnobirthing.co.uk; www.natalhypnotherapy.co.uk
Doulas: www.doula.org.uk; 0871 4333103
Information and support on all aspects of Caesareans:
www.caesarean.org.uk
Caesarean procedure and mothers' rights information:
www.csections.org

Multiple births
Twins and Multiple Birth Association: www.tamba.org.uk;
0800 138 0509

Premature and poorly babies
Special care baby charity: www.bliss.org.uk; 0500 618 140

Breastfeeding
NCT breastfeeding helpline: 0300 330 0771
La Leche League Helpline: 0845 120 2918
National Breastfeeding Helpline: www.nationalbreastfeedinghelpline.
org.uk; 0300 100 0212

Safety
The Lullaby Trust: www.lullabytrust.org.uk
Child Accident Prevention Trust: www.capt.org.uk

Bibliography

CMACE. 2011. *Saving Mothers' Lives: reviewing maternal deaths to make motherhood safer (2003–2005)*. London: Wiley-Blackwell. www.oaa-anaes.ac.uk

CMACE/RCOG. 2010. *Management of women with obesity in pregnancy*. London: RCOG Press. www.rcog.org.uk

Demos. 2011. The Home Front. www.demos.co.uk/publications/thehomefront

Downe S. 2009. The transition and the second stage of labour. In: Fraser DM, Cooper MA. eds. *Myles Textbook for Midwives*. 15th ed. Edinburgh: Churchill Livingstone, 509–30

McCormick C. 2009. The first stage of labour: physiology and early care. In: Fraser DM, Cooper MA. eds. *Myles Textbook for Midwives*. 15th ed. Edinburgh: Churchill Livingstone, 457–75

McDonald S. 2009. Physiology and management of the third stage of labour. In: Fraser DM, Cooper MA. eds. *Myles Textbook for Midwives*. 15th ed. Edinburgh: Churchill Livingstone, 531–54

Murray I, Hassall J. 2009. Change and adaptation in pregnancy. In: Fraser DM, Cooper MA. eds. *Myles Textbook for Midwives*. 15th ed. Edinburgh: Churchill Livingstone, 189–225

NCCWCH. 2007. *Intrapartum care: care of healthy women and their babies during childbirth*. National Collaborating Centre for Women's and Children's Health, clinical guideline. London: RCOG Press. www.nice.org.uk

RCOG. 2011. *Ultrasound Screening for Fetal Abnormalities*. London: RCOG Press. www.rcog.org.uk

Index